THE CITY IN ANCIENT ISRAEL

SOCIETY OF BIBLICAL LITERATURE
DISSERTATION SERIES

edited by
Howard C. Kee
and
Douglas A. Knight

Number 36
THE CITY IN ANCIENT ISRAEL

by
Frank S. Frick

SCHOLARS PRESS
Missoula, Montana

THE CITY IN ANCIENT ISRAEL

by
Frank S. Frick

Published by
SCHOLARS PRESS
for
The Society of Biblical Literature

Distributed by

SCHOLARS PRESS
Missoula, Montana 59806

THE CITY IN ANCIENT ISRAEL

by
Frank S. Frick
Albion College
Albion, Michigan 49224

Ph.D., 1970
Princeton University

Advisor:
R. B. Y. Scott

Library of Congress Cataloging in Publication Data

Frick, Frank S
  The city in ancient Israel.

  (Society of Biblical Literature dissertation series ;
no. 36)
  A revision of the author's thesis, Princeton, 1970,
presented under title: The city in the Old Testament.
  Bibliography: p.
  Includes index.
  1. Cities and towns—Biblical teaching. 2. ᶜIr (The
Hebrew word) 3. Cities and towns—Palestine. I.
Title. II. Series: Society of Biblical Literature.
Dissertation series ; no. 36.
BS680.C5F74 1977 221.8'30136'3'0933   77-21984
ISBN 0-89130-149-6

Printed in the United States of America
1 2 3 4 5 6

Printing Department
University of Montana
Missoula, Montana 59812

5557 UM Printing Services

TABLE OF CONTENTS

vi

FOR BONNIE, KIMBERLY, AND RACHEL LYNN

PREFACE

In the seven years since I completed this dissertation at Princeton, there has been a growing interest among biblical scholars in the social world of ancient Israel. I am most grateful to Scholars Press and to Douglas A. Knight, editor of the SBL Dissertation Series, for the opportunity to publish my study. It is my hope that it will make at least a small contribution to scholarly understanding of urban aspects of the social world of ancient Israel. While the guidelines of this Series do not allow extensive, substantive revision, I have included references to literature relevant to the subject which has appeared or come to my attention in the intervening seven years. The reader will find such citations in the notes and in the bibliography, enclosed in square brackets.

The translations of the Hebrew in this work are mine, unless otherwise noted. Where the *RSV* has been found to contain a suitable translation, I have generally followed it. Likewise, the translations of foreign authors are mine, unless otherwise indicated. In the citation of biblical references, the enumeration of verses in the Hebrew text has been used. The text form utilized is that found in *BHK*.

While I cannot here acknowledge my personal debt of gratitude to all those persons who have assisted me in the various stages of work on this study, I would like to express special appreciation to some persons whose assistance has been invaluable.

In the beginning stages of research, the comments and suggestions of Paul M. Harrison of the Pennsylvania State University and of John S. Holladay of the University College of Toronto were especially helpful. Formative study in the history and culture of the ancient Near East was done under the thoughtful guidance of John H. Marks, whom I thank for his personal interest and direction throughout my years at Princeton. I would also like to thank A. Thomas Kirsch of the Program in Anthropology at Princeton for his assistance in some of the interdisciplinary aspects of this work.

Above all, I am grateful to my adviser, R. B. Y. Scott, Professor Emeritus of Religion at Princeton, who guided me in matters of both style and content in ways far beyond what duty would require. Beyond this, his interest in me as a person, as well as a fledgling scholar, supplied the kind of encouragement which enabled me to persevere in my research and writing.

At Albion, my colleagues have provided support in innumerable ways. Finally, I cannot forget our departmental secretary, Nancy Wireman, who was so understanding and diligent as we worked together in the preparation of the manuscript.

The original title of this dissertation was *The City in the Old Testament*. The present title better reflects the fact that I have drawn heavily on archaeological and historical as well, as general sociological data, and not just on OT materials.

F. S. F.

Albion, Michigan
June 3, 1977

ABBREVIATIONS

AASOR	Annual of the American Schools of Oriental Research.
AB	Anchor Bible
AfO	*Archiv für Orientforschung*
AJOS	*American Journal of Oriental Studies*
AJSL	*American Journal of Semitic Languages and Literature*
AnBib	Analecta biblica
ANET	J. B. Pritchard (ed.), *Ancient Near Eastern Texts*
AnOr	Analecta orientalia
AOTS	D. W. Thomas (ed.), *Archaeology and Old Testament Study*
ARM	Archives royales de Mari
ArOr	*Archiv orientální*
ARW	*Archiv für Religionswissenschaft*
ASV	*American Standard Version*
ATD	Das Alte Testament Deutsch
BA	*Biblical Archaeologist*
BAR	*Biblical Archaeologist Reader*
BASOR	*Bulletin of the American Schools of Oriental Research*
BDB	F. Brown, S. R. Driver, and C. A. Briggs, *A Hebrew and English Lexicon of the Old Testament*
BHK	R. Kittel, *Biblia Hebraica*
Bib	*Biblica*
BJRL	*Bulletin of the John Rylands University Library of Manchester*
BWANT	Beiträge zur Wissenschaft vom Alten und Neuen Testament
BZAW	Beihefte zur *ZAW*
CAD	*The Assyrian Dictionary of the Oriental Institute of the University of Chicago*
CAH	*Cambridge Ancient History*
CBQ	*Catholic Biblical Quarterly*
EA	J. A. Knudtzon (ed.), *Die El-Amarna Tafeln*
GKC	*Gesenius' Hebrew Grammar*, ed. E. Kautzch, tr. A. E. Cowley
HAT	Handbuch zum Alten Testament

HKAT	Handkommentar zum Alten Testament
HTR	*Harvard Theological Review*
HUCA	*Hebrew Union College Annual*
IB	*Interpreter's Bible*
ICC	International Critical Commentary
IDB	G. A. Buttrick (ed.), *Interpreter's Dictionary of the Bible*
IDBSup	Supplementary volume to *IDB*
IEJ	*Israel Exploration Journal*
IZBG	*Internationale Zeitschriftenschau für Bibelwissenschaft und Grenzgebiete*
JAOS	*Journal of the American Oriental Society*
JB	A. Jones (ed.), *Jerusalem Bible*
JBL	*Journal of Biblical Literature*
JBR	*Journal of Bible and Religion*
JCS	*Journal of Cuneiform Studies*
JNES	*Journal of Near Eastern Studies*
JPOS	*Journal of the Palestine Oriental Society*
JQR	*Jewish Quarterly Review*
JR	*Journal of Religion*
JRH	*Journal of Religious History*
JSS	*Journal of Semitic Studies*
JTS	*Journal of Theological Studies*
KAI	H. Donner and W. Röllig, *Kanaanäische und aramäische Inschriften*
KB	L. Köhler and W. Baumgartner, *Lexicon in Veteris Testamenti Libros*
KB³	Köhler and Baumgartner, *Hebräisches und aramäisches Lexikon zum Alten Testament*
KJV	*King James Version*
KS	A. Alt, *Kleine Schriften zur Geschichte des Volkes Israel*
LXX	Septuagint
Magnalia Dei	F. M. Cross, W. E. Lemke, and P. D. Miller, Jr. (eds.), *Magnalia Dei: The Might Acts of God*
MT	Masoretic text
NEATC	J. A. Sanders (ed.), *Near Eastern Archaeology in the Twentieth Century*
Or	*Orientalia* (Rome)
PCB	M. Black and H. H. Rowley (eds.), *Peake's*

CHAPTER I

URBAN STUDIES AND OLD TESTAMENT STUDIES:
INTRODUCTION TO THE PROBLEM

At first glance, the title of this study may suggest to
the reader an improbable mix of two rather disparate fields,
urban studies and OT studies.   Therefore some sort of
apologia is perhaps required for their confluence in the
present instance.

The city is commonly acknowledged to have been the
crowning achievement of the ancient world in the organization of human society.   That such relatively permanent,
large-population agglomerations have always made their mark
on a society's way of life has been recognized nearly as long
as there have been cities.   The analysis of the role of the
city in a society's life is perhaps above all the task of the
urban sociologist.   Louis Wirth in fact defines the task of
his discipline in these terms:

> The central problem of the sociologist of the city is to
> discover the forms of social action and organization
> that typically emerge in relatively permanent, compact
> settlements of large numbers of heterogeneous
> individuals.[1]

Robert Ezra Park, one of the patriarchs of modern urban
studies, writing in 1916, spoke of the city as: ". . . a
state of mind, a body of customs and traditions, and of un-
organized attitudes and sentiments that inhere in those
customs and are transmitted with this tradition."[2]

While neither of these statements gives a comprehensive
definition of the city or of the disciplines which study it,
they do suffice to indicate something of the prominence that
has been given in this century to the phenomena of urbanization and urbanism as independent variables in the explanation
of social phenomena.   But in the course of these studies it
has been increasingly realized that urbanization and urbanism
as such are complex variables which must be further analyzed,
particularly with due consideration to the historical perspective.   Thus, urban studies has in fact become a synoptic

discipline in which the borderlines between fields of
inquiry are not always well defined. While the literature
on cities is becoming increasingly sociological in tone in
our day, there is at the same time a widening awareness of
the possibility that here, in the study of the way in which
urban society has organized itself spatially and structurally
and has developed a variety of social systems, there exists
an incomparable arena in which to bring together more explic-
itly a number of converging disciplines.[3]

Among those scholars in other fields which have converged
upon the study of the city is the historian, and in particular
the relatively new sub-species of that field, the urban
historian.[4] Because the contemporary city is the focus of so
many problems, it has been natural to look back to the past
for origins and parallels. The goal of the urban historian
is not directly to illuminate the present, but rather to
explain the past. The inspiration for historical studies not
only of particular cities, but of cities as a category and of
urban processes in society, seems to have sprung from changes
within history itself and the recognition of the need to
examine in detail social structure and change in the most
meaningful units that historians can discover. Obviously,
the city is one of those units. It may well be, however,
that some historians in general and OT historians in
particular, have in the past attributed to cities what is
better attributed to economic and social groups within them
or have not probed deeply enough into the social influences
of "class" or religion. We shall certainly have to ask
whether or not this has been so with respect to historians
of the OT period.

If then we were to characterize this study in terms of
that branch of scholarly endeavor known generically as urban
studies, it could be said that we are here attempting to
write a chapter in urban history, in which use is made of a
theoretical framework supplied by urban sociology. The framework so supplied will be particularly useful in the attempt
to arrive at a working definition of the city and of the
process of urbanization. In this study we shall bring
together two methodologies. The first of these is what

Milton Singer has described as the "functionally causal analysis" which is the method of the sociologist and the social anthropologist. This methodology "seeks to establish functionally causal relations between the physical and 'moral' density
of settlement units and the social and cultural characteristics
generally associated with them."[5] The second methodology is
termed a "historical-contextual" one by Singer and belongs to
the culture historian and the archaeologist. It is characterized by the recognition that:

> . . .urban centers of similar density may differ in impor-
> tant social and cultural characteristics if they are lo-
> cated in different historical and environmental contexts
> and if they play different cultural roles in the network
> of settlement units in which they are located. This meth-
> od views the city as a locus of interaction of diverse
> cultural traditions and tries to trace the conditions and
> consequences of such interaction in the formation and
> transformation of new cultural traditions.[6]

The particular past which this study seeks to illumine
through the application of an urban studies framework is delim-
ited with respect to both time and space. In terms of time,
our bracket will be what is usually called the pre-exilic period in Israelite history, with only minor excursions outside of
that bracket. While the *terminus a quo* of the period depends
to some degree on one's definition of the beginning of Israelite history, we shall here adopt the late thirteenth century
B.C. as our starting point. The *terminus ad quem* can be set
with more precision, being confirmed by Neo-Babylonian chronicles which record the destruction of Jerusalem in 587 B.C.
Within this period the city was the setting of a great part of
the historical experience of the Israelite people, and furthermore, it furnished the foundation of a great religious symbol
which was still further developed in the religion that emerged
from this period--the image of the City of God.

Before proceeding to our analysis of the place of the city
in Israelite society, we should first of all characterize the
nature of the theoretical framework upon which many of our observations about the city in the OT will rest.

In much of the nineteenth-century literature, including
material which can be regarded as prolegomena for the emergence
of sociology, systematic efforts were made to explain differences between urban and pre-urban life-styles. The pioneer

urban theorist was the French scholar Numa Denis Fustel de
Coulanges, whose *La cité antique* appeared in 1882 and has become something of a classic in the field of urban studies.
His work is of particular interest here because he took religion to be the critical institution in the analysis of urban
origins. The purpose of *La cité antique* was to show point-by-
point correspondences between religion and the constitution of
society in ancient Greece and Rome, and how in the course of
history the two changed together. In line with other nineteenth-century thinkers, Fustel de Coulanges saw the correlation in terms of cause and effect. The original nucleus of
pre-urban society in his analysis was the family hearth, the
religious symbol of the family in which the father served as
priest.

> The tribe, like the family and the phratry, was estab-
> lished as an independent body, since it had a special wor-
> ship from which the stranger was excluded. Once formed,
> no new family could be admitted to it. Just as several
> phratries were united in a tribe, several tribes might as-
> sociate together, on condition that the religion of each
> should be respected. The day in which this alliance took
> place the city existed.[7]

Thus, for Fustel de Coulanges, the ancient city was primarily a religious community. While his assumption that religion is the cause and the other institutions are the effect
cannot be accepted uncritically, the assessment of A. R. Radcliffe-Brown provides a fair perspective on the work of this
pioneer. While he rejects the cause-effect sequence of Fustel
de Coulanges, he says:

> We can . . . retain as a valuable and permanent contribu-
> tion to our subject a great deal of what Fustel de Cou-
> langes wrote. We can say that he has produced evidence
> that in ancient Greece and Rome the religion on the one
> side and the many important institutions on the other are
> closely united as interdependent parts of a coherent and
> unified system.[8]

Many of our observations on the place of religion in the
OT city will draw on the work of the contemporary sociologist
Gideon Sjoberg. Like Fustel de Coulanges, he emphasizes the
importance of religion in the ancient city. Writing in his
magnum opus, *The Preindustrial City: Past and Present*, he says:

> The religious norms [in the preindustrial city], deriving
> from the religious values and in turn reinforcing them are
> highly prescriptive. One's day-by-day behavior is

largely governed by religious injunctions, and few areas of activity--be these family life, politics, economics, education or whatever--escape their pervasive influence. Moreover, the periodic religious ceremonies, in which a large segment of the community may participate, are one of the few mechanisms the city possesses for integrating disparate groups in an otherwise segmented community.[9]

Henry Sumner Maine in his *Ancient Law*, saw a differentiation between two principles of social organization which were operative in the ancient city.[10] On the one hand he posited an organization based on kinship in which status in the family was the key determinative. On the other hand, there was a principle of territoriality which tended to be substituted for the kinship base in an urban setting, thus freeing the individual to enter into "contractual" relations. The effect of this analysis, according to Don Martindale, was to bring the relations of kinship and territory into focus institutionally, shifting the attention of urban theory to the evolution of law. This then was the starting point for rich additional developments and the consideration of the importance of a whole series of legal or semi-legal phenomena for the development of the city. Maine's theory pervades the work of such OT scholars as Antonin Causse, and has been modified only in more recent times.[11] Again, the work of Sjoberg cited above will be informative for our study with respect to the nature of the family in the urban sphere. Sjoberg is one of those who has modified earlier theory regarding the urban family. Instead of maintaining that kinship was replaced as an organizational principle in the pre-industrial urban setting, he holds that the preindustrial urbanite functioned within a family system and subordinated himself to it.

Another of the early European urban theorists was Henri Pirenne.[13] His analysis of the ancient city centered on urban economic institutions. For him the *sine qua non* of the city was the development of a class of merchants who were the promulgators of a distinct communal organization. Thus, for Pirenne, the city was above all the community of merchants.

While these scholars are only representatives of a wider body of early urban theorists, their approach is certainly typical of the whole group. Martindale characterizes early European urban theory in the following terms:

There are two general properties of the theories of the
city emerging in the late nineteenth and early twentieth
centuries in Europe--they all assume that the characteristics of any unit of social life are determined by institutions. Secondly, they all generally assume that human society is an evolutionary or historical product, hence explanation of social events consists in a discovery of origins. Thus, in contrast both to the ecological theory of
the city and the rather fragmentary social-psychological
theory of the city, European urban theory at the turn of
the century held an institutional theory of the city. The
explanation of the city was found in the peculiar order
and historical primacy of its institutions. The various
special theories differed in terms of the particular institution they took to be central or original.[14]

In addition to the emphasis on institutions, another focus
of urban theory has been a continuing attempt to differentiate
urban life from pre- or extra-urban life in terms of the construction of a rural-urban or folk-urban dichotomy. One of the
first systematic attempts to elaborate such differences was
that of Ferdinand Tönnies in his *Gemeinschaft und Gesellschaft*,
published in 1887.[15] Like Maine, Tönnies attached fundamental
significance to the difference between small-scale communities
based on kinship ties and large-scale societies which transcen-
ded such ties. While Maine's key terms were "status" and "contract," Tönnies used the two German words *Gemeinschaft*, "community," to describe the former type of societal organization,
and *Gesellschaft*, "society," to characterize the latter. These
basic terms were then elaborated with considerable specificity
as to their differentiating characteristics.

Emile Durkheim in *De division du travail social*, and in
subsequent works, described this differentiation in terms of a
"mechanical" and an "organic" solidarity and sought to deline-
ate the significance of such criteria as volume, mass, and density in forms of social organization.[16]

These germinal thinkers were followed by numerous others
in the early period of urban theory, and this means of concept-
ualization has carried over into modern sociological theory
where there has come into being a whole series of paired terms,
some suggesting a dichotomy, but more often, a continuum, and
all involving either directly or indirectly characteristics im-
puted to a "rural" or "urban" social morphology. Richard Dewey
has observed that it has become common to equate the general
terms "rural-urban" with such classifications as "sacred-

secular," *Gemeinschaft-Gesellschaft*," "folk-urban," "static-dynamic," "agricultural-non-agricultural," "pre-literate-literate," "primitive-civilized," etc.[17] But Dewey *et al.* have criticized the use that has been made of such differentiations. P. M. Hauser expresses the tone of this critique when he says:

> Differentiation between the folk and urban society and the urban and rural social orders became so widely diffused in the literature of sociology and anthropology, in the literature of general education, and in the general lay literature, as well, that they were accepted as generalizations resulting from sociological and anthropological research. Yet the fact is that most of the scholars who contributed to the emergence of these concepts regarded them not as generalizations based on research but, rather as 'ideal type constructs. [18]

Hauser's conclusion, which is particularly relevant for our purposes, is that the usefulness of folk-urban and rural-urban dichotomies is limited by the fact that they are ideal-type constructs which are products of modern Western writers. Hauser's opinion is also reflected in the writing of Sjoberg, who believes that many of the generalizations with regard to rural-urban differences are in need of a thorough overhauling. Like Hauser, Dewey, *et al.*, Sjoberg believes that this situation is the result of the erroneous assumption that numerous patterns on the American scene can be read back into earlier times. The crucial part of Sjoberg's critique which makes his work of particular relevance for our study of the OT city is his recognition that many rural-urban differences are typical only of industrial-urban, not of preindustrial societies. Although industrial and preindustrial orders exhibit some common rural-urban divergencies, there are others that are seen by Sjoberg as peculiar to preindustrial societies:

> Such a category as 'urban society' may require still further breakdown, inasmuch as some rural-urban differences appear to be valid only for specific types of societies--e.g. for either industrial or preindustrial civilizations. Thus in preindustrial (or feudal) societies, the familial and religious organizations in their most highly developed and integrated forms are urban rather than rural, a fact that contravenes many generalizations based solely upon research in the United States. . . The fact is that sociologists need to give much more attention to defining the precise limits of their generalizations concerning rural-urban phenomena.[19]

Sjoberg's thesis has gained empirical support in the work of Oscar Lewis, which is based primarily on his research in

Mexico City. Lewis' findings provide evidence that urbanization is not a single, unitary, universally homogeneous process
but assumes different forms and meanings, depending on the prevailing historic, economic, and cultural conditions. Among
other things, Lewis found that peasants adapted to city life
with far greater ease than one would have expected judging from
folk-urban theory. Family life remained quite stable and extended family ties increased rather than decreased. Religious
life became more Catholic and disciplined, indicating the reverse of the anticipated secularization process. Lewis then
concluded that in place of, or in addition to, the handy designations of "folk society," "peasant society," "urban society,"
etc., we need a larger number of subtypes based on better-de-
fined variables and perhaps the addition of new ones.[20]

There is thus evidence to show that many of the things
which have been uncritically taken as part and parcel of urbanism do not depend upon cities for their existence, at least in-
sofar as the preindustrial city is concerned. What then are
the distinctive traits or cultural universals of the preindustrial city as a city-type which can serve the formulation of a
definition of the city and of urbanization so far as the OT is
concerned? In seeking to isolate such criteria, we shall follow Sjoberg's basic thesis:

> Preindustrial cities everywhere display strikingly similar
> social and ecological structures, not necessarily in spe-
> cific cultural content, but certainly in basic form. Ad-
> mittedly the idiosyncratic values of any given culture do
> induce some unique urban patterns. But all too much em-
> phasis has been given to the aberrant, especially by wri-
> ters imbued with the humanistic tradition. . . We seek to
> isolate for preindustrial cities structural universals,
> those elements that transcend cultural boundaries. These
> cities share numerous patterns in the realms of ecology,
> class, and the family, as well as in their economic, pol-
> itical, religious, and educational structures, arrange-
> ments that diverge sharply from their counterparts in ma-
> ture industrial cities.[21]

Sjoberg takes technology, that is the available energy,
tools, and know-how, as his key independent variable in distinguishing the preindustrial city from its industrial succes-
sor, without however committing himself to a technological determinism or a unilinear evolutionary schema, a trap that other
urban theorists are not so successful in avoiding.[22]

One definition of the city which is frequently quoted is that of Louis Wirth, which he developed in the well-known essay which was cited above. Parts of his protracted definition are incorporated into many currently used definitions of urbanism, and, by implication, of ruralism as well. In short, Wirth's idea was that:

. . . on the basis of the three variables, number, density of settlement, and degree of heterogeneity of the urban population, it appears possible to explain the characteristics of urban life and to account for the differences between cities of various sizes and types.[23]

Certainly Wirth's criteria have some validity, but they are hardly sufficient in themselves to constitute a definition of the city and, as Martindale has observed, when taken by themselves there sets in "a strong tendency for the relevant world of action to be reduced to mere matters of increase, density, and heterogeneity of population which have psychological effects."[24]

One of the most comprehensive lists of definitive urban criteria is that of V. Gordon Childe, which incorporates Wirth's citeria along with several other.[25] We shall set forth Childe's criteria here as a framework for discussion. Childe enumerates a total of ten criteria, both social and cultural in nature, which he then subdivides into two groups of five each. The first five criteria deal with the importance of full-time specialists, supported ultimately by the ability of farmers to produce a food "surplus," as an index of complex societal structure. The second five criteria deal with ways in which the surplus produce was collected and used, other than for the support of specialists. The criteria, stated in concise form, are as follows:

(1) The presence of full-time specialists. These specialists exchange their services for food produced by the farmers, but this was a mediated rather than a direct exchange. Only a small portion of the population lived in cities after they emerged or engaged in specialized urban tasks.

(2) Larger, denser populations [à la Wirth et al.]. This demographic situation is made possible by the fact that urbanites do not need space to produce food.

(3) Great art, produced by specialists.

(4) The presence of writing and numerical notation.

(5) Exact and predictive sciences, such as arithmetic, geometry and astronomy.

(6) Tribute or taxes paid by farmers to a religious or secular administration, thus allowing for the concentration of the surplus product.

(7) A society organized on the basis of residence instead of, or on top of, a basis of kinship.

(8) Monumental public buildings symbolizing the society's surplus.

(9) "Foreign" trade made possible by the surplus.

(10) A class-structured society which emerged from the unequal distribution of more plentiful property and from specialized activities. The elite contributed important functions to the society--usually religious, political or military--but nevertheless the gap between their life and that of the peasant-farmer was very wide.

Since we shall have occasion to discuss most of these criteria in some detail in the chapters which follow, we shall here make only some general comments concerning them.

At the outset, we should amend this list to include a criterion which certainly must be included in the definition of the city in the OT, namely, the fact that a city must be bounded by walls or fortifications. These walls can be seen as both symbolic of and preservative of the social organization which resulted in a sense of the corporate individuality of the urban unit. Wolf Schneider refers to an inscription of Urnanshe of Lagash which gives one of the earliest written definitions of the essentials of a city in the ancient Near East: "The king built the temple and the walls, erected statues, dug a canal, and filled the storehouse with grain."[26] This early definition of the city names physical structures which were examples of monumental architecture. The importance of social organization in the definition of urbanization is emphasized by Eric Lampard:

> Urbanization may be regarded as the organization component of a population's achieved capacity for adaptation. It is a way of ordering a population to attain a certain level of subsistence and security in a given environment. The technological component is always a direct constituent of social organization but is distinct from it. Technology is the *sine qua non* of urbanization,

as of every other form of community organization, but it is not the exclusive property of the city. Thus the demographic approach not only defines the process of urbanization with absolute parsimony but, by the addition of one 'cultural' variable, technology, it elucidates the role of a fourth 'social' variable, organization. Together the four variables--population, technology, organization and environment--may explain the prevailing pattern of urbanization and indicate how that pattern emerged in the past.[27]

While technological achievements are in evidence in Childe's criteria, Lampard's statement regarding the relationship between technology and other variables is well taken. In some of Childe's earlier works, technology was seen as developing apart from, rather than as a human creation which both required some changes in social organization and made others possible. We shall have cause to give further attention to this aspect of urbanization in our sketch of the history of urbanization as it pertains to the OT in our fourth chapter.

The second of Childe's criteria, the demographic one, is of limited applicability to the OT. While the OT city was densely populated, relatively speaking, there are as we shall see in Chapter III peculiarities which make it extremely questionable to speak of large "resident" urban populations. In many cases, the city in the OT is not so much a place of residence as a fortified place of refuge. Thus the population of a city could fluctuate as a function of the presence or absence of threats to its populace. The criterion of size is of even less relevance for defining the OT city. As we shall demonstrate in Chapter II, the urban vocabulary of the OT centers on the defensive structures instead of size in assigning the designation "city" to a community.

The question of the existence of writing as an urban criterion has occasioned some disagreement among scholars. Redfield is among those who believe this to be a critical factor in distinguishing the "urban" from the "folk:"

> . . . an aspect of the isolation of the folk society is the absence of books. The folk communicate only by word of mouth; therefore the communication upon which understanding is built is only that which takes place among neighbors, within the little society itself . . . With no form of belief established by written record, there can be no historical sense . . . no theology, and no basis for science in recorded experiment.[28]

In this statement, Redfield brings together the fourth and
fifth of Childe's criteria. Sjoberg would also include a
literate group as a necessary part of Childe's group of full-
time urban specialists, but he admits that the criterion of
literacy does not in itself resolve all difficulties in classi-
fying communities as urban or not.[29] While this criterion
would appear to be an objective one, in that it can be inferred
with high probability and in a detached way from material
remains, its necessity has been placed in question principally
by the discoveries of Neolithic Jericho.

The archaeological remains at Jericho provide evidence
for all of those criteria which can be so deduced, including
a central social organization capable of constructing elaborate public works of monumental proportions and of exploiting
an environment which was far from ideal, agriculturally speaking. There is also evidence of considerable artistic skill.
It would thus seem probable that this community may have had
at least some system of numerical notation used by the "ruling
class" to facilitate administration. The lack of evidence
for such a system may just be an accident of archaeology.
But it also remains at least theoretically possible that writing preceded the emergence of cities. If writing is seen as
an expression of invention and creativity, it may not be a
definitive urban factor. A. J. Reiss, Jr., for example,
suggests that if the invention of the wheel, the domestication
of animals, or the use of another man's labor are preconditions to urbanization, then they must have arisen under non-
urbanized conditions. Thus urbanization itself cannot be a
sufficient source of invention or creativity.[30] The bibliography of this controversy will be cited in Chapter IV.

Total employment in urban (that is, non-agricultural)
functions is an unsatisfactory criterion for defining the
OT city. In this connection we would agree with C. T. Stewart,
Jr., who proposes that the use of the employment pattern be
extended to distinguish between urban and rural functions and
maintains that a minimum percentage of the resident population
must be engaged in urban functions to give the settlement a
mainly urban character.[31] Certainly the OT city contained a
small stratum of religious and governmental officials, traders

and artisans, whose residence in the city was made possible
because their livelihood did not depend upon their presence on
the land.[32] As we shall see in Chapter III, there is considerable evidence in the OT for a "commuting" pattern on the part
of urban dwellers. This pattern involved the city as a "bed-
room community," to use contemporary parlance. A not inconsid-
erable proportion of the city's lower class would leave the
city in the morning to spend the daylight hours as agricultural laborers then return to the city for the night. Thus,
a rigid rural-urban pattern cannot be imposed upon the OT.

Childe's sixth criterion defines the city in relation to
its hinterland. Lampard describes this relationship in the
following terms:

> Definitive urbanization was the organization and appropri-
> ation of an agricultural surplus. The capacity to real-
> ize and invest the net social saving was the primary
> achievement of the first cities; it involved prolonged
> and many-sided operations beyond the capabilities of
> other known forms of sedentary adaptation. Hamlets and
> villages could neither store nor protect a large and
> varied social product. Thus the realization and control
> of saving--whether instituted by bureaucratic, military,
> commercial, or fiduciary means--became the strategic
> function that established the framework within which other
> routinized roles would be performed. Herein lies the
> explanation of why decisions emanating from the center
> had such a profound dominance over the population area as
> a whole.[33]

This statement certainly serves to illustrate the effect
of the city on the pattern of social life. Itself a product
of basic economic and technological developments, the city in
turn tends to exercise influence not only over aspects of
existence within the city proper but in the rural hinterland
as well. In assessing such a situation, one should be careful
not to read into the term "surplus" the modern connotation of
the word which derives from a highly-mechanized agricultural
system in which one farmer is capable of supporting a large
number of urban dwellers. In preindustrial times just the
reverse was true and there was no real "surplus" in the modern
sense of the word. Certainly the city could not exist until
food production had reached the stage where the farmer could
produce more than he could consume, but as Kingsley Davis has
observed, high productivity per acre does not necessarily
mean high per capita productivity. Instead of producing a

surplus for urban dwellers, the cultivators could, at least
theoretically, multiply on the land until they produced just
enough to sustain themselves.[34] Thus the existence of the
city depended upon the ability of the ruling class to extract
the "surplus" from the hinterland in the form of tribute or
taxes. Speaking of the problem of motivating farmers to
surrender food to urbanites, Sjoberg says:

> It is erroneous to assume that surpluses are constituted
> simply as the result of technological forces, although
> relatively advanced technology is necessary if a surplus
> is to be produced. Through an appropriate ideology,
> reinforced by coercion in the form of taxes and tributes,
> the elite induces the peasantry to increase its produc-
> tion and to relinquish some of its harvest to the urban
> community. In other words, it must persuade many persons
> subsisting, relative to industrial standards, on the very
> margins of existence, under conditions of near starvation
> or malnutrition, to surrender food and other items that
> they themselves could readily use.[35]

The interplay between technological and organizational
factors is well put in the following statement:

> We must guard against invoking cultural determinism, i.e.
> viewing religious, political, or other features of social
> organization as the sole determinants of . . . cities.
> No amount of religious exaltation or of political control
> could have originally concentrated and administered a
> surplus product if environmental and technological con-
> ditions had not made such a surplus possible. Neverthe-
> less, the creation [and continuance] of cities was not
> an inevitable consequence of a society's possession of
> such surpluses alone; rather it was through the interac-
> tion of social, technological, and environmental factors
> that cities were formed. But the catalytic function of
> political and religious organization, and the seemingly
> more 'abstract' aspects of social structure, exemplifies
> the role of new, complex forms of society in making
> efficient use of surpluses.[36]

Max Weber's perspective on the city is especially relevant
at this juncture. Sjoberg, in his classification of urban
theorists by the particular variable to which their "school"
gives priority, assigns Weber to what he terms the "value-
orientation school." This school stresses values, social or
cultural, as key determinants in the study of land use and
urban social structure. In essence, Weber is said to have
taken the values of sociocultural systems as his explanatory
variable and the social structure of the city as his dependent
variable.[37] Weber's approach has been defended by Gerhard
Lenski who perceives that Weber was careful to point out that

he was not trying to substitute a theory of religious determinism, nor was he attempting to deny the role of economic institutions in the process of social change. Rather his goal was simply to challenge what he regarded as an unrealistic and over-simplified theory of social change advocated by the economic determinists and to propose a more adequate alternative.[38]

Certainly we shall have to take cultural and social values into consideration in our attempt to account for the ecological, physical, and social structures of the OT city. While the OT city does have much in common with other preindustrial cities, the technological variable alone cannot explain all aspects of Israelite urban structures. Surely the distinctive value orientation stemming from the Yahwistic religion contributed to the uniqueness of the OT city. But in saying this, we are not committing ourselves to a kind of one-to-one correlation between values and social structures. Such a simplistic assumption stands behind much of the writing of those who have read into the OT a thoroughgoing "anti-urbanism," based primarily on the idea that the Yahwistic value system included a positive valuation of the nomadic life and a corresponding antipathy for the settled life of the city. In Chapter IV we shall examine the Israelite assessment of the city. In this examination we shall challenge the assumption that there is a normative "nomadic ideal" in the OT and shall seek, at the same time, to make discernible the effect of cultural values on the Israelite concept of the city.

Since we have introduced Max Weber into our discussion, Weber's definition of the city can serve as a transition to the discussion of the criterion of trade in Childe's set of *propia* of the city. For Weber, in order to constitute a full urban community a settlement must:

> . . . display a relative predominance of trade-commercial relations with the settlement as a whole displaying the following features: (1) a fortification; (2) a market; (3) a court of its own and at least partially autonomous law; (4) a related form of association; and (5) at least partial autonomy and autocephaly, thus also an administration by authorities in the election of whom the burghers participated.[39]

While Childe includes "foreign" trade among his criteria, Weber speaks more in terms of the local commercial enterprise.

There is certainly evidence for the existence of local markets in the OT, although it is questionable whether it can be said that as a rule there was "a relative predominance of trade-commercial relations" in the OT city, since even urban economy retains an agricultural base throughout the OT period. "Foreign trade" as such in the OT was virtually a royal monopoly, and was for the most part limited to luxury goods which were not really a commodity sold on the open market, but whose distribution was limited to the elite urban stratum. Sjoberg's conception of the place of commercial activity in the preindustrial city is relevant here:

> Economic activity is poorly developed in the preindustrial city, for manual labor, or indeed any that requires one to mingle with the humbler folk is depreciated and eschewed by the elite. Except for a few large-scale merchants, who may succeed in buying their way into the elite, persons engaged in economic activity are either of the lower class (artisans, laborers, and some shopkeepers) or outcastes (some businessmen, and those who carry out the especially degrading and arduous tasks in the city.)[40]

In his analysis of urban industrial-commercial enterprises, Sjoberg considers the guild, itself a uniquely urban phenomenon, to be the key unit in the urban economic realm. Accordingly, in Chapter III we shall collect and evaluate the evidence for the existence of guilds in the OT city.

In his definition of the city Weber also mentions another factor which is of importance in defining the OT city, namely, the feature of at least partial autonomy and autocephaly in legal and administrative matters. While the development of municipal politics, in the sense of a self-conscious corporate body with autonomous, secular institutions for its own administration, was not consummated until classical times, we will inquire into the OT precursor of the Greek *polis*. The Israelites were heirs of the Canaanite city-state system of administration. André Piganiol defines the city-state as: "An autonomous state composed of a city and its outskirts and revealing a more or less clearly defined distinction between a bourgeois and a peasant class."[41] In a sense, the city-state, comprising the city proper and its hinterland, including the city's fields and villages was a self-contained, self-sufficient, independent unit of human society where sovereignty was vested in the city dwellers and their representatives. Historically, this concept of the city-state had considerable durability in the ancient Near East, and the experiments at empire succeeded only with some difficulty.

In the OT the principal urban legal-administrative body was that of the elders, who met at the city gate. Like the institution of the city-state, the elders were a rather durable institution, outlasting the monarchy so far as Israel was concerned. In Chapter III, we shall discuss the constitution of this body, its role, and the relationships between municipal and central authority under the Israelite monarchy. In the same chapter, the interplay between residence and kinship as organizational factors will be considered, and the continuing role of kinship in determining the community leadership will be assessed.

The last of Childe's criteria cites a bifurcated class structure as an urban characteristic. While the OT does bear witness to a system of social stratification which emerged in the intensive urbanization of the monarchical period and at last partially as a result of unequal property distribution, part of our problem will be to determine the degree to which such a bifurcation is indicative of a rural-urban split and thus to what degree it was a factor in any anti-urban sentiments. Sjoberg agrees that the preindustrial city was characterized by a bifurcated class structure, but he merges the peasantry, or rural population, with the lower urban caste to form one broad, lower class group:

> Few aspects of daily activity [in the preindustrial city] escape the pervasive influence of class. A small urbanized, privileged group commands the local community and the society and is nourished by the lower class. . . Social mobility in the city . . . seems, relative to the industrial norms, inconsequential. The small upper class . . . controls the key organizational units of government, religion and education in the city and society.[42]

In Chapter III we shall discuss the urban social structure in the OT. There we shall make use of Sjoberg's framework and shall seek to determine the degree to which the two classes interacted, the existence of leveling factors, etc. It is in connection with the class structure that much of the city's influence in society can be seen. The elite class was an urban class, and their influence far surpassed what might be expected on the basis of their small number relative to the total population. The preponderant role which the city played in the process of cultural change is due largely to their activity and influence.

Robert Redfield and Milton Singer have suggested two basically different roles which cities and their elite can play in relation to cultural change, both of which we shall see operative in the OT. The first of these roles is called "orthogenetic," and in this role the city serves to carry forward an older culture into a systematic and reflective dimension. The second role is termed "heterogenetic" and characterizes the role of the city in creating original modes of thought beyond or in conflict with those of an older culture.

> Insofar as the city has an orthogenetic role, it is not to maintain culture as it was; the orthogenetic city is not static; it is the place where religious, philosophic, and literary specialist reflect, synthesize and create out of the traditional material new arrangements and developments that are felt by the people to be outgrowths of the old. What is changed is a further statement of what was there before. Insofar as the city has a hetero-genetic role, it is a place of differing traditions, a center of heresy, heterodoxy and dissent, of interruption and destruction of ancient tradition. . . Cities are both these things, and the same events may appear to particular people or groups to be representative of heterogenesis. The predominant trend may be in one of two directions, and so allow us to characterize the city, or that phase of the history of the city, as the one or the other.[43]

The way in which the OT city fulfills both of these roles will be one of our foci throughout this study.

Childe's ten criteria can thus serve, with the provisos and amendments suggested, as a provisional definition of the city in the OT. The foregoing critique of this definition is only introductory to a continuing examination of the concept of the city in the OT which will occupy us throughout our study. We shall consider the city basically from three perspectives: (1) We shall consider the relationship between people and the urban physical environment; (2) we shall consider those aspects of social organization for which the urban society of the OT is noteworthy; and, (3) we shall consider the ways in which the city affects the Israelites' thinking. In giving attention to the first two of these perspectives, we shall approach the city and urbanization in a way which reflects the position of Wirth:

> Urbanization denotes not just the process by which persons are attracted to a place called the city and incorporated into its system of life. It refers also to that cumulative accentuation of the characteristics distinctive of the mode of life which is associated with the growth of cities, and finally to the changes in the direction of modes of life recognized as urban which are apparent among people, wherever they may be, who have come under the spell of the influences which the city exerts by virtue of the power of its institutions and personalities.[44]

The third perspective will lead us to consider the city as a symbol. Gist and Fava have set forth this aspect of the city in the following terms:

> The emotional and moral qualities assigned to urban life are an illustration of the symbolic meaning of the city. The city has been viewed as the embodiment of good or evil; as representing progress or decline; as being the arena of human alienation or human salvation. There can be no factually correct answers to the normative questions posed by such opposed views of urban life. The significance of such questions lies in their being asked at all, for this significance is that man is not neutral to cities, but surrounds them with values and beliefs. Hence cities become symbols, as well as things.[45]

In sum, we propose to do for the OT city what Sjoberg has suggested in his conclusion to *The Preindustrial City* as to the utility of his typology:

> The ultimate test of our constructed type . . . is its long-run utility for interpreting empirical phenomena. . . . the typology should prove useful to historians, anthropologists, and archaeologists attempting to reconstruct the social arrangements in cities long since dead. Certain aspects of their life-ways lie forever beyond our grasp. The only reasonable alternative is extrapolation to the past from data on more recent feudal cities, utilizing in the process, recent advances in the social scientist's knowledge of social systems. Knowing what to expect in earlier cities imparts fuller meaning to written records and permits more satisfactory reconstructions where gaps exist in the data. A salient weakness in much historical research is the tendency to assume uniqueness for much of the social phenomena encountered; all manner of false interpretations ensue. Such is historicism, ultimately a denial of objective generalization as the goal of social science.[46]

NOTES

[1] Louis Wirth, "Urbanism as a Way of Life," *Reader in Urban Sociology* (eds. P. K. Hatt and A. J. Reiss; Glencoe, Ill.: Free Press, 1951) 37.

[2] R. E. Park, "The City: Suggestions for the Investigation of Human Behavior in the Urban Environment," *Reader in Urban Sociology*, 2.

[3] Cf. Wirth, "The Urban Society and Civilization," *AJOS* XLV (1940) 743-755.

[4] For a comprehensive survey of the field of urban history see H. J. Dyos ("Agenda for Urban Historians," *The Study of Urban History* [H. J. Dyos; London: Ed. Arnold, 1968] 1-46).

[5] Milton Singer, "The Expansion of Society and its Cultural Implications," *The City Invincible: A Symposium on Urbanization and Cultural Development in the Ancient Near East* (C. H. Kraeling and R. M. Adams; Chicago: The University of Chicago Press, 1960) 260-261.

[6] Ibid., 261.

[7] N. D. Fustel de Coulanges, *The Ancient City: A Study of Religion, Laws and Institutions of Greece and Rome* (N. Y.: Chas. T. Dillingham, 1882) 126-127.

[8] A. R. Radcliffe-Brown, "Religion and Society," *Structure and Function in Primitive Society* (N. Y.: Free Press, 1965) 162.

[9] Gideon Sjoberg, *The Preindustrial City: Past and Present* (Glencoe, Ill.: Free Press, 1960) 327. Cf. also Chapter IX, "Religious Structure," 256-284.

[10] Henry Sumner Maine, *Ancient Law* (London: J. Murray, 1861).

[11] Cf. esp. Antonin Causse, *Du groupe ethnique à la communaute religieuse. Le problème sociologique de la religion d'Israel* (Paris: Alcan, 1937).

[12] Sjoberg, *Preindustrial City*, Chapter VI, "Marriage and the Family," 145-181.

[13] Pirenne's major work is *Medieval Cities: Their Origins and the Revival of Trade* (Princeton: Princeton University Press, 1925).

[14] Don Martindale, "Prefatory Remarks: The Theory of the City," Max Weber, *The City*, trans. and ed. by Don Martindale and Gertrude Neuwirth (N. Y.: Free Press, 1966) 46.

[15] F. Tönnies, *Community and Association* (London: Routledge and Kegan Paul, 1955).

[16]
E. Durkheim, *The Division of Labor in Society* (N. Y.: Free Press, 1947). For an excellent discussion of the theories of Tönnies, Durkheim, *et al.*, see Peter H. Mann

(An Approach to Urban Sociology [London: Routledge and Kegan Paul, 1965] 191-205).

[17]Richard Dewey, "The Rural-urban Continuum: Real but Relatively Unimportant," *AJOS* LXVI (1960), 62.

[18]P. M. Hauser, "Observations on the Urban-Folk and Urban-Rural Dichotomies as Forms of Western Ethnocentrism," *The Study of Urbanization* (eds. P. M. Hauser and L. F. Schnore; N. Y.: John Wiley and Sons, 1965) 504.

[19]Sjoberg, "Comparative Urban Sociology," *Sociology Today: Problems and Prospects, II* (eds. Robert K. Merton, *et al.*; N. Y.: Harper and Row, 1959) 342-343.

[20]Oscar Lewis, "Further Observations on the Folk-Urban Continuum and Urbanization with Special Reference to Mexico City," *The Study of Urbanization,* 494-495. [For a cross-cultural statement on the role of corporate kin groups see Paul Wheatley (*The Pivot of the Four Quarters* [Chicago: Aldine, 1971] 374-377).]

[21]Sjoberg, *Preindustrial City,* 5-6.

[22]Ibid., 7-13.

[23]Wirth, "Urbanism as a Way of Life," 44.

[24]Martindale, "Prefatory Remarks," 42.

[25]Childe's list appears in its most comprehensive form in "The Urban Revolution," *Town Planning Review* XXI (1950) 3-17. He adds a short note in "Civilization, Cities and Towns," *Antiquity* XXXI (1957) 36-38.

[26]Wolf Schneider, *Überall ist Babylon: die Stadt als Schicksal des Menschen von Ur bis Utopia* (Düsseldorf: Econ Verlag, 1960) 35.

[27]Eric Lampard, "Historical Aspects of Urbanization," in *The Study of Urbanization,* 521-522.

[28]Robert Redfield, "The Folk Society," *AJOS* LII (1947) 296-297.

[29]Sjoberg, *Preindustrial City,* 32-33. [For a succint discussion of writing as an index of urban status see Wheatley (*Pivot of the Four Quarters,* 377-383).]

[30]A. J. Reiss, Jr., "An Analysis of Urban Phenomena," *The Metropolis and Modern Life* (ed. R. M. Fisher; Garden City: Doubleday, 1955) 42. Cf. also Dewey ("The Rural-Urban Continuum," 63).

[31]C. T. Steward, Jr., "The Rural-urban Dichotomy: Concepts and Uses," *AJOS* LXIV (1958) 152.

[32]Cf. Kingsley Davis, "The Origin and Growth of Urbanism in the World," *AJOS* LX (1955) 429-437.

[33]Lampard, "Historical Aspects of Urbanization," 542.

[34]Davis, "The Origin and Growth of Urbanism," 430. Cf. also Clifford Geertz, *Agricultural Involution* (Berkeley: University of California Press, 1963).

[35]Sjoberg, *Preindustrial City,* 118. For a discussion of the difficulties in defining what a "surplus" is, see Marvin

Harris, "The Economy Has No Surplus?" *American Anthropologist* LXI (1959) 185-199.

[36] N. P. Gist and S. F. Fava, *Urban Society* (5th ed.; N. Y.: Thomas Crowell, 1964) 18.

[37] Sjoberg, "Theory and Research in Urban Sociology," *The Study of Urbanization*, 157-189.

[38] Gerhard E. Lenski, *The Religious Factor: A Sociological Study of Religion's Impact on Politics, Economics, and Family Life* (Garden City: Doubleday: 1963) 5-6.

[39] Max Weber, *The City*, 80.

[40] Sjoberg, *Preindustrial City*, 325.

[41] André Piganiol, "City-State," *Reader in Urban Sociology*, 71.

[42] Sjoberg, *Preindustrial City*, 324.

[43] Robert Redfield and Milton Singer, *The Cultural Role of Cities* (Chicago: University of Chicago Press, 1961) 169-170.

[44] Wirth, "Urbanism as a Way of Life," 34.

[45] Gist and Fava, *Urban Society*, 524.

[46] Sjoberg, *Preindustrial City*, 333.

THE URBAN TERMINOLOGY OF THE OLD TESTAMENT

In this section, the principal focus will be on a philological investigation of the most frequently used OT word for
"city," ʿîr, its synonyms, homonyms, and cognates in related
Semitic languages, as well as its particular use in the OT
text. In attempting to examine the etymology of this word, an
earnest effort is made to avoid what James Barr has termed the
"over-etymological approach" in which the endeavor to state the
meaning in the actual language under study (in our case, Hebrew) has often been biased by an attempt to fit this meaning
into a possible derivative process starting from the comparative material.[1] The meanings of the word ʿîr obtained here are
hopefully those which can be derived from the use of the word
in the actual OT literature. It is thus assumed that a Hebrew
word has corresponding Hebrew meanings which belong intrinsically to that language and are not somehow "naturally" determined by derivation from a supposed root meaning of a cognate
word in another Semitic language. Comparative philology will
be used here, nevertheless, as a tool in helping to determine
the general semantic field in which a word may lie. This general meaning will then be tested over against the use of the
word in the OT text in order to determine more subtle nuances
it may have there.

The Term ʿîr, Its Frequency and Characteristics

The most frequently occurring term for "city" in the OT,
ʿîr, is found some 1,090 times, spread over the entire historical range of the literature.[2]

The word ʿîr is feminine in gender, corresponding to the
gender of places in Hebrew generally. GKC lists several classes of ideas which are generally regarded as feminine. The
reason given for the names of countries and towns being so regarded is that they were thought of as the mothers and nurses
of their inhabitants. The same reasoning can then be applied
to appellative nouns which denote a circumscribed space, but

are not proper nouns, e.g., *'ereṣ* and *'ǐr*.[3]

An unresolved problem in connection with *'ǐr* is the peculiar divergence between its singular and plural forms. The
singular is consistently read *'ǐr*, with the *ḥǐreq yôd*, while
the plural regularly appears as *'ārǐm* (construct, *'ārê*).[4] The
most satisfactory explanation yet set forth is that of GKC,
where it is contended that the plural is not formed from *'ǐr*,
but rather from a related singular, *'ār*, which occurs in the
OT only in proper names.[5] In other words, there is a possibility that the actual form *'ār* may have existed in Hebrew but was
a dialectic or archaic form which was used only in the formation of proper nouns.[6] City names in the OT formed with *'ār*
include Ar, or Ar-Moab (Num 21:15, 28; Deut 2:9, 18, 29; Isa
15:1) and Aroer (Deut 4:48; Josh 12:2). The Hebrew noun *yôm*,
"day," whose plural is *yāmǐm* is cited by GKC as another noun
whose plural is formed on a different base word. Bauer-Leander
suggests the possibility that *'ārǐm* is perhaps analogous to
bātǐm, "houses," which is the plural of the singular *bayit*
(construct, *bêt*), or, alternatively, that both words stem from
a dialect in which the *ay* was contracted to *ā*.[7]

Another type of explanation for this divergence of singular and plural forms is the one which seeks to determine the
root on which *'ǐr* is formed. Fuerst sees such a possible root
in *'wr*, with the meaning "to surround, circle, enclose." The
plural *'ārǐm* then is formed from a singular *'ôr*, with *ô>ā* as in
yôm.[8] The absence of any root with this meaning in Hebrew,
however, would seem to militate against this possibility.
Gesenius has also suggested that *'ǐr* may be derived from a
root *'wr*, which bears the meaning "to awake, be awake, be
roused." He then drew from this that significance that in its
origins the city was an *Alarmplatz* for the neighboring shepherds when they were "roused."[9] While in this case the existence of a root *'wr*, "to be roused," cannot be doubted, this
does not mean that the noun *'ǐr* with a corresponding meaning
was in use in Hebrew, since the etymology of any particular
word does not necessarily establish the existence of other for-
mations on the same root. It must then be concluded that there
is no definite solution to the difficulty posed by the seemingly divergent forms of this word in the singular and plural, and

that the above suggestion of GKC seems the most probable of
those set forth.

The Etymology and Semitic Cognates of ‘îr

At the outset it should be stated that any suggested etymology for the word ‘îr should be regarded as tentative in view
of the repeated assertions of its uncertainty. Since, following the suggestion of GKC above, there are in reality two words
involved in the case of the singular and plural of ‘îr, one
might expect a dual etymology, one based on ‘îr and another
based on ‘ār. This possibility will be examined below.

In the case of such a universal cultural term as "city,"
a cross-cultural examination of urban terminology and etymologically related terms is certainly called for. If the ancient
Near East had been composed of isolated nation-states with
their own unique cultures and languages this would be a dubious
procedure at best, but it seems safe to state that, in fact,
there was a very real cultural unity in the ancient Near East.

A particular phenomenon which must be considered in the
case of a word such as ‘îr/ ‘ār which contains the laryngeal
consonant ‘ is that of phoneme merger in Hebrew, which results
in the formation of homonyms. In both Arabic and Ugaritic,
e.g., there are the two phonemes ‘ and ġ, which correspond to
an assumed similar phonemic distinction in proto-Semitic, but
which are merged in Hebrew into the one phoneme, ‘ .[10]

One of the earliest suggestions for a cognate of the Hebrew ‘îr/ ‘ār was that of Franz Praetorius in 1872 in his discussion of Himyarite (now more commonly called Sabean) inscriptions:

> The Himyarite ‘r does not seem to have the common meaning
> of 'city;' for which the Himyarite, in agreement with
> Ethiopic used the word hgr; but the meaning of 'fortified
> place, fortress,' from which the Hebrew ‘yr developed its
> general meaning.[11]

Joseph Halévy translates the same word as a "chateau fort
construit sur une montagne."[12] Both the lexica of KB and of
BDB cite this word as cognate of the Hebrew ‘îr.[13] Thus there
appears in this cognate the dual aspect of an elevated location
as well as of fortification. Both of these traits will appear
again in the following discussion, and their frequent conjunction in the meaing of the Hebrew word for "city" will hopefully

be demonstrated.

In Phoenician, the word ʿr occurs in a sixth century B.C. inscription of Eshmunyaton, a Sidonian. Here the word clearly has the meaning "city" as it appears, in a construct relationship with the proper name of the city, *SHRW*, in the phrase: ʾnk ʾsmnytn . . . wʿlt ʿr SHRW, "I am Eshmunyaton . . . and I went up to the city SHRW."[14]

It is, however, with the development of Ugaritic studies in recent decades that the candidates for cognates of this Hebrew word have significantly multiplied. Barr, while offering some critical remarks on the trend toward multiplication of homonyms, has cataloged some nine different homonyms that have been proposed for ʿyr/ ʿrym.[15] While some of these obviously have nothing to do with the root word for "city," the list bears close inspection in line with our stated purpose of discovering a general frame of meaning in which our word can be set. The first of these supposed homonyms germane to this section is that one first proposed by H. L. Ginsberg, which he derived from ġyr, which means "to protect" in Ugaritic and "to be jealous" in Arabic.[16] Ginsberg later expressed certain misgivings about this equation, but his original suggestion has been supported by a number of scholars.[17] Among those who have supported Ginsberg's derivation, John Gray has made the specific suggestion that the word ʿtr is likely to be derived from a root ʿyr, which is a cognate of the Ugaritic ġyr.[18] He finds this verbal root in a Ugaritic benediction: "ilm tġrk tslmk," "May the gods protect you and keep you safe."[19] Both Aistleitner and Gordon interpret the verb here as the *Qal* of the root nġr.[20] Driver recognizes a verbal root ġyr, but translates it "envy."[21] The root ġyr in Ugaritic, cognate to a biblical root ʿyr "to protect," is also discussed by Raphael Serra.[22]

Verbal forms based on the root ʿyr in the OT can be found in Job 8:6;[23] Deut 32:11;[24] 1 Sam 28:16;[25] and Ps 139:20.[26] Nominal forms based on this root are to be found in Isa 14:21; 33:8; Dan 4:10, 20; Mic 5:13[27] and Mal 2:12.[28]

Of these suggestions for the occurrence of the root ʿyr in the OT, the nominal form usually translated "cities" occurs only in Isa 14:21; Mic 5:13; and Jer 2:28; 19:15. It would seem that in these cases Dahood's decision to alter the

translation to "protectors" or "protective divinities" is a
rather arbitrary one. Why is this translation chosen for these
verses but is not suggested as well for the numerous other passages in the prophetic literature where the destruction of
ʿārîm, "cities," is spoken of? Instead of proposing a different translation, a sounder procedure would be to see the Hebrew
noun ʿîr/ʿārîm as derived from a root ʿyr, cognate of the Ugaritic ġyr, and then deduce from this that the word for "city"
includes within its general frame of meaning the connotation of
protection for its inhabitants and those of the immediate envi-
rons.

Another of the Ugaritic words which the Hebrew ʿîr/
ʿārîm may be related to is ġr.[29] Driver has suggested that the
noun ġr is derived from the root ġwr, which is in turn cognate
with the Arabic ġawr, "to sink in the earth," whence ġār,
"hole, pit, cavern."[30] But antithetically, Gordon suggests
that the corresponding Arabic term is rather ṣwr, "mountain,
rounded place."[31] Rössler is in agreement with Driver as to
the Arabic cognate, but suggests that the Ugaritic word with
its meaning "mountain, rounded place" developed as the result
of the phenomenon in which two supposedly opposite meanings develop from a common root.[32] He also finds it significant that
the Ugaritic synonym of ġr, "mountain," viz. gbʿ, likewise goes
back to a root with such a double meaning.[33] Gray would emphasize the first meaning of ġr as "inmost recess." He sees this
meaning especially in the following text:[34]

> klat tġrt bht ʿnt   Anat has closed the gate of the tem-
> wtqry ġlmm bst ġr   ple,
>   Gathering (her) ministrants into the
>   inmost recesses of the penetralia.

Loren Fisher, on the other hand, would emphasize the other
meaning, "hill," and relate this to the S. Arabic and Phoenician cognates mentioned above and to the Hebrew ʿîr, all of
which have the meaning of a "hill" or a "city/building on a
hill."[35]

Relating the foregoing to the stated purpose of determing
a general frame of meaning for ʿîr/ʿārîm, two more elements are
to be added, viz., the use of the word to refer to a citadel-
like structure, set in the interior of a surrounding area, and
to a structure situated on a hill or mountain. These two

elements are certainly consistent with the Phoenician and S. Arabic cognates.

In addition to these possible Ugaritic cognates, there is one other Ugaritic word which should be considered as a cognate of *ʿr̂r*/*ʿār̂îm*. This word is *ʿr*, the most common word in Ugaritic for "city."[36] Neither Aistleitner nor Driver suggest a root for this word, but Gordon proposes its derivation from a root *ʿyr*, which, however does not occur in any extant Ugaritic materials, and for which he suggests no particular meaning. All three scholars are nevertheless unanimous in translating the word "city," and both Aistleitner and Gordon list the Old S. Arabic *ʿr* as a cognate, which Gordon translates "acropolis." The translation "city" is supported by the fact that *ʿrm* appears in a number of texts in parallel with *pdrm*, plural of *pdr*, another word for "city."[37] The word *ʿr* also occurs in Ugaritic in conjunction with a proper noun, e.g., *ʿr qdm*, or *ʿr dqdm*.[38] The connotation of this word as a general term for a permanent settlement, perhaps the most common meaning for "city," can thus be added to our general frame of meaning.

The Meanings of *ʿr̂r*/*ʿār̂îm* in the Old Testament

Having briefly explored some possible cognates of *ʿr̂r*, the next task is to examine the OT text itself with a view to testing the above-suggested meanings and more precisely determining what range of meanings is attached to the word in its actual use. While the factors to be employed in developing a rural-urban typology will be spelled out in detail in the following chapter, for the purpose of the section at hand an elementary distinction will be made between the two categories of establishments. The terms which apply more specifically to "rural" settlements will be understood provisionally as denoting unwalled, or at the most, temporarily enclosed settlements. The term "city" will be used here in its most general sense in the OT--a fixed settlement which is rendered inaccessible to assailants by a wall and/or other defense works. This usage of the term "city" makes no distinction as to size, and includes within its scope a simple fortified enclosure which constituted a refuge for rural inhabitants in time of emergencies,[39] as well as the larger city with more elaborate defense works.[40]

Max Weber is probably correct in his thesis that, historically speaking, neither the palisaded village nor the emergency fortification is the primary forerunner of the city fortress. This forerunner was rather the citadel.[41] However, it
is also probably correct to say that by the time the Israelites
came into contact with the Canaanite cities, most of these communities had expanded to include more than just a citadel, and
probably included the citadel together with its surrounding
settlement and outer wall. Hence, while not the earliest use
for "city," historically speaking, this general meaning is certainly one of the earliest and most consistent in the OT, and
is the one out of which the more specialized and symbolic connotations develop to a considerable degree.

This general use of the word "city" is so prevalent in the
OT as to make its comprehensive documentation an unmanageable
task. Instead, we will limit ourselves to the citing of scattered references in different strata of the OT literature which
bring out this aspect of the city, including those which refer
to the defensive works of a given settlement.[42]

The enumeration of fortification features of a city, as a
way of defining the city, is evident throughout the OT. Such
lists usually include the fact that the city is walled and that
its gate, the place at which an attack was generally centered,
was secure.[43] The adjective *mibsār* is frequently used as a
modifier of "city," and as Gray indicates, this adjective usually points to "something cut off abruptly," so as to be isolated, and thus aptly describes a fortified city with walls
rising sheer above a steep escarpment.[44] This adjective is also used a great deal in a metaphorical or symbolic sense. When
employed in this way it communicates the fearful impression
which the "heaven-high" fortifications of the Canaanite cities
made on the Israelites.[45] Such an impression is recorded in 2
Kgs 17:9: בכל-עריהם ממגדל נוצרים עד-עיר מבצר, "In all their
cities, from watchtower to fortified city," illustrates something of the spectrum of meaning for the word *'îr*, with the
'îr mibsār representing the ultimate in a well-fortified establishment.[46] The prophets also make use of this adjective for
emphasis in some of their polemics against the city as an object of false trust.[47]

Another adjective seemingly connected with the idea of the city as a fortified place in which people dwell is $g\check{e}d\hat{o}l\hat{a}$. While this adjective generally has the meaning "large," it also seems to have the connotation "strong," and in this meaning it is related to the Arabic root gdl, "to make firm, strong."[48] The use of this adjective with "city" corresponds closely to that of $mib\d{s}\bar{a}r$.[49]

The aspect of the city as a protected dwelling place can also be seen in the significant number of proper names of cities in the OT which are compounded with some fortification characteristic, or are simply a fortification feature. Wilhelm Borée has cataloged fifteen such names. His list includes, among others, the place-name $s\check{e}d\hat{o}m\hat{a}$, Sodom, which, along with Gomorrah, becomes the type of the wicked city par excellence.[50] Borée suggests that this city name is derived from an early Semitic word related to the Arabic $sadama$, "to fortify."

The city as a walled place of refuge is thus a very early and very predominant way of understanding the city in the OT. The walls of a city were not intended to be the demarcation of the city limits; they rather signified the cooperative attempt of a social unit to find complete security for the place of its abode.

From this broad concept of the city, we move to a more limited one, viz., the use of $\u{r}$ to designate not the entire fortified settlement, but a particular part thereof, a city quarter. The two key passages on which the determination of such a meaning of $\u{r}$ rests are 1 Kgs 20:30 and 2 Kgs 10:25. Both Fisher and Gray deal with these passages in the present context.[51] The text of 1 Kgs 20:30 reads:

וינסו הנותרים אפקה אל-העיר ותפל החומה על-עשרים ושבעה אלף איש הנותרים ובן-הדד נס ויבא אל-העיר חדר בחדר

> And those remaining fled into the city of Aphek; but the wall [of the city] fell upon the twenty-seven thousand men who were left. But Ben-hadad had fled and entered into the citadel of the city.

The key phrase in this verse is the concluding one, $\u{e}l$-$h\bar{a}\u{r}$ $\h{e}der$ $b\check{e}\h{a}der$. This idiomatic phrase can be read literally as "into the city, room by room," and probably indicates a structure located in the city's center which was entered only after passing through other dwellings surrounding it. The expression *ḥeder bĕḥāder* also occurs in 1 Kgs 22:25 and 2 Kgs 9:2. In the first of these passages it again refers to a structure in Samaria and in the latter passage to what must have been the citadel of Ramoth-Gilead.

Fisher contends that the translation "an inner chamber in the city" (so *RSV*) is too vague here, and on the basis of the two other occurrences of the phrase he argues that we are here dealing with a case where *'îr* means specifically the temple or temple quarter. He says:

> *ḥeder bĕheder* seems to be an explanation of *hā'îr*. It is the temple quarter which contains the inner chamber. On the other hand, the second possibility, that the city is to be equated with the inner room, is not entirely inadmissible.[52]

We would agree that *'îr* is used in a specialized sense in the latter part of 1 Kgs 20:30. But it seems more likely that it refers to the inner quarter of the city, the citadel containing the king's palace, the temple, and other administrative headquarters, and, in connection with the phrase *ḥeder bĕheder*, is used to designate a room somewhere within this complex, but not necessarily the temple.

In 2 Kgs 10:25 there occurs the difficult phrase *'ad 'îr bêt habā'al* in the context of Jehu's slaughter of the Baal worshipers. The *RSV* here has emended the *'îr* of the MT to read *dĕbîr*, "inner room." Gray sees *'îr* here as a cognate of the Ugaritic *ġr*, with the sense of the inmost recess, or shrine, of the temple.[53] Fisher, on the other hand, opts for the translation "temple quarter," arguing on the basis of parallels in the Nuzi texts.[54] The sense of the verb then would be that Jehu's men entered the temple quarter of the house of Baal, which probably means that the phrase "the city of the house of Baal" here defines a particular temple quarter of the city of Samaria, where there was quite possibly more than one such *'îr* or temple quarter.[55] But again, in this passage it is questionable whether *'îr* can be translated so specifically as "temple quarter," or whether it would be more accurate to translate it "citadel," bearing in mind that the citadel was in fact a sort of city within a city, containing, among other things, a temple or temples.

If one accepts the *kĕtîb* of 2 Kgs 20:4, it can be adduced as further evidence of the use of *'îr* in the sense of "citadel." The entire phrase with the qĕrê/kĕtîb alternative reads: ויחי ישעיהו לא יצא העיר (חצר) החיכנה, "Isaiah had not yet left the citadel." Isaiah had been visiting Hezekiah in his royal quarters, and this phrase refers to the fact that a fresh oracle from Yahweh came to the prophet before he was even out of the citadel. Most critics have followed the qĕrê here on the grounds that the ʿ of hāʿēr represents a scribal error for the ṣ of ḥāṣēr. The RSV follows the qĕrê as does the LXX, which however may translate a different Vorlage, and translates the phrase, "And before Isaiah had gone out of the middle court." Orlinsky cites Keil as one of the few who accepted the kĕtîb and translated hāʿēr as the "königlicher Burg," the royal citadel, after the analogy of 2 Kgs 10:25. Orlinsky also cites rabbinic interpretations which support the kĕtîb.[56] Fisher cites this passage and again admits the possibility of the meaning "temple quarter."[57] It seems best to retain the kĕtîb here and translate the phrase, "Before Isaiah had gone out of the inner city" (i.e., the royal citadel).

The adjective rabbâ is affixed to the names of two cities in the OT, viz., Sidon and Hamath. The names of these two cities appear as ṣîdôn rabbâ and ḥamat rabbâ, and might be translated "Greater Sidon" and "Greater Hamath." Gottwald believes that this particular designation of Hamath is intended to distinguish the city proper from its "suburbs" in a manner somewhat analogous to, although not identical with, the construction Rabbath Bene-Ammon, the chief city of the Ammonites in 2 Sam 12:26-27.[58] A more complete explanation of this urban terminology is set forth by Gordon who cites the constructions udm rbt. . .udm trrt and ḫbr rbt. . .ḫbr trrt in the KRT text from Ugarit, which he translates "Udum the Great. . .Udum the Small" and "Hubur the Great. . .Hubur the Small."[59] He interprets the "Great" city as the metropolitan area in general, while the "Small" city is seen as the citadel or fortified temple-palace area. Since the "Small" city was the best defended and contained the most sacred area, it was regarded as the most important, as witnessed to by the fact that it appears as the second or climactic element in the Ugaritic texts. Fisher cites a parallel usage in the Nuzi texts, where "great" and "little" appear as postpositive determinatives of city names. The Terms *GAL* and *TUR* (read *rabû*, "great" and *ṣeḫru*, "little") are used in this way.[60]

While there is apparently no usage corresponding to the "small" city in connection with city names in the OT, it seems probable that a similar usage is witnessed to in Gen 19:20, where the *RSV* reads: "Behold, yonder city is near enough to flee to, and it is a little one. Let me escape there--is it not a little one?--and my life will be saved!" The word "little" in this verse is *miṣʿār*, from the root *ṣʿr*. It is usually interpreted as "little" in the sense of insignificant, and indeed this appears to be its meaning in other contexts in the OT. But it is only here that this adjective is coupled with the noun "city," and the sense of insignificant does not really explain why Lot would want to flee there in order to save his life.[61] BDB cites the Akkadian *ṣeḫeru* as a cognate of the Hebrew *ṣʿr*.[62] If this relationship is accepted and compared with the above mentioned usage at Ugarit and Nuzi, then the sense of Gen 19:20 is that the city was not small in the sense of being insignificant, but rather just the opposite, viz., the best defended and most important part of a city, probably a citadel, or citadel-like structure.

Before leaving this discussion of *ʿr* in its more specialized meaning as referring to a particular section of a larger city, mention should be made of two expressions which are of particular relevance vis-à-vis the Jerusalem traditions of the OT. These two expressions, which both refer to the citadel area containing the quarters of the king and the house or temple of God, are "City of David" and "City of God." Fisher observes that the name "the city of the gods" is applied to the city of Arrapha in the texts from Nuzi, and that in this name one is dealing with the sum of the temple quarters of the different deities, which together equalled the entire city.[63] Albright translates *EA* 254.28-30: "I will resist my foe(s), the men who captured the city of god (*āl ili*), the despoilers of my father," and believes that the expression *āl ili* refers to the temenos or sacred enclosure of fourteenth-century Shechem.[64] C. J. Gadd, in commenting on the use of the phrase "city of the gods" in Akkadian, says that the place at which the tablets were found in the mound of Kirkuk was constantly called by this

name and that "It may with confidence be assumed that this appellation belongs only to a certain part of the city, and is
not the general name of the place."[65] Something of the same
situation may also be preserved in the OT in the use of *bet*
together with a theophoric element in city names. Examples of
such names are: Beth-Anath (Josh 19:38); Beth-Baal-Meon (Josh
13:17); Beth-Dagon (Josh 15:41); Bethel (Josh 18:21). These
names may originally have been applied to a temple or sacred
area, and subsequently came to refer to the entire city in
which the temple was located.

Proceeding from this consideration of *ʿîr* in its more circumscribed meaning, we must now consider the expressions, in
addition to *rabbâ*, which denote the "greater" city, or the city
with its surrounding lands and villages. Such expressions apparently stem from the typical city-state conception of the
Canaanite period in which the country was subdivided into small
principalities in which a city was the capital of an area, including the urban hinterland with its estates, pastures, cultivated fields, villages, and other rural establishments.

In the above sense, the Hebrew word *ʾereṣ* can be employed
to refer to a city, or city-state, in a way which finds analogies in the ancient Near East. Understood in this way, this
meaning of *ʾereṣ* must be added to its more general meanings,
"the surface of the earth" or "country, territory."[66] This
identification of *ʾereṣ* with "city-state" has been proposed by
Dahood *et al.*[67] Dahood cites, as epigraphic evidence for this
identification, two Phoenician inscriptions.[68] The first of
these is the sarcophagus inscription of Eshmunʿazar, king of
Sidon.[69] In Phoenician, the pertinent phrase is: *ṣdn ʾrṣ ym*,
which Dahood translates "Sidon, city by the sea." The other
inscription is that of Yehawmilik of Byblos,[70] which refers to
the residents of Byblos as the *ʿm ʾrṣ z*, which is translated
"the people of this city-state." To this epigraphic evidence
cited by Dahood, there can be added two instances in the Moabite Stone where the name of a city is joined to the word *ʾrṣ*,
viz., *ʾrṣ mhdbʾ* and *ʾrṣ ʿṭrt*.[71]

Most of the passages which are mentioned by Dahood *et al.*
in support of their proposed translation of *ʾrṣ* as "city" or
"city-state," are drawn from the Psalms and the Wisdom

Literature.[72] In two of these instances, Eccl 10:16 and 2 Chr 32:4, the LXX translates the Hebrew 'rṣ with *polis*. In Prov 8:26, 'rṣ is used in connection with ḥûṣôt, a word commonly used to denote city "streets" or "suburbs."[73] Prov 31:23 uses the word 'rṣ in connection with another urban institution, the gate of the city, in its function as the seat of the local court.[74] In Jonah 2:7, 'rṣ appears in conjunction with one of the features of the fortifications of the city gate, the běrîaḥ, "bars."

While Dahood's translation seems to be borne out by the evidence, his further suggestion that it indicates a dialect in which 'ereṣ came to mean "city" remains questionable.[75] To the list of passages cited above where 'ereṣ may mean "city," the following verses might be added: Gen 11:28 (referring to the city of Ur); Gen 34:2 (Shechem); 1 Kgs 8:37 (MT = bě'ereṣ šeʿārāyw, cf. the LXX, *en mia ton poleōn autou*); 1 Kgs 22:36; Jer 29:7 (MT = šělôm hāʿîr; LXX = *eirēnēn tēs gēs*. In this case, the LXX may represent a different Hebrew *Vorlage* which had the word 'ereṣ); Jer 15:7 (běšaʿărê hāʾāreṣ); Jer 51:4 (cf. Prov 8:26); and Ezek 22:30.[76]

Another use of 'îr is involved in the identification of 'ereṣ and 'îr in several of the passages cited in the preceding paragraphs, viz., in Jonah 2:7 and Ps 141:7. In these passages 'ereṣ is understood as the nether city, or the city of the dead. Mesopotamian parallels which refer to the dwelling place of the dead as a city are numerous. Since it was a common belief that the gathering place of the dead was situated within the earth, the Sumerians referred to it as *KUR*, and the Semites in Babylonia called it *irṣitu* (cf. the Hebrew 'ereṣ in Exod 15:12 and Isa 14:12), both of which mean "earth." The name *URU.GAL*, "the great city," was another of the Sumerian designations.[77] The city of the dead was described in Mesopotamia as a great metropolis surrounded by seven walls, each wall having a gate guarded by a demon.[78] In Canaanite mythology as well, the underground realm of Mot, the god of death at Ugarit, is called his "city" in a passage which again indicates the parallel use of the words for "land" and "city:"

idk al ttn	Then of a truth do you set your faces
pnm tk qrth	[towards Mot son of El] within his city,
hmry mk ksu	but the throne on which he sits [is] deep

tbth ḥḥ arṣ	in the mire and the land of his
nḥlth. . .	heritage. . .[79]

There are numerous instances of the application of urban terminology to the realm of the dead in the OT. E.g., there are references to the "gates of She'ol" (Isa 38:10) and to the "bars of She'ol" (Job 17:6). The expression "the gates of death" occurs in Ps 9:14; 107:18, and in Job 17:6.

Using the fact that the realm of the dead is pictured as a city elsewhere in the OT, Dahood offers an interesting explanation of the problematic verse, Ps 73:20.[80] In the MT this verse reads: כחלום מהקיץ אדני בעיר צלמם תבזה. While a discussion of all the problems associated with this verse would not be to the point, the important focus is on the word *bāʿîr*. Most translators render this word as a verbal form of the root *ʿwr*.[81] But Dahood is supported by the LXX and three versions in his translation, "in the city."[82] He thus translates the entire verse: "Like a dream after awaking, O Lord, you will value them lightly in the city of phantoms." This translation seems to require the fewest emendations, and is commended by the support of the versions.

Still another use of *ʿîr* is hinted at in 2 Kgs 17:9, which reads: בכל-עריהם ממגדל נוצרים עד-עיר מבצר, "In all their cities, from watchtower to fortified city."[83] Here we are concerned with the smaller end of the spectrum, i.e., the use of the word "city" in reference to a small defensive installation such as a watchtower. The author of 2 Sam 17:13 must have had some such structure in mind when he speaks of dragging an *ʿîr* into the valley with ropes. In the account of Joab's attack on Rabbah of the Ammonites, it is reported that he took the *ʿîr hammāyim*, the site of the royal gardens, after the analogy of Jerusalem.[85] But I would follow Gray's suggestion here, and translate *ʿîr hammāyim* as "the water fortress."[86] The structure so designated was probably some type of installation which defended the city's water supply, the source of which stood outside the walls of the city.[87]

To conclude this section of our study, some uses of *ʿîr* which are not references to any specific structure, or place of human settlement, should be noted. The first of these is the use of *ʿîr* as synonomous with the population of a settlement.

It is used in this way in Judg 9:31; 1 Sam 4:13; 5:11-12; Ruth 1:19; Isa 22:2; Jer 4:29; 26:2; Zech 2:15; 3:1; and Prov 11:10. The other use is a symbolic one, in which the city, or a feature of the city's fortifications, is used as a symbol of strength. In the blessing of Asher contained within the Benediction of Moses (Deut 33:25), the imagery of a city gate is used in the phrase, "Your bars shall be iron and bronze."[88] Judg 18:7, in referring to the people of Laish, says: "They dwelt in security, after the manner of the Sidonians." It may well be that Sidon became the "type" of a fortified city, just as Sodom and Gomorrah became "types" of the wicked city.[89] Urban imagery is also used to describe an individual made strong by Yahweh, as in Jer 1:18: "I make you this day a fortified city, an iron pillar, and bronze walls" (cf. also Jer 15:20).

To summarize the preceding section, it can be said that the word ʿîr covers the following range of meaning in the OT: (1) a fortified structure for defensive purposes; (2) a walled, permanent settlement; (3) a quarter within such a settlement, especially the citadel containing the temple or temples and the administrative quarters; and (4) in a more comprehensive political and economic sense, the city includes the citadel, the fixed settlement, and is the center of and marketplace for the surrounding secondary settlements of a less permanent nature.

The Use of ʿîr in Particular Phrases

Before proceeding to the discussion of the synonyms of ʿîr and other related words, brief mention should be made of two particular phrases in the OT in which the word ʿîr occurs, which are important for an understanding of OT city concepts.

The first of these phrases combines the noun ʿîr with the verbal root bnh. The basic meaning of this verb is "to build," but it has, in addition, auxiliary meanings when used with certain objects.[90] The literal meaning of "to build," in the sense of constructing something for the first time, is used in connection with such structures as houses (including palaces and temples), high places (bāmōt), altars, and to a limited degree, in connection with the founding of cities. The use of this verb with "city" occurs principally in the annalistic references to the building activities of the kings of Judah and

Israel. Such a meaning of *bnh* is, however, often difficult to
establish, in that it assumes that there was no previous settlement on the site, a fact which can only be established archaeologically.[91] For this reason, most of the instances of
the occurrence of *ʿîr* with *bnh* fall under one of the other
meanings of the verb.

A second meaning of the verb *bnh* is a figurative one, used
principally with a human object, usually meaning "to perpetuate,
build up, or establish a person, a national group which is personified, or a family line."[92] A third meaning, and the most
important one in connection with *ʿîr*, is *bnh* with its meaning
"to rebuild, expand, or add to the fortifications of." This
meaning of "to rebuild" or "to expand" is obviously used to refer to the reconstruction of a place or structure which has
been destroyed.[93] But it should be noted that in some cases
the idea is not just that of repairing, but also of expanding.
It is the particular meaning of "to fortify" or "to construct
fortifications" that is the most pertinent here. In this sense
the verb *bnh* has as its object a whole range of fortification
or anti-fortification features, including walls (1 Kgs 3:1),
gates (2 Kgs 15:35 = 2 Chr 27:3), towers (both those within a
city as a part of its defensive system as in Judg 9:51, and
those which are independent defensive structures as in 2 Chr
26:10), the *millô'* (2 Sam 5:9),[94] and siegeworks (2 Kgs 25:1 =
Jer 52:4). This sense of the verb *bnh* is also apparent in
those cases where it is used in connection with the name of a
city with a long history behind it, e.g., Jericho (1 Kgs 16:34)
and Shechem (1 Kgs 12:25).[95]

In support of the thesis that the city in the OT is basically thought of as a fortified settlement, it is perhaps significant to observe that the verb *bnh* is used only with the
noun *ʿîr* in the OT, and not with any of the other words used
to designate human communities. A most interesting passage in
this regard is 1 Kgs 16:24. In this verse Omri's purchase of
a mountain for the site of his capital is related. There then
follows this phrase:

ויבן את-ההר ויקרא את-שם העיר אשר בנה על שם-שמר אדני ההר שמרון,

"And he (Omri) fortified the *mountain*, and he called the name
of the *city* which he had (thus) built after the name of Shemer,

the owner of the *mountain* Samaria." On the basis of the interplay here between *ʿîr* and *hār*, there appears to be a close relationship between these two terms. The city here is quite
literally a fortified mountain, or, in other words, a mountain
becomes a city by the erection of fortifications.[96]

The other phrase to be discussed here is *qrʾ šm*, meaning
"to name" or "to call by one's name," used with *ʿîr* as its object. The most important passage for determining the significance of this expression is 2 Sam 12:28, where, after having
taken the *ʿîr hammāyim*, Joab sends a message to David to the
effect that David should come with his troops and take the city
proper, פן-אלכד אני את-העיר ונקרא שמי עליה, "lest I (Joab) take
the city and it be called by my name." What is involved here
is apparently the phenomenon alluded to by R. Abba, in which to
be called by a person's name implies ownership by that person.[97] In addition to the ownership of the city, by this act
one also incurs the responsibility for its protection. K. Galling sees in the phenomenon of "die Ausrufung des Namens" a
measure taken over from private law into public law as a way of
designating an exchange of property.[98] Thus, in his message,
Joab is alerting David to the fact that if he (Joab) proceeds
with the capture of the city proper, it will be called by his
name, i.e., it will come under his ownership, authority, and
protection.[99] Other examples of the taking of a city and a
consequent "calling by one's name" are to be found, e.g., in
such passages as Deut 3:14, "Jair. . .took all the region of
Argob. . .and called the villages after his own name, Havvoth-
jair."[100] David's capture of the Jebusite citadel of Zion in
2 Sam 5:9 is likewise followed by the renaming of it the "city
of David."

In addition to the use of the phrase *qrʾ šm* to denote ownership in connection with the capture of a city, it is also
used with *bnh*, probably in its connotation of "to build for the
first time," in Gen 4:17, where it is said that Cain named the
city which he had built after the name of his son, Enoch, thus
implying that Enoch became the *ʾadôn*, i.e., the proprietor and
master of the city which bore his name.[101] A city, or city
site, could also come into one's possession by outright purchase from its previous owner.[102] Note should be made of the

fact that a capital city or a city under a monarch's control is often called by the king's name.[103]

Synonyms of ʿîr and other Words
Designating Secondary Settlements
and Fortified Structures in the Old Testament

In the following section, terms will be examined, some of which are used synonomously with ʿîr (or nearly so), and others which designate some form of community of a secondary or less permanent type than a city. Consideration will also be given to a group of words which are used to denote fortified structures akin to the citadel of the city, or at least a part thereof. This section will be limited to a definition of such terms, and where it is relevant, to an evaluation of their relationship to the principal word ʿîr. The more precise definition of a rural-urban typology and of the physical, political, social, and economic characteristics associated with these communities and structures will be deferred until the following chapter.

The first term to be noted in this connection is the word *qiryâ*.[104] The principal use of this term is in poetic contexts where it is often found in parallel with ʿîr, or in a setting which indicates that its meaning is identical to that of ʿîr.[105] Another use of the term, even more numerous in occurrence than the preceding one, is its application in the formation of proper names of cities. It is used in this way in reference to the pre-Israelite names of Hebron (Kiriath-Arba, Josh 14:15), Debir (Kiriath-Sepher, Josh 15:15) and of other non-Israelite cities.[106] This application of the term *qiryâ* may well point to its non-Israelite origin. This word, which was in rather common use in Canaan as a word for "city," never acquired currency in the ordinary language of the Israelites. Instead, its use was preserved in the names of some localities, and it enjoyed a certain revival in the poetic literature where a viable synonym for ʿîr was needed for the sake of poetic variety. It has been suggested that this noun derives from the root *qrh* and thus means a "meeting place for men."[107] But it is more probably to be connected with the masculine noun *qîr*, "wall," and thus designates in its most basic sense a walled settlement.[108]

There are, in fact, references in the OT where *qir* appears to be an alternative for *qiryâ*. KB, e.g., lists the forms *qîr hereś* (Jer 48:31, 36), *qîr ḥăreśet* (Isa 16:7), and *qir moʾāb* (Isa 15:1). Also listed is the form *qr*, one of the ordinary Moabite words for "city" which occurs in the inscription of Mesha.[109] In the Isa 15:1 passage the form *qîr* appears in parallel with *ʿār* in an oracle against Moab. While the *RSV* here renders both *ʿār* and *qîr* as proper nouns, they are more likely to represent "the city of Moab," a way of referring to a country's principal city, in this case probably Kir-hareseth, an ancient capital of Moab. Amos mentions a *qîr* in two instances. In Amos 1:5 *qîr* is named as the place to which the people of Syria will be exiled. In Amos 9:7 a *qîr* is mentioned as the original home of the Arameans. The form *qîrâ* occurs in 2 Kgs 16:9 as the place to which the Damascenes were exiled, with the *a* ending being a locative one. The Lucianic rescension of the LXX here reads *tēn polin*, "the city" for the MT *qîrâ*.[110] It is, however, generally accepted that the reference in 2 Kings is a gloss from Amos, to emphasize the fulfillment of Amos' prophecy.[111] If *qîr* is to be seen as a place name, the location of the place so designated is extremely uncertain. In Isa 22:6 *qîr* occurs in parallel with Elam and may indicate a place in the distant northeast of Mesopotamia. If, however, *qîr* is not to be taken as a proper name, at least not in every instance, it may simply be a common noun for "city."[112]

The idea of the Canaanite origin of this term is supported by the existence of obvious cognates of this term in other Semitic languages, especially those of the northwest group.[113] Rabin has suggested that in this group of cognates the Moabite *qr* has nothing to do with the others, but Van Zyl maintains, to the contrary, that the substantive *qr* is derived from the root *qyr* and is related to the Hebrew word *qîr*, "wall." This word originally meant wall, but it could also designate a city, as the settlement was changed into a city by the addition of a surrounding wall.[114]

In support of the view that the Hebrew word *qiryâ*, as well as its Semitic cognates, is used to designate a fortified place, Rabin sets forth the idea that *qrt* is a derivative of the Hittite *gurta*, "fortress." He would also see this Hittite

word as related to the Sanskrit term *kṛta*, with the same meaning.[115] But he denies any connection with the Ugaritic word
grdš, a term of uncertain meaning.[116]

While the relatively limited use of this term in the OT
would suggest caution, the conclusion would seem to be justified, on the basis of its use and that of its cognates, that the
term *qiryâ* (and its variant forms) is a Canaanite survival, and
is virtually synonymous with the word *ʿîr*.

The next term to be discussed is *šaʿar*, the word which
ordinarily designates the city gate, but which in some places
becomes a synonym for *ʿîr* on the pattern of *pars pro toto* or
synecdoche, in which a part of an object is used to stand for
the entire entity. The explanation for this phenomenon lies
in the fact that the gate of the city was considered to be the
very nerve center of much of the commercial and social life
life of the city's population. In at least some of the instances where *šaʿar* stands for "city," there is the military
aspect of the gate as the critical point at which the defense
of and attacks upon the city were concentrated. This fact is
echoed in an Akkadian proverb: "From before the gate of the
city whose armament is not powerful the enemy cannot be re-
pulsed."[117] Isa 28:6 also points to two aspects of the gate's
importance: ". . .a spirit of justice to him who sits in judgment, and strength to those who turn back the battle at the
gate." In terms of numbers, the great preponderance of the
use of the term *šaʿar* as a synonym for *ʿîr* is found in the work
of the Deuteronomist.[118] In fact, Driver lists "your gates,"
in the sense of the cities of Israel as a phrase which is peculiarly characteristic of the Deuteronomist.[119] The use of
šaʿar in this way outside the work of the Deuteronomist is con-
fined to those instances where the gates stand for the whole
underground realm of the dead.[120] The equation of *šaʿar* and
ʿîr is attested to by the LXX translation of nearly all of the
Deuteronomic passages (with the exception of Deut 12:12; 23:17;
and Exod 20:10) where instead of the expected *pulē*, "gate," the
translation is *polis*, "city." A parallel to this OT usage of
šaʿar is to be seen in the Akkadian use of *bābu*, "gate," in referring to a city quarter or to persons living within the confines of a city.[121] There is also another possible parallel in

Ugaritic usage where the king of a city-state is referred to as the *mlk tǵr*, "king of the gate."[122] Thus, while *šaʿar* is not to be considered as a synonym of *ʿîr* in every instance, it does appear to be used in this way in those passages which we have cited.

A similar instance in which a word does not communicate the specific information "city," but where in some instances it may have the referent "city" is the term *māqôm*, "place." As the lexica attest, this word has a wide range of meaning in the OT, ranging from the most specific to the most general.[123] When used in the sense of "city," the connotation is basically that of a place of human abode. It is sometimes used in parallel with *ʿîr* in this sense (Gen 18:24, 26; Deut 21:19; Amos 4:6), and in its more specific sense is applied to the place where Yahweh dwells (Hos 5:15; Jer 7:12; Isa 26:21; Mic 1:3). This term thus always refers to a fixed locality, whether large or small in extent.

Yet a third instance of a term which does not specifically mean "city" but which sometimes is used in a way that it means "city," is the word *har*, "mountain, hill, mountainous region." The relationship between these two words has already been suggested above. The word *har* has obvious mythological implications. Mountains are generally regarded as dwelling places of gods in the ancient Near East, and consequently as sites of cultic significance. It has been observed that there is, so far as is known, no word for "mountain" common to the various Semitic languages. However, Rössler does point out that there is a certain compatibility in the sense that the word for mountain appears to be what he calls a *Mythologem*.[125] As such, in addition to its usual meaning, the term bears the very old connotation of "country, territory, site." It is in this sense that the word for mountain can be associated with "city." This association can be seen especially in connection with terms associated with the realm of the dead. As we have seen, the designation of the underworld as a "city" was a common one in the ancient Near East. At the same time, however, it is also called a mountain. Tallqvist, e.g., observes that the most frequent term in Akkadian for the kingdom of the dead is *arallû, aralû*, or the mountain of *arallû*, which in turn is to be equated with the Akkadian *irṣitu* (= Hebrew *'ereṣ*), whose meaning "city-state" has already been pointed out.[126] Clements cites a Ugaritic parallel, in which Mot's dwelling is described by three parallel terms -- his city, the throne where he sits, and the land of his inheritance.[127] But in another passage which describes the dwelling place of Baal, the third expression becomes "the mountain of my inheritance."[128] M. Pope cites the parallelism of *qr bt il* and *ǵr bt il* in the Ugaritic texts.[129] One might also note in this context a passage in which the Mesopotamian city of Der is referred to as "The (Sumerian, "my") city, the mountain of the land of Sumer and Akkad, (which offers) protection to the entire world."[130] The connection of city and mountain can also be seen in the name of the town Halbu in an Akkadian passage, *āl Ḫal-bi ḪUR.SAG Ḫa-zi*, which Albright has translated, "the town of Halbu (of) Mount Hazi.[131]

The connection between the terms "mountain" and "city" may well rest on a more pragmatic than mythological base. This connection may stem from the fact that the city, as a fortified settlement for the protection of its inhabitants, was so often situated on a hill or mountain on the strategic consideration that such a site provided the optimal prospect for security. Certainly this was one of the major factors in the choice of Jerusalem and Samaria as the sites for the capitals of Judah and Israel. Samaria, in fact, continued to be known as *har šōmĕrôn*, and Amos proclaims against those "who feel secure on the mountain of Samaria."[132] The mountain-city as an unconquerable fortress became proverbial material in the book of Ahiqar: "A man of becoming conduct whose heart is good is like a mighty city which is situated upon a mountain."[133] Samaria was not alone in having the word "mountain" as an element in its name. Borée has compiled a list of place names that have one of the Hebrew words for "hill" or "mountain" as their base word.[134] These can be divided into three groups, according to the base word: (1) *gibeʿâ*, "hill." The list includes Gibeath Ammah (2 Sam 2:24); Gibeath Benjamin (1 Sam 13:2, 15, etc.); Gibeath Hamorah (Judg 7:1); Gibeath Phineas (Josh 24:33); Gibeath Saul (1 Sam 11:4; 15:34); Gibeath Hachilah (1 Sam 23:19; 26:1, 3); and Geba (Josh 18:24; Ezra 2:26; Neh 7:30). (2) *har*, "mountain, hill." Har-heres (Judg 1:35; cf. Josh 19:41, where the name of this city is given as *'ir šemeš*); Har jearim (Josh 15:10. In this verse the other name of this mountain-city is given as *kĕsālôn* from the root *ksl*, "confidence."); and (3) *rāmâ*, "height, high place." Ramath Lehi (Judg 15:7; Ramath Negeb (Josh 19:8); Ramath Mizpeh (Josh 13:26).

The word for "mountain" is apparently used in place names at Ugarit in a manner similar to that of the OT use.[135]

While the conclusion can be drawn that there is, indeed, a close relationship between the words "mountain" and "city," it does not seem likely that one should go so far as Fisher, who suggests that *'ir* might, in some places, be translated "the hill of God" or "the altar of God."[136]

Before discussing those terms which designate communities of a secondary or less permanent nature, some words which designate structures which formed an important part of the city's fortifications and/or independent fortification structures should be noted. The first term to be noted in this context is the word usually translated "tower," *migdāl*. In this sense, *migdāl* is apparently related to the Arabic root *gdl*, cited earlier, with its sense of "to make strong, firm."[137] While this term is used to designate the towers or bastions erected as a part of the city walls, particularly those flanking the city's gates (cf. Jer 31:38; 2 Chr 14:6; 26:9, 15; 32:5; Neh 3:1, 11, 25), this use is apparently a later one than the use of this term to designate the citadel.[138] The earlier use of this word to designate the citadel of a city corresponds to the fact that this structure was, at least in many instances, the kernel around which the rest of the city grew. This use of *migdāl* is probably to be applied also to the independent structures which were built during the divided monarchy outside of existing cities in order to secure a line of defense.[139] De Vaux, e.g., identifies two such structures at Qedeirat and Khirbet Ghassa.[140] Such structures may then have become the nuclei for new urban settlements.

The use of the term *migdāl* as the first element in place names probably serves to indicate small urban settlements that were grouped around a nuclear citadel. Examples of such place names are: Migdal-Penuel (Judg 8:9, 17); Migdal-El (Josh

19:38); Migdal-Gad (Josh 15:37); Migdal-Eder (Gen 35:21; Mic 4:8); and Migdol (Ex 14:2, etc.). A parallel to such OT place names is perhaps to be seen in the Ugaritic toponym *mgdly* and in the reference to the city Qart-abilim as *ablm qrt zbl yrḫ d mgdl*.[141] De Vaux also observes that in the case of those place names which have a theophoric element in the second part of the name, this "castle" would be a fortified temple, like that of Baal-berith in Shechem.[142] G. E. Wright reports that B. Mazar has argued in an unpublished article that a study of place names suggests that there were buildings in several cities which belonged to a class of *migdāl* or fortress-temples. The name of the Galilean town Migdal-El is thus apparently derived from a fortress of the god El, a fortress that was also a temple. Wright maintains that the fortress-like function of such a temple may possibly be seen in the story of Abimelech's siege of Thebez (Judg 9:50-55). While the English versions simply speak about the building as a "strong tower," its Hebrew name, *migdal-ʿōz* may well be that of a temple since *ʿōz* is a very common divine epithet.[143]

The use of *migdāl* is also to be noted in the case of the citadel in larger, well-known cities.[144] *Migdāl*, like *ʿîr*, also has a symbolic usage in Psalms and Proverbs in the description of Yahweh as a refuge.[145]

In connection with *migdāl*, attention should also be drawn to a later word which is used synonomously, viz., *bîrâ*.[146] B. Mazar considers this word to be a loan word from the Akkadian *bîrtu*, "fortress," by way of the Aramaic *bîrâ/bîrtāʾ*, "fortress, fortified city."[147] The term *bîrâ* thus takes the place of *migdāl* in a later period, and is used in referring to a citadel within a city,[148] or perhaps to an entire fortified city.[149] The *hapáx legomenon*, *baḥan*, "watchtower" in Isa 32:14 is probably an Egyptian loanword, and is to be considered as synonomous with *migdāl*.[150]

Another term, whose probable meaning is "citadel," is the problematic word *ṣĕrîaḥ*, which occurs only three times in the OT.[151] In Judg 9:46 this term is set within the phrase: ויבאו אל-צריח בית אל ברית.[152] This phrase bears a striking resemblance to the one mentioned earlier in 2 Kgs 10:25, where one reads: וילכו עד-עיר בית-הבעל, and it is likely that the two terms, *şĕrîaḥ* and *'îr*, in these two passages refer to similar structures, viz., a fortress-temple which was equivalent to, or at least part of, the citadel of the city. Again, with regard to the occurrences of this term in Judges, Wright points out that 9:45 is a natural conclusion to the Abimelech story. Accordingly, 9:46-49 thus forms an appendix which probably represents a separate fragment of tradition containing additional details about the battle.[153] Thus, the *şĕrîaḥ* (vv 46, 49), the *bêt millô'* (vv 6, 20), and the *migdal šĕkem* (v 46) probably all refer to the citadel of Shechem, the final point of the city's defense.[154] That the word *şeriaḥ* means citadel or fortress is also supported by the Alexandrian family of LXX manuscripts, which read *ochurōma*, "fortress," in the Judges account, and by the Arabic cognate cited by KB, *şarḥun*, "tower."[155]

The next word to be considered is also closely connected with the citadel area of a city. It is the term *'armôn*.[156] In the singular, this term appears to denote the citadel. This seems clear in two occurrences in Kings (1 Kgs 16:18; 2 Kgs 15:25), where it is found in the phrase, *'armôn bêt-hammelek*, which should be translated "the citadel of the king's house," referring to the central fortified installation of the city, which included the king's palace, together with other buildings. The translation of *'armôn* as "palace" would be tautologous.

In the great majority of its occurrences, the term *'armôn* is in the plural, and among these occurrences, a great majority again are found in the context of prophetic threats against man-made fortifications as a false refuge and as an expression of lack of faith in Yahweh, who is regarded by the prophets as the only dependable defense for his people.[157] A verse which is illustrative of such threats, as well as instructive for a determination of the meaning of *'armôn*, is Hos 8:14:

> For Israel has forgotten his Maker, and built palaces (*hêkālôt*);
> And Judah has multiplied fortified cities (*'ārîm bĕsurôt*);
> But I will send a fire upon his cities (*'ārāyw*),
> And it shall devour his strongholds (*'armĕnōtêhā*).

In this passage, as well as others, *'armôn* appears in a poetic context in parallel with other terms designating a fortified dwelling place or some particular part of such a place.[158] The parallelism in the above passage is a clear example of

50

chiastic parallelism, following the pattern A.B.B.A.

That the term *'armôn* indicates a dwelling place, doubtless fortified, is supported by the etymology suggested by E. Speiser. He compares *'armôn* to the Akkadian noun *rimîtû*, "dwelling," which is formed on the root *ramû*, which is principally used in the sense of "to found a dwelling," and means "to dwell," when used without an object.[159] When used in the plural, the term becomes practically synonomous with *'ārîm*, meaning "fortified dwelling places," not necessarily palaces in particular.[160]

A term which is closely related to *'armôn*, both morphologically and in meaning as well, is the term *'almĕnôt*, which occurs in Isa 13:22 and Ezek 19:7. There are two ways of dealing with this word. The first assumes that the reading *'almĕnôt* represents a scribal error and should be emended to read as the plural of *'armôn*. The second way of dealing with this term is to assume that *'almôn* and *'armôn* coexisted as words with the same referent. Delitszch defends the MT reading and sees it as a cognate of the Akkadian *almattu*, "fortress."[162] Linguistically, the liquid consonants *l* and *r* are subject to confusion both due to the similarity of their phonetic value and to a certain interchangeability on the same bases in Semitic languages.[163] Thus a decision on how to account for the existence of the form *'almĕnôt* cannot be made with certainty.

Still another term which may well have to do with the citadel area of a city is the word *ya'ar*. This word is homonymous according to the lexica, and its two basic meanings are given as "forest, thicket" and "honeycomb."[164] However, there are instances where neither of these meanings renders a satisfactory translation, or at the most, leads to an unstrained one. The suggestion set forth here is that, in addition to its more literal meanings, this term acquired a more figurative one during the monarchical period, a meaning which carried the information of a thick, woodlike structure which was nearly impenetrable, or at least quite difficult of access for the would-be attacker. This meaning may have resulted from a construction technique in which heavy timbers or beams were used for the construction of this structure which was a part of the citadel. In the account of Solomon's building activity in 1 Kgs 7:2-3, it is stated that:

> He built the House of the Forest of Lebanon (yaʿar hal-lĕbānôn. . .and it was built upon three [reading with the LXX instead of the MT, "four"] rows of cedar pillars, with cedar beams upon the pillars. And it was covered with cedar above the chambers that were upon the forty-five pillars, fifteen in each row.

This same structure is referred to in 1 Kgs 10:17, where it is reported that Solomon made ". . .three hundred shields of beaten gold. . .and put them in the House of the Forest of Lebanon." Isaiah speaks of this same structure in 22:8: "In that day you looked to the weapons of the house of the forest (bet hayyāʿar)."[165] On the basis of these passages, it is reasonable to conclude that this Solomonic building must have served as an armory, being an especially well-fortified building within the citadel.[166] In addition to these references to the particular structure in Solomonic Jerusalem, there are other instances in preexilic literature where the term yaʿar is used in a similar way. In Jer 21:14, in the context of an oracle against Jerusalem and her inhabitants for their belief in her impregnability, there is the phrase: "I will kindle a fire in her forest (bĕyaʿĕrâ) and it shall devour all that is round about it."[167] J. Bright, in commenting on this verse, says that this is probably a reference to Jerusalem's great buildings of cedar, rather than literally to adjacent woodlands.[168] That yaʿar is equivalent to ʿîr, in the sense of a fortified structure which was a part of the citadel, can be seen also in the parallelism in Jer 50:32: "I will kindle a fire in his cities (bĕʿārāyw), and it will devour all that is round about it."[169] In Isa 32:19, although the MT is obviously corrupt, the *RSV* reading can be adopted, and the verse read: "And the forest (hayyāʿar) will utterly go down, and the city will be utterly laid low."[170] In its present context, this verse is out of place, and is within a section which was a later addition to Isaiah's work.[171] But, this verse, with its reference to the complete destruction of even the most secure part of the city, is reminiscent of the "anti-urban" materials in the preexilic prophets, and may well be drawn from an earlier context. That the term yaʿar was indeed used in such a figurative sense can also be recognized in its application in a description of the Assyrian army as "the glory of his forest," or "the trees of his forest."[172]

The term *ya'ar* also occurs in place names in the OT, e.g., Kiriath-jearim (Josh 15:10), which might then bear the connotation of an especially well-fortified city. In Josh 9:17, this city appears as a member of the Gibeonite confederacy of four strategically located fortress cities.[173] Another toponym containing the word *ya'ar* is Har-jearim (Josh 15:10), whose alternate name is given as Chesalon, "confidence."

The term *ya'ar* also refers to some particularly well-fortified structure in the Moabite stone. In the recounting of his royal building activities, Mesha says: "It was I (who) built Qarhoh, the wall of *the forests* (*hy'rn*) and the wall of the citadel (*h'pl*); I also built its gates and I built its towers."[174] Some sort of fortified structure seems to be implied by the inclusion of *y'r* within the series of walls, gates, and towers. R. J. Williams would translate this line: "It was I who built Qericho, the wall of the two honeycombs (i.e., the two mounds honeycombed with cisterns; or forests?) and the wall of the citadel; I who built its gates; I who built its towers."[175] His own question mark indicates Williams' uncertainty with his reading, but the translation "two honeycombs" (taking *hy'rn* as a dual) hardly seems plausible. The translation here of *y'r* as "arsenal" makes much better sense.

That *y'r* is connected with an arsenal-like structure can also be inferred from a passage in the Ugaritic texts which Gordon translates:

> The enemies of Baal seize the forests (*y'rm*)
> > The foes of Hadd, the fringes [or the 'innermost
> > parts' with Driver[176]] of the mountain.
> And Aliyn Baal declares:
> > 'Enemies of Hadd, why do ye invade,
> > > Why do ye invade the arsenal (*ntq*) of our de-
> > > fense?'[177]

If the meaning for *y'r* which has been suggested is accepted, then the Hebrew, Moabite, and Ugaritic words may all be etymologically related to the Arabic root *wa'ar*, "to be rugged," from which the noun *wa'arun*, "rough or difficult place (in the sense of access), mountain" is derived.[178]

Before concluding this discussion of terms which have the city's citadel, or a part thereof, as their referent, two more terms need to be mentioned. The terms *'ōpel* and *millô'* are

most commonly rendered in English as proper nouns, referring to
particular structures in Jerusalem. But, in addition to this
use, both of these terms are associated with structures in other Israelite cities.

Outside of Jerusalem, ʿōpel occurs in connection with Samaria in 2 Kgs 5:24, and in a more general context in Isa 32:
14.[179] In the 2 Kings passage, the term appears with the definite article, and thus should probably be taken more specifically than the RSV translation of "the hill" would suggest.[180]
The basic options for the translation of ʿōpel seem to be the
one which takes it as a word denoting "hill"[181] and the other
which would see it as referring to a specific fortified installation or quarter of a city located on a hill.[182] Those who
would translate ōpel as "hill " do so more on the basis of its
etymology than on its use. As cognates, the Akkadian uplu,
"boil, tumor" and the Arabic ʿafalun, "tumor" are cited.[183]
Among those who support the second option, Gray suggests that
the ʿōpel in 2 Kgs 5:24 was the citadel of Samaria, ". . .
crowned by the inner wall and palace of Omri and Ahab, just as
'the Ophel' at Jerusalem refers specifically to the citadel of
the pre-Davidic and Davidic city."[184] Gray's suggestion is
supported by the use of ʿōpel in Isa 32:14 and Mic 4:8, where
it is mentioned along with other fortification features in both
instances.[185] The meaning of ʿōpel as a fortified area of limited extent, thus a citadel, is further supported by its use in
the Moabite stone, where the construction of the "wall of the
ʿpl" is related. Albright translates this expression with "the
wall of the citadel."[186] Again, our term occurs in a series
with other fortification features.

The term millōʾ is exceedingly problematic. Speaking of
the Millo at Jerusalem, J. Simons comments: "As usual, the
great number of theories claiming to have solved these problems
is inversely proportional to the amount of clear data."[187]
Fortunately, the scope of this inquiry puts most of the problems associated with this word beyond our immediate concern.
Our aim here is only to determine what, if any, specific information is conveyed by the term in reference to the OT city
in general. The root from which this noun is derived has certain cognates in nearly every Semitic language, all having the

basic meaning "to fill, be full" and, in the nominal form, "fullness, something which is filled." Etymologically, the definition proposed for this term supports the explanation of Barrois, who says that the word refers to "a structure built on an artificial platform of stamped earth."[189]

The great preponderance of use of this term is associated with a particular structure in Jerusalem.[190] There are, however, as in the case of $\check{o}pel$, a few instances where the reference is to a structure outside of Jerusalem.[191] In all of these, the allusion is to a $b\hat{e}t$ $mill\hat{o}$. In his discussion of the $b\hat{e}t$ $mill\hat{o}$ at Shechem, Wright concludes that the Beth-Millo and the Migdal-Shechem are to be equated:

> Millo means a fortification set upon a 'filling.' One existed in Jerusalem. Other examples may have been found in the tenth century district headquarters of the central government in Lachish and Beth-Shemesh, where the governor's palace was erected on a filling, perhaps to raise the building above the others in the city. The contexts of both the references to Migdal-Shechem and Beth-Millo, however, suggests that the whole temenos or sacred area is referred to, not simply to its most important building.[192]

While Wright's evidence for this conclusion is mainly archaeological and not linguistic, his analysis would appear to be supported by the construction $b\hat{e}t$ $mill\hat{o}$, in which the $b\hat{e}t$ most likely refers to a city quarter, quite possibly one of houses which were built on terraces.[193] Considered from a linguistic standpoint, there seems to be evidence that the Millo of Jerusalem also refers to a citadel-like structure in the oldest section of the city, viz., the southeast hill. The LXX, while sometimes leaving "the Millo" untranslated (1 Kgs 9:15, 24), at other times offers the interpretive translation, $akra$, "citadel" (2 Sam 5:9; 1 Kgs 11:27; 9:15 [LXX^A]; 10:22 [LXX^B]). The Targums have the word $mlyt$', as a translation for $mill\hat{o}$', the same word which they use to translate $s\check{o}lla$, the mound of earth cast up by the besiegers of a city.[194] Without examining the archaeological suggestions as to the nature of the Millo in more detail, it is difficult to say anything much more definite than that the Millo at Jerusalem, by analogy with the $b\hat{e}t$ $mill\hat{o}$' at Shechem, and on the basis of its use and the LXX translation, constituted an important part in the defenses of the city of David, and probably was a citadel-like structure at a

location which needed some special protection, probably the
northern part of the hill on which the city of David stood, the
only really vulnerable approach to the city.[195]

In view of these numerous candidates for terms which can
refer to the city's citadel in its entirety, or to an important
part of it, the conclusion would seem to be justified that the
citadel of the Israelite city constituted a vital part, if not
the most vital part of the city. This conclusion does not rest
on linguistic grounds alone, for as we shall see in the following chapters, it has other bases as well.

Terms Designating Secondary Settlements

Having examined the principal words designating the city
in the OT, as well as those which denote an important section
or feature of these communities, the final part of this chapter
will be given over to an investigation of OT terms which are
used to refer to settlements which are of a subsidiary type in
relation to the city proper. Such settlements are not necessarily smaller in terms of area, but are either of a less permanent nature, or are at least dependent upon the city in certain ways, and thus can be categorized as secondary establishments. While these settlements might be called "rural," this
term can be applied to them only with the provisos which will
be set forth in the formation of an urban-rural typology which
is applicable to the ancient city.[196]

Of all these terms, undoubtedly the most important is the
noun ḥāṣēr. While this is the term for "village" which is used
with the highest frequency in the OT, not all of the incidences
of the term concern a village-type settlement. This is due to
the fact that the word ḥāṣēr is homonymous, owing to the phenomenon of phoneme merger in Hebrew, a circumstance not reflected in concordances which commonly lump the two homonyms together under one entry. According to Orlinsky, the two roots.
which have merged are: (1) the proto-Semitic ḥẓr; Arabic ḥaṣara
[so also Phoenician ḥẓr; Syriac ḥeṣāra; Ugaritic ḥẓr; and probably the Aramaic ḥuṭra and the Akkadian uṣurtu, which appears
in the Mari dialect as ḥaṣarum].[197] The verbal form of these
terms has the meaning "to encompass, surround," with the corresponding nominal form denoting an "enclosure" (for animals)

or a "court"; (2) proto-Semitic *ḥḍr*; Arabic *ḥaḍara*; S. Arabic *hḍr*. This word has the verbal meaning "be present, dwell, settle" and the nominal one of "dwelling, settlement, village," in this case a dwelling not for animals, but primarily for humans.[198]

The use of *ḥāṣēr* in the OT fortunately contains a built-in key which makes it possible to differentiate between the two roots. This clue is the fact that the word which derives from the second root, "to settle," always occurs in the plural and is always masculine in gender. In the instances of the term which are related to the first root, there is, on the other hand, no such consistency of number or gender.[199] The only exception to the occurrence of *ḥāṣēr*, "village or settlement" in the plural in the OT is its use in the formation of place names, e.g., Hazar-Enan (Num 34:7, the modern Hadr); Hazar-Gaddah (Josh 15:27); Hazar-Shual (Josh 19:3); Hazar-Susah (Josh 19:5); etc. The biblical name of Hazor may be regarded as expressing the word *ḥaṣār*, with the characteristic Canaanite vowel shift of *ā* to *ō*.

Save for those of the Israelite tribes, references to the *ḥăṣērîm*, "settlements, villages," occur only in connection with the semipermanent habitations of seminomadic tribes.[200] That the *ḥăṣērîm* were unwalled settlements seems clear from such references as Lev 25:31, which clearly distinguishes them from "walled cities": "But the houses of the villages (*ḥăṣērîm*) which have no wall around them shall be reckoned with the fields of the country." That the *ḥăṣērîm* were settlements which were subsidiary to cities, is witnessed to by the frequent occurrence of the term as a designation for settlements in the vicinity of a city, particularly in Joshua, where the phrase *ʿārîm wĕḥăṣrêhen* "cities and their villages," occurs repeatedly.[201] In only one instance are *ʿārîm* attributed to another city. This occurs in Josh 10:39, where they are attributed to Debir. Orlinsky has observed that the LXX here reads *kōmas*, "villages," in place of the MT *ʿārehā*. He also notes that this translation of *kōme* for *ʿîr* would be unique among the 150-odd occurrences of this term in Joshua, and that in Josh 15:49 Debir is listed with ten other cities and is there assigned *ḥaṣrê* in accord with the usual pattern. This

is accounted for by Orlinsky by supposing that the LXX here
translates a *Vorlage* in which a cursive script allowed no possibility for the confusion between ע and צ, as did that of the
square script from which the MT was copied, in which the צ was
mistaken for an ע, with the resulting translation "its cities."[202]

Closely related to the phrase *ʿārîm wĕhaṣrehen*, and sometimes occurring in conjunction with it, is the use of the term
bĕnōtĕhā, "its daughters," in conjunction with a city's name,
forming the expression "the city 'X' and its daughters," which
means "the city 'X' and its dependent villages."[203]

The designation of the villages in the vicinity of a city
as "its daughters" is instructive with regard to the relationship which existed between city and village. We have earlier
alluded to the significance of the feminine gender of the noun
for "city." In 2 Sam 20:19, the city of Abel is called a
"mother in Israel." In addition to this appellation of a city
as a "mother," there is the phrase *meteg hāʾammâ* in 2 Sam 8:1,
which the *RSV* takes as a place name. However, no such place
has been identified. The literal translation "the bridle (or
authority) of the mother-city" has been suggested.[204]   While
one cannot be certain that the Chronicler's rendering here is
correct, or merely a "brave guess" as Caird suggests,[205] his
reading of "Gath and its villages" in the parallel of 1 Chr
18:1 in 2 Sam 8:1, could well render the following sense when
the two verses are conflated: "After this David defeated the
Philistines and subdued them; he assumed (or took) the authority of the mother-city Gath and its villages."

Feminine imagery is also used in an extended metaphor to
illustrate the relationship between "peoples" and "cities." In
Ezek 16:44-63, Jerusalem is pictured as the "daughter" of two
"peoples," the Amorites and the Hittites. Samaria and Sodom
are called her "sisters."[206] But, in the frequent references
to Jerusalem as the *bat-ṣîyyōn*, the intention is probably not
what is implied by the usual English translation "daughter of
Zion." Stinespring is probably correct in asserting that this
phrase refers to Zion herself, and should be considered an appositional genitive.[207] This use of an appositional genitive
is even clearer in the references to Jerusalem as the *bat*

yĕrûšālāim (Lam 2:13, 15), where the translation "daughter of
Jerusalem" would be nonsensical. In this construction then,
Jerusalem is personified as "the maiden Zion," the usual con-
notation being that of pity for a ravished maiden.

In speaking of cities and their villages as "mothers" and
"daughters," there are implications from the status of women in
Hebrew society that should not go unnoticed here. Both the
mother and daughter play a clearly subordinate, but nevertheless important role in the Hebrew family. The mother, while
having the primary function of producing children, also had
considerable authority over her daughters, hence the analogical
control of a mother-city over the dependent daughter-villages.
The mother had major reponsibilities in caring for the children, and similarly, the city provided protection for its dependent daughter-villages.

In addition to the mother-daughter imagery of the city-
village relationship, the Semitic propensity for expressing relationships in familial terms is also exhibited in the expressions which speak of a city's founder as the "father" of the
city.[208] In speaking of Shechem, e.g., as a person whose father was Hamor, one personalizes the city, its origins, and the
name of its present inhabitants after a manner typical of Israelite "corporate personality." Shechem is a corporate entity
whose "father" or founder was Hamor, and whose present inhabitants are thus called the *bĕnê ḥāmōr*, the "sons of Hamor" (Gen
33:19), or the *'anšê ḥāmōr*, the "men of Hamor" (Judg 9:28).
Wright contends that Hamor as the "father" of Shechem suggests
that either the founding of the city, or else something constituent of its very being, had to do, not with a person named
Hamor, but with a covenant or treaty. Thus the expression
bĕnê-ḥāmōr designates the members of an urban confederation
which had been ritually confirmed by the killing of an ass.[209]

Albright also sees the application of family terminology
in the enigmatic expression of Gen 15:2, *ben-mešeq*, which is
applied to Abraham's prospective heir, Eliezer of Damascus. He
observes that the designation of a person as *ben* with the name
of a city was common usage in Ugaritic and Akkadian to indicate
a native of a given town.[210] In the preexilic period, the inhabitants of Jerusalem are regularly called the *bĕnê* Jerusalem

or the *bĕnê* Zion.   But elsewhere *bĕnê* is used in connection
with a city only in later literature, e.g., Joel 2:33; 4:6;
Lam 4:2; and Ps 149:2.   Its more common use in earlier literature is in connection with the names of peoples or lands.   Albright also observes that in later Aramaic and Akkadian, the
words *bir*, *bar*, and *mār*, "son of," regularly took the place of
bêt, "house of," in place names beginning with this element.
The Assyrians, e.g., called Jehu the "son of Omri," which meant
merely "native of Beth-Omri," the official name for Samaria.[211]

In concluding this section on terms designating settlements of a status inferior to that of the city, several terms
are yet to be mentioned which are used infrequently in the OT
to denote small settlements of an impermanent type.

The noun *ḥawwa* occurs in the OT only in the plural and in
references to certain rural establishments in Gilead which are
called the *ḥawwōt yāʾir*.[212]   That these were rural establishments of some kind is generally supposed on the basis of the
etymology of *ḥawwâ*.   The Arabic verb *ḥaway*, "to assemble, collect, gather," and the derivative noun in Arabic, *ḥiwāʾ*, "circle of tents," are cited as cognates of the Hebrew term.[213]
While the term probably originally designated impermanent settlements, the settlements lasted long enough to be preserved
in several traditions.   It seems likely that this designation
as "tent villages" was at first descriptive of the actual nature of the settlements, but later assumed the character of a
proper name which remained even after they had become cities.[214]   These settlements may have been similar to the *alānu*
which are spoken of frequently in the Mari texts.[215]   Like
Transjordan, where there were tribal groups, so these settlements around Mari were associated with tribal groups.   They are
to be thought of as more or less permanent settlements, mainly
of tents, established in groups in the vicinity of an already
existing urban center.[216]   As such, they supplied a fixed point
of return for tribesmen, as well as a suitable place for them
to leave their women and children.[217]

Another term which may designate a type of settlement
which was subordinate to the city is the term *nāweh*.   This term
is also related to a term from Mari, *nawûm*, which was often
used in contrast with the usual term for city, *ālum*.[218]   The

nawûm was central to the tribal organization mentioned in the
Mari documents. Malamat observes that in standard Akkadian,
this term has a variety of meanings, such as "desert, uncultivated field, ruin, savage," but that at Mari it specifically
designated the status of the seminomadic tribe.[219] Edzard defines the *nawûm* around Mari as "the encampments of nomadic
tribes together with the existing tribal members and those who
were moving with them."[220] The term in the OT, like its cognate, is found in a pastoral context, and probably had its origin in such a setting. Its use in the OT is in the denotation
of the pasture land of the shepherd (Jer 23:10; 9:9; Ezek 34:
14; Ps 23:2; 65:13), the sheepfolds in the pastures (Jer 23:3;
25:30, 37), and with reference to the abode of shepherds while
they were with their sheep in the pasture. From this latter
meaning there developed, chiefly in metaphors and in poetry,
the use of the term to designate a more fixed dwelling or home,
either of man or of Yahweh.[221] In Jer 49:19 (= 50:44), the
term appears with the adjective *ʾêtān*, "durable, lasting, permanent," and suggests a structure which was built for the protection of sheep and shepherd in emergencies.[222] With respect
to the city in the OT, this term has one especially interesting
use. This is the one in which *nāweh* is used in the description
of a destroyed city, in a context which closely resembles that
of the treaty-curse formula. An example of this is found in
Ezek 25:5: "I will make Rabbah a yard (*linwēh*) for camels, and
the cities of the Ammonites a fold for flocks."[223] Edzard
cites a parallel to this OT expression in an old Babylonian o-
men which he translates, "the city has been made a *nawû*."[224]
The imagery conveyed in such expressions is that of a well-fortified city whose walls have been demolished and thus is fit to
serve only as a dwelling place for animals.

A final term in the OT which finds a parallel at Mari as
a designation of a villagelike settlement is the Hebrew *kāpār*
or *kōper*, which corresponds to *kaprum* at Mari. The form *kōper*,
with the characteristic Canaanite vowel shift, is found in an
early occurrence in 1 Sam 6:18, where the "unwalled villages,"
kōper happĕrāzî, of the Philistines are contrasted with their
"fortified cities," *ʿîr mibṣār*. In 1 Chr 27:25, the term
occurs in a series: הָאֲצָרוֹת בַּשָּׂדֶה בֶּעָרִים וּבַכְּפָרִים וּבַמִּגְדָּלוֹת, "the

treasuries in the field, in the cities and in the villages and in the citadels," where it designates a rural community. The term is also used in the formation of place names.[225] De Vaux considers the word to be an Aramaism in late Hebrew and in Aramean place names.[226] However, it is not necessarily late, especially in view of its use in Samuel, Joshua, and Chronicles in contexts dating from the monarchy.[227] KB considers the term to be an Akkadian loanword.[228] That the term was part of the early Aramaic lexicon is witnessed to by its occurrence in two eighth-century B.C. inscriptions.[229] This term must have been one which, while probably having been known to the Israelites at a relatively early period, never acquired currency in their everyday language. Like its cognate at Mari, this term, in contrast to *nawûm/nāweh*, is not used for the seminomadic type of settlement.[230]

Having examined those terms in the OT which designate secondary settlements, it should be said that there seems to be little basis for drawing distinctions among them on the basis of lingusitic criteria. With the exception of *ḥāṣēr*, their use is so limited as to make any kind of precise definition uncertain. The most that can be said is that these terms do designate originally unwalled, or at the most provisionally walled settlements, which were subordinate to urban centers in specific ways which remain to be seen.

CHAPTER II

NOTES

[1] James Barr, *Comparative Philology and the Text of the Old Testament* (Oxford: Clarendon Press, 1968) 90.

[2] KB, 701.

[3] GKC, 122h. Cf. 2 Sam 20:19, where the city Abel is called an ʾēm in Israel and Ezek 23:2, where Samaria and Jerusalem are pictured as two women, "the daughters of one mother." Babylon is called a "mother" in Jer 50:12.

[4] The plural form ʿayārîm occurs in Judg 10:4. GKC, 96, correctly observes that this is a case of erroneous pointing in order to bring the word into harmony with the preceding ʿăyā-rîm, "ass colts."

[5] GKC, 96.

[6] On the analogous use of other nouns, cf. Barr, *Comparative Philology*, 181-184.

[7] Hans Bauer and Pontus Leander, *Historische Grammatik der hebräischen Sprache des Alten Testaments*, I (Hildesheim: G. Olms, 1962) 78.r; 17.1.

[8] Julius Fuerst, *A Hebrew and Chaldee Lexicon to the Old Testament* (3rd ed.; Leipzig: Bernhard Tauchnitz, 1867) 1043.

[9] Wilhem Gesenius, *A Hebrew and English Lexicon of the Old Testament* (Boston: Crocker and Brewster, 1954) 774. This derivation was abandoned after the tenth edition of Gesenius' *Handwörterbuch*, and those editions of this work edited by Frants Buhl maintain that the derivation is unknown.

[10] On the phonemic pattern in Semitic languages see Sabatino Moscati (*An Introduction to the Comparative Grammar of the Semitic Languages* [Wiesbaden: Harrasowitz, 1964] 8.59, 60). [H. J. Dreyer ("The Roots qr, ʿr, ġr, and s/tr = 'stone wall, city,' etc." *De Fructu Oris Sui* [ed. I. H. Eybers *et al.*; Leiden: E. J. Brill, 1971] 17-25) has argued that the Semitic roots mentioned in his article's title are cognates, i.e., they originated from the same basic radicals in Proto-Semitic, and that the biconsonantal words containing these roots, viz., qûr; ʿtr; ġr (Ugaritic); and sûr/tûr, belong to the oldest stock of the Semitic vocabulary.]

[11] Franz Prätorius, "Himjarische Inschriften," *ZDMG* XXVI (1872) 437. Himyarite or Sabean is a S. Arabic language which occurs in inscriptions from ca. 700 B.C. - A.D. 550. The inscription discussed by Prätorius is not dated by him.

[12] Joseph Halévy, *Etudes Sabéenes* (Paris: Imprimerie nationale, 1875) 159. Cf. also J. H. Mordtmann, *Himjarische Inschriften* (Berlin: W. Spemman, 1893) 29; and Ed. Ullendorff, "The Contribution of South Semitics to Hebrew Lexicography," *VT* VI (1956) 196.

[13] KB, 701. BDB, 786.

[14] J. M. de Saulcy, *et al.*, eds. *Corpus Inscriptionum Semiticarum*, I (Paris: E Rei Publicae Typographeo, 1881) No. 113.

[15] Barr, *Comparative Philology*, 125.

[16] H. L. Ginsberg, "Two North-Canaanite Letters from Ugarit," *BASOR* 72(1938) 19.

[17] H. L. Ginsberg, "Baal's Two Messengers," *BASOR* 95(1944) 28. Ginsberg's original suggestion has been supported by S. E. Löwenstamm ("*tkstym hdsym blswn ɔawgryt*," *Tarbis* XXVIII[1958] 248-249); H. N. Richardson ("A Ugaritic Letter of a King to his Mother," *JBL* LXVI[1947] 322); O. Rössler "Ghain im Ugaritischen," *ZA* XX 1961 164-166); Mitchel Dahood (*Bib* XLIII[1962] 226); Dahood (*Psalms I*, AB, Vol. 16 [Garden City: Doubleday, 1965] 55-56); Benedikt Hartmann ("Mögen die Götter dich behüten und unversehrt bewahren," *Hebräische Wortforschung*, VTSup XVI [Leiden: E. J. Brill, 1967] 102-106); and John Gray (*I and II Kings* [Phila.: Westminster Press, 1963] 223).

[18] Gray, *I and II Kings*, 223.

[19] The text of this benediction is found in *UT*, 2009.3-4; 2059.4-5; and 95.8-9.

[20] *WUS*, No. 1811 and *UT* 19.1670.

[21] G. R. Driver, *Canaanite Myths and Legends* (Edinburgh: T. and T. Clark, 1956) 142.

[22] Raphael Serra, "Una raiz, afin a la raiz ugaritica *ġyr* 'guardar', en algunos textos biblicos," *Claretianum* IV(1964) 161-176.

[23] Those works cited in n. 17 excluding those of Ginsberg and Lowenstamm see the root *ʿyr* here. Gray (*I and II Kings*, 223) points out the collocation of *ʿîr* and *šilləm* here as in the Ugaritic benediction mentioned above.

[24] Cf. n. 17 except Gray but contra Gerhard von Rad (*Deuteronomy* [London: SCM Press, 1966] ad loc.) who sees the root *ʿwr* here.

[25] Dahood, *Psalms I*, 56.

[26] Ibid., 56. Subsequently, Dahood (*Psalms II*, AB, Vol. 17 [Garden City: Doubleday, 1968] 243) has added the aspect of "to nurture" to this root and finds it also in Isa 43:13.

[27] Dahood, *Psalms I*, 56. In the case of the verses in Daniel, Dahood observes that the Syriac word for "angel," *ʿirā*, is probably derived from this root. Cf. Marcus Jastrow (*A Dictionary of the Targum, the Talmud Babli and Yerushalmi, and the Midrashic Literature*, II [N.Y.: Pardes, 1950] 1075) on *ʿîr* as "guardian angel" in New Hebrew. With reference to the Micah passage, Dahood takes the parallelism with *ɔăšərêkā* as evidence for his supposition that *ʿārêkā* here means "pagan divinities" or "protectors" and compares this with the phrase in Jer 2:28; 19:15, where he thinks *ʿārîm* is intended in a double sense, since both pagan idols and cities could be destroyed.

[28] Hartmann ("Mögen die Götter," 104) maintains that *ʿēr* here signifies a "guardian, protector."

[29] *WUS*, Nos. 2166-68; *UT*, 19.1953, 1983, 1984.

[30] G. R. Driver, "Hebrew Notes on Prophets and Proverbs," *JTS* XLI(1940) 164.

[31] *UT*, 463, 19.1953.

[32] Rössler, "Ghain im Ugaritischen," 164-166. This phenomenon, for which the technical term ʾaddād is used in Arabic, is discussed by Barr (*Comparative Philology*, 173-177).

[33] *UT*, 76:III.29; ʾnt:III.28.

[34] Gray, *I and II Kings*, 507-508. The text is found in *UT*, ʾnt:II.3-5.

[35] Loren Fisher, "The Temple Quarter," *JSS* VIII(1963) 37. Although Fisher mentions the har ʾēl of Ezek 43:15 in this connection, there does not appear to be any etymological relationship between hār, "mountain," and ʾīr/ǧr.

[36] *WUS*, No. 2091; *UT*, 19.1847; Driver, *Canaanite Myths*, 141.

[37] *UT*, 19.2019; *WUS*, No. 2200; Driver, *Canaanite Myths*, 163. Driver and Aistleitner derive pdr from the Urartian patari, "city."

[38] *UT*, 19.1847.

[39] Cf. Deut 3:19 and Josh 2:5.

[40] Cf. A. L. Oppenheim (*Ancient Mesopotamia* [Chicago: University of Chicago, 1964] 115) for a similar pattern of use for the Sumerian *URU* and the Akkadian ālu.

[41] Max Weber, *The City* (N.Y.: The Free Press, 1966) 75-76.

[42] It should be noted here that while the rule seems to have included an enclosing wall for the city, it does not seem to have been the absolute prerequisite in every period. Witness to this can be seen in the few instances in which the noun ʿīr is modified by the adjective prz, thus designating an "unwalled city." Cf. Deut 3:5 and the LXX translation of Num 13:19.

[43] Cf. 1 Sam 23:7; Deut 3:5; 1 Kgs 4:13; Ezek 38:11.

[44] Gray, *I and II Kings*, 437. While the concept of the city as a fortified place is an early one, this particular adjective finds its most prevalent use in the work of the Deuteronomic historian and later, with only four occurrences in the "Tetrateuch," which may themselves be the work of a Deuteronomic editor. This may mean that in the earlier strata of the OT it was superfluous to apply this adjective, the word "city" already meaning in itself a fortified place.

[45] Cf. Num 13:19; Deut 1:28; 9:1; Josh 14:12.

[46] Cf. also 2 Kgs 18:8, 13; Isa 36:1.

[47] E.g., Jer 5:17; 8:14; Isa 27:10; Hos 8:14.

[48] BDB, 152. So also the New Hebrew, cf. Jastrow, *Dictionary*, 213, gdl II.

[49] Cf. Deut 1:28; 9:1; Num 13:28; Josh 10:2; 14:12; 1 Kgs 4:13.

[50] Wilhelm Borée, *Die alten Ortsnamen Palästinas* (Leipzig:

Eduard Pfeiffer, 1930) 108-109.

[51]Fisher, "The Temple Quarter, 34-37. Gray, *I and II Kings*, 381, 507-508.

[52]Fisher, "The Temple Quarter," 38.

[53]Cf. above, 29.

[54]Fisher, "The Temple Quarter," 37-38.

[55]It should be admitted that the uncertainty of the text here suggests caution. R. B. Y. Scott has suggested, in a private communication to the author, that an alternative explanation of the text could see '*îr* here as a corruption of *'ad*. If this were the case then either the corrupt word and the correction have been preserved, or the error originated in a dittograph of which there are several examples in Samuel-Kings. For a list see B. J. Roberts (*The Old Testament Text and Versions* [Cardiff: University of Wales, 1951] 93).

[56]For a listing of those who follow the *qĕrê*, see H. M. Orlinsky ("The Kings-Isaiah Rescensions of the Hezekiah Story," *JQR*, N.S. XXX[1939] 34-35).

[57]Fisher, "The Temple Quarter," 38. However, he prefers the meaning of "the city or altar within the temple" in this instance.

[58]Norman K. Gottwald, *All the Kingdoms of the Earth* (N.Y.: Harper and Row, 1964) 96n.

[59]*UT*, 19.85, 924. Cf. also C. H. Gordon (*The Common Background of Greek and Hebrew Civilizations* [N.Y.: W. W. Norton and Co., 1965] 137-138) and John Gray (*The Krt Text in the Literature of Ras Shamra* [2d ed. rev.; Leiden: E. J. Brill, 1964] 45).

[60]Fisher, "The Temple Quarter," 35. Cf. the similar use of the "outer city" and the "inner city" in the "Lamentation over the Destruction of Ur," lines 260-262, *ANET*, 460. See also M. Witzel ("Die Klage über Ur," *Orientalia* XIV [1945] 215, 217).

[61]The Targum senses some difficulty here and gives the interpretive translation: "It is small, and the guilt thereof light." The translation here is that of J. W. Etheridge (*The Targums of Onkelos and Jonathan ben Uzziel on the Pentateuch* [N.Y.: Ktav, 1968]).

[62]BDB, 858.

[63]Fisher, "The Temple Quarter," 36.

[64]W. F. Albright, *The Cambridge Ancient History*, II, ch. XX (rev. ed.; Cambridge: The University Press, 1966) 19.

[65]C. J. Gadd, "Tablets from Kirkuk," *RA* XXIII (1926) 64.

[66]Cf. BDB, 75-76.

[67]Mitchell Dahood, *Proverbs and Northwest Semitic Philology*, (Rome: Pontifical Biblical Institute, 1963) 62-63; Dahood, "The Phoenician Background of Qoheleth," *Bib* XLVII (1966) 280; Dahood, *Psalms II*, 208; Dahood, "Congruity of Metaphors," *Hebräische Wortforschung*, 46-47. Cf. also R. B. Y. Scott (*Proverbs-Ecclesiastes*, AB, Vol. 18 [Garden City: Doubleday, 1965]

and André Barucq (*Le livre des Proverbes* [Paris: Gabalda, 1964] 234.

[68] Dahood, "The Phoenician Background of Qoheleth," 280.

[69] The text of this inscription can be found in *KAI*, No. 14.16, 18. Translation in *ANET*, 502.

[70] Text in *KAI*, No. 10.10-11. Translation in *ANET*, 505.

[71] *KAI*, No. 181.7-8, 10. It might also be observed that in the Sumerian myth, "Enki and Ninhursag," (*ANET*, 37-38) which opens with a eulogy for Dilmun, this mythical place is called both a "land" and a "city."

[72] Prov 8:26; 31:23; Eccl. 10:16; Sir 51:9; Ps 74:20; 141: 7; Jonah 2:7; 2 Chr 32:4.

[73] S. Yeivin, *A Decade of Archaeology in Israel: 1948-1958* (Istanbul: Nederlands Historisch-Archaeologisch Institut in het Nabige Oosten, 1960), 29.

[74] On the gate as the site of the urban court, see below 125-127.

[75] Dahood, "The Phoenician Background of Qoheleth," 280.

[76] In light of the above interchangeability of "land/city," it would seem that caution is urged in identifying the "people of the land" in all cases as a rural population group. On this issue, see below, 100-102.

[77] Alexander Heidel, *The Gilgamesh Epic and Old Testament Parallels* (Chicago: University of Chicago Press, 1949) 171-172.

[78] See the story of Ishtar's descent in *ANET*, 106-109.

[79] *UT*, 51:VIII.10-14. Translation follows Driver, *Canaanite Myths*, 102-103. The word "city" here is *qryt*, a synonym of *ʿr* in Ugaritic and cognate of the Hebrew *qrt/qryh*, which will be discussed below as a synonym of *ʿîr*.

[80] Dahood, *Psalms II*, 193-194.

[81] So *RSV*, Artur Weiser (*The Psalms* [Phila.:Westminster, 1962] 506), and *JB*.

[82] The evidence from the versions is cited by Fisher ("The Temple Quarter," 39). He retains the MT *bāʿir*, but does not connect it with the city of the dead as does Dahood.

[83] Cf. 2 Kgs 18:8.

[84] On the significance of the phrase, "lest. . .it be called by my name" in v 28, cf. below, 41-42.

[85] H. W. Hertzberg, *I and II Samuel* (London: SCM, 1964) 318.

[86] Gray, *I and II Kings*, 223. Cf. also A. S. Brockington ("I and II Samuel," *PCB*, 334) and G. B. Caird ("I and II Samuel," *IB*, II, 1107).

[87] Cf. the place name *qr mym* in *UT*, 1 Aqht. 151-152.

[88] Cf. Prov 10:15; 18:11, 19; 25:28.

[89] Cf. the name of Tyre in Josh 19:29, etc., *mibṣar-ṣōr*.

[90] BDB, 124-125.

[91]For such a confirmation with regard to Samaria, see J. A. Montgomery (*A Critical and Exegetical Commentary on the Book of Kings*, ed. H. S. Gehman, ICC [Edinburgh: T. and T. Clark, 1951] 285) and the archaeological reports cited there.

[92]Deut 25:9; 1 Sam 2:35; Am 9:11; Jer 24:6; etc.

[93]Josh 6:26; Am 9:14; Isa 45:13; 58:12; etc. Cf. also the Moabite stone, lines 27-30.

[94]On the meaning of this term, see below, 53-55.

[95]Cf. the similar usage in the Moabite stone, lines 21-23.

[96]The LXX here reads *horos*, "mountain," for the MT ʿ*îr*.

[97]R. Abba, "Name," *IDB*, III, 502.

[98]Kurt Galling, "Die Ausrufung des Namens als Rechtsakt in Israel," *TLZ* LXXXL (1956) col. 67.

[99]Cf. Hertzberg, *I and II Samuel*, 319.

[100]Cf. also Num 32:41. On *hwh* as a designation for "village," see below, 59. The translation of Deut 3:14 here follows the suggestion of the critical apparatus in *BHK*.

[101]Cf. also Gen 34:2.

[102]Cf. 1 Kgs 16:24. It would seem to be anomalous that after Omri purchases the city site from Shemer, the city which is built there is called Samaria, after the name of its previous owner, instead of after its new owner. This probably points to the fact that the name Shemer is a case of popular etymology, since *šōmĕrōn* means "watchpost" or "protector." Cf. also the place name Mizpah, which means "watchtower."

[103]Cf. Num 21:25-26; 2 Sam 8:8 = 1 Chr 18:8; and the numerous references to the "City of David."

[104]Although this is the most common form of the word, cf. the form *qeret*, which occurs in Job and Proverbs only (Job 29: 7; Prov 8:3; 9:3, 14).

[105]The term occurs only once in the "Tetrateuch," in parallel with ʿ*îr*, in some of the preexilic prophets (principally Isaiah), only four times in the Deuteronomic history work, twice in the Psalms, in Job and Proverbs, and not at all in the post-exilic prophets or other works dated in the post-exilic era.

[106]E.g., Kiriathaim (Jer 48:1; cf. *qrytn* in the Moabite stone, *KAI*, No. 181,10) and Kiriath-Huzoth (Num 22:39), which were Moabite cities. Cf. also Kiriath-Jearim (Josh 9:17) which is characterized as a Hivite (probably Hittite or Hurrian) city.

[107]BDB, 900. But contra I. Eitan ("The Crux in Prov 27: 16," *JQR*, N. S. XV [1924-25] 421). Cf. also Chaim Rabin ("Hittite Words in Hebrew," *Or* XXXII [1963] 126) who observes that this root means only "to meet by coming towards one," not "to gather in one place."

[108]So A. G. Barrois (*Manuel d'archaéologie biblique*, I [Paris: A. Picard, 1939] 89-90) and A. H. Van Zyl (*The Moabites* [Leiden: E. J. Brill, 1960] 175).

[109]KB, 838, $q\hat{t}r$ II. For the text of the Moabite stone see *KAI*, No. 181, lines 11-12, 24. Cf. also the form *ḥqrt* in a Phoenician inscription, *KAI*, No. 26A:II.9, 17.

[110]Montgomery-Gehman, *Kings*, 463.

[111]Ibid., 459. Cf. Gray (*I and II Kings*, 574) who sees $q\hat{t}r$ as a common noun, "the city," i. e. Nineveh.

[112]Gray, *I and II Kings*, 574.

[113]Cf. Biblical Aramaic, *qiryāh* (cf. also *KAI*, No. 222.33 and No. 215.4, 15); Syriac, *qrē* (*qe/uryat*); Phoenician, *qart*; Arabic, *qaryah*; Ugaritic, *qryt* and *qrt* (cf. *UT*, 19.2278 and the references cited there). On all these cognates, cf. Rabin, "Hittite Words," 125-126.

[114]Van Zyl, *The Moabites*, 175. [Dreyer ("The Roots *qr*, *ʿr*, *ġr* and *s/tr*," 18-19) maintains that the form *qirya* can best be explained as a Pa'yal formation from the root *qr*. The function of the Pa'yal is to intensify the meaning of the noun. *qirya* originally had the special meaning of "a large or well forti-fied town."]

[115]Rabin, "Hittite Words," 125-126.

[116]Cf. Gray, *The KRT Text*, 31.

[117]*ANET*, 425.

[118]Deut 12:12, 15, etc.; 14:21, 27, etc.; 15:7, 22; etc.; Exod 20:10 = Deut 5:14; 1 Kgs 8:37; and possibly Jer 14:2.

[119]S. R. Driver, *A Critical and Exegetical Commentary on Deuteronomy*, ICC, Vol. 5 (N.Y.: Scribner's Sons, 1902) lxxix.

[120]Isa 38:10; Ps 9:14; 107:18; Job 38:17.

[121]*CAD*, Vol. 2, 20-21.

[122]*UT*, 1007.6.

[123]KB, 559-560; BDB, 879-881.

[124]Rössler, "Ghain im Ugaritischen," 165-166.

[125]Ibid., 166.

[126]Tallqvist, "Namen der Totenwelt," 6-8.

[127]R. E. Clements, *God and Temple* (Oxford: Blackwell, 1965) 53. The text is found in *UT*, 51:VII.13-15.

[128]*UT* ʾnt:III.26, 27.

[129]M. H. Pope, *El in the Ugaritic Texts* (Leiden: E. J. Brill, 1955) 59-60. The texts are in *UT*, 75:II.61 and 1 *Aqht* 153.

[130]*CAD*, Vol. 1, part 1, 379.

[131]W. F. Albright, "Baal Zaphon," *Festschrift Alfred Ber-tholet zum 80. Geburtstag* (eds. W. Baumgartner *et al.*; Tübing-en: J. C. B. Mohr, 1950) 2.

[132]Amos 3:9; 6:1. In 3:9, the reading follows the singu-lar with the LXX.

[133]Ahiqar 11:159-160. Translation is that of H. L. Gins-berg in *ANET*, 429. For the Aramaic text see A. E. Cowley

(*Aramaic Papyri of the Fifth Century B.C.* [Oxford: Clarendon, 1923] 204-208).

[134] Borée, *Ortsnamen Palästinas*, 82.

[135] *UT*, 19.1984 and the textual references cited there.

[136] Fisher, "The Temple Quarter," 37. His sole basis for such a translation appears to be the *har'ēl* in Ezek 43:15, where he emphasizes the aspect of the "hill" and says that the *'ēr* within the temple is the "hill," "altar," or "inner room."

[137] See above, 32.

[138] Roland de Vaux (*Ancient Israel*, I [N.Y.: McGraw-Hill, 1961] 235), who suggests the translation "castle" in the sense of the Latin, *castellum*.

[139] Cf. 2 Chr 26:10; 27:4, where there are annalistic references to such structures built by Jotham and Uzziah.

[140] De Vaux, *Ancient Israel*, I, 235.

[141] *mgdly*, *UT*, 1081.10; the reference to Qart-abilim, *UT*, *3 Aqht*, rev. 30-31.

[142] De Vaux, *Ancient Israel*, I, 235.

[143] G. E. Wright, "Shechem," *AOTS*, 361.

[144] E.g., Shechem (Judg 9:46-49). *migdal-'ēder*, "tower of the flock," may be an ancient name for the Jebusite citadel which became the city of David. D. W. Thomas ("Micah," *PCB*, 632) identifies *migdal-'ēder*, which appears in parallel with the "hill of the daughter Zion" in Mic 4:8, with Jerusalem, as does Artur Weiser (*Das Buch der zwölf kleinen Propheten*, I, ATD, Vol. 24, [Gottingen: Vandenhoeck und Ruprecht, 1963] 268). A *migdal-'ēder* is mentioned in Gen 35:21, which is apparently in the vicinity of Bethlehem. The Migdal-David in Cant 4:4 may be another name for the city of David.

[145] Prov 18:10; Ps 61:4.

[146] *bîrâ* is found only in Chronicles, Nehemiah, Daniel, and Esther.

[147] B. Mazar, "The Tobiads," *IEJ*, VII(1957) 140. Cf. also the name of Elephantine in the Elephantine papyri, Yeb the fortress, *yb-byrt'*.

[148] Neh 2:8; 7:2. J. M. Myers (*Ezra-Nehemiah*, AB, Vol. 14, [Garden City: Doubleday, 1965] 97) translates Neh 2:8: ". . . timber for the beams of the gates of the citadel guarding the house. . ." This structure was probably the predecessor of the Antonia fortress of Herodian times and, as such, stood to the north of the temple area which was vulnerable to attack from high ground in that direction. Cf. L. H. Vincent, *Jerusalem de l'Ancien Testament*, I (Paris: J. Gabalda, 1954-56) 242.

[149] Used thus in reference to Susa (*passim* in Esther).

[150] So KB, 117.

[151] Judg 9:46, 49; 1 Sam 13:6

[152] Reading *ba'al* instead of the MT *'el* with LXX[A] and OL and by analogy with v 4 of this chapter.

[153]G. E. Wright, *Shechem* (N.Y.: McGraw-Hill, 1965) 106.

[154]By analogy, in 1 Sam 13:6 the reference then would be to the citadels of unnamed cities.

[155]KB, 816. BDB, 863 cites the Arabic noun *darīhun*, sepulchral chamber, as cognate with the Hebrew term, which is then given the special sense of underground cave. Cf. also S. R. Driver (*Notes on the Hebrew Text and Topography of Samuel* [Oxford: Clarendon Press, 1913] 99) and Eduard Nielsen (*Shechem* [Copenhagen: Gad, 1955] 164). It is apparently this latter cognate which has led to the translation of "tombs" in the *RSV* of 1 Sam 13:6, where the *KJV* has "high places." The derivation from *sarhun* with its meaning of "tower," seems to provide a closer parallel to *migdāl*, and is less contrived than "cave of refuge."

[156]The term *'armōn* does not occur in the Pentateuch and only occurs twice in the Deuteronomic history work (both times in the singular). It finds its widest use in the eighth century prophets and in Jeremiah and occurs a few times in Psalms, Proverbs, Lamentations, and once in Chronicles. In these books the plural outnumbers the singular nearly seven to one.

[157]Cf., e.g., the number of occurrences of the verb *'akl*, "to consume," in connection with *'armōnōt*: Jer 17:27; 49:27; Hos 8:14; Amos 1:4, 7, 10, 12, 14; 2:2, 5.

[158]Cf. Amos 3:11; 6:8; Isa 34:13; 23:13; Jer 49:27.

[159]Ephraim A. Speiser, "The Etymology of *'armōn*," *JQR*, N.S. XIV (1924) 329.

[160]Cf. Ginsberg ("The Ugaritic Texts and Textual Criticism," 113-114) and Montgomery-Gehman (*Kings*, 290).

[161]So BHK and Walther Eichrodt (*Der Prophet Hesekiel*, ATD [Göttingen: Vandenhoeck and Ruprecht, 1959-66] 159), with Targum and Theodotion.

[162]Cited by BDB, 74. Others who defend the MT reading are H. G. May ("Ezekiel," *IB*, VI, 165-166) and C. G. Howie (*The Date and Composition of Ezekiel* [Philadelphia: The Society of Biblical Literature, 1950] 62).

[163]A. Sperber, *A Historical Grammar of Biblical Hebrew* (Leiden: E. J. Brill, 1966) 481. Cf. also Barr (*Comparative Philology*, 96-98).

[164]BDB, 420-421; KB, 391.

[165]Cf. the LXX, *oikous tēs poleōs*, being a translation of the Hebrew *bātē hā'îr*, "houses of the city," where *'îr* bears its more specialized meaning, "citadel."

[166]Gray (*I and II Kings*, 167-168) concurs in this and cites C. Watzinger (*Denkmäler Palästinas* [Leipzig: Hinrichs, 1933-35] 96), who refers to an analogous structure in Athens.

[167]According to BHK, the Syriac here has a translation which would reflect the Hebrew *bĕ'arĕhā*, "in her cities." Again, this may witness to a more specialized connotation of *'îr*. Cf. also Jer 50:32, where the same line reads *bĕ'arāyw bĕya'rah*.

[168]John Bright, *Jeremiah*, AB, Vol. 21 (Garden City:

Doubleday, 1965) 141.

[169]The LXX here translates the Hebrew *bĕyǎʿrô*.

[170]Reading *wĕyārad* with the Targum instead of the MT *ubā-rad*. Cf. 1QIsa which reads *hyʿr* in both places.

[171]So John Bright ("Isaiah," *PCB*, 512) and R. B. Y. Scott ("Isaiah 1-39," *IB*, V, 346).

[172]Isa 10:18, 19. Cf. also 10:33-34 for possible similar imagery.

[173]Cf. also Ezr 2:25, where the name of this city becomes *qiryat ʿārîm*. The name of this city may appear in one of the Amarna letters, *EA* 333.10, as *aluia-ra-mi*.

[174]For the text see *KAI*, No. 181.21-22. The translation here is Albright's in *ANET*, 320. The italics represent Albright's italics, evidently registering his dissatisfaction with his translation at this point.

[175]R. J. Williams, "The Mobite Stone," *IDB*, III, 420.

[176]Driver, *Canaanite Myths*, 101.

[177]*UT*, 51:VII.35-39. The translation here is that of Cyrus Gordon (*Ugaritic Literature* [Rome: Pontifical Biblical Institute, 1949] 36). On *ntq*, cf. Aistleitner (*WUS*, No. 1876), who compares this term with the Hebrew *neseq*, "weapons" or "armory."

[178]So *WUS*, No. 1200. Cf. BDB, 420, Fuerst (*Lexicon*, 588), and KB, 391.

[179]All other occurrences of *ʿōpel* either refer specifically to Jerusalem, or are plural in form and have a completely different meaning, viz., "tumor." Cf. BDB, 779.

[180]In Isa 32:14, *ʿōpel* is anarthrous, but the *RSV* again translates it "the hill." Cf. the *KJV* which translates the word in both cases as some sort of fortification, "tower" or "fort."

[181]So J. Mauchline, "I and II Kings," *PCB*, 349. Cf. KB, 723 and *RSV*.

[182]So Gray (*I and II Kings*, 458), Scott ("Isaiah 1-39," 344) and Snaith ("I and II Kings," 214). Among the versions, the LXX, Targum, and OL would seem to support this translation.

[183]BDB, 779, and KB, 723.

[184]Gray, *I and II Kings*, 458. Cf. also Neh 3:27. Gray observes that Gehazi's residence within the royal citadel would be consonant with Elisha's status as a royal seer.

[185]With *baḥan*, "tower," in Isa 32:14 and *migdal*, "tower," in Mic 4:8. Cf. the translation of Scott ("Isaiah 1-39") of Isa 32:14, where he reads "acropolis."

[186]*ANET*, 320.

[187]J. J. Simons, *Jerusalem in the Old Testament* (Leiden: E. J. Brill, 1952) 131.

[188]BDB, 569-570.

[189]G. A. Barrois, "Millo," *IDB*, III, 383. [K. Kenyon

(*Royal Cities of the Old Testament* [London: Barrie and Jenkins, 1971] 34) maintains that the present archaeological evidence suggests that *millô'* was a terrace structure, in the most exact sense a filling.]

[190] 2 Sam 5:9; 1 Chr 11:8; 1 Kgs 9:15, 24; 11:27; 2 Chr 32: 5. In all of these references, with the exception of the last, *millô'* is joined with the verb *bnh* in its sense "to repair" or "to rebuild the fortifications of."

[191] Judg 9:6, 20 (Shechem); 2 Kgs 12:21 (where the reference is to a *bêt millô' hayyôrēd sillā, sillā* being an indeterminate place. On the latter reference cf. Montgomery-Gehman (*Kings*, 431-432) and Mauchline ("I and II Kings," 351) contra Barrois ("Millo," 383).

[192] Wright, *Shechem*, 126. Cf. also Eduard Nielsen (*Shechem*, 165-166) who concurs with Wright in this identification and convincingly refutes arguments which oppose such an equation.

[193] The word *bêt* in this sense was probably used, in its original sense, to refer to a settlement of consanguinous persons and alternatively to the sanctuary round which the settlement grew. Cf., e.g., the use of *bêt* in numerous place names.

[194] Driver, *Notes on Samuel*, 261-262.

[195] Certainly the S.E. hill of Jerusalem is not simply a downward slope from the temple area, but seems to have a secondary elevation, possibly marked off by a fosse. Cf. Simons (*Jerusalem*, 64-67) and R. P. S. Hubbard ("Topography of Ancient Jerusalem," *PEQ* [1966] 130-154).

[196] See below, Chapter III.

[197] Cf. *CAD*, VI, 130b.

[198] H. M. Orlinsky, "*Hāsēr* in the Old Testament," *JAOS*, LIX (1939) 22-23. Cf. also Abraham Malamat ("Mari and the Bible: Some Patterns of Tribal Organization and Institutions," *JAOS*, LXXXII [1962] 146-147) and BDB, 346-347, contra Buhl (in the 15th ed. of Gesenius' *Worterbuch*, 250) who does not recognize different roots for *hāsēr*.

[199] Orlinsky ("*Hāsēr*,") further observes that *hāsēr*, "court," originally and normally feminine, came to be confused with the masculine *hāsēr*, "settled abode," when the court in question was that of the temple, since the temple was the "abode" of the deity. Cf. Ps 92:14; 135:2; Zech 3:7; 1 Chr 28: 6, and also *UT*, 129.19-20 and *KRT*. 203-204. This identification is one which dates from exilic or post-exilic times.

[200] Gen 25:16 (where it occurs with the word *tîrâ*); Deut 2: 23.

[201] 15:32-62; 18:24, 28; 19:6-23; etc. Cf. also 1 Chr 4:33. The instance in Isa 42:11 where the "village" is contrasted with the "city," would appear to be an anomalous one, resulting from "poetic license."

[202] Orlinsky, "*Hāsēr*," 34.

[203] Josh 15:45, 47; Num 21:25; 32:42; Judg 1:27; Jer 49:2; Ezek 26:6; etc. Cf. also the parallel in the 8th century B.C. treaty from Sfire, *'rpd wbnth*, "Arpad and its daughters," *KAI*

No. 222 A.35.

[204] BDB, 52, and so the *ASV*.

[205] Caird, "I and II Samuel," 1089.

[206] Cf. the expression *bat-ʿammî* applied to Jerusalem in Isa 22:4; Jer 8:21-23; Lam 2:11; etc., contra W. F. Stinespring ("No Daughter of Zion," *Encounter*, XXVI, 137).

[207] Stinespring, "No Daughter of Zion," 133-141. Cf. also GKC, 391-392, 416, and R. J. Williams (*Hebrew Syntax* [Toronto: University of Toronto, 1967] 42.

[208] Josh 21:11 (Hebron); Judg 9:28; Gen 33:18-20 (Shechem); cf. also Gen 4, where Cain is understood as the "father" of the city "Enoch."

[209] Wright, *Shechem*, 130-131. On this means of ratifying a covenant cf. Martin Noth ("Old Testament Covenant-Making in the Light of a Text from Mari," *The Laws of the Pentateuch and other Studies* [Philadelphia: Fortress, 1966] 108-117).

[210] W. F. Albright, "Abram the Hebrew: A New Archaeological Interpretation," *BASOR*, 163(1961) 47. If so, this would be an unusual case in the OT where the singular form of son would be used in this way. Cf. possibly Jer 35:8.

[211] Ibid., 47.

[212] There are three different explanations given for the name Havvoth-jair, representing three independent traditions: Num 32:41 = Deut 3:14; Judg 10:3-4; and 1 Chr 2:21-24. S. Cohen ("Havvoth-Jair," *IDB*, II, 537-538) correctly attributes the greatest historical probability to the first of these in which the conquest is made by the Jair clan, here personified.

[213] BDB, 295; KB, 280.

[214] They are included among a varying number of cities in Josh 13:30; Judg 10:4; 1 Kgs 4:13; and 1 Chr 2:23.

[215] ARM, II:92.12; 102.7; III:12,17; 16.5; etc.

[216] Cf. especially ARM, III:16.5.

[217] Cf. J. C. L. Gibson, "Light from Mari on the Patriarchs," *JSS* VII (1962) 56-57.

[218] ARM, II:48.8-9; 27.3-5; etc.

[219] Malamat, "Mari and the Bible," 146.

[220] D. O. Edzard, "Altbabylonisch *nawûm*," *ZA*, N.F. LIII (1959) 168-173.

[221] Exod 15:13; Isa 32:18; 33:20; Jer 31:23; Prov 21:20; 24:15; etc.

[222] Such a structure may be reflected in the "desert kites" discussed by A. S. Kirkbride ("Desert Kites," *JPOS* XX [1946] 1-5). Cf. also Yigael Yadin (*The Art of Warfare in Biblical Lands* [London: Weidenfeld and Nicolson, 1963] 124) who believes that the kite-shaped enclosure on the reverse side of the Narmer Palette symbolizes trans-Jordanian territory. These enclosures were often built of stone and as such were semi-permanent.

[223]Reading "cities" with *BHK*. Similar expressions can be found in Isa 34:13 and 27:10. For destroyed cities as the dwelling place of animals in treaty-curses, cf. Delbert Hillers (*Treaty Curses and the Old Testament Prophets* [Rome: Pontifical Biblical Institute, 1964] 43-46).

[224]Edzard, "Altbabylonisch *nawûm*," 169.

[225]Cf. Chephirah in Josh 9:17; 18:26, where it is listed as one of the Hivite cities, which probably indicates that it was a village that had become a city by the addition of fortifications. Mizpah (Tell en-Nasbeh), e.g., began as a village in the 12th-11th centuries, and ca. 900 a strong wall was built around it, and it became a "city." On this, see David Diringer ("Mizpah," *AOTS*, 332). The city Chephirah is also mentioned in Ezr 2:25 = Neh 7:29. Josh 18:24 refers to a Chephar-ammoni as one of the "cities" of Benjamin, probably so called because it was originally an Ammonite village.

[226]R. de Vaux, "Les patriarchs hébreux et l'histoire," *RB* LXXII (1965) 14.

[227]For this dating of the Chronicles passage, cf. J. M. Myers (*I Chronicles*, AB, Vol. 12 [Garden City: Doubleday, 1965] 185).

[228]KB, 452.

[229]*KAI*, No. 215.10 and No. 224.23, 26.

[230]Edzard, "Altbabylonisch *nawûm*," 170.

CHAPTER III

THE OLD TESTAMENT CITY:
ITS NATURE AS SEEN IN ITS PHYSICAL, SOCIAL, ECONOMIC,
AND POLITICAL STRUCTURES IN THE ISRAELITE MONARCHY

Pursuant to the investigation of the philological data
pertaining to the city in the OT, and preceding the discussion
of the historical aspects of urbanization in ancient Israel
with its attendant valuation of the city, the focus of this
chapter will be on a functional description of the ancient Israelite city in its "fully developed" form. This description
will be formulated on the basis of the physical, social, economic, and political structures associated with the city so
far as such structures can be discerned in the literature of
the OT and on the basis of archaeological and comparative urban
studies.

Our aim in this chapter is basically a functional one.
Through the description and analysis of the various structures
associated with the city in the OT, we hope to be able to see
something of the role which the city played in Israelite society.

In this chapter, as was indicated in our first chapter,
extensive use will be made of the thesis of Gideon Sjoberg,
which he states in the following terms:

> Our principal hypothesis is that in their structure, or
> form, preindustrial cities. . . resemble one another
> closely and in turn differ markedly from modern industrial
> urban centers.
>   Preindustrial cities everywhere display strikingly sim-
> ilar social and ecological structures, not necessarily in
> specific cultural content, but certainly in basic form.
> . . . We seek to isolate for preindustrial cities struc-
> tural universals, those elements that transcend cultural
> boundaries. These cities share numerous patterns in the
> realms of ecology, class, and the family, as well as in
> their economic, political, religious and educational
> structures, arrangements that diverge sharply from their
> counterparts in mature industrial centers.[1]

An attempt will be made to utilize Sjoberg's findings concerning the preindustrial city, while at the same time testing
the applicability of such data to the city in ancient Israel by

utilizing the descriptions of urban structures which are found in the pages of the OT and those which can be derived from the established results of archaeology. Furthermore, Sjoberg's hypothesis will be examined in the light of data concerning the Near Eastern city in antiquity, with which the ancient Israelite city shares a considerable degree of cultural affinity.

Physical Aspects of the City in Ancient Israel

The physical layout of the typical Palestinian city is a matter of prime importance in seeking to discover the nature of the city in the OT traditions. While it is beyond the scope of this study to analyze the architectural details of specific sites, for which purpose archaeological reports on such sites should be consulted, such physical details cannot be ignored altogether.[2] A. L. Oppenheim has aptly put the rationale for giving attention to the physical aspects of the city:

> Urbanization as a sociological phenomenon creates in every civilization in which it materializes a characteristic projection in the physical design of the typical urban settlement. The arrangement of the private and public buildings of a city and that of the intracity arteries of communication and fortifications reflect the needs as well as the aspirations of the community as they find their realization within the existing frame of the ecological and technological contingencies of period and region.[3]

Among the factors which influenced the form which the ancient Israelite city took, one of the most prominent was that of the location of the city. Yohanan Aharoni lists four main factors which determined the original choice of a Palestinian city site and contributed to the continuity of occupation on the same site. The four contributing factors are: (1) strategic considerations involving the defensibility of the site, (2) an adequate water supply, (3) situation on thoroughfares or interurban arteries, and (4) nearness and ease of access to agricultural lands.[4]

Though not all of equal importance, these four factors were givens which tended to produce a certain degree of uniformity among Palestinian cities. The prime factor among the four seems to have been the strategic one, which might be expected on the basis of the philological study in which the importance of the aspect of fortification was stressed again and again. Having said this, however, the proviso should be added

that the requirement of defensibility and its consequent limiting influence was not constant throughout the pre-exilic period, due to changes in the political situation. The imposing
city fortifications of the Early and Middle Bronze Ages had
been dictated by the fact that the city-state political system
of totally or partially independent city-states had put the
prime responsibility for security on the individual city. This
situation was modified to some extent in the period of the Israelite tribal confederacy, one of whose major roles was that
of common defense, and which relieved the individual city of
some of the responsibility for security.[5] This situation was
again altered in the period of the two states of Israel and Judah, as is attested in the references to the activities of
kings in improving the fortifications of certain cities.[6]

The most easily defended site was that of a hill isolated
on all sides, or, alternatively, a spur connected with a larger
hill by a narrow neck of land. J. J. Simons sees examples of
the former type in the cities of Lachish and Jericho; of the
latter in Megiddo and Davidic Jerusalem.[7] But there were few
hill sites which offered much space for the expansion of a
city, and thus the strategic factor also influenced the size of
the city. Since city building in Palestine followed the nearly
universal custom in the ancient Near East of rebuilding on the
same site, the result was the well-known tell. The higher the
tell became, the smaller the inhabitable area of the city which
could be built on its crown. In time this development thus resulted in either an expansion of the city down the sides of the
tell or in the abandonment of the site. If the former alternative was chosen, the natural topographic features which had enhanced the city's security were no longer so effective and thus
had to be further supplemented with man-made fortifications.[8]
Where the site did not permit such expansion, the size of the
city was severely limited. Yadin has estimated that in the
early Israelite period the average area of most cities was
between five and ten acres. On the basis of the figure of 240
inhabitants per urban acre, the population of such cities would
then range from 1,000-3,000.[9] However, caution is urged in any
computation of the population of an ancient Israelite city at
any given moment in time, due to the circumstance that in time

of peace many city dwellers would be transient and would not
live continually within the city walls, but for extended periods in the city's "daughter-villages." In addition to the
strategic factor, there were others which limited the size of
the city, as we shall see below.

The second factor which tended to determine the location
of the city was that of an adequate water supply. Obviously,
when the strategic factor suggested a location on an elevated
site, this was more often than not in conflict with the provision for an adequate source of drinking water which the concentration of population in a city demanded. The preferred
source of water was a fresh spring, but since springs do not
flow from hilltops, they were usually located outside of the
city walls and provisions had to be made both for their protection and for access to them in case of enemy siege.[10] The conflict between security requirements and an adequate water supply was mitigated somewhat early in the Israelite period by the
invention of a plastering and whitewashing technique which made
it possible for a city to store an entire year's water supply
in cisterns within its walls, and which also made possible the
establishment of settlements independent of springs.[11]

The situation of a city on a major trade route was an economic factor, which again was not necessarily consistent with
the demands of security. But, in cases where a city was located both on a defensible site and, at the same time, at the in-
tersection of trade routes, the development of the city into a
center of some size and historical consequence was the likely
result. Notable examples of such cities in the OT are Hebron,
Gibeon, Bethel, Shechem, and especially Samaria.[12]

The final factor which influenced the location of the city
was that of the nearness and ease of access to the fields of
the city. We have already asserted, on philological grounds,
that the city and its hinterland formed a unit.[13] Here, this
unity is seen from an economic perspective. The inhabitants
of the city are basically dependent on the produce from the
fields immediately surrounding the city, with some goods being
brought in from a greater distance. This fact again places a
limitation on the size of the city. As the population of a
city grew, the acreage of the fields on which the city depended

had to increase proportionally, barring any significant technological advance in agriculture. As this expansion continued, the fields soon became so distant from the city that they could not be protected. The result in this instance was a movement from the city to the villages,[14] or alternatively, the establishment of "cities" (i.e., fortified settlements) which were still subservient to and allied with the "mother city."[15]

The four factors which we have discussed are not active agents in the formation of cities at particular sites so much as they are restrictive agents. Since the requirements were not easily met, particularly in the hill country regions, suitable possibilities for urban location were greatly limited.[16]

While the change in the fortifications of a typical city in the different periods of Israelite history is admitted, still, fortification was one of the primary features of the city throughout the period with which we are concerned. From the beginnings of the city in the fourth millennium, the distinguishing mark of the urban settlement in the ancient Near East--with the exception of Egypt--seems to have been the presence of a rampart. As we have seen, the primary linguistic distinction between "city" and "village" in the OT was that the former was walled and the latter was not.

There was an evolution in the technique used in the construction of walls, ranging from the use of unhewn or roughly hewn stones employed in city walls at the beginning of the Israelite period to the smooth stones, which were hewn by hand, used in city walls and important buildings in the later period of the monarchy.[17] These stone foundation walls were usually topped by a wall of sun-dried bricks, whose architectural details have mostly been deduced from pictorial representations of cities of the period, due to the fact that there are few archaeological remains of such clay structures.[18]

Although the Israelite period did witness an evolution in wall-building techniques, apart from the repairing of extant Canaanite walls, the Israelites constructed two basic types of walls: casemate walls and walls with redans, or offset-inset projections from the line of the wall.[19]

The wall with redans was apparently a development from the original attempt to make maximum use of the natural

defenses provided by the topographical situation of the site.
In building their walls, the Canaanites tried to follow, as
closely as possible, the escarpment of the hill. This resulted
in the necessity of breaking the straight line of the wall;
thus obtaining a series of redans. This procedure was then
adopted in some Israelite fortifications. These redans
provided salients for the defense of the walls, but their main
function was to strengthen the wall without increasing the
thickness.[20] These walls with redans were then reinforced
with towers.[21] As a rule, the city gates were also flanked
by a tower or towers, since they were the foci of any attack.

The other basic type of Israelite wall was the casemate
wall. This type of wall construction apparently did not
originate with the Israelites, but seems to have come from
Asia Minor. De Vaux states that the casemate wall was generally replaced by the type with redans in Palestine and
suggests that the main reason for the change in type was a
chronological one, while at the same time he admits to the
continuation of the casemate type into the ninth century
B.C.[22] Aharoni has challenged the usual assertion that casemate walls were Davidic or earlier and were used only rarely
in later periods:

> It is now obvious that casemate-walls continued in use
> and were constructed after the tenth century no less
> than before. It seems that Solomon built different
> walls in different cities: casemate walls in Hazor,
> Gezer and Tell Qasile but a solid wall with projections
> and recesses in Megiddo.[23]

In place of a chronological division between the two types of
walls, Aharoni sets forth a functional one. Functionally, the
casemate wall was intended primarily for storage. It had no
strategic advantage over the solid wall, but did require less
material for its construction, and the resulting magazine rooms
preempted the need for independent storage buildings. Thus,
casemate walls were used for the typical store-city.[24]

In addition to the storage function of the casemate wall
and the obvious defensive function of both types of city wall,
there were also other functions which were served by the city
wall.

Oppenheim emphasizes, e.g., the monumental aspect of the
walls of a city, in that they were the dominant feature of

urban architecture. Their size and arrangement were a testimony to the importance and strength of the city. In Mesopotamia, these carefully maintained walls were placed under the protection of deities.[25]

A further function of the city wall was a regulatory one. In this role the walls served to regulate the activities of merchants and other would-be visitors to the city. Within the city, walls could also be used to circumvallate distinct districts or quarters.[26]

The city wall, for which the usual Hebrew designation is ḥômâ, was sometimes protected by means of a glacis, a sloping reinforcement at the outer base of the wall, designed primarily as a defense against the battering ram.[27] This reinforcement of the ḥômâ was called a ḥēl.[28] The spatial relationship between the ḥēl and the ḥômâ is perhaps indicated in the unaltered MT of 2 Sam 20:15-16, which describes Joab's attack against Beth-maacah: "They cast up a mound against the city, and it stood against the rampart (ḥēl) . . . Then they began tunnelling (JB = 'sapping,' RSV = 'battering') to bring down the wall (ḥômâ)."[29]

The city gate, like the walls, had as one of its functions, the dominant one of defense.[30] The number of gates which a city had seems to have been dependent to some degree upon the defense requirements placed upon the city in different periods. The Late Bronze and Iron Age cities normally had no more than one or two gates. Judg 16:3, for instance, implies that Gaza had but one gate.

The typical parts of the gate can be seen in the stereotyped expression which enumerates the doors, bolts and bars of the gate in Deut 3:5; Judg 16:3; 1 Sam 23:7; 2 Chr 8:5; etc.[31] The doors, delet, often found in the dual form dĕlātayim, were the wooden gate leaves which were placed at the outer entrance of the gate. Being made of wood, as a rule, there are no archaeological remains of them from the Israelite period. These wooden leaves were hinged on either side and were fastened to the posts, mĕzûzôt (Judg 16:3). When closed, these doors were secured by means of bars or bolts, bĕrîaḥ (compare also the manˁûl in Cant 5:5; Neh 6:3, 6; and the minˁāl in Deut 33:25). This bolt was often made of metal (1 Kgs 4:13; Ps 107:16).

In addition to these structures closely associated with the actual opening of the gate, there was also a number of other features designed to protect this vulnerable spot in a city's defense system. While in some individual instances these features could become quite elaborate and exhibit considerable ingenuity on the part of their builders, features common to most city gates were the flanking of the gate on either side with towers and the providing of the gate with a series of "guard rooms."[32] In Canaanite cities, the gate with tenailles or narrows in the entryway was a classical type. This was formed by two or three pairs of opposing abuttments which protruded into the area on the city side of the gate. The Israelites kept this type of gate in service, with or without modification, e.g., in Shechem, Beth Shemesh, Hazor, Gezer, Megiddo, and Tirzah.[33] By the further extension of these pilasters, the Israelites formed small guard rooms within the gate, a physical feature of no little importance in the social, economic and judicial structures of the Israelite city.

Another feature associated with the gate, at least in some larger cities, which made the gate a multi-functional structure, was the rĕḥ̄b, which is defined as "a broad open place or plaza in a city (usually near the gate), for various private and public uses."[34] In cities where there is little or no evidence of city planning, such as was often the case in the pre-Hellenistic city of Palestine, this rĕḥ̄b was the only extensive free space in the otherwise highly congested city.[35] This space is designated the rĕḥ̄b šaʿar hāʿîr in 2 Chr 32:6.[36] Such an area is attested archaeologically at Tell en-Naṣbeh (Mizpah)[37] and also at Tell el-Farʿah (Tirzah).[38]

In the absence of extensive city planning, many Palestinian cities simply grew, usually becoming quite crowded in order to bring as many families as possible within the walls.[39] As we have suggested above, the layout of the city was dictated to a considerable degree by its topographical situation. When there is planning in evidence, it appears to be concentrated mostly in the part of the city which contained administrative quarters or public buildings, or in that part of the city where the homes of the "upper class" were located.[40]

So far as city streets are concerned, C. C. McCown
believes it significant that there is no Hebrew word for
"street" which clearly means a narrow, clearly bounded strip
of land set aside for the traveler within the city.[41] The
Hebrew term most often translated "street" in English is *ḥûṣ*,
whose meaning is actually quite ambiguous. The specific information which it conveys is simply that of being "outside" an
enclosure of some sort. The enclosure intended is usually
either a house or a city, but it is often not specified.[42] A
more precise term for "street" is *šûq*, which occurs only four
times in the OT,[43] and then only in the Wisdom literature.
The translation "street" for either of these terms is mislead-
ing, since it conveys the impression of a continuous roadway,
when the actual situation was that the *ḥûṣôt* were only occa-
sional spaces between individual houses. When the houses were
not arranged according to a regular plan, the resulting
"streets" were little more than an irregular maze of alleys.[44]
Lacking provisions for sanitation, other than the rather
accidental one sometimes provided by the slope of the tell,
these "streets" served in many cases as refuse dumps.[45]

A function often served by the *ḥûṣôt* of the city is indicated in 1 Kgs 20:34: "The cities which my father took from
your father I will restore; and you may establish bazaars
(ḥûṣôt) for yourself in Damascus, as my father did in Samaria."
This implies that in large cities there were areas set aside
for merchants.[46] Such areas within the city are witnessed to
elsewhere in the OT.[47]

The central area of the typical preindustrial city was
in most cases, both physically and symbolically, the dominant
one:

> Both physically and symbolically, the central gov-
> ernmental and religious structures dominate the urban
> horizon. Because political and religious activities
> in preindustrial cities have more status than the
> economic, the commerical structures in no way rival the
> religious and political. The central area is also the
> chief residence of the elite, the poor are concentrated
> on the outskirts. Assuming that the upper-class persons
> strive to maintain their prerogatives in the community
> and society, they must isolate themselves from the non-
> elite and be centrally located to ensure ready access
> to the headquarters of the governmental, religious and
> educational organizations. The highly valued residence,

then, is where fullest advantage may be taken of the
city's strategic facilities. This locale is, moreover,
the best-protected sector of the city, often enclosed by
a wall of its own.[48]

Sjoberg's description of the typical preindustrial city is
certainly applicable to the early Mesopotamian city. A. J.
Jawad offers the following description of Gawra, apparently the
earliest known walled city in northern Mesopotamia:

> In the center of the settlement stood an inner massive-
> walled citadel having a circular plan, and single ramp-
> protected entrance. . . closely packed, wall-to-wall
> houses were erected in the eastern sector. The main
> building standing in the center of the town was not the
> temple but rather the citadel. A superior position thus
> seems indicated for the political focus of the settle-
> ment.[49]

One of the issues at stake in determining the features
shared by the Mesopotamian and Palestinian city is hinted at in
the closing line of Jawad's statement. This issue concerns
the relationship of the religious and political structures and
their relative positions in relation to the physical layout of
the city.

In the old cities of the alluvial plains in Mesopotamia
there was a significant separation between the temple and the
palace. The main sanctuary, with its temple-tower, courts,
granary, and storehouses, together with the living quarters of
its personnel, was encircled by a wall and separated from the
palace. But in later Upper Mesopotamia, Syria, Asia Minor, and
Palestine, this separation disappears. Temple and palace move
together and often form a city within a city, either occupying
the central position of the city or becoming a part of the outer wall of the city. Where these two institutions and their
several dependencies have moved together, the remainder of the
city's inhabitants live outside the enclosure, segregated from
their more elite governmental and religious leaders. A city
formed on such a pattern can thus be designated a citadel
city.[50]

That the Israelites adopted the citadel city plan is evidenced above all by the archaeological findings at Samaria.
Samaria is of particular relevance in this regard because it is
the only major city which was founded by the Israelites *de no-
vo*. Excavation of the site has shown that Samaria was built
by Omri on a virgin site. Samaria thus provides for us an

example of how the Israelites laid out a city when they were
not restricted by buildings or remains from earlier occupation
of the site.[51]

At Samaria, the entire hilltop was laid out as a royal
quarter, with a wall separating it from the rest of the city.
That the wall which separated the citadel from the remainder of
the city was not originally defensive in function is confirmed
by the fact that this wall, in the first building phase, was
only about five feet thick.[52] One non-defensive function
served by the wall can perhaps be seen by comparing this wall
to the retaining walls discovered in recent excavations in Jerusalem. These excavations have established the existence of
retaining walls which ran at right angles to the slope of the
hill of the Davidic city site, forming terraces which thus increased the habitable area of the hill.[53] But, in addition to
this utilitarian function, the walls surrounding the citadel
could and did serve a more symbolic one as well. While in
physical form the Israelite citadel bears a close resemblance
to the acropolis of the typical Greek city, its socio-political
function is rather different. In the Greek city, the acropolis
served as the defensible civic center of a democratic community. But, in the case of Samaria, the layout makes it quite
clear that the area within the citadel wall was in no sense a
civic center, but rather an exclusive enclosure reserved for
an autocratic king and his servants.[54] The citadel thus stood
as the symbol of the wide social gap between the ruler and his
elite administrative personnel on the one hand, and the bulk of
the common people on the other.[55] Within the citadel, as a
rule, the layout was regular and spacious. The buildings were
aligned on the enclosure wall, and the rooms were fairly
large.[56]

While the citadel at Samaria did not apparently have a defensive function in its original construction, it soon acquired
one. The building operations, which are probably to be attributed to Ahab, included the extension of the area occupied by
the citadel and the erection of a casemate wall which was
clearly defensive in purpose, varying in thickness from twelve
to thirty-two feet.[57]

The citadel at Samaria, as elsewhere, contained not only the living quarters of the king and his administrative staff, but was also the site of the royal necropolis. Just as it is repeatedly mentioned in the concluding formulae concerning the Judean kings that they were buried "in the City of David," the burial of the Israelite kings within their royal citadel receives the same mention (1 Kgs 16:28, etc.) This practice of burial within the city, again served to set the king apart from the people, the general rule being to locate burial places outside the city walls. At Samaria, the graves of the common people were so located.[58]

Unfortunately excavations at Samaria provide no definitive information for the resolution of the problem as to whether or not the citadel of the typical Israelite city contained a temple. There is a literary tradition which mentions a temple in Samaria: "He [Ahab] erected an altar for Baal in the house of Baal which he had built in Samaria" (1 Kgs 16:32). No real evidence of this shrine has been discovered, however.[59]

All assumptions regarding the presence or absence of a temple within the citadel of Israelite cities now stand in need of revision in the light of revolutionary finds at Arad. Such statements as the one of Noth, that "Not even one plan has yet been disclosed in any Iron Age level in Palestine which can definitely be described as a temple," are no longer valid.[60] McCown's statement that "No temple or provisions for worship are found in Hebrew cities outside of Jerusalem," can also no longer be accepted. Concerning the discovery of a sanctuary in the citadel of Arad, Aharoni, the excavator of Arad, says:

> One fact seems to be beyond doubt, that the sanctuary at Arad was a genuinely Israelite temple, a 'House of Yahweh' in the language of the Bible. . . This is borne out by its plan and contents, especially the Hebrew ostraca with names of priestly families, and by the mere fact that it was an integral part of the royal fortress, built and rebuilt together with it, beginning with the first fortress in the days of Solomon.[62]

The history of Arad as an urban settlement goes back to EB II (ca. 2,900 to 2,700 B.C.). This Early Bronze Age city was destroyed before the end of EB II, and it lay deserted until the eleventh century, when a village grew up on the site of the earlier city. A citadel was erected on this site in the

tenth century, probably during the reign of Solomon. While the
settlement outside the citadel has not, as yet, been fully excavated, it appears to have had the character of an open settlement.[63]

The buildings within the citadel at Arad, in addition to
the temple, consisted of a storehouse, living quarters (seven
units), and various workshops. Access to any but the two public buildings appears to have been limited by the location of
the citadel gate.[64]

The question raised by the discovery of a Yahwistic temple
within the citadel of Arad is whether this instance of the existence of a temple within an Israelite city outside the capital is typical or atypical, i.e., whether the temple at Arad
represents a unique instance of a Judean temple outside of Jerusalem, or whether it represents only one of several temple
which existed in Judah during the monarchy. Aharoni associates
the *bāmôt* mentioned in connection with Israelite cities (1 Kgs
12:31; 2 Kgs 23:8, 9, 15) with urban sanctuaries such as the
one at Arad:

> All the places singled out for the erection of temples
> have one common geographic feature, which is true also for
> Arad: all are near the borders of the kingdom, either of
> Israel or of Judah. Is this merely accidental? Or may we
> assume that a temple was an indispensable institution at
> the royal administrative and military centers dominating
> the borders?[65]

Aharoni goes on to answer his own rhetorical questions by
asserting that in the royal citadels which dominated the border
areas there was a royal and sanctified temple which was a vital part of each of them.[66]

So long as no other temples like the one at Arad are
found, Aharoni's thesis can stand as a tentative conclusion.
It certainly has the merit of being in agreement with the general theses of Sjoberg and Oppenheim which we have cited, both
of which see a close relationship between the religious and political institutions in the urban setting, having their center
of operation in the citadel of the city. But, by his own ad-
mission, Aharoni's hypothesis awaits further archaeological
confirmation.[67]

While the existence of temples in Israelite cities is disputed, the *bāmâ*, "high place," should also be considered as a

center for urban worship.[68] These open air sanctuaries were
not necessarily within the city, but could be located near the
city. That such sanctuaries were regarded as legitimate places
of worship by a substantial element of the population, at least
until the end of the seventh century B.C., can be inferred from
the Josianic provision for the centralization of worship in
Jerusalem, which legislated the elimination of such shrines.[69]
Since these "high places" were modestly furnished, probably
having few or no permanent structures or furnishings, it is
quite possible that their presence or absence in or near Israelite cities cannot be established archaeologically.

Two other important examples of the citadel city in the
OT are Megiddo and Hazor. In strata III and IV at Megiddo, as
at Samaria, the top of the hill was employed during the monarchy for official buildings. Domestic quarters may well have
existed on the slopes outside the citadel, but the official
quarter dominates the town.[70] One large building within the
citadel of Megiddo is aptly described by Schofield as a "temple fortress," its construction resembling that of the Solomonic temple at Jerusalem. But there is some disagreement as to
whether this building served a secular or religious purpose.
Schofield maintains that it served both kinds of function.[71]
Kenyon says, with regard to the citadel at Shechem, that the
emphasis there was on garrison purposes rather than on royal
residence.[72] However, one should keep in mind, as Sjoberg suggests, that in the city of antiquity the political-administra-
tive functions were almost inseparable from the military ones:

> The ruling group must command military power if it is to
> maintain dominance over the populace within the society
> and protect itself from attack from without. It is hard-
> ly accidental that many cities have grown up around for-
> tresses.[73]

At Hazor, a whole series of citadels were excavated, one
on top of another in succeeding periods. The latest of these
was from the Hellenistic period, and beneath it was a citadel
which was constructed by the Israelites in the ninth century
and later reused during the Persian period. The Israelite citadel was composed of two parts. In the center was the fort
proper, and surrounding it was an annex containing the living
quarters of its occupants.[74] The outstanding feature of the

citadel at Hazor was the strength of the walls. In some places
they were up to six-and-one-half feet thick and had foundations
of some ten feet below the floor level.[75] There are apparently
no signs of a temple within the citadel of Hazor in any of the
Israelite strata.[76]

There are, however, other instances in which manifestly
administrative buildings are not located within a citadel. In
stratum IIa (ca. 1,000 to 587) at Beth-Shemesh, there was a
governor's residence, and adjacent to it a large, thick-walled
building which probably served as a district storehouse for
goods and produce.[77] There is also evidence for the location
of public buildings near the city gate, e.g., at Tirzah, a location which was evidently advantageous for regulatory reasons.[78]

In addition to the security considerations which favored
the location of administrative headquarters within a citadel,
the creature comforts of the more elite administrators were
catered to in the numerous instances in which their quarters
are located on the western edge of a city site. This location
made use of the natural "air conditioning" provided by the prevailing westerly breezes.[79]

A Rural-Urban Typology for the Old Testament

As was indicated in our first chapter, the subject of a
rural-urban typology has not lacked for attention on the part
of urban sociologists. Many of the rural-urban dichotomies
which are in evidence in studies of social structures in the
OT have served to emphasize the great divergence between city
and countryside, between urban and rural life. Such divergence is, to some degree, the result of observations based on
rural-urban relationships in the form which they have taken
since the industrial revolution, and as such are not directly
applicable to the preindustrial city of the OT, but serve only
to mar our perspective. Sjoberg sets forth the following critique of such typologies:

> Many of the generalizations with regard to rural-urban
> differences resulting from the early influence of Wirth
> and Redfield, *intra alia*, reflected in current sociology,
> require a thorough overhauling. Numerous patterns on the
> American scene are erroneously thought to hold for other
> societies as well, when in fact many of these rural-urban

> differences are typical only of industrial-urban, not of
> feudal [i.e., preindustrial] civilized societies. Al-
> though industrial and feudal orders reveal some of the
> same kind of rural-urban divergencies, there are others
> . . . that are peculiar to preindustrial civilized soci-
> eties. The city is in many ways molded by the social sys-
> tem of which it is a part, i.e. the city is a dependent
> rather than an independent variable.[80]

The city in ancient Israel is only part of a total rural-
urban system which included the "mother city" together with its
"daughter villages" and the city's fields. The city could not
survive without the produce of its hinterland. Thus, in any
attempt to construct a rural-urban typology which will be applicable to the OT situation, one must guard against contrasting that which is only part of a system with another part of
the same system, as if one were contrasting two independent
systems. The interdependence of city and village is one of the
central theses of a work by Carleton Coon in which he maintains
that perhaps the greatest accomplishment of Middle Eastern peoples was their development of a rather complicated way of living which consisted basically of treating the various segments
of the landscape as parts of a coordinated whole, rather than
as separate economic realms. He affirms a division into three
mutually dependent kinds of communities:

> . . . the village, the nomadic camp, and the city, which
> distinctively offer each other, in the same order, vege-
> table foodstuffs, animals suited for transport, and pro-
> cessed goods including tools. Both village and camp sup-
> ply the city with meat, milk products, skins, and wool.
> Not only is each of these three types of community depen-
> dent on the others for the maintenance of its way of life,
> but each is equally specialized. . . Both the city people
> and the nomads need vegetable foodstuffs, which they con-
> sume chiefly in the form of grain. Although the cities
> include (among other specialists) enough farmers to till
> the soil immediately outside the walls, as well as rich
> men who raise fruits in their gardens, these efforts do
> not produce one-tenth of the food eaten.[81]

Having discussed the city with regard to its physical
characteristics, our purpose here is to define more closely the
city as a part of a city-village system. Unfortunately, the
OT nowhere delineates laws regarding city-village relationships,
nor is the village an entity for which there is a precise definition.

A legal distinction is drawn, however, between the city
and the village in a passage providing for the redemption of

urban property in the jubilee year (Lev 25:29-34). In this legal maxim the houses in unwalled villages are under the same law as the "fields of the country" (śĕdēh hā'āreṣ. Could this expression be the equivalent of śĕdēh hā'ᶜr, where 'ereṣ = 'ᶜr as we have noted above?).[82]

The village was generally unwalled and dependent upon the walled city as a place of refuge for its inhabitants. A passage in the *KRT* text from Ras Shamra describes what must have been a familiar scene in Palestine at the approach of an enemy. The inhabitants of the city 'Udm are pictured as working outside the city. In time of emergency, alarm would be given from the city walls, and those who were outside the walls performing various tasks would rush inside the city in response to the alarm. The passage reads:

> The wood-cutting women are rushing from the open
> country, Likewise those who congregate in the open
> thoroughfare, The water-drawing women are rushing
> from the well, Even from the spring those who fill
> (their jars).[83]

We have observed that two basic terms are used to designate the villages associated with cities, ḥăṣērîm and bānôt.[84] Another term for villages, and in slightly modified form for their inhabitants, is the term pĕrāzôt, which occurs only in the plural and is formed on a root prz. This term occurs in Ezek 38:11; Zech 2:4 ; and Esth 9:19. In the Ezekiel passage it is specified that such settlements were without walls, bars or gates. An adjectival form, pĕrāzî occurs in Deut 3:5 where it is used rather indiscriminately to modify ᶜārê and in 1 Sam 6:18 where it modifies kōper. In both cases such settlements are contrasted with walled or fortified cities. The form pĕrāzôn, "dwellers of open country," or "peasantry" (so *RSV*), occurs in a very old context in the Song of Deborah (Judg 5:7, 11). Some Hebrew manuscripts however read pĕrāzôt here. The *JB* adopts this latter reading and translates:

> Dead, dead were Israel's villages
> until you rose up, O Deborah,
> you rose up, a mother in Israel.

Jacob Myers reports that it has been held that there may have been some confusion here between Deborah and "mother in Israel," which appears to mean "metropolis" or "main city," and that Deborah may have been Dabareh or Dabarittha, near

Mount Tabor.[85]   Even if the possibility of such a confusion is rejected, the likelihood remains that Deborah was spoken of here in a way which made use of city-village terminology to portray the role of Deborah in restoring security to the villages/peasantry just as the city provided security for its daughter-villages.

Archaeological information on the nature of the village is almost nonexistent owing to the lack of permanent structures in the villages and their extremely fluid population.[86]   While the village was distinguished from the city by the fact that it had no wall, in some instances villages may well have centered on a *migdāl*.[87]

Every city which dominated a particular natural region must have had its "daughters" even though they are not always mentioned.   Few names of such secondary establishments survive, and we are not informed whether they in fact always had separate names or whether they were merely subsumed under the name of the mother-city.[88]   However, it can probably be inferred that in some cases villages had their own names, like the modern Silwan (Hebrew, *šelaḥ*; New Testament, Sil m), a village opposite the southeastern hill of Jerusalem.

Closely associated with the "daughters" of a city were its fields.   Note, e.g., the following passage: "But the fields of the city (*śĕdēh hāʿr*) and its villages (*ḥăṣerehā*) had been given to Caleb the son of Jephuneh as his possession."[89]   The village in this sense was a sort of agricultural sub-station of the city and, as such, would naturally perform, e.g., such functions as the threshing of grain.[90]

There is evidently a distinction drawn between the "fields" (*śādeh*) of a city and a city's "pasture lands" (*migrāš*).[91]   This distinction can be seen in those passages concerning the Levitical cities.[92]   Josh 21:11-12 (= 1 Chr 6:55-56) is especially relevant in this connection:

> They gave them Kiriath-arba, Arba being the father of Anak (that is, Hebron), in the hill country of Judah, along with the pasture lands (*migrāš*) round about it. But the fields of the city and its villages had been given to Caleb the son of Jephuneh as his possession.[93]

That the pasture lands represented a very circumscribed area adjacent to the city, in contrast to the fields of the

city which represented the broader expanse of arable land controlled by the city is indicated by the dimensions of such
pasture lands given in Num 35:5:

> And you shall measure outside the city, for the east side
> 2,000 cubits, and for the south side 2,000 cubits, and
> for the west side 2,000 cubits, and for the north side
> 2,000 cubits, the city being in the middle; this shall
> belong to them as pasture land for their cities.

According to R. B. Y. Scott, the "cubits" of the Levitical
pasture lands must be understood as cubit frontages of land
if the passage is not to be reduced to absurdity; i.e., on
each side of the city there was to be a block of land with a
frontage of 2,000 cubits and a depth of 1,000 cubits.[94]   That
such land was not considered to be included in the arable land
assigned to the city may thus explain those passages which
say that the priests are to have no inheritance or portion in
the land.[95]

We have previously noted that the dependence of the city
on its fields was a limiting factor on the size of the ancient
Israelite city. In addition to the factor of protection for
the fields there is also the element of economic feasibility.
The pattern of life was that those who worked in the fields
would leave the city in the morning to go out to the fields,
returning in the late afternoon. The farther the outermost
fields, the longer the walk each way. Since much of the work
required oxen or donkeys, progress was held down to their speed
which was seldom more than a slow walk. Four hours a day
"commuting" time would represent a feasible limit, which would
mean that the periphery of the city's cultivated fields should
not be much more than four miles distant.[96]   This limit could
be extended in peaceful times when the security provided by
the city was not necessary and more of the population could
move out of the city and establish temporary residence in
villages.

Sociologists have often made use of certain variables of
community formation in setting up their rural-urban typologies.
Among the four variables most frequently considered in this
context is that of agricultural and non-agricultural pursuits.[97]
The city, according to this criterion, is distinguished by a
complex division of labor based on non-agricultural pursuits.
The unsuitability of a rigid application of this criterion has

been pointed out by other sociologists.[98] With respect to the ancient Israelite city, a certain degree of division of labor can be demonstrated, but, despite the growth of urban life in the monarchical period, the economy of Israelite society retained its predominantly pastoral base throughout the period of history represented by the literature of the OT.[99] Even the latest priestly law presupposes only simple forms of commercial transaction. The only explicit evidence we possess about the exports of Israel and Judah implies an agricultural community (Ezek 27:17 and 2 Kgs 18:31, 32).

The city and the village in the OT cannot then be distinguished by the use of the criterion of non-agricultural pursuits since economically the urban groupings of the OT were basically involved in functions connected with agricultural production.[100] Thus instead of a radical dichotomy between the city and the village, the close relationship of the city to agricultural activities in its villages and fields produced an urban-rural interdependence:

> The notion that cities are not only apart from, but opposed to the life and livelihood of the country is unfounded in ecological theory. At their most 'unmutual,' urban-rural relations are always reciprocal. When exploiting landlords raise rents or when terms of trade turn against farm produce, the urban-rural relation is still one of interdependence. Through performance of its nodal functions, the center gives definition and structure to outlying parts. Without focus and direction, sedentary life outside the city would stultify or relapse into folkish independence, a comparatively uniform order of subsistence unrelieved by the stimulus of difference.[101]

The close affiliation of the city with agriculture is also reflected in the religion of the Canaanite cities and that of their Mesopotamian counterparts. Frankfort, e.g., comments on the seeming contradiction in the worship of nature gods in the Near Eastern cities which would seem to be more suitable for worship by countrymen and farmers than by city-dwellers. He observes that this apparent contradiction only results from a theory of rural-urban divergence which is a product of the industrial revolution.[102] Pedersen, while positing a distinction between what he terms the "old Israel of the small communities and the remodelled Israel of the great towns," and observing that there were conflicts between these two groups, at the same time admits that the two types were not sharply defined.[103]

Just as the city was dependent upon its hinterland for its food supply, the food-producing hinterland was also dependent upon the city for a market. The bulk of the wares which were offered for sale in the urban market consisted of agricultural produce not actually consumed by the farmer, who offered it on the market in exchange for the few indispensable artifacts manufactured by the urban specialists.[104] Historians have characteristically used the word "peasant" for this type of small-scale agricultural producer. Redfield would emphasize the fact that the peasant represents a type of person whose existence is dependent upon the city: "The peasant is a rural native whose long established order of life takes important account of the city--economically, politically, and morally."[105]

Thus, seen from the perspective of an economy with a base which was preponderantly agricultural, the city was a distinct social institution; but it was intimately related to the land, and even as recently as the European Middle Ages a rural-urban contrast has very limited applicability.[106]

Urban Social Structure in the Old Testament

As we noted in our first chapter, another of the criteria often used to define the city is the appearance of social differentiation and stratification. Again we quote Sjoberg's statement concerning the class structure of the preindustrial city:

> The preindustrial city is characterized by a fiburcated class structure comprising the elite or upper class, that which manifests the highly valued criteria, and the lower class, or mass populace, that which does not. The elite, though small, forming perhaps less than five to ten per cent of the total social order, dominates both city and society. At the minimum, this literate group comprises the upper ranks of the governmental, religious and educational bureaucracies. The bulk of the lower-status urbanites and the vast peasantry, two groups that share many traits, form the great commoner, or lower-class group.[107]

With regard to Sjoberg's observations, it should be pointed out that he does not disregard the character of the city which was observed in the preceding section by bifurcating the preindustrial social order along rural-urban lines. Rather, he groups the lower-status urbanites with the peasantry:

> Although the urban lower class is usually a notch
> above the peasantry, looking down on the latter as
> backward and rustic, from a societal perspective
> the two merge to form one broad, lower-class group.[108]

Sjoberg's basic statement, as well as his further observations, must now be examined with a view to establishing their
applicability to the city in ancient Israel. Any leveling
tendencies operative within Israelite society which would have
tended to modify the rather rigid stratification proposed by
Sjoberg *et al*., must be sought out and explicated.[109] We shall
also attempt to ascertain the degree to which a social pathology resting on a class division formed a basis for the critique
of Israelite life offered by the classical prophets.

While the somewhat complex subject of the origins of
cities is beyond the scope of this study, and will be treated
only summarily in the following chapter, it is important at
this point to observe that the rise of cities was preeminently
a social process; i.e., it was more an expression of changes
in man's interaction with his fellows than with his environment. The city was dependent upon food surpluses beyond the
needs of the farmer, but there was also a whole new series of
institutions and more complex social organization involved.
Logically, changes in social structure preceded the creation
of cities, which in turn are one of the results of these social
changes. The emergence of cities in turn brings about a whole
second order of social changes. It is with this second order
of changes that we are concerned.[110]

In order to analyze the urban social structure of the
ancient Israelite city, we must first of all look at some of
the more important terms used to designate social classes or
groups. One of the most important of these is the term
ḥopšt.[111] This term obviously has the connotation "free" in
the numerous instances where it is used in speaking of the
emancipation of a slave.[112] Elsewhere, the term is used less
specifically, but still with a root meaning of being "set free"
or "separate." Gray, however, believes that the term has a
different connotation in 1 Sam 17:25 and would understand the
term there as referring to a class set apart for military
service and enjoying certain privileges, as a result, which are

usually associated with a feudal system. Saul does not here promise emancipation in the general sense of the term, but he does undertake the release of the would-be champion from the limitations of his family ties and his investiture with the status and substance of a feudatory. This, like the grant of land to the *mrynm* at Ugarit, was to be to his family, and as such *in perpetuum*.[113]

With respect to the term *ḥopšî* in the OT, it thus seems that a double application is to be reckoned with. The instance in Samuel is apparently the only explicit instance in which the term has an obvious reference to a person whose attachment was no longer to his ancestral land but to the king.[114] In addition to this term in Samuel with its feudatory connotations, there are other indications that certain features of the Bronze Age system were adopted and adapted by Israel in the early monarchy, coinciding with the period of intensified urbaniza-in Israel. John Bright observes:

> Early Israel had been . . . a clan society with none of the feudalism of the Canaanite states, she had no ruling class, no social distinctions or extremes of wealth and poverty. This was all changed [in the monarchy]. Solomon's commercial and industrial ventures, though state monopolies, raised the living standard of the nation and allowed some . . . to grow rich. The court grew very rich. As royal projects drew people to the cities, urban population grew apace, with an attendant weakening of tribal ties and traditions. . . Plagued by a chronic fiscal dilemma, Solomon ultimately drafted his subjects into forced labor for the state (1 Kgs 5:13-18)--a wholly 'un-Israelite' measure. As life was regulated under the crown, and as Canaanites with a feudal background and no conception of the covenant order were absorbed, notions of aristocracy and class distinction began to intrude (1 Kgs 2:1-15).[115]

Gray sees the beginnings of the adoption of the old Canaanite system already in the time of Saul, as implied in his interpretation of 1 Sam 17:25, and in such texts as 1 Sam 22:7, which speaks of the granting of "fields and vine-yards" by Saul.[116]

David himself was a professional soldier who attached himself to the king. It is especially in the reign of David that urban social structure begins to make a significant impact upon Hebrew life, especially after the incorporation of the Canaanite cities into the Davidic state. Weber, in particular, views the civic society of Palestine at this time as

a variation of ancient Mediterranean urbanism. In describing
David's relationship to the urban class structure, Weber says:

> Conditions differed when a charismatic war lord succeeded
> as lord of the city in making himself independent of the
> aristocracy of elders by winning a personal following, or
> by hiring paid, frequently foreign-born mercenaries, who
> constituted a bodyguard only to him. He might recruit
> personally devoted officials (*śarîm*) from his following
> . . . If he based his power completely on these power
> sources, that form of princely ruler emerged which in
> later inimical perspective, was associated with
> 'kingship.'[117]

Weber sees in the emergence of the Israelite monarchy, a
ruling class of wealthy urban families who, by the accumulation
of wealth, become "economically expendable" and thus able to
devote themselves to politics and war. The ancient free peasantry was disarmed in the process, as Weber illustrates with
his comparison of the peasant summons in the Song of Deborah
with the chariot cities of Solomon. In this situation which
gave rise to typical class antagonisms, urban patricians were
pitted against socially, economically, and militarily descend-
ing peasants. The so-called "biblical social evils" which the
prophets chastize are then connected with this social
tension.[118]

It is Weber's analysis which has set the tone for most of
the subsequent analyses of the Israelite social structure.
Edward Neufeld, e.g., appears to be dependent upon Weber in
his analysis of the development of an aristocracy in Israel.
He observes that even in premonarchical times there were indeed
prominent persons within the tribal society, but that it is
under the monarchy that there developed a proper aristocracy.[119]
This aristocracy is often mentioned jointly with the king,[120]
and is kept apart from the ordinary people.[121] The French
scholar Antonin Causse also presents an analysis of the social
organization of Israel in the monarchy which is quite similar,
in many respects, to that of Neufeld and Weber.[122]

Any attempt to analyze the social structure of the
Israelites must certainly reckon with the problematic
expression *'am hā'āres*, which is applied to a group of people
some seventy times in the OT. The problem is to ascertain to
what particular group, if any one group, the term is applied.
The history of the interpretation of this expression is a

rather involved one, and the various suggestions set forth cover a wide gamut. De Vaux has categorized the various interpretations:

> Certains y ont vu une espèce de Parlement, un corps représentatif des groupes locaux, une sorte de Chambre des Communes; d'autres au contraire y ont reconnu la noblesse terrienne, la 'Landsadel,' une sorte de Chambre des Lords; d'autres encore les campagnards opposés aux citadins, en fait aux habitants de la capitale, ou la plèbe opposée à l'aristocratie, la partie pauvre et méprisée de la population. Cette opinion, qui a été assez répandue, est influencée, je pense, par l'usage rabbinique de l'expression.[123]

E. W. Nicholson observes that these varied interpretations have one thing in common, namely, their insistence that the expression is a *terminus technicus* used to designate a fixed and special social or political class or group within the population of the country. With this observation he also points a way out of the maze of interpretations by suggesting that the expression is not a technical term but is used in a very general manner, varying in meaning from context to context.[124]

In the use of this term in the OT, three periods are discernible. Of these three periods, we are here interested only in the monarchy. In this period, the use of this expression is mainly in three books: 2 Kings, Jeremiah and Ezekiel.[125] In these books, the "people of the land" is distinguished from, or contrasted with: (1) the king or prince; (2) the king and his servants; (3) the chiefs and the priests; and (4) the chiefs, the priests and the prophets.[126] The cleavage witnessed to in these texts is basically one between subjects and the ruling element, including the priests and prophets associated with the latter. In those instances where a rural-urban cleavage has been suggested, another explanation is preferable. In 2 Kgs 11:20 there appears the phrase: "So all the people of the land rejoiced; but the city was quiet after Athaliah had been slain with the sword in the king's house." De Vaux is probably correct in his suggestion that the contrast implied here is nothing more than a distinction between the city as the seat of the regime which had just been overthrown and the rest of the country which had remained loyal to the Davidic house.[127] Thus the expression *'am hā'āres* has here a general meaning and does not refer to a particular class or group within the population. De Vaux goes on to suggest that the opposition implied in the above passage is neither more nor less than that implied in Jer 25:2: "All the people of Judah and all the inhabitants of Jerusalem."[128]

Another instance where a rural-urban cleavage has been suggested is in 2 Kgs 25:3: " . . . the famine was so severe in the city that there was no food for the people of the land." There is again no need for reading into this verse a rural-urban split. A simpler interpretation of this verse is to take the second half of the verse as standing in apposition to the first half so that both refer to the same location: "The famine was so severe in the city that there was no food for the people living there."[129] One other passage in 2 Kings is instructive for our purpose here: "But the people of the land slew all those who had conspired against King Amon, and the people of the land made Josiah, his son, King in his stead" (21:24). Our expression has a political significance here, in that the action of the "people of the land" represents a movement on the part of the native free Israelites over against the action of the "servants" of King Amon who had put him to death.[130]

The "people of the land" thus most generally represents the free Israelite community, constituted on the basis of kinship as the etymology of ʿam suggests, as distinct from the royal entourage, Israelite or alien, who owed their status not to membership in the kinship group of Israel, but to the royal favor.[131] Nicholson's conclusion is thus probably accurate;

> . . . the term has no fixed and rigid meaning but is used rather in a purely general and fluid manner and varies in meaning from context to context. To regard it as a technical term designating a specific class or group within the population of Judah is to read far too much into its meaning.[132]

The expression is thus little more than an alternate one for the "people of Judah."[133]

Those attempts which have made this expression the basis of discerning a social cleavage between rural and urban elements in the monarchy have read too much into this expression from its later use which originated, no doubt, with the self-consciousness of the postexilic Jewish community over

against the local population of Palestine who did not endorse
their program of restoration. The only cleavage witnessed to
in the use of this expression in preexilic times is one which
is primarily politically based and is typical of the preindustrial city, i.e., the separation of the ruler and the ruled.
As de Vaux remarks:

> The king's officials formed a kind of caste, detached
> from, and sometimes opposed to municipal interests. Above
> all, the play of economic life, business deals and the
> sale of land destroyed the equality between families.
> But it would be a mistake to see in ancient Israelite
> society the contrasts found in other societies past or
> present between 'nobles' and 'plebeians,' 'capitalists'
> and 'proletariat.' In Israel there never really existed
> social classes in the modern sense of groups conscious
> of their particular interests and opposed to one
> another. It is to avoid such misleading comparisons
> that we prefer to speak here of 'divisions of the popu-
> lation.'[134]

De Vaux's statement would seem to imply that there were
at work within Israelite society certain leveling forces which
tended to reduce stratification. That there were different
degrees of stratification in different parts of the country,
due to the varied economic capabilities of a given area, seems
evident from the results of archaeology. At Tirzah, as we have
mentioned above, the uniform houses of the tenth century
suggest an equal standard, but two hundred years later there
is a marked division between well-built residences and "slums."
There was also a "better" part of eighth-century Shechem. But,
by contrast, no such disparity is evident at the Judean city
of Debir. This lack of any marked social division might be
due to the fact that in the southern kingdom private enterprise developed less rapidly, and with less violation of the
traditional social structure than was the case in the northern
kingdom. Heaton observes that it is intrinsically probable
that in the southern kingdom, with its limited natural resources and its relatively isolated cantons in the mountains,
fewer individuals were in a position to exploit their countrymen and get rich quick.[135] The situation in the southern kingdom was also regulated by the existence of a relatively stable
monarchy at Jerusalem, something which was never really
achieved in the northern kingdom. Certainly there is nothing
in the southern kingdom's history to compare with Jehu's

revolution which was brought on, at least in part, by social and economic tensions.[136] That the northern kingdom was less stable socially can also be seen in the fact that the preponderance of prophetic activity was centered on the social pathology of this region.

In addition to regional leveling factors, another such factor in Israelite society was the concept of community identity which was operative in the Yahwistic religion:

> Israel's community identity was the basis of an internal leveling tendency. The Kingdom of Solomon was rigidly stratified according to the pattern of ancient times. As Israel's special nature and status became more salient, however, greater pressure developed to define all Hebrews as having the same problem. Hence, the distinction between belonging and not belonging became emphasized, rather than differentiations within the community of Israel itself.[137]

The covenant of the Israelite people with Yahweh was within the sphere of kinship ideas so prevalent among the ancient Semites, and it created a people which could be called an extended family:

> Israel became ideally a 'people' in the strict sense of the Hebrew word ʿam, which means those who together form an entity, a whole, and whose members are united by 'fellow-feeling' as brothers and comrades.[138]

Such a religious concept of community was certainly a leveling tendency and also assisted the Israelites in the incorporation of the heterogeneous groups which existed in the Canaanite cities. The real question is just how far such leveling tendencies went in an urban setting. We shall return to this question below.

At this point it might be useful to insert a brief discussion of the family in urbanized Israelite society. Such a discussion has its place within the treatment of the urban social structure in that, as a microcosm of the social whole, the family is a convenient unit through which to trace some of the influences of the city on social institutions. Louis Wirth observed that the distinctive features of the urban mode of life have often been described as consisting of the substitution of secondary for primary contacts, the weakening of bonds of kinship, and the declining social significance of the family.[139]

Sjoberg has presented a rather convincing argument, contra

Wirth *et al.* who have posited that the extended family unit is
a rural phenomenon and, as a corollary, have maintained that
the city is deleterious to such groups. Sjoberg again believes
that such popular assumptions have grown out of observations
of the industrial city and do not hold true for the preindustrial city. As he states:

> Herein resides one of the most striking diferences
> between rural and urban communities in preindustrial
> orders, one that supports as well the argument that the
> elite is preeminently urban, not rural.[140]

Sjoberg's observations here are again closely related to the
technological base of the preindustrial society. In such a
society, the lower class is less able to maintain large house-
holds than the urban upper class because the peasant's land
holdings are too small to support a large family unit, with
the result that many of the sons must seek occupational
opportunities elsewhere. At best they can maintain a "limited"
extended family system consisting of one or two elders (usually
grandparents), one married son, his wife and children. Sjoberg
observes that this is the sociologists' *famille souche*.[141]
On the other hand, in its ideal form, the preindustrial city's
extended family includes a man and his wife (or wives), their
unmarried children, married sons, and the latters' wives and
children, and perhaps other relatives such as widowed daughters
or sisters of the family head, as well as numerous servants.
The conjugal, or nuclear family as a separate social unit,
which is the prevailing form in industrial cities, is not
found by Sjoberg to be the typical upper-class form for any
preindustrial city.[142] Maintaining a broad kinship group as
a single functioning entity requires extensive financial
resources and a stable power position. In turn, the elite's
extended family aids and abets its members' formal education
and entrance into the high-status occupations, for these
positions are filled primarily by selection according to the
particularistic criteria of family or friendship ties.[143]
With regard to the functions of such an extended family, it can
be said that it filled many of the functions that are assumed
primarily by governmental welfare agencies in industrial
orders. But, in addition to its welfare role, the extended
family performs strategic economic and political functions.

Often it is only the maintenance of the extended family that keeps property, especially landholdings, intact. This, in turn, unquestionably promotes the extended family's survival. Moreover, the elite strives to place members of the kinship unit in key political, educational, and religious posts in the community and society, thereby ensuring the continuance of the extended organization.[144] Still another function of the extended family is that of sustaining ties with the past, which in turn reinforces its status. Authority in the preindustrial order being legitimized by appeal to tradition, families justify their claim to present superiority in terms of their former eminence. A favorite device for achieving this end has been the construction and maintenance of genealogies.[145]

While it is beyond the scope of this study to examine in detail all of the sociological implications of Sjoberg's theses, it seems relevant to observe those points at which his observations are substantiated by evidence from the OT.

There is certainly evidence in the OT for the existence of large families among the ruling elite. Both Gideon (Jerubbaal) and Ahab are said to have had seventy sons.[146] That the sons of such families received some sort of formal education from their guardians or tutors (ʾōmnîm) is implied in several instances.[147]

The practice of the elite's attempts to place members of their kinship unit in key posts is evident as well. Saul's commander, Abner was a relative of Saul's, although the exact relationship is difficult to determine.[148] A similar situation can be seen in Joab, the commander of David's army, who was David's nephew (2 Sam 2:18; 1 Chr 2:16). Jonathan, David's uncle was a counselor (yôʿēṣ) in David's court (1 Chr 27:32-33). The list of David's principal officials concludes with the phrase: "and David's sons were priests" (2 Sam 8:18).[149] The names of these "sons of David" are not given, and in the parallel list of David's officers in 2 Sam 20:23-26, the "sons of David" are replaced by "Ira the Jairite was also David's priest." With regard to these "sons of David," de Vaux is probably correct when he says that the most we can presume is that they assisted or did duty for their father in those sacerdotal functions which were sometimes performed by the king.[150]

Other instances of the custom of placing a member of one's family in an important post are seen under Solomon and Rehoboam. Solomon appointed two of his sons-in-law as commissioners of Dor and of Naphtali.[151] Rehoboam secured his position and sought to guard against disloyalty when he: "dealt wisely, and distributed some of his sons through all the districts of Judah and Benjamin, in all the fortified cities . . ." (2 Chr 11:23).

A term which probably indicates the choice of an official from members of the king's family is the title *ben hammelek*, "son of the king," which is used in several places where the context indicates that "son" is not being used in the strict sense of the king's biological offspring.[152] That this term can denote an office is supported by the discovery of a seal and a ring-stamp, both of which have inscribed on them a proper name followed by *bn hmlk*. The expression *bn hmlk* thus occurs in the place where other seals mention their owner's office. De Vaux, who mentions these seals, concludes that the officials so designated were not of very high rank and were probably some kind of police officer who was perhaps originally chosen from among the king's sons.[153]

Certainly, the device of legitimizing authority by appeal to tradition, and the justification of the claim to present superiority in terms of former eminence were well known among the Israelites. M. Burrows says:

> For the ancient Hebrew, as for the Semites in general and other peoples also, a curse or a blessing is not merely the expression of a wish; it is a powerful instrument for good or evil. Consequently the prosperity of a tribe can be explained naturally by saying that its ancestor pronounced a blessing on it.
> A poem in the form of such a blessing is then an effective vehicle for describing the group's history and present condition.[154]

The use of the past to legitimize the current ruling power is also evident in one of the sources which went into the formation of Samuel-Kings. One of the purposes of the so-called "Succession Document" (2 Sam 7; 9:1-20:22; 1 Kgs 1:2) is to show how three sons of David were set aside to make way for Solomon. Embedded within the history of the monarchy is a prophetic "word of God history" which is not necessarily a continuous story but the interpretation of critical transitions

in historical material already extant. In this history there
is a succession of prophets who commission, and/or curse, not
only kings, but dynasties as well. Disaster is seen in this
interpretation as a result of a past curse on the dynasty.[155]

The device of constructing and maintaining genealogies
as a means of establishing authority is well attested. Among
the motives responsible for the compilation of genealogies in
the Old Testament are: (1) establishment of right to such
social positions as nobility, kinship, and priesthood
(Ezra 2:59-63); (2) prideful demonstration of relationship to
an eminent worthy of the past; and (3) the strengthening of
position or authority by tracing its origin back to an important ancestral appointment to that post.[156] The techniques
used in compiling genealogies in the OT show that where actual
determination of kinship was not possible, then the fiction of
blood relationship was created by various means.[157] This
concern with genealogies comes only with the more complex
social organization of the settled, permanent community:

> Because of concern with succession to power and with
> order of rank, . . . people learn to keep track of their
> genealogies. In a band or tribe, people cannot usually
> trace back their genealogies more than about three
> generations.[158]

Another indicator of the state of the family often applied
in the OT is the institution of family property, or the patrimony. Such family property was the norm in Israel. Land
really belonged to the individual only as a representative of
the family unit. According to Abraham Malamat, the patrimony
was an essentially inalienable piece of land possessed solely
by a gentilic unit, whether large or small; hence, this land
could not, at least in theory, be sold to any one, and its
transfer could only be effected through inheritance.[159] This
system of land tenure has its basis in a settled agricultural
society, not in a purely nomadic society where real property
either does not exist or is of insignificant proportions.
Evidence from Ugarit indicates that such a system existed
among the Canaanites, from whom the Hebrews must have adopted
it.[160]

While the scattered indications of inheritance customs
and practices in the OT are not sufficient for constructing a

systematic description, there are indications in the laws aimed
at the control of inheritance that the measures taken to preserve the family patrimony, and to facilitate its recovery if
lost, were strict.[161] The strictness with which this system
of land tenure was applied in Israel can be illustrated with
the familiar story of Naboth's vineyard in 1 Kgs 21. Without
attempting to survey the various interpretations of this story,
it will suffice here to say that the simplest and most straightforward understanding of this story, with relation to the
system of property laws, is the one suggested by E. Hammershaimb. He maintains that Naboth's conception of his ancestral
inheritance was in fact respected by the king when Naboth
refused to sell it. The protest of Elijah then is not directed
against the fact that the king failed to recognize the law of
property, but against the devious and cruel means by which the
king attained his end.[162] There is also the possibility that
Ahab had some collateral right of inheritance in this instance,
which he could legally exercise after the owner's death.[163]
Even if this possibility is not accepted, the Naboth incident
does not seem to provide positive evidence that the traditional
system of land tenure was disregarded by the rulers in Israel.
On the contrary, as Sjoberg suggests, the maintenance of the
extended family by the ruling strata would be to their particular advantage in such a system of land tenure, for it would
make it possible for them to keep their landholdings intact,
which in turn would promote the survival of the extended
family.[164]

While the law of familial land tenure was applied to the
agricultural land, there is some evidence that this law was
felt to be inapplicable to property within cities. The basis
for this is seen in the exception of urban property from the
privilege of redemption in the jubilee.[165] But, even in this
apparent exclusion, it should be noted that it is expressly
said that if it is not redeemed within the redemption year,
"then the house that is in the walled city shall be made sure
*in perpetuity to him who bought it, throughout his genera-
tions.*" This would seem to indicate that family ownership of
property in cities was the rule rather than the exception.
Again, this rule would be of use to the urban upper class in

maintaining property which they had acquired within the city as well as without.[166]

In addition to the laws dealing with land, there are other laws in Deuteronomy in which "we are dealing with ordinances which regulate a definite sociological form of community life, namely the living together in the framework of the 'extended family.'"[167] The so-called Levirate law in Deut 25:5-10, e.g., opens with the significant expression, "If (or "when") brothers dwell together," implying an extended family situation.[168] Whatever the primary purpose of the Levirate law, the statement of Josephus seems to state its function:

> For this procedure will be for the benefit of the public, because thereby families will not fail, and the estate will continue among the kindred; and this will be for the solace of wives under their affliction.[169]

The conclusion to be gained from the above discussion is that while urbanization brought about social changes for the Israelites, the deleterious effect on the family was not so much the result of urbanization as such, but more the consequence of the economic policies of the monarchy, which were designed to draw the wealth from the land.

Having completed this brief digression on the family, we must now return to the discussion of the more general aspects of urban social structure in the OT. While we have admitted the existence of certain leveling tendencies which were at work in Israelite society, it should not be inferred from this that the social structure of the Israelite city is to be understood as atypical in comparison with that form commonly found in the ancient preindustrial city. De Vaux is basically correct when he insists that we should not speak of social classes in the OT in the modern sense of a closed class into which one is born. Sjoberg's definition of a social class, therefore, is probably applicable to the Old Testament. He says that a social class is:

> A large body of persons who occupy a position in a social hierarchy by reason of their manifesting similarly valued objective criteria. These latter include kinship affiliation, power and authority, achievements, possessions and moral and personal attributes. Achievements involve a person's occupational and educational attainments; possessions refer to material evidences of wealth; moral attributes include one's religious and ethical beliefs and actions; and personal attributes involve

speech, dress, and personal mannerisms.[170]

It is evident from Sjoberg's definition that one's class was
not determined solely, or even primarily by birth.[171] The
account of 2 Sam 3:8-39 shows, e.g., how status could be won
by military exploits. The proverbs in 1 Sam 10:12 point to
family distinction as status. Thus an upper class, constituted on the basis of family connection, wealth, military
distinction, royal favor, experience, and particular skills
such as those of the "wise," is manifest in the OT. As we have
already seen in our discussion of the expression "people of the
land," a distinction can legitimately be drawn between the
upper ruling class and the remainder of the population, a
distinction which groups the lower-status urbanites together
with the peasants living in the city's hinterland. That the
formation of an upper class is an urban phenomenon is attested
to both by Sjoberg and in the history of the OT itself by the
fact that the formation of this stratum, within a society which
was previously quite egalitarian, coincided with the urbanization of Israelite society under the impetus of the monarchy.
Thus the ruling element was concentrated in the cities.

That administrative personnel concentrate in cities seems
only too obvious, but in the preindustrial city there were
cogent reasons for this apparently self-evident fact. The
nobility congregated in cities, and within the city in citadels, for the security offered there against enemies, both
foreign and domestic. Before the advent of mass communication
the residence of the ruling element in a relatively compact
area was essential. Location in the city also enabled the
elite to profit from the presence of merchants, servants,
craftsmen and others offering a wide variety of services.[172]

The ruling class as a whole is called by several names
in the OT, all of which indicate their privileged position in
the society. One of these labels is $\dot{h}\bar{o}r\hat{\imath}m$, which is usually
translated "nobles."[173] While $\dot{h}\bar{o}r\hat{\imath}m$ occurs in parallel with
$\dot{s}\bar{a}r\hat{\imath}m$, "royal officials" or "chiefs" in several instances
(Isa 34:12; Eccl 10:17), a key verse for determining its
meaning is Jer 27:20, where $\dot{h}\bar{o}r\hat{\imath}m$ replaces the $\dot{s}\bar{a}r\hat{\imath}m$ of the
parallel text in 2 Kgs 24:14.[174] On the basis of this verse
and the occurrence of $\dot{h}\bar{o}r\hat{\imath}m$ only in late contexts, this term

should probably be considered to be a synonym of *śārîm*.[175]

Another appellative of the upper class is the term
nĕdîbîm, which is formed on a root *ndb*.[176] Like *hōrîm*, this
term is also used in close conjunction with *śārîm* in a number
of poetic passages (Num 21:18; Ps 83:12; Prov 8:16). A
particularly instructive passage is found in Job 34:17-19:

> Shall one who hates justice govern?
>   Will you condemn him who is righteous and mighty,
> who says to a king, 'Worthless one,'
>   and to nobles (*nĕdîbîm*), 'Wicked man;'
> who shows no partiality to princes,
>   nor regards the rich more than the poor,
> for they are all the work of his hands?

This passage reveals both the connection of the *nĕdîbîm* with
the ruling class and something of their status in Israelite
society. De Vaux says of the relationship of *hōrîm* and
nĕdîbîm:

> These words . . . are almost synonomous and denote the
> ruling class of the monarchical period, administrators
> and heads of influential families--in short, the men of
> position.[177]

While it is probably justifiable to speak of this upper
class of officials produced by the concurrent phenomena of
urbanization and the development of the court as a social class
it is not necessarily correct to posit the existence of the
poor as a separate social class in contrast to them. As we
have already seen, the "people of the land" cannot be thought
of in such terms. Certainly there was not an equal distribution of wealth, and the greatest inequality was probably in
the areas surrounding the capital cities of Jerusalem and
Samaria. These cities, particularly Jerusalem, with their
large numbers of personnel in the royal court, could not be
supported by the produce of their immediate hinterland, and
thus had to draw upon the economic surplus of the whole land.
Again, we can see the close concurrence of urbanization and
the monarchy, as the monarchy provided the power structure
without which such relatively populous cities could not be
sustained. As Sjoberg observes, farmers rarely produce and
give up a surplus willingly, but tribute must be exacted if
cities are to gain the wherewithal to support their population.[178]

The policies instituted in the monarchy to draw the

wealth from the land are mirrored in the antimonarchical
document of 1 Sam, which describes royal policy:

> He will take the best of your fields and vineyards and
> olive orchards and give them to his servants [i.e.,
> the royal administrative personnel]. He will take the
> tenth of your grain and of your vineyards and give it
> to his officers and to his servants. He will take your
> menservants and maid servants, and the best of your
> cattle and your asses, and put them to his work. He
> will take the tenth of your flocks, and you shall be
> his slaves.[179]

The effect of such massing of wealth and services around
the urban centers, particularly the capitals, is aptly put by
Scott:

> Once a people loses its organic relationship with its
> means of subsistence, . . . once individual wealth and
> power become the accepted goal of endeavor within the
> community--poverty, injustice and social strife have
> come to stay . . . With the establishment of the
> court . . . there began a concentration of wealth which
> drained off the economic surplus of the community . . .
> Vast quantities of food, goods, and services were now
> taken for the upkeep of the royal establishment and
> the army, while the conscript labor which built chariot
> cities and embellished Jerusalem, left crops and
> herds untended. The importing of great new quantities of
> gold and silver . . . forced prices upward in a sudden
> inflation. Men were compelled to mortgage their lands,
> their persons, or their children to pay the exactions
> demanded. The interest was usurious, and many free
> Israelites lost their land and became slaves, while
> those who had an initial advantage amassed lands and
> money.[180]

The existence of the poor in Israel is presupposed in the
monarchical period by the essentially urban legislation of the
basic framework of Deuteronomy which reflects the social
conditions of its period and seeks to provide laws whose aim
was to eliminate abject poverty among the Israelites.[181]
While it is difficult to determine the degree to which such
social legislation was actually put into practice, the legislation itself at least indicates that there was a concern about
poverty and a feeling of responsibility for its alleviation at
work within the Yahwistic religion.[182] Typical examples of
such legislation are those laws aimed at the protection of two
"unlanded" groups within Israelite society, the $g\bar{e}r\hat{i}m$,
"resident aliens," and the Levites. Marmorstein defines the
$g\bar{e}r$ as "an agricultural laborer in the service of a hereditary
landowner, paid with a share of his produce and dependent on

the kindness of his patron."[183] While they had originally been
of different ethnic backgrounds, including autochthonous
Canaanites along with immigrants from various countries, they
became known collectively as *gērîm*, and constituted landless
peasants who worked as sharecroppers.[184] Again it was the
Israelite conception of community that assisted the assimilation of such persons in the society and sought to provide at
least a modicum of legal protection for them as persons who
could not share in the normal economic process.

The above section is an admittedly oversimplified attempt
to present the organizing principles of the Israelite social
order as it was centered in the cities in the monarchical
period. As we shall see in the following chapter, the condemnation of the social order by the prophets had an essentially
religious base; but this religious base had, in turn, its
grounding in a particular social order created by the intensified urbanization of the period and its effects on social
values:

> The desire for security and satisfaction, then, was
> the mainspring of social action, and determined most
> decisively the form of the social order and the quality
> of its human relationships. Within the Israelite society
> certain individuals, groups and classes had attained a
> position of dominance and privilege through the exercise
> of power, the influence of prestige and the possession
> of wealth; and the latter means were continually being
> sought for the former ends. The interests of society as
> a whole were . . . too easily identified with the
> interests of the ruling classes in maintaining their
> position and privileges . . . the final faith of the
> nation was not in Yahweh . . . . Hence the social evils
> which the prophets denounced were not political and
> economic merely; they were at the same time religious
> evils. . . Political forms, economic activities, legal
> and judicial practice, social institutions, public
> morals, culture and religion—all were deformed by a
> basic error as to the meaning, values and direction of
> life.[185]

Urban Government in the Old Testament

In view of the fact that the upper class was basically
constituted of the urban administrative personnel, it is only
natural that the discussion of urban government in the OT
follow on that of the urban social structure. Government in
its earliest form in the ancient Near East primarily performed the function of distributing the agricultural surplus

which made aggregative living possible. Early government also embodied defense and police functions, and in collaboration with the religious hierarchy, played some role in respect to the welfare and spiritual life of the people.[186]

Certainly some of these early urban governmental functions continued into later periods. Sjoberg attributes three primary functions to the governmental apparatus in the preindustrial city: (1) social control or the maintenance of order; (2) the provision of services; and (3) the exaction of tribute from the populace to finance the operations of government and to underwrite the elite, or more narrowly the ruling group.[187]

The number of ruling families who executed such functions in most preindustrial societies was small. In the early Israelite period, the OT traditions preserve a situation in which, as a rule, it was a single extended family which dominated a city, such as the Abiezrites in the city of Ophrah and the sons of Hamor in Shechem.[188]

A major concern in the analysis of urban governmental structures is the relationship between the ruling stratum and the citizenry in general. We have already maintained that socially there was a cleavage between these two groups. Our concern here is to ascertain how these groups were related politically, i.e. what was the role played by each group in urban administration. In the following analysis of Israelite urban administration, we are dealing, in the main, with the Israelite city during the monarchy. In so doing, the disintegration of the tribe as the basic political unit is assumed. As Israel settled in the areas which bore the tribal names, the tribes (šebātîm or maṭṭôt) themselves retained importance as territorially determined groups of the communities in which the clans (mišpāḥôt) and families (bêt-'abôt) lived, but it was the urban community which early became the basic political unit.[189]

There is no certain information as to whether a tribal organization ever existed among the Canaanites. But, even if there were such an organization, it can be said with certainty that it was not the dominant one when the Israelites came into contact with the Canaanite city. The city-state was the predominant form of political organization in Palestine-Syria in

this period.[190] The tenacity of this political system is
probably to be explained, at least in part, by the fact that
the land of Canaan possessed little geographical unity.
Instead, the systems of mountains and valleys subdivided the
land and tended to accentuate local differences. There was
no unified Canaanite state before the Israelites, and the
history of the Israelites shows the relatively short-lived
nature of the attempts to create and maintain a national state
on Palestinian soil.[191]

From the OT sources, we learn that these Canaanite city-
states were governed either by a king, or by a local aristocracy, the elders.[192] The traditions regarding the offer of
kingship to Gideon and Abimelech may well represent, as Wright
suggests, a proposal to return Shechem to the city-state
pattern of government with a local king who still would remain
within the Israelite confederation.[193] It is, however, with
the role of the elders that we are basically concerned, since
the city controlled by elders remained the central core of
Israelite political life up to the exilic period.[194]

In seeking to outline the role of the elders in the urban
administration in the OT, we are assisted by references to
analogous groups in the ancient Near East. These same references are also useful in determining the relationship of the
elders to other urban assemblages. Elders existed among the
Hittites as a local ruling group:

> . . . the elders are the governing body of the city, the
> town council, with whom provincial governors on tour are
> required to collaborate in judicial and other affairs.
> The conclusion seems to be clear: the Hittite state was
> the creation of an exclusive caste superimposed on the
> indigenous population of the country, which had originally
> been loosely organized in a number of independent town-
> ships, each governed by a body of elders.[195]

Here is an example of the continuation of the rule of local
elders under a provincial system, similar in some ways to that
of Solomon, which supplemented rather than replaced an already
existing local administrative system.

At Mari, there is a bare mention of the elders of a city,
whose name is lost, and of Iamrus-El and the elders of Qa.[196]
On the basis of these and other scattered references, McKenzie
concludes that the organization of the city government at Mari

consisted of a mayor, who was equivalent to the Israelite
śārîm, and a council of elders.[197]

Phoenician cities also had their assemblies of elders,
attested at Byblos and Tyre by non-biblical documents, and in
the passing reference in the oracle of Ezekiel against Tyre.[198]
The elders as a local judicial body are also attested in Babylonia in the period of Hammurapi, sometimes together with the
royal governor of the city. The elders as a judicial body
also appear in the Neo-Babylonian period.[199]

In light of this evidence for the institution of the
elders, McKenzie concludes:

> This evidence leaves room for the conclusion that the
> institution was widespread in the ancient Near East,
> that the allusions of the OT to the elders of Moab and
> of a Canaanite city are based on fact, and that it is a
> mere accident that we have no reference to the elders
> in the Amarna letters or in Ugaritic literature.[200]

While the existence of elders in the ancient Near Eastern
city can hardly be questioned, there is considerable difference of opinion as to their precise composition and function,
particularly in relation to a supposed popular assembly or
assemblies. In seeking to arrive at a workable definition of
the functions of the elders in the OT, the caution of Evans
should be heeded when he points out that in an age before the
refinement of political theory, there is little or no fine
line of distinction drawn between the elders acting as a court
of law and the same men serving as an advisory body on matters
of local policy. Neither does there appear to be a distinction drawn between the group's acting as witnesses for a
commercial transaction or its deciding on peace or war.[201]

A number of scholars have posited the existence of two
distinct local assemblies in the ancient Israelite city, after
the analogy of the existence of such a "bicameral" body in the
ancient Mesopotamian communities.[202] The two bodies which
together constituted the urban administration were the council
of elders and the general assembly of adult men. The under-
lying concept of these twin bodies is quite ancient and is to
be traced to the Sumerians. In the Gilgamesh Epic, it is
related that Agga, the king of Kish, sent envoys to Gilgamesh,
the ruler of the rival city-state of Erech, with an ultimatum
demanding the surrender of his city.[203] Before he can engage

in combat with Agga, Gilgamesh must consult with two bodies.
He first seeks the counsel of the assembly of elders, urging
upon them a military response to the demands of Agga rather
than submission.[204] Nevertheless, the elders recommend surrender. That their recommendation was not binding is made evident
in Gilgamesh's next move. He turns to the assembly of the
"able-bodied men," that is, of arms-bearing males, with his
request for a military response.[205] In a rather lengthy statement, the assembly of "men" overrules the decision of the
elders and declares itself for a military response.[206] The
important thing to be noted in this episode is that when the
two bodies were in disagreement, it is the word of the general
assembly of arms-bearing males which prevailed over that of
the elders.

The ultimate authority of the large body is also docu-
mented in the sources from the Assyrian trading colony at
Kanesh in Cappadocia.[207] At Kanesh there is an apparent decline in power of the assembly and a shift of the balance of
legal powers from the full assembly to that of the elders.
The latter were not chosen simply on the basis of age, which
the term "elder" implies, but probably on the basis of a
position of influence within the community, gained on the
basis of their commercial success.[208]

Speiser draws upon two distinctive phrases in the OT to
build his case for the existence of a bipartite assembly in
Israel. The two phrases are "All those who went in at the
gate of the city" (Gen 23:10, 18; etc.) and "All those who went
out the gate of the city" (Gen 34:24; etc.).[209] He sees the
term $\check{s}a\hat{r}ar$ in such instances as meaning "assembly, community."[210] The phrase, "All those who went out by the gate
of the city" is equated with "those capable of bearing arms."
To go out of the gate of one's city thus means to represent
one's community in battle.[211] This group in the OT is then
held to be analogous to the assembly of "men" in the Gilgamesh
Epic. Speiser equates "All those who went in at the gate of
the city" with the body of elders.

While it is possible that "those who went out of the gate"
are to be regarded as the armed men of the community, the
identification of "all those who went in" with the elders does

not seem so probable. As Evans observes, such a particularistic definition of this phrase cannot really be supported,
and it is probably better to be taken as meaning simply "all
the citizens," and not just the elders.[212] Thus it cannot be
maintained that "those who went in" and "those who went out"
correspond to two groups which jointly represented the source
of urban authority. But having said this is not to deny altogether the existence of an assembly of some kind which was
not limited to the elders. Wilson has called attention to
the mention of a city assembly in the story of Wen-Amon:

> When morning came, he (Zakar-Ba al) had his assembly
> summoned and he stood in their midst . . .

Wilson also sees a reference to this city council of Byblos
in a phrase in Ezek 27:9: "the elders of Gebal and her wise
men."[213] Unfortunately, however, this verse provides little
information for the determination of the makeup of a similar
body in the Israelite city.[214]

Another explanation which attempts to explain the relationship of the local elders to a broader assembly is the one
offered by Wolf. He sees the expressions "men of Israel" and
"the elders" as being used interchangeably and reflecting a
situation in which the elders represented the people so fully
that either term could be used with the general meaning of
the total male population.[215] In support of his thesis he
notes that although the number of elders in a given community
is only rarely given, when it is mentioned, it is often in
the seventies.[216] He then interprets this number as being
representative of the entire free male population of a town,
holding that such an explanation is more plausible than the
one which interprets the number as determined by the number
of families that were able to establish their right to be
represented in the council.[217] Admitting that we may not say
positively that every reference to "elders" in the OT is to
the entire town assembly, Wolf concludes his study by quoting
Pedersen with favor: "The elders are identical with the city
and comprise the whole body of citizens helping to support its
life."[218]

McKenzie, however, advances a telling critique of
Wolf's proposal. He questions, first of all, the assumption
that the Israelites used the term "elders" without precise

determination. Secondly, he observes that the weight of the passages in which elders are mentioned in a way which apparently contrasts them with the "men" or the "people" is against this identification. He also doubts whether the number of elders in a given community is correctly preserved.[219] Finally, he states that the identification of the elders with the entire adult male population is not in harmony with the analogous institutions in the ancient Near East.[220]

Such an identification of the elders with all the adult men of a community also goes against Sjoberg's thesis that the number of ruling families in most preindustrial cities is small, not a few local communities being dominated by one, or at the best a few elite families.[221]

The problem of determining the relationship of the elders to any other supposed groups would seem then to hinge on the objective criteria which were used to constitute the body of elders in a community. The degree to which these criteria were spelled out is questionable, but certainly "We are not to look on this institution as an artificial one. The elders do not form a council, chosen, and governing according to automatic rules."[222] Based on the etymology of $z\bar{a}q\bar{e}n$, "elder," the term could signify little more than an adult male with a $z\bar{a}q\bar{a}n$, "beard." But in the framework of the family, it is the adult male who is the elder member of the family that yields authority in the particular unit. As parents wield authority as a result of their wisdom and experience, which is in turn a product of their greater age, so "elders" as a technical term refers to those who exercise authority in the life of the clan, tribe, or local community. The respect of experience is thus the origin of the authority of the elder. But, while this is the origin of the authority of the elder, it did not remain the sole basis of authority in an urban setting. In the cities of Israel in the monarchical era, with the breakdown of the tribe as a working political unit and the development of the city as a basic administrative unit, different clans and tribes coalesced in the same city. In such a situation the term "elder" lost its original physiological basis and came to be used to indicate a class distinction based on rank, wealth, or heritage.[223] The elders became the

men of the powerful families who de facto had the power to
rule.[224]   The elders as a group thus became able to determine
their membership by cooption.[225]   In this cooption, the factor
of ownership of real property must have been a highly valued
criterion, if not the decisive one.[226]   With the concentration
of land ownership, there would thus have been a corresponding
decrease in the number of elders. By the eighth century B.C.,
the elders must have been a small minority, consisting of
landlords or those entirely dependent   on landlords.[227]
However, it is difficult to say in many cases whether the
elders were a duly constituted group or simply an ad hoc group
who felt sure enough of its prestige in a given instance to
make some administrative move. While the term "elder" can
have a rather precise definition when placed in the framework
of a tribal hierarchy, with the disappearance of the tribal
unit as a political structure, this definition loses some of
its sharpness. When the "elders" of a city are spoken of, the
reference is probably to the heads of the leading family or
families of that city who formed a sort of city council.[228]

The expression "elders of a city" is used for the first
time in the period of the judges, a time of political transition.[229]   The numerous references to the "elders of the
people," "elders of the land," "elders of Judah," and "elders
of Israel" apparently refer to a body, called together at
various times, which was made up of one or more elders from
each city or settlement within the tribal or regional area
named.[230]   An interesting example of the use of the expression
"elders of Judah" occurs in 1 Sam 30:26-31:

> When David came to Ziklag, he sent part of the spoil to
> his friends, the elders of Judah, saying, 'Here is a
> present for you from the spoil of the enemies of the
> Lord;' it was for those in Bethel, in Ramoth of Negeb,
> in Jattir, in Aroer, in Siphmoth, in Eshtemoa, in Racal,
> in the cities of the Jerahmeelites, in the cities of the
> Kenites, in Hormah, in Borashan, in Athach, in Hebron,
> for all the places where David and his men had roamed.

Here, "elders of Judah" is a territorial definition and apparently includes the elders of the various cities named.[231]
Another passage which demonstrates a certain flexibility of
use is found in Ruth 4:1-4, 9, 11:

> And Boaz went up to the gate. . . And he took ten men of
> *the elders of the city*. . . Then he said to the next of

kin, 'Naomi, who has come back from the country of Moab, is selling the parcel of land which belonged to our kinsman Elimelech. So I thought I would tell you of it, and say, 'Buy it' in the presence of those sitting here, and in the presence of *the elders of my people* . . . Then Boaz said to *the elders and all the people*, 'You are witnesses this day that I have bought from the hand of Naomi all that belonged to Elimelech and all that belonged to Chilion and to Mahlon'. . . Then *all the people who were at the gate, and the elders*, said, 'We are witnesses.'

In this passage, the elders in question are the elders of Bethlehem. It is they who made legal the transaction between Boaz and his kinsman. The role of the random group of people who happened to gather at the city gate at this particular time, appears to have been limited to that of serving as corroborative witnesses to the legal transaction, for which only the elders were absolutely necessary.[232] In addition to the role of the elders in this passage as the representative of the community in a legal transaction, they also fulfilled other functions which are summarized by McKenzie under five headings: (1) They represent the entire people of a community in political or religious activity. (2) They are associated with the leader, or accompany him when he exercises authority. (3) They appear as a governing body; this function overlaps their representative function and their association with the leader. (4) They constitute a part of the royal council. (5) They are a judicial body.[233]

In their representative role in the period of the monarchy, the elders of the land could be assembled to participate with the king in a council of war (1 Kgs 20:7-9), they participated in the election of a king in the case of Saul (1 Sam 8:4) and David (2 Sam 5:3), and they participated in religious processions (1 Kgs 8:1, 3 = 2 Chr 5:4).[234]

In seeking to determine the administrative relationship of the elders to the central authority, it is imperative to examine the instances in which the term "elder" appears in conjunction with other terms denoting officials of the central government or other local officers.

The officers most frequently mentioned with the elders are the śārîm.[235] The Hebrew word has a cognate in the Akkadian šarru, which in the singular means "king," but the

Akkadian is more directly related to our Hebrew term in the plural, where it means "viceroys, thereafter chieftain, leader of a group or commission, official; . . . finally designates a rank, the caste of officials."[236] In the premonarchical period, the śārîm are virtually synonymous with the "elders.[237] But, in the monarchy śārîm designates, like its Akkadian cognate, a class of Unterkönige, who were not completely self-regulating, but were dependent upon the king to some extent. Pedersen says, concerning this class of officials:

> They form a new aristocracy, a limited class as opposed
> to the people. . . In the small towns this new aris-
> tocracy may not have made itself felt. But in the large
> cities, and above all in Jerusalem, the new class
> dissolved the power of the old families . . . . The king
> could raise men who pleased him, and the old order of
> property was not respected. It is very likely that the
> Israelite king tried to do the same thing that was done
> in Egypt in the 17th and 18th dynasties, i.e. to create
> a feudalistic state and to supplant the old proprietors
> with his officials, thus maintaining these as his
> feudals.[238]

While Pedersen is probably correct in his analysis of the śārîm as a kind of feudal aristocracy, he probably exaggerates the extent to which they "dissolved the power of the old families." There is some evidence that even in the monarchy, there is a degree of overlapping in the two groups.[239] In one passage in which civic officials are listed, the śārîm appear to be practically synonymous with the elders in function.[240] The śārîm, as royal officials, were probably found in the larger towns, where they had a limited function, consisting basically of protecting the king's interest and being respon-sible for the collection of the royal tribute.[241] Whether these royal śārîm are always to be distinguished from the local śārîm is not clear. In some cases the royal officials may have been recruited from the old leading families. McKenzie, building on the suggestion of van der Ploeg that the śār, by definition, is the one who has the power to command, holds that it is likely that both the tribes and cities of Israel were organized into military units even in non-military affairs, and thus the śārîm would be the military officers of the tribal, clan, or local units. In this sense, then, the elders and the śārîm touch or overlap to some extent. The elders would form the larger group from which the śārîm were

drawn.[242] In the functions served by governmental apparatus,
there is certainly a rationale for such a close relationship
between the administrative and military arms. As a king's
tentacles of control extended into the urban communities of his
realm, one of the first of his appointed officials, quite
often related to the head of state, was a representative of the
military arm.[243] Certainly, the governmental apparatus would
be totally ineffective without the backing of a loyal military
arm that both protects the society from external aggression
and assists in maintaining law and order within. Army garrisons are usually found in large cities, with the most powerful forces being stationed in the capital to protect the king
and his court. As Sjoberg observes, capital cities have
historically been vulnerable to attack for they are the prime
targets of an invading army. The surrender of the capital and
the king is tantamount to the society's collapse.[244] In this
regard, the *śar hā'îr* as a royal official located in the
capital city, may have had, in part, a military function.
While the references to this official do not provide much
information as to his function, he was obviously an important
person, and in one instance where his role is alluded to, he
is in charge of the prison at Samaria.[245]

It is particularly in their role as a municipal judicial
body that the elders exercise a continuing independent
function in the city of the Israelite monarchy. It is also
here that we can see a degree of unity prevailing within the
city, in contradistinction to those who hold that the city
necessarily brings with it a lack of cooperation.[246] There
were provisions for appeal from the local legal assembly to a
higher authority, as is attested by the story of the wise
woman of Tekoa in 2 Sam 14.[247] The story also shows that in
David's time, questions of blood revenge could still be
settled without recourse to the legal assembly. This practice
is in agreement with Sjoberg's idea that although there were
judicial bodies in the preindustrial city, in actual practice,
people tended to avoid recourse to the courts, and it was
deemed preferable to settle disputes privately, that is,
between families, guilds and the like.[248]

The unity of the urban community was strong enough that

there was a sense of collective communal responsibility operative. Deuteronomy is municipal law in the proper sense of the
word, for it reckons with the city as the responsible body.[249]
The classic instance of communal responsibility is the relating
of the ritual to be observed in the event of a murder by an
unknown person in Deut 21:1-9.[250] The elders of the city
which is nearest the spot of the crime perform a rite which
involves the killing of a heifer in order to purge their community from any possible responsibility for the crime by
diverting judgment for the deed to the uncultivated area outside the city. There are parallels to this community law in
the ancient Near Eastern cities of Nuzi and Ugarit. In one
instance at Nuzi, a whole town is held accountable for the
death of an ass.[251] A parallel to the Israelite procedure of
Deut 21 is mentioned by Gaster in connection with a homicide
by an unknown hand at Ugarit.[252] But, instead of the "elders"
performing the rite, it is the king who does it at Ugarit. For
each of the three suspect cities, the king pronounces a
collective curse, invoking upon the city the penalty which
would normally be inflicted on the individual malefactor.[253]
In another case in Deut, the entire population of an Israelite
city which was guilty of apostasy is deemed responsible and
the city is treated as though it were under the ban (*herem*) of
holy war.[254]

In the physical description of the city which we have
outlined above, we observed that due to the lack of extensive
city planning there was little if any open space within the
typical Palestinian city. Consequently, the place of assembly
was around the city gate, to a limited extent inside, but
usually outside, where the converging tracks made a well-worn
area which was the scene of much of the activity of a public
nature.[255] According to Evans, it is the difference in layout
of an eastern, as opposed to a classical city that has contributed to many of the false contrasts which have been drawn
between the two. It has been pointed out, e.g., that an
oriental city lacked the central open spaces of the type of
the Greek agora or the Roman forum. Evans holds that while
this is true enough, the inferences which are drawn from this
fact may be false since the gate was the scene of many

activities which, in a Western city, were carried on in a central square.[256]

In addition to the practical considerations which led to the use of the gate as a place of public assembly and hence a site of considerable social importance in the OT, the gate also had a peculiar religious significance:

> . . . the threshold that separates the two spaces (sacred and profane) also indicates the distance between two modes of being, the profane and the religious. The threshold is the limit, the boundary, the frontier that distinguishes and opposes two worlds--and at the same time the paradoxical place where those two worlds communicate, where passage from the profane to the sacred world becomes possible. Here too certain palaeo-oriental cultures (Babylon, Egypt, Israel) situated the judgment place. The threshold, the door *show* the solution of continuity in space immediately and concretely; hence their great religious importance, for they are symbols and at the same time vehicles of *passage* from the one space to the other.[257]

With regard to the Israelite city gate in particular, evidence of the religious significance of the gate can be seen in the excavation of an Israelite stratum (III) at Tell el Farʿah (Tirzah) where, in the axis of the city gate, there was a square piece of masonry or platform and nearby a small stone basin. De Vaux believes that this platform was the support of a stone pillar which was found in the last Israelite stratum at the same spot near a basin built up with slabs. He maintains that this pillar was a *maṣṣēbāh* and, with the basin, marked a place of worship at the entrance to the city.[258]

An indication of the gate as the dividing point between the "sacred" and the "profane" is also to be seen in the reference to the place of the execution of the death penalty which had been imposed by the elders as being "outside the city."[259]

The problem of the relationship between the local ruling group and the central authority of the king recurs with regard to the elders as administrators of justice. In Deut 16:18 there occurs the problematic expression, "You shall appoint judges (*šōpĕṭîm*) and officers (*šōṭĕrîm*) in all your towns."[260] These "officers" were, like the *śārîm*, royal officials, whose sphere of operation lay chiefly in the affairs of the army.[261] The "judges" who are paired with these royal "officers" are thus probably to be regarded as royal officials as well.[262] These references in Deuteronomy to the appointment of judges

in the cities have thus been connected with the judicial reforms of Jehoshaphat in the ninth century.[263]   According to 2
Chr 19:5, Jehoshaphat "appointed judges in the land, in all the
fortified cities of Judah, city by city."[264]   Thus, it would
seem that, with regard to the local judicial system, the crown
at first intervened to the extent of selecting magistrates
from among the "elders." Albright is thus correct when he
asserts that there is nothing to indicate that Jehoshaphat's
reform went farther than the designation of certain local
dignitaries as royally appointed judges.[265]

To conclude our discussion of this aspect of local administration, we shall quote von Rad, who, in commenting upon the
appointment of royal judges, says:

> The rise of such a body of officials shows a trend for the
> machinery of administration to come under the control of
> the monarchy, a trend which can be perceived in other
> spheres of life as well. But it seems as if this trend
> did not get beyond certain early stages. Even the Israel
> of the period of the monarchy never achieved a complete
> constitution as a state.[266]

To von Rad's statement we might simply add the observation that
the OT city thus retained its importance throughout the
monarchy as a social, governmental and judicial center which
the monarchy had always to reckon with.

Urban Specialization in the Old Testament

We must now bring this chapter to a conclusion with a
discussion of two rather closely related matters: the specialization of labor that occurred in the Israelite city, and the
development of city-types, which is related to the specialization. As we have indicated in our first chapter, the criterion
of the division of labor is an oft-cited one in the definition
of the city. In the ten criteria of Childe, the first five
deal with the importance of "full-time specialists," supported
ultimately by the ability of the farmers to produce a food
surplus. While we must reiterate the fact that throughout the
biblical period the economy of Palestine remained principally
pastoral-agarian, we must at the same time draw upon such
evidence as there is in the text of the OT and from the results
of archaeology to ascertain the presence of urbanites who
engaged in various kinds of manufacturing and commerce. Again,

we must clear the terms "manufacturing" and "commerce" from
their industrial connotations and define what they meant in a
preindustrial setting:

> Manufacturing in the feudal society, overwhelmingly
> dependent upon animate sources of energy, is of the handi-
> craft type. It is a small-scale undertaking, confined
> usually to the homes of craftsmen or small shops in the
> market place. A few 'large' workshops have existed in
> preindustrial centers, but even these have rarely enclosed
> more than a few score of workers. The generally small
> size of the productive unit reflects the simple technol-
> ogy, one that sets barriers to capital formation and
> prohibits the development of a mass market for goods.
> Specialization in production occurs in the product,
> not in the process. Specialization in product is often
> carried to the point that craftsmen devote their full time
> to producing items made from a particular raw material;
> thus we have goldsmiths, coppersmiths, wool weavers, etc.,
> each with their own guild.
> Manufactured goods are intended primarily for con-
> sumption by urbanites. Although some of the city's prod-
> ucts are conveyed to the countryside by travelling
> merchants, they constitute but a small fraction of the
> total urban manufactures. Contrariwise, the feudal city
> recieves far more from the rural hinterland, subsisting
> largely on the fruits of the peasant's labor--the
> 'surplus' food and raw materials he produces and the
> taxes or tribute he renders.[267]

This definition of manufacturing and commerce appears to
be generally applicable to the OT situation. Certainly, there
is evidence for home industry. In a study of ancient Palestinian dwellings, Beebe testifies to the extradomestic use of
houses in the Israelite period. In many cases homes served
as industrial and commercial shops as well as household
quarters.[268]

Before discussing the types of industry in the Israelite
city in greater detail, we shall first describe the class of
persons who engaged in such non-agricultural pursuits. The
general term for "craftsman" in the OT is $h\bar{a}r\bar{a}\check{s}$.[269] This
term is used to denote a worker in wood (a wood carver), a
worker in stone, and especially a worker in metals (a smith
or a founder).[270] In addition to this general term for
"craftsman" there are a number of specific trades listed in
the OT.[271]

With regard to the organization of trades in preindustrial
cities, Sjoberg states that the most obvious aspect of the
preindustrial city's economic organization is the guild system

which pervades manufacturing, trade and services. Such guilds
are peculiar to towns and cities, not to villages; only in the
former are full-time specialists to be found in numbers significant enough to warrant organization. The few extra-urban
craftsmen usually combine their function as artisan with part-
time farming and do not organize into economic associations.[272]

Definitive evidence for the existence of guilds in the
OT comes from the post-exilic period when, following the model
of the family system from which they had originated, the
craftsmen organized themselves into families or clans,
$mišpāḥôt$.[273] The heads of such guilds were given the familial
designation "father," while the journeymen were termed "sons."
This familial terminology may well represent the origins of
this system of organization in the family workshop, where the
father was expected to teach his own trade to his son. In
the family workshop it was thus the ideal and usual pattern
for a son to follow in the footsteps of his father.[274]

At Ugarit, artisans were in the royal service. They received the raw materials with which they worked from the royal
stores and received their sustenance and compensation from
them as well. The royal administration also distributed and
redistributed land among them. Each specialty or group of
related specialties had its chief (rb) and the central authority often dealt with the specialty group as a whole body,
demanding from them military and other services not directly
related to their professions.[275]

The evidence for the existence of guilds in pre-exilic
Israel points to a similar relationship to the central authority of the king. This evidence consists chiefly of the existence of "trade-marks" which were engraved on pottery. At
Gibeon (el-Jib), for example, a large number of jar handles
have been found bearing the word gdr and a proper name,
following the name of Gibeon, $gbᶜn$. Both the reading and the
interpretation of gdr have been disputed. Avigad has read gdd
and sees in this term a personal name.[276] The preferred reading, however, seems to be gdr.[277] With the reading gdr,
Pritchard favors a meaning similar to the French $clos$, "a
section of a vineyard, a walled enclosure or vineyard."[278] The
basic meaning of gdr as a walled enclosure may also refer

simply to a particular walled settlement, and may thus be a
place name which limits Gibeon as a section of a general
area.[279] The personal names may then be the "trade-marks" of
particular groups of vintners.[280]

Another example of what may be a hallmark stamp has been
found at Beth Haccherem (Ramat Rahel). Aharoni has called
these phw' stamps.[281] Several of these stamps have only the
words $yhwd/phw'$, but others contain personal names and read
$yhwd/hyw$ zr/phw' or l hzy/phw'. Aharoni believes that these
stamps were the property of a functionary in the fiscal administration of the province and would read the seals: "Yehud,
the governor;" "Yehud, Yehoezer, the governor;" and "belonging
to Ahzai the governor" respectively.[282] Cross, however, has
offered an alternative explanation, in which he reads phr',
"the potter," instead of phw' and suggests that the jars in
question belonged to a pottery workshop which manufactured jars
for tax collection.[283] The personal names would then presumably be those of the heads of particular workshops, working
under royal patronage as did the artisans at Ugarit. Cross'
interpretation of the seals is also in harmony with Diringer's
explanation of the so-called "royal seals," bearing the
inscription $lmlk$, "belonging to the king, royal." At Lachish,
seals were found bearing $lmlk$ in combination with the city
names Hebron, Ziph, Socoh, as well as a fourth city, $mmst$,
whose location is unknown. It is probable that these jar
handle stamps belonged to jars which were made in the royal
factories similar to those mentioned in 1 Chr 4:23. [284] In
addition to designating these jars as products of a royal
pottery, these stamps also were probably intended to serve as
a royal guarantee of the capacity of the container.[285]

There were several factors operative in the concentration
of particular trades in given localities. As with modern
industry, manufacturing plants in ancient Palestine were
located in places where appropriate raw materials were access-
ible. For example, in the sheep-raising country of southern
Judah, the cities of Lachish and Debir (Tell Beit Mirsim)
exhibit industrial specialization based on the ready availability of wool in the area. Several dyeing plants were
discovered in the excavations of Iron Age Tell Beit Mirsim,

and dyeing seems to have been the main occupation of the local inhabitants.[286] Heaton describes this industry as a "cottage industry" carried on by about 1,000 inhabitants occupying some two hundred houses.[287] A similar textile industry existed at Lachish.

Another industry under royal patronage seems to have been established in the oasis of En-gedi on the western shore of the Dead Sea. During the reign of Josiah, En-gedi became a royal estate, its inhabitants being employed mainly in the growing and manufacture of balm. The workshops were located in the nearby settlement of Tell el-jurn, and the perfumers were apparently organized in a guild. The excavation of Tell el-jurn has revealed the presence of manufacturing installations, including ovens, which appear to have been connected with a perfume industry.[288]

Estimates of an extensive Solomonic industry at the port city of Ezion-geber can no longer be maintained. The supposed "copper smelter and refinery" of Solomon, which enjoyed so much notoriety in the numerous archaeological manuals of the OT of the last decade or so, is no longer conceived of as an "advanced type of smelter-refinery" by its excavator, Nelson Glueck. Glueck has revised his former estimate and now believes that this structure was designed as a citadel, and was also employed as a storehouse and/or a granary. Solomon's Ezion-geber thus served in a comparatively modest way as the southernmost of the fortified district and chariot cities that Solomon built in more elaborate fashion at Hazor, Megiddo and Gezer. Glueck still maintains, however, that industrial and metallurgical operations did take place at Ezion-geber, as evidenced by the finding of copper slag and the remains of a hand-bellows furnace. This is more in line with the smelting operations which were done *in situ* throughout the coal. Ezion-geber was thus probably only a final processing station which formed the copper into ingots.[289] Thus the idea of a large, state-owned smelting plant at Ezion-geber loses its archaeological support, and, as Heaton remarks, "Although Solomon was capable of most things . . . his royal monopoly in metals for export, must remain, like his wisdom a matter for debate."[290]

In the face of this reinterpretation of Ezion-geber's industry, the largest industrial installation so far discovered in an Israelite city was apparently the one at Gibeon, which is associated with the jar handles mentioned above. The extent of this installation is indicated in the following description:

> An industrial area, designated by the excavators as the winery, was cleared. . . The installation contained numerous winepresses, fermenters, and sixty-three cellars capable of serving as cool storage places for large wine jars. The winery, occupying more than 1,100 square yards, contained many cuttings in the limestone, some of the cellars being more than seven feet deep and equipped with stone covers; the entire installation was capable of storing wine in jars to the amount of 25,000 gallons (U.S.). . . The discovery of the winery with its numerous cellars, wine jars, more than forty clay stoppers, and a clay funnel, supported the view that the inscribed jar handles were from wine jars which had originally been in use in Gibeon and had been returned to be refilled.[291]

It is quite difficult to determine whether this industry at Gibeon was controlled by the king, or was, as Heaton classifies it, an example of private enterprise.[292] Such a determination depends, to some degree, on how one interprets the jar-handle inscriptions. In addition to the inscriptions mentioned above, there was also found at Gibeon a group of some eighty handles stamped with the royal seal, *lmlk*.[293] If one interprets such seals to mean that the jars so stamped were used for the delivery of royal revenues, and were thus connected with the management of a royal enterprise, then Gibeon's winery could be called a state industry. But, as de Vaux observes, while these jars could have been used for the delivery of revenue, it is simpler and less hazardous to explain the stamp on them as the hallmark of a royal pottery.[294] If this explantion is adopted, it may also explain the *gdr* on the Gibeonite jars. This *gdr* may be a reference to the royal pottery at Gederah, mentioned in 1 Chr 4:23. According to Aharoni, sufformatives were not permanent elements of a name, that is to say, many names were formed by the addition of sufformatives which can be changed without altering the geographic meaning of the term. Sufformatives may have possessed a locative force and could be altered or dropped.[295] Although Gederah has not been identified positively, Morton believes that it may be identified with the modern Khirbet

Jedireh, about ten miles southeast of Lod, near Gibeon.[296]

Within the city, each branch of a trade or industry was usually carried on in a specific quarter. In Jerusalem, potters were apparently concentrated in the southern "suburbs," as may be inferred from the toponymn Potsherd Gate, which may refer to an exit from the city to a dump for broken pottery (Jer 19:2). A field just outside Jerusalem was called the Fuller's Field (2 Kgs 18:17; Isa 7:3), and probably indicates the presence of a fuller's plant in the vicinity. The location of fullers outside the city walls was probably required by the unpleasant odors associated with their trade.[297] A section of Jerusalem was also given over to the bakers (Jer 37:21), from which the Tower of the Ovens presumably got its name (Neh 3:11; 12:38). There was also a goldsmith's quarter in Jerusalem (Neh 3:32).

In 1 Kgs 7:45-46 (compare 2 Chr 4:7) there is a reference to bronze casting "in the clay ground between Succoth and Zarethan." The OT Succoth has been identified with Tell Deir ʿAlla and Zarethan with Tell es-Saʿidiyeh. In excavations at Tell Deir ʿAlla conducted by H. J. Franken, there is evidence that an advanced metallurgical industry for the smelting and casting of iron and copper existed there both prior to, during, and after the Solomonic period.[298] There is also evidence for a similar industry at Tell es-Saʿideyeh.[299]

Other instances of localities, or parts of localities, noted for a particular group of specialists are evidenced in the postexilic period, and may well have their roots in a preexilic situation. Examples of these are: wood-workers at Lod and Ono (Neh 11:35), linen-weavers in Beth-asbea (1 Chr 4:21), metal-workers in Ge-harashim (1 Chr 4:14) and gold-smiths in a quarter in Jerusalem (Neh 3:32).

Such a concentration in a particular part of a community no doubt assisted the guilds in the fulfillment of several of their salient functions, as they have been outlined by Sjoberg.[300] Certainly, in a day of limited communication facilities, concentration was necessary in making it possible for the guilds to regulate the activities of the members with responsibility to the occupation in question. It would also aid the carrying out of the welfare function of such guilds

which were a social security agency on the local level, ranking
next to the family. It is this latter function which was
particularly important for those craftsmen and merchants who
had no family connections.[301] The guilds, with their terminology borrowed from the family, also served some of the
functions of the family.

The OT provides little information on the administrative
and social position of artisans and merchants. If, as we have
seen at least with reference to potters, Israelite artisans
were in the royal service, they may have been dealt with as
specialty groups by the central administration, as we have seen
was the case at Ugarit. As such they would be royal dependents
whose social position would not differ in principle
from other groups in the royal service.

In 1 Kgs 20:34 there is an allusion to the fact that
trading concessions were granted to alien merchants. In this
case the reference is to a reciprocal trade agreement between
Ahab and Ben-hadad, which permitted the former to establish
"bazaars" in Damascus, just as the latter's father had set up
similar establishments in Samaria.[302] Since the context makes
it clear that this represents part of the terms of concession
on the part of Ben-hadad, it would seem that such "bazaars"
constituted a royal enterprise which would have funneled off
some of the economic resources of Damascus and diverted them
to Ahab's treasury.[303] It is also likely that these alien
merchants were granted other privileges in the host city,
even including freedom from taxation.[304]

Weber has classed the artisans and merchants with the
gērîm, or resident aliens, and held that they were metics
whose position was sharply differentiated from the total for-
eigner. The *gēr* was of foreign stock, but was legally
protected:

> Whatever his position with respect to the ownership of
> land, the sources regularly mean by 'ger' a denizen who
> was not only under the private protection of an individu-
> al with the religious protection of guest right, but a
> man whose rights were regulated and protected by the
> political organization. This legal situation was termed
> *ger asher bish'arecha*[sic] in the old legal collections,
> 'the metic in your gates.' This is to say, the metic
> belonged to the bailiwick of the city and stood under
> its regular protection.[305]

It is true that there was really no merchant class among the Israelites and that real commerce was, for the most part, in the hands of foreigners.[306] But, having said this, it is questionable whether the OT evidence would support Weber's position that craftsmen and merchants were classed with the $g\bar{e}r\hat{i}m$. Marmorstein, on the contrary, has defined the $g\bar{e}r$ as "an agricultural laborer in the service of a hereditary land-owner paid with a share of his produce and dependent on the kindness of his patron." He adds that this class of $g\bar{e}r\hat{i}m$ formed the great mass of the agricultural population.[307] Thus, in this analysis, the $g\bar{e}r\hat{i}m$ are to be equated with the land-less peasants. Nowhere in the OT do $g\bar{e}r\hat{i}m$ appear specifically as either craftsmen or merchants.[308] On the contrary, the $g\bar{e}r\hat{i}m$ are, as a rule, poor unskilled persons who were forced to hire themselves out as paid day-laborers and were dependent upon the charity of the more well-to-do.[309] They certainly do not represent a skilled class of persons such as artisans or an economically sound class such as merchants. While there is no definite evidence as to the social rank of the craftsman in the urban society of the OT neither is there any indication that he would have been consigned to the bottom of the city's social structure.

While the above examples are illustrative, and are by no means exhaustive, they serve to demonstarate some of the areas in which there was non-agricultural specialization in the Israelite city. Although the concentration of certain industries in given localities has been noted, and was no doubt instrumental in the formation of guilds, it should be pointed out that among the city-types of the OT there is no mention of an industrial city as such. As was the case at Ugarit, so in Israel industry was, to a great degree, under the patronage of the king, who supported those who engaged in such nonagricultural pursuits from the royal treasury. McCown's statement that Ezion-geber was the only "industrial city" can, as we have seen, no longer be maintained, and the industry of the OT is much more along the lines suggested by Sjoberg above, that is, a small-scale undertaking of the handicraft type.[310]

City-types in the Old Testament

Although we are probably not justified in singling out
the industrial city as a specific city-type in the OT, there
are a number of city-types mentioned in the OT. The connection
of most of these with the monarchy is apparent in one reference
to cities which served special functions: ". . . all the
cities that Solomon had, and the cities for his chariots and
horses."[311]

The store-city is always mentioned in connection with
royal activity.[312] This city-type was a site where warehouses
were built for the storage of government supplies of various
kinds.[313] Wright, for example, would translate the usual expression for "store-cities," ʿārê miskěnôt, as "cities of
granaries."[314] The construction of a "store-city" refers then
to the building of royal granaries or warehouses in already
existing cities rather than to the building of an entire city.
Such structures were probably used to store the taxes of grain,
wine and oil collected by the government.[315] Some of these
supplies were probably used as provisions for royal garrisons
stationed in the cities. We have no list of the cities in
which such warehouses were located, but they must have been
in most of the larger cities, and certainly in those cities
which served as administrative centers in the monarchy.[316]

Archaeologically, there is adequate evidence for the
presence of such structures in Israelite cities. At Beth-
Shemesh, in stratum IIa (ca. 950-825 B.C.), a large house was
excavated, which was constructed in the tenth century and
remained in use in later periods. The size of this building
suggests that it was not a private dwelling, but was connected
with the royal administration. This function is also attested
by the adjacent silo, whose dimensions are given as 5.7 by 6.5
by 7.5 meters.[317] The walls of Beth-Shemesh of this period
were of the casemate type, which served a storage function.

Storage facilities also appear to have been erected at
Lachish at the beginning of the monarchy. Again, as at Beth-
Shemesh, there are two closely associated structures, the one
being a large building, the other a long-roomed storehouse
nearby.[318] Other examples of such storage facilities can be
seen at Shechem, Mizpah and Hazor.[319]

Under Solomon a strong chariot force was established, and thus there arose a need for "cities for his chariots and horses," or "garrison towns" as they are called by de Vaux.[320] These "chariot cities," as they are called in 1 Kgs 10:26, are listed in 1 Kgs 9:15-19 and include Hazor, Megiddo, Gezer, Lower Beth-Horon, Baalath and Tamar.[321] Like other cities in the OT which were constructed or fortified for defense purposes, these cities were strategically located. Megiddo and Hazor were intended to protect the northeast border from Syrian advances, Lower Beth-Horon, Gezer and Baalath fronted on Philistia, and Tamar protected the southern flank. In addition to the six chariot cities listed in 1 Kgs 9, there was also a garrison for the royal force in the capital.

The "cities for defense" ($^c\bar{a}r\hat{i}m$ $l\check{e}m\bar{a}s\hat{o}r$), built by Rehoboam, like Solomon's fortified cities, represent an attempt to secure certain cities which formed a continuous line of defense for his kingdom to the west, south and the east, as well as at important intersections. These "fortress cities" thus do not represent a peculiar type of city, but are simply cities whose fortifications received particular attention in critical times. That the defense function of a city and its use as a garrison also included the provision for storage is indicated in the reference to Rehoboam's cities:

> He made the fortresses strong, and put commanders in them, and stores of food, oil, and wine. And he put shields and spears in all the cities, and made them very strong.[322]

There are two references to a "royal city" ($^c\hat{i}r$ $hammam-l\bar{a}k\bar{a}h$) in the OT.[323] In Josh 10:2 the reference is to Gibeon which was "like one of the royal cities." Gibeon itself was not a "royal city," that is a city which was the residence of the king of a city-state. It was more likely a dependency of Jerusalem in this period, and was ruled by elders (Josh 9:11). Saying that it was like a royal city was evidently a way of expressing the fact that it was an especially strong city, like the well-fortified cities in which kings resided. In 1 Sam 27:5 the expression "royal city" designates the residence of Achish, the *seren* of Gath.[324]

"Cities of refuge" are mentioned in four places: Num 35:9-34; Deut 4:41-43; 19:1-13; Josh 20:1-9. One of the problems in dealing with this urban type is that of sorting

out the material in these pericopes in order to determine early
strata and later additions. If one views these passages in
the perspective of the uncritical historical schema set forth
in the Pentateuch, the development of this institution would
unfold in the following manner:

> The command of Nb 35, associated with the period on the
> steppes of Moab, fixes the rules but states neither the
> number nor the names of the cities: the land is not yet
> conquered. In Dt 4, Moses chooses three cities in the
> land of Canaan, which has still to be conquered, but
> does not name them; the additional verses, 8 and 9,
> provide for three other unnamed cities in order to com-
> plete the traditional number of six, without seeing that
> the three missing cities are those of Dt 4. Finally,
> when the conquest is complete, Jos 20 recalls the rules
> proclaimed earlier and at last gives the names of the
> six cities with their geographical positions.[325]

But, when viewed critically, this schematized picture does
not bear up. A detailed examination of the contexts and
vocabulary of each of these passages cannot be presented here,
but we accept the conclusions of those scholars who maintain
that nothing in these passages necessitates a postexilic date
for this institution.[326]

In terms of our stated purpose of illuminating urban
institutions *per se* and the concept of the city in the OT, the
Deuteronomy 19 passage is probably the most relevant.[327] It is
this passage which places the greatest responsibility on the
local community and its elders, and thus sets forth a high
valuation of the city. A twofold responsibility is laid on
the community. The prime responsibility is to make available
a place of refuge (*miqlāt*) for the person guilty of accidental
homicide. And, related to this responsibility, there was also
the duty of regulation, so that the privilege of asylum might
not be granted to murderers. This passage is also important
in demonstrating the way in which the old custom of blood-
revenge was not abolished in the urban setting, but indeed
was woven into municipal law.

Wellhausen made the establishment of cities of refuge in
Deuteronomy a logical and necessary result of the policy of
cult centralization: "in order not to abolish the right of
asylum along with the altars, he [the Deuteronomist] appoints
special cities of refuge for the innocent who are pursued by
the avenger of blood."[328] But it is certainly questionable

whether the establishment of cities of refuge was a Deuteronomic innovation. It seems more likely that the law of Deuteronomy was rather an attempt to modify an already existing
institution. It is not to be denied that the rite of asylum
in the OT is connected with the seeking of protection at an
altar.[329] The question seems to be whether the city of refuge
was meant to supplant the custom of seeking refuge at an altar,
or whether it was meant to be a supplement and necessary
adjunct to this old rite. Critics of Wellhausen's position
have pointed out that the altar cannot have provided a permanent refuge for the manslayer, so that there was a practical
basis for the city as a place of refuge even before the elimination of local shrines.[330] Greenberg takes cognizance of the
fact that the altar could not be considered as a permanent
place of refuge and views the institution of the city of refuge
as a means of securing the life of the manslayer for an
indefinite period. He sees, in addition to the security
provided by the provision for a prolonged stay in the city of
refuge, a punitive purpose as well. One of the principal
merits of Greenberg's study is that he takes the parallel
notions of bloodguilt and asylum which were present among other
peoples into consideration.[331] One particular law concerning
involuntary homicide is quoted by Greenberg:

> The man who is convicted of involuntary homicide
> shall, on certain appointed days, leave the country by
> a prescribed route, and remain in exile until he is
> reconciled to one of the relatives of the deceased.
> Then the law permits him to return.[332]

Applying this parallel to the biblical situation, where banishment or exile is never prescribed as a legal penalty, Greenberg thus regards the enforced stay in the city of refuge as
a punitive measure adopted in lieu of banishment and designed
to provide expiation for the guilt incurred in the slaying.[333]
Greenberg concludes:

> It appears, the city of refuge . . . is the necessary
> adjunct to, rather than a replacement of, the local
> altars. The altar gives temporary asylum from the
> immediate danger of pursuit by the avenger; the city
> alone provides for the expiation of bloodguilt which
> every stratum of biblical law associates with homicide.[334]

Greenberg's use of analogies seems justified in view of the
fact that the Israelites had no monopoly on the system of

asylum, nor was it in any way peculiar to nomadic peoples and thus a part of the "nomadic heritage" of Israel. De Vaux observes that the list of cities of refuge in Joshua 20 cannot be traced back to the tribal federation, for the towns are chosen and determined by their geographical situation, not by their attachment to a tribe. He thus concludes that the institution is independent of tribal organization and does not antedate the monarchy.[335] Certainly all of the cities listed were not Israelite cities, at least until the time of David. It is interesting to observe that all six of the cities listed as cities of refuge also appear in the list of Levitical cities in Joshua 21. Since the cities mentioned were reckoned as sacred places by the Canaanites, one might ask what influence the Canaanite concept of the city as being under the protection of its tutelary deity had on the expansion of the concept of the invocation of divine protection at the altar to include the protection afforded by the city as a whole? Could the city itself be thought of as the "sacred" area so that, in a sense, the whole city and not just the altar and temple were considered to be under the special protection of a god? If such a concept was operative, then one might say that the institution of the city of refuge constitutes a "sacralization" of the city rather than a "secularization."

There remains one OT city-type to be considered, viz., the Levitical city. Lists of Levitical cities appear in Joshua 21 and in 1 Chronicles 6.[336] The problems associated with these texts in any kind of *traditionsgeschichtliche* investigation are numerous, and probably cannot all be brought to a satisfactory solution. Our aim here is to ascertain whether there is a functional concept behind this city-type and, if so, what its nature is.[337] For our purpose it is sufficient to note that although utopian features are obviously present in the schematized form of the list, the institution itself has a historical basis. Just as was the case in the instance of store cities, the name "levitical city" should not be taken exclusively as meaning that only Levites lived there. The name rather stems from the fact that there were apparently Levites living there who performed a particular function in that city.[338]

Functionally, the Levitical cities most likely represent administrative and fiscal centers. Mazar and Aharoni are the principal advocates of this functional description of the Levitical cities. Mazar's position is stated in the following quotation:

> Levitic cities are a kind of provincial administrative cities, in which the Levites were appointed 'for all the work of the Lord and for the service of the king;' they were largely responsible for the supervision of the royal estates and the collection of taxes. It seems that the purpose of these cities was different from that of such cities as Megiddo and Hazor--fortified strongholds with military units stationed there, and in the case of Megiddo, chariots.[339]

Mazar draws on parallels for such practice in Egypt and on traditions of Levites being employed in "secular tasks" which are preserved in Chronicles. As an example of an analogous practice in Egypt, he cites the Harris papyrus from the time of Ramses III, which records the estates of the god Amon.[340] Among the cities listed, there are nine in Canaan. According to the payrus, these cities contained storehouses for the collection of tribute from the local population. Each city had a temple which was staffed by priests who were occupied with the cult and with secular administration as well. Mazar sees a link between this Egyptian practice, which continued in operation as late as the twelfth century A.D., and the plan carried out in Israel under the united monarchy to establish Levites in administrative centers.[341]

The biblical basis for this kind of employment of the Levites is seen by Mazar in 1 Chr 26:29-32, which states that they were appointed to:

> . . . outside duties for Israel, as officers and judges . . . (they) had the oversight of Israel. . . for all the work of the Lord and for the service of the king. . . for everything pertaining to God and for the affairs of the king.[342]

Aharoni essentially adopts Mazar's position and adds:

> The Levitical cities were established probably principally as royal Israelite centers near the borders intended for strengthening the kingdom's authority by promulgating Yahwistic worship, national solidarity, and loyalty to the Davidic dynasty at Jerusalem.[343]

Aharoni at first maintained that the Levitical cities served such a function only until the division of the kingdom.[344] But, on the basis of the result of archaeological work at Arad,

he has modified his position and now suggests that the storehouse at Arad, with which the ostraca were connected, may well
have been connected with the service of the Levitical administration in the last days of the Judean monarchy.[345]

While the puzzling nature of the biblical material would
suggest caution with regard to any dogmatic conclusions about
the nature of these cities, Mazar's thesis seems to be the most
satisfactory one yet set forth, and seems best to take account
of the materials which are available.

[1]Sjoberg, *The Preindustrial City*, 4-5.

[2]For summary reports on the major Palestinian sites which have been excavated see D. Winton Thomas, ed., *Archaeology and Old Testament Study* (Oxford: Clarendon Press, 1967) and the bibliographies on individual sites cited therein.

[3]Oppenheim, *Ancient Mesopotamia*, 125-126.

[4]Yohanan Aharoni, *The Land of the Bible: A Historical Geography* (London: Burns and Oates, 1962) 95-96.

[5]Aharoni (*Land of the Bible*, 96) observes that we almost never hear of settlements being besieged in this period. On the defensive function of the tribal amphictyony cf. Gerhard von Rad (*Der Heilige Krieg im alten Israel* (4. Auflage; Göttingen: Vandenhoeck und Ruprecht, 1965), esp. the section entitled "Der heilige Krieg in der Geschichte des alten Israel," 14-32).[Aharoni ("Nothing Early and Nothing Late: Re-Writing Israel's Conquest," *BA* 39 [May, 1976] 55-76), has concluded, on the basis of a thirteen-year, five-tel campaign in the Megeb, that although the size and character of the new thirteenth-century B.C. settlements differed, they were, without exception, unfortified.]

[6]Cf., e.g., 1 Kgs 9:15-19 (Solomon); 2 Chr 11:5-12. Martin Noth (*Old Testament World*, [Phila.: Fortress Press, 1966] 146) observes that in the changed conditions of the Persian, Hellenistic and Roman periods local fortifications were in most cases completely dropped.

[7]Simons, *Jerusalem in the Old Testament*, 51. Samaria is another example of the second type.

[8]Yadin, *The Art of Warfare*, 18-19.

[9]Ibid., 19-20. On the basis of dimensions given by Simons (*Jerusalem in the Old Testament*, 50-51) the following acreage figures can be calculated: Gibeah, ca. 2.5; Tell eṣ-ṣāfi (Libnah ?), ca. 20; Megiddo, ca. 15; Jericho (in the time of Joshua), ca. 7; Tell beit mirsim (Qiryath-sepher ?), ca. 9. Cf. also the similar figures cited by Noth (*Old Testament World*, 147).

[10]For an example of a "water-fort" protecting the water supply of the city Rabbah, see above, 41-42. On the water-works of Jerusalem, Ibleam, Gezer, Megiddo, Etam, Lachish and Gibeon see Noth, *Old Testament World*, 154-158.

[11]On the development of the lime-plastered cistern see W. F. Albright (*The Archaeology of Palestine*, Pelican Books [rev. ed.; Harmondsworth: Penguin Books, 1956], 113). Cf. also R. W. Hamilton ("Waters Works," *IDB*, IV, 813). The preference for fresh water over the staler-tasting cistern water is figuratively described in Jer 2:13.

[12] A notable exception is Jerusalem. [Cf. K. Kenyon, "Israelite Jerusalem," *NEATC*, 232-253.]

[13] See above, 36-38.

[14] Cf. Ludwig Köhler, *Hebrew Man* (London: SCM Press, 1956) 69-70.

[15] Wright (*Schechem* 4) suggests that at the period of its greatest power, Shechem controlled an area of at least 1,000 sq. mi. This large area was managed by the establishment of dependent "cities." In a series of statements in Josh 15:45-47, the Philistine cities Ekron, Ashdod and Gaza are uniquely credited with both "daughters" and "villages." In this case the *bēnōt* may well represent intermediate settlements, between city and village.

[16] Cf. the settlement pattern and the list of major urban centers according to the four longitudinal zones of Palestine in Aharoni (*The Land of the Bible*, 19-22).

[17] Noth, *Old Testament World*, 147-151, esp. the illustration on 149.

[18] Two well-preserved examples of mudbrick walls have been excavated at Tell el Far ah and Jericho. Cf. A. G. Barrois, *Manuel d'archaeologie biblique*, I (Paris: A. Picard, 1939), 175, 177.

[19] De Vaux, *Ancient Israel*, I, 232-233. For examples of Israelite fortifications see Yadin (*The Art of Warfare*, 16) and Barrois (*Manuel d'archaeologie*, I, ch. IV).

[20] De Vaux, *Ancient Israel*, I, 232-233. Tell en-Nasbeh (Mizpah), Megiddo and Lachish are cited as examples.

[21] Cf. 2 Chr 26:9, 15 where the salient is called either *hammiqsō'a* or *pinnāh*. In either case it is fortified with a tower, *migdal*. A pictorial representation of such structures can be seen in the Assyrian bas-relief which portrays the fortifications of Lachish, which is reproduced by Yadin (*The Art of Warfare*, 428-430). In bas-reliefs at Khorsabad, temple-attendants carry models which are generic representations of cities. In appearance the models are precisely alike, a wall in the form of a square which is surmounted by four towers. On these bas-reliefs, see E. Douglas Van Buren ("The *salmê* in Mesopotamian Art and Religion," *Orientalia*, X [1941], 85-86).

[22] De Vaux, *Ancient Israel*, I, 233. He cites evidence for this type wall at Boghazköy, the Hittite capital, and at Mirsin, both in the 14th-13th centuries, and at a slightly later date at Senjirlis and Carchemish. Ninth-century Israelite examples are cited at Samaria and Ramat Rahel. On casemate walls cf. also Albright (*Archaeology of Palestine*, 120-122). [Nancy L. Lapp ("Casemate Walls in Palestine and the Late Iron II Casemate at Tell el-ful (Gibeah)", *BASOR*, No. 223 [Oct., 1976] 25-42) documents casemate walls in Palestine ranging in date from MB II C to the early sixth century B. C.]

[23] Y. Aharoni, "The Date of Casemate Walls in Judah and Their Purpose," *BASOR*, 154 (1959) 35-30.

[24]On the classification of royal cities according to their main function as "chariot-cities," "store-cities," etc., see below, 136-142.

[25]Oppenheim, *Ancient Mesopotamia*, 127-128.

[26]Sjoberg, *Preindustrial City*, 91-92. Cf. also de Vaux ("Tirzah," *AOTS*, 378) and Yigael Yadin ("Some Aspects of the Material Culture of Northern Israel during the Canaanite and Israel Periods in the Light of Excavations at Hazor," *Antiquity and Survival*, II (1957) 165-166) on such divisions in the lower city at Hazor.

[27]Noth, *Old Testament World*, 148. For examples of the glacis see Yadin (*The Art of Warfare*, 323) and Barrois (*Manuel d'archaeologie*, I, 107, 145, 149, 179).

[28]Rabin ("Hittite Words in Hebrew," 115-116) denies the usual connection of the Hebrew/term with the Arabic ḥaula, "round about," which he says is a specifically South-Semitic development of a root meaning "to dance," and can hardly be used as an etymon for the Hebrew term unless a like development can be shown in Hebrew. In place of this Arabic derivation, he suggests a cognate in the Hittite ḥila, ḥēla, "fence, court, halo" and would translate the Hebrew term "ring of fortifications surrounding a wall." However, the most straightforward derivation of ḥēl/ḥêl would seem to be from the verbal root ḥwl/ḥyl, "to be firm, strong" since the ḥēl was a "strengthening" of the city wall.

[29]Cf. de Vaux, *Ancient Israel*, I, 233. Cf. also the LXX translation of ḥēl with *proteichisma*, "an advanced work, an outwork." KB[3], 299, also cites the Syriac rendering of ḥēl with bar šûrā, "son of the wall" and the Vulgate *antemurale*. Cf. the use of this term in Isa 26:1; Lam 2:8 and Nahum 3:8. Gray (*The KRT Text*, 65) sees a cognate in the Ugaritic ḥlm, with an enclitic m, but it is difficult to see any resemblance of meaning in the use of this term in the Ugaritic texts. See *UT*, 125.7-9.

[30]See below, 125-126

[31]This expression is a literary convention for emphasis on the fact that a city was well fortified. Just as the repetition of the phrase "walled cities" does not imply that there were any unwalled cities, neither does this expression imply that there were cities without gates. Cf. C. C. McCown, "City," *IDB*, I, 633. Cf. also the use of this phrase to indicate a certain smugness on the part of cities in Jer 49:31 and Ezek 38:11: "I will fall upon the quiet people who dwell securely, all of them dwelling without walls, and having no bars or gates."

[32]Some particularly interesting gate construction can be seen at Tell en-Nasbeh (Mizpah). See McCown ("City," 634-635) and McCown et al. (*Tell en-Nasbeh*, I [Berkeley: Palestinian Schools of Oriental Research, 1947] 198 and the survey map). Cf. also the descriptions of the gates at Tell Beit Mirsim (Kiriath-sepher or Debir) in W.F. Albright et al. (*The Excavation of Tell Beit Mirsim, III, The Iron Age, AASOR* XXI-XXII [1941-43], 118-119);of Megiddo in G. Loud (*Megiddo II: Seasons of 1935-39* [Chicago: Oriental Institute, 1948]

fig. 105 and accompanying text); and of Hazor and Gezer
(stratum X) in Yadin ("Solomon's City Wall and Gate at Gezer,"
IEJ, VIII [1958] 80-86).

[33]De Vaux, *Ancient Israel*, I 233-234; and Kurt Galling, ed.
Biblisches Reallexikon (Tübingen: J. C. B. Mohr, 1937), cols.
523-524.

[34]BDB, 932; and KB, 884.

[35]Noth, *Old Testament World*, 151.

[36]Cf. also Deut 13:17; Judg 19:15, 17; Esth 4:6; Cant 3.2
and Jer 5:1.

[37]McCown, "City," 636.

[38]De Vaux, "Tirzah," 377. [Avram Biran ("Tell Dan," *BA*
XXXVII [1974] 26-51) reports that the gate complex at Dan, which
he dates at the end of the tenth century, included a protected
square measuring 19.5 by 9.4 meters.]

[39]While instances of city planning seem to be the exception rather than the rule, E. W. Heaton (*The Hebrew Kingdoms*,
New Clarendon Bible, vol. III [London: Oxford University Press,
1968] 35-36) reports that a measure of town-planning can be
seen at Tell es-Sa'idiyeh (Zarethan). He notes that there were
ten almost identical houses on a residential street. [Y.
Aharoni ("Excavations at Tel Beer-sheba," *BA* XXV [1972]
111-127) reports that Beersheba of the United Monarchy was a
well-planned city from the time of its inception. The salient
feature was a street encircling the city, always equidistant
from the casemate wall, with rows of buildings on either side.]

[40]Cf. for example stratum II at Tell el-Far'ah. De Vaux
("Tirzah," 376-378) notes that the houses in the rich quarter
stand in an orderly fashion along well-marked streets with a
uniform pattern for the houses, all of which were constructed
around a courtyard. By contrast, in the poorer quarter, the
houses were smaller and were simply huddled together with no
evidence of planning.

[41]McCown, "City," 636.

[42]Cf. the phrase *bĕḥūṣôt yĕrūšalaim*, which occurs frequently in Jeremiah (33:10; 44:17; 21; etc.) and is usually
translated "the streets of Jerusalem." However, this expression
should be compared with two other expressions in Jeremiah: "In
the cities of Judah and the *bĕḥūṣôt* (LXX = *exothen*) of
Jerusalem" (33:10) and "In the places about Jerusalem (*sĕbîbê
yĕrūšalaim*)" (32:44). These two expressions appear in similar
contexts and probably have the same referent. Cf. also the
Aramaic synonym *bar*. This Aramaic term may be related to the
Sumerian designation of the "outer city" as *URU.BAR.RA*.
Oppenheim (*Ancient Mesopotamia*, 116) describes these "suburbs"
of the Mesopotamian city as containing agglomerations of
houses, farms, cattle folds, fields and gardens which extended
for an indeterminate distance outside the city walls.

[43]Prov 7:8; Cant 3.2; Eccl 12:4, 5. The term is
apparently an "Aramaism." On the Aramaic influence on the
language of Qoheleth, cf. Scott (*Proverbs-Ecclesiastes*, 192).
On such influence in Song of Songs, cf. Norman Gottwald ("Song
of Songs," *IDB*, IV, 421).

[44]Noth, *Old Testament World*, 154.

[45]De Vaux documents an eighteen-inch rise in the street level at Tell el-Far'ah ("Tirzah," 376). Undoubtedly one of the reasons for such a rise was the gradual accumulation of debris which had been thrown from the houses.

[46]Yeivin (*A Decade of Archaeology*, 29) suggests that the presence of a series of large commercial (?) buildings outside the city proper at Hazor, but apparently within a fortified enclosure, may indicate that this "suburb" was assigned to an extraterritorial foreign merchant colony. Due to the ambiguity of the word *ḥûṣ* mentioned above, it could well mean a district outside the city proper.

[47]Cf. the discussion below on "city quarters," and that on the economic areas associated with the city gate. Oppenheim (*Ancient Mesopotamia*, 116) cites the existence of a harbor section in Mesopotamian cities on the rivers. This district functioned as the center of commercial activities and had administrative independence. He also observes that this shows a difference between the *URU* city concept and that of Syria-Palestine, where the foreign merchants could operate within the city.

[48]Sjoberg, *Preindustrial City*, 96-98.

[49]Abdul Jalil Jawad, *The Advent of the Era of Townships in Northern Mesopotamia* (Leiden: E. J. Brill, 1965), 54-55.

[50]Oppenheim (*Ancient Mesopotamia*, 132) observes that the term designating the citadel city is non-Semitic, suggesting alien origin. Wright (*Shechem*, 94) also suggests a foreign origin for the citadel as a fortress-temple (*migdal*). It appeared for the first time in the 17th century, at the same time as the Indo-European migrations. [Giovanni Pettinato ("The Royal Archives of Tell Mardikh--Ebla," *BA*, Vol. 39, No. 2 [May, 1976] 44-52) reports that according to a text from Tell Mardikh (TM. 75 Gr. 336) the EB city was divided into two sectors: the acropolis and the lower city. On the acropolis are located the four administrative centers which are called: "Palace of the City," "Palace of the King," "Stables," and "Palace of the Servants." All four administrative centers are together called *e-MI+SITA*, "Governorship."]

[51]Kathleen M. Kenyon, *Archaeology in the Holy Land* (N.Y.: Frederick A. Praeger, 1960) 262. R. B. Y. Scott ("Postscript on the Cubit," *JBL* LXXIX [1960], 328) shows that the original enclosure wall at Samaria had dimensions in round numbers of cubits, viz., 400 by 200.

[52]Kenyon, *Archaeology*, by 263.

[53]Kenyon, *Jerusalem: Excavating 3000 Years of History* (London: Thames, 1967) 32, 49.

[54]Kenyon, *Archaeology*, 263.

[55]On the correlation between the development of a sharply bifurcated class structure and urbanization, cf. the section below on the social structure of the city.

[56]Cf., e.g., J. W. Crowfoot *et al.*, *Samaria-Sebaste II: The Buildings at Samaria*, 5-8.

[57] G. W. Van Beek, "Samaria," *IDB*, IV, 184.

[58] Cf. fig. 9 in Van Beek, "Samaria," p. 182. See also Noth (*Old Testament World*, 168-169) who cites instances of the burial places of nobility in Bronze Age Megiddo and Gezer.

[59] Peter Ackroyd, "Samaria," *AOTS*, 345. Cf. also 2 Kgs 10:18-28. The case of Samaria is not, however, a unique one in which literary evidence for the existence of a temple has not been corrobrated by archaeological discovery. A similar situation exists with regard to the temple at Shiloh (1 Sam 1:9; 3:3; Jer 26:6, 9; 7:12, 14), the temples in Dan and Bethel (1 Kgs 12:29; Amos 7:13), and even the Jerusalem temple itself, for which we are completely dependent on the rather detailed, but at the same time ambiguous description of 1 Kgs 6-7.

[60] Noth, *Old Testament World*, 176.

[61] McCown, "City," 636.

[62] Aharoni, "Arad: Its Inscriptions and Temple," *BA* XXXI (1968) 25-26.

[63] Ibid., 3-5.

[64] Ibid., 7-8 and fig. 5. The layout of the main buildings remained basically constant through all of the six Iron Age strata.

[65] Ibid., 28.

[66] Ibid., 29-30. He goes on to analyze the role which such border sanctuaries played in the reforms of Josiah, related to the centralization of worship in Jerusalem.

[67] Ibid., 32. He sees likely candidates for such confirmation in the so-called "Solar Shrine" at Lachish, cf. the preliminary report of Yadin (*IEJ* XVI [1966] 280-281).

[68] Cf. 1 Kgs 12:31; 2 Kgs 23:5; 17:9; 2 Chr 28:25. [Biran ("Tel Dan," 40-43) describes a *bāmā* at Dan which had two stages in the Israelite period.]

[69] Deut 12:13-14. Cf. also Noth (*Old Testament World*, 177-178) on the *bāmôt* and their furnishings.

[70] Kenyon, *Archaeology*, 271. The plan of Megiddo is said to bear close resemblance to that of Samaria.

[71] J. N. Schofield, "Megiddo," *AOTS*, 324. Cf. also the discussion of Wright on "fortress-temples" on 361 of the same volume.

[72] Kenyon, *Archaeology*, 271.

[73] Sjoberg, *Preindustrial City*, 88. Cf. David's bodyguard of foreign mercenaries in Jerusalem.

[74] Yadin, "Excavations at Hazor," *BA Reader*, II (eds. E. F. Campbell, Jr., and D. N. Freedman; Garden City: Doubleday, 1964), 202-203.

[75] Ibid., 203.

[76] Four superimposed Canaanite temples were found in the "Lower City." This part of the citadel was not rebuilt after the destruction of the second LB city, according to V. R. Gold

("Hazor," *IDB*, II, 540). At Shechem, the sacred area of the Canaanite citadel was "secularized" by the Israelites who constructed a government warehouse on the ruins of a temple in the late ninth-eighth century. See Wright, "Shechem," 366. Other Israelite citadels are attested at Tell el-Ful (Gibeah), Tell Zakariyah (Azekah), Tell el-Hesy (Eglon ?), Tell Taannach, and Ramat Rahel (Beth-haccherem). Cf. de Vaux (*Ancient Israel*, I, 243-245) and Aharoni ("Beth-haccherem," *AOTS*, 172).

[77]V. R. Gold, "Beth-Shemesh," *IDB*, I, 402. Emerton ("Beth-Shemesh," *AOTS*, 205, n. 14) states that the theory was held at one time that this building was a temple.

[78]De Vauz, "Tirzah," 377.

[79]Cf., e.g., the location of such quarters at Ramat Rahel in de Vaux, "Tirzah," 374, 377.

[80]Sjoberg, *Preindustrial City*, 14-15. [John Gulick ("Village and City: Cultural Continuities in Twentieth Century Middle Eastern Cultures," [ed. I. M. Lapidus, *Middle Eastern Cities*; Berkeley: University of California, 1969] 123) cites factual differences between even the contemporary Western and Middle Eastern rural and urban subcultures.]

[81]C. S. Coon, *Caravan: The Story of the Middle East* (N.Y.: Holt, 1958), 171. The relationship of nomadic groups to the city will be investigated in the following chapter. On the existence of gardens within Israelite cities, cf. Aharoni ("Beth-haccherema," 172) and the statement that "Naboth the Jezreelite had a vineyard in Jezreel, beside the palace of Ahab king of Samaria" (1 Kgs 21:1).

[82]According to the law, urban property was redeemable, but village property was considered inalienable in the same way as the fields. The Levites' property was in a different position, since they possessed no fields. Cf. 94-95 below on the *migraš*, "pasture lands" associated with the Levitical cities. [On Lev 25:29-34, cf. M. 'Arak. 9:3, 5, 7.]

[83]Translation following Gray (*The KRT Text*, lines 110-113, 13). Cf. also Amos 3:6; etc.

[84]The only apparent distinction between these two terms is the one recognized by McCown ("City," 633) who observes that the use of *bānôt* seems to be preferred for non-Israelite cities in Judges, e.g., Judg 1:27.

[85]Myers, "Judges," *IB*, II, 721-722. The possibility of such a confusion here was held by Albright in "A Revision of Early Hebrew Chronology," *JPOS* I (1921) 61 and in his "Earliest Forms of Hebrew Verse," *JPOS* II (1922), 81, n 3. Albright later refuted his own argument ("The Names 'Nazareth' and 'Nazorean,'" *JBL* LXV [1946] 399-400, esp. n. 4).

[86]The early Israelite villages are doubly problematic in this regard according to Kenyon (*Archaeology*, 263-264). These villages were located in the hill country, at some distance from Canaanite cities and at sites which do not present the same thick deposits of successive strata as do sites in flat country.

[87]E.g., during the eleventh century, Arad was a small open village. In the tenth century a strong fortress was erected,

but the settlement around this central fortress was an open
one. Cf. Aharoni, "Arad," 4-5. Kenyon (*Archaeology*, 237)
cites Tell el Fûl (Gibeah) as an example of this type of
settlement. Wolf ("Village," *IDB*, IV, 784) suggests that
cities having two walls may represent the incorporation of
originally unwalled villages or "suburbs." Cf. the two walls
at Hazor, mentioned by Yadin ("Hazor," in *AOTS*, 246-248).

[88] Aharoni, *Land of the Bible*, 94.

[89] Josh 21:12. Cf. also Lev 25:31. Other passages which
indicate a connection of fields to a city are Gen 41:48; Deut
28:3; Neh 11:30; 12:29 (where *RSV* translates "region"), 44; Jer
32:7. Cf. also a similar use of *śĕdēmāh*, "field," in Deut 32:
32:22.

[90] On the extra-urban location of the threshing floor,
specifically just outside the city, cf. Ruth 3:2, 15; 1 Sam
23:1; 2 Sam 6:6; 24:16.

[91] G.R. Castellino ("Les origines de la civilisation selon
les textes bibliques et les textes cuneiformes," *VTSup*, IV
(1957), 120-121) would make *śādeh* mean specifically "steppe,"
to which he would then contrast *ʾădāmā*, the "portion of the
earth where man lives, which he cultivates and works." That
such a contrast is not valid is evident from the passages cited
by both BDB, 961, *śādeh*, 2.a. and KB, 915, *śādæh*, 3.d, in
which *śādeh* means "arable or cultivated land."

[92] Num 35:1-8; Josh 20:7-8; 21:1-42; Lev 25:33-34; 1 Chr
5:16; 6:40-66. For the purpose of our discussion here, we
accept the judgment of de Vaux (*Ancient Israel*, II, 366) that
the Joshua 21 passage should be given priority, the others
being dependent upon it.

[93] H. G. May ("Joshua," *PCB*, 302) suggests that these
verses may represent an editorial expansion, reconciling the
giving of Hebron to the Aaronitic Kohathites in view of the
fact that it had been earlier given to Caleb (Josh 14:14-15).

[94] R. B. Y. Scott, "Weights, Measures, Money and Time,"
PCB, 37.

[95] Cf. Num 18:20; 26:62; Deut 10:9 and esp. Josh 14:4.
Cf. also Ezek 48:17, where the *migrāš* of the city extends only
250 cubits. C.G. Howie ("Pasture Land," *IDB*, III, 675) defines
the term as designating "Open country around the villages to
be used freely in common by the herdsmen and shepherds in the
village." In this sense the word can be compared to the
English word "commons" as designating a piece of land held in
common by the inhabitants of a city. In the Mishnah (Mak 2.7)
the "Sabbath limit" of a city was 2,000 cubits beyond the
city's confines and was provided the same right of asylum as
the area within the city's confines: "As the city grants
asylum so does [all the space within] its Sabbath limit grant
asylum." The translation here is that of Herbert Danby (*The
Mishnah* [London: Oxford University Press, 1933] 405. Jastrow
(*Dictionary*, 730) quotes a Talmudic injunction:"You must not
change a cultivated field (outside a town of refuge) into an
open space (*migrāš*)."

[96] Coon, *Caravan*, 175-176. Cf. the greeting, "Yahweh
keep your going out and your coming in" (Ps 121:8), where

going out from the city to work in the fields in the morning and coming in from the fields in the evening is suggested.

[97]Cf. Chapter I, 12-13.

[98]Cf., e.g., A. J. Reiss, Jr., "An Analysis of Urban Phenomena," (ed. R. M. Fisher, *The Metropolis in Modern Life*; Garden City: Doubleday, 1955) 42. Reiss' observations are not limited to the industrial city.

[99]See below, 127-135.

[100]Cf. W. L. Westerman ("Concerning Urbanism and Anti-Urbanism in Antiquity," *Bulletin of the Faculty of Arts, Farouk I University*, V[1949] 81), who asserts the agricultural nature of pre-Hellenic cities in general. Cf. also Weber (*The City*, 70-73) for a similar characterization of the ancient city.

[101]E. E. Lampard, "Historical Aspects of Urbanization," (eds. P. M. Hauser and L. F. Schnore, *The Study of Urbanization*; N.Y.: Wiley, 1965) 540. Cf. also Baron's critique of Robert Gordis ("Sectional Rivalry in the Kingdom of Judah," *JQR* XXV[1934-35] 237-59) in which he criticizes attempts to explain many conflicts in Israel on the basis of the contrast between town and village on the grounds that he fails to take cognizance of the agricultural base of the Israelite city. Baron's critique is in his *A Social and Religious History of the Jews*, III (N.Y.: Columbia University Press, 1937) 17, 60.

[102]Henri Frankfort, *The Birth of Civilization in the Near East*. Anchor Book (Garden City: Doubleday, 1956) 61.

[103]Johannes Pedersen, *Israel, Its Life and Culture*, I-II (London: Cumberlege, 1946-7) 25.

[104]Barrois, "Trade and Commerce," *IDB*, IV, 678-679.

[105]Robert Redfield, *The Primitive World and its Transformation* (N.Y.: Great Seal Books, 1953) 31-33. Cf. also his article, "The Folk Society," *AJOS* LII (1947) 296-308. [See also E. R. Wolf, *Peasants* (Englewood Cliffs, N.J.: Prentice-Hall, 1966) and G. E. Mendenhall, "Social Organization in Early Israel," *Magnalia Dei*, 132-151.]

[106]Frankfort (*Birth of Civilization*, 62) quotes in this connection a passage from G. M. Trevelyan's *English Social History*:

> In the fourteenth century the English town was still a rural and agricultural community as well as a centre of industry and commerce . . . outside lay the 'townfields,' . . . where each citizen-farmer cultivated his own strips of cornland; and each grazed his cattle and sheep.

[107]Sjoberg, *Preindustrial City*, 110.

[108]Ibid., 122.

[109]Basically, we are speaking here of the Israelite city in its most "fully-developed" form, i.e., the shape which it assumed in the monarchical period.

[110]R. M. Adams, "The Origin of Cities," *Scientific American*, Sept., 1960, 153-172. Cf. also N. P. Gist and S. F. Fava, *Urban Society* (5th ed., N.Y.: Thomas Y. Crowell, 1964) 10.

[111]This term has a considerable background in Syria in the

period preceding the Israelite monarchy. It is used in the
Amarna letters, at Alalakh, and Ugarit. In the MB II period of
"re-urbanization," the rulers of the city-states of Syria and
Palestine created a class of feudal barons on whom they con-
ferred heritable fiefs and privileges. The resultant class
structure was a noble class led by the king, and a lower class
comprising the rest of the free population. At Alalakh, the
lower class was subdivided into two groups, the ḫupšena (ḫupšu)
and the ḫanyaḥena, according to I. Mendelsohn ("New Light on
the Ḫupšu," *BASOR* 139 [1955] 9). At Ugarit, there seems to
have been a social structure analogous to that of Alalakh. In
the *KRT* text from Ugarit there are two terms which denote two
categories or classes of people, ḥpt and tnn. The term ḫubšu
is found in the Amarna letters, and should be compared to ḫupšu
and ḥpt. Cf. *EA* 85.12; 114.21-23; 130.41-43; etc. Pedersen
(*Israel I-II*, 7 n.2) saw in this term at Amarna a social class
of considerable importance, who were not mercenaries, but who
were, in all likelihood, aristocrats. His linguistic arguments
are found in his "Note on Hebrew Ḥofšt," *JPOS* VI (1926) 103-
105. Albright ("Canaanite Ḥapši and Hebrew Ḥofšt Again," *JPOS*
VI[1926] 106-109), in a response to Pedersen's analysis, connected ḫubšu with the Akkadian ḫabašu, the Hebrew ḥbš, and the
Arabic ḥbs, all of which have the meaning "to bind." He therefore suggested that the primary meaning of ḫubšu was a "serf
who was bound to the land." Secondarily, the term referred to
a peasant landholder as distinguished from a serf. Albright's
conclusion was that the Hebrews were familiar with the term in
its secondary application. Albright's analysis is probably
correct in view of the unstable social and political situation
in Palestine which is reflected in the Amarna materials. The
nobles in the Palestinian city-states were losing their power
and authority in the face of a rising tide of dissidence within their areas. In this situation there is an evident increase
in the power of the people. Plots against a ruling prince were
organized by the lower class, by other members of the nobility,
and even by the prince's own family. In this situation, the
word which had meant "feudal serf" in the Canaanite documents
acquired the secondary meaning "freedman" because the "bound"
serfs had acquired their freedom. Cf. Albright, *From the Stone
Age to Christianity*, Anchor Book (Garden City: Doubleday, 1957)
285. [See also D. J. Wiseman, "Alalakh Texts," *IDB Sup*, 16-17].

[112]Cf., e.g., Ex 21:2, 5; Deut 15:12, 13, 18; Jer 34:9.

[113]Gray, "Feudalism in Ugarit and Early Israel," *ZAW* LXIV
(1952) 55. Cf. also his *The Legacy of Canaan* (2d ed. rev.,
Leiden: E. J. Brill, 1965) 236.

[114]The cognate of ḥopšt remained current in Assyria, where,
at the time of Shalmaneser and Sargon, it referred to soldiers
who were not freemen, but bound to the king. In this connection, Pedersen (*Israel, I-II*, 7, n.2) cites an inscription of
Sargon, in which he complains that the corvee has been laid on
the city of Ashur and that its inhabitants have been treated
as ḫubšu.

[115]John Bright, "Hebrew Religion, History of," *IDB*, II,
564.

[116]Gray, "Feudalism," 52. Cf. also Albrecht Alt, "The
Formation of the Israelite State in Palestine," *Essays on*

Old Testament History and Religion, (Garden City: Doubleday, 1967) 258-259.

[117]Max Weber, *Ancient Judaism*(Glencoe, Ill.: Free Press, 1952) 18.

[118]Ibid., the introduction to Weber's thought by Gerth and Martindale, esp. xviii.

[119]Edward Neufeld, "The Emergence of a Royal Urban Society in Ancient Israel," *HUCA* XXXI (1960) 31-53, esp. 39-44.

[120]Jer 4:9; 49:38; Hos 3:4; 13:10; Amos 1:15. Neufeld ("Royal Urban Society," 39) observes that while this class occupied high-ranking military office, Job 29:9 reflects a situation in which they were not exculsively limited to the military. Cf. also *UT*, 2 Aqht V. 6-7 with this text in Job.

[121]Jer 26:11-12, 16; 34:10.

[122]Antonin Causse, *Du groupe ethnique à la communauté religieuse. Le problème sociologique de la religion d'Israel* (Paris: Alcan, 1937) esp. 41. For an analysis and critique of the work of Causse see S. T. Kimbrough (*The Place of Antonin Causse in Old Testament Studies* [unpublished Th. D. dissertation, Princeton Theological Seminary, 1966]).

[123]De Vaux, "Le sens de l'expression 'peuple de pays'dans l'ancien testament et le rôle politique du peuple en Israël," *RA* LVIII (1964) 167.

[124]E. W. Nicholson, "The Meaning of the Expression ʿm hʾrṣ in the Old Testament," *JSS* X (1965), 60. Cf. also de Vaux, *Ancient Israel*, I, 70-71.

[125]In the later rabbinic literature, the expression became a term of contempt for the religiously illiterate, but the expression lacks any such religious connotation in our period. Solomon Zeitlin ("The Am Haarez," *JQR* XXIII [1932] 45-61) argues back from this rabbinic use of the expression and concludes that the word originally applied to the farmers who lived in the villages and thus were ignorant in contrast to the better-educated city dwellers. Robert Gordis ("Sectional Rivalry," 245) also uses the term to designate a rural-urban split, arguing that ʾereṣ has the specialized meaning "country-side," i.e. the rural area. Both Zeitlin and Gordis draw too great a contrast between the urban and rural elements in the light of the agricultural nature of the preindustrial city.

[126](1) 2 Kgs 16:15; Ezek 7:27; 45:22; (2) Jer 37:2; (3) Jer 1:18; 34:19; 44:21; (4) Ezek 22:24-29.

[127]De Vaux, *Ancient Israel*, I, 71. Cf. also Gray (*Kings*, 526) who adopts de Vaux's interpretation and adds to it the fact that Jerusalem, as a royal demesne, was inhabited to a large extent by dependents of the palace.

[128]De Vaux, "'peuple de pays,'" 169.

[129]Nicholson, "The Meaning of ʿm hʾrṣ," 65.

[130]Gray, *Kings*, 522, 648. Gray suggests that the "servants of the king" represent feudal retainers of varying degrees in the crown property of Jerusalem. On this technical use of ʿebed, cf. Curt Lindhagen (*The Servant Motif in the Old*

Testament [Uppsala: Lundequistska bokhandeln, 1950] 62); Jonas Greenfield ("Some Treaty Terminology in the Bible," *Fourth World Congress of Jewish Studies*, I [1967], 117-119); and Ziony Zeivit ("The Use of *ʿebed* as a Diplomatic Term in Jeremiah," *JBL* LXXXVIII [1969] 75).

[131]Gray, *Kings*, 522-523. On the basis of 2 Kgs 23:35 and 25:39, Gray observes that the expression could also be applied to the representatives of the freemen of Judah rather than to the people in general. On this, cf. Alt ("Neue assyrische Nachrichten über Palästina," *KS*, II, 237 n.) and de Vaux ("'peuple de pays,'" 171).

[132]Nicholson, "The Meaning of *ʿm hʾrṣ*," 66.

[133]Cf. 2 Kgs 14:21 and 2 Kgs 23:30. Ernst Würthwein (*Der ʿam haʾareṣ im Alten Testament*, BWANT, 4 Folge. 17 Heft [Stuttgart: W. Kohlhammer, 1936]) has argued that since the word *ʿam* in the expression designates the responsible male citizenry of a country it can also be replaced by the word *ʾanšê*, so the *ʿam-haʾareṣ* of Judah is equivalent to the *ʾanšê yehûdâ* in 2 Sam 2:4; etc. It is further argued that every country has its *ʿam*, and thus, the word *haʾareṣ* can be replaced by the actual name of the country to which it refers.

[134]De Vaux, *Ancient Israel*, I, 68.

[135]Heaton, *The Hebrew Kingdoms*, 38-39.

[136]Causse, *Du groupe ethnique*, 47-48.

[137]Talcott Parsons, *Societies: Evolutionary and Comparative Perspectives* (Englewood Cliffs, N.J.: Prentice-Hall, 1966) 100.

[138]R. B. Y. Scott, *The Relevance of the Prophets* (rev. ed., N.Y.: Macmillan, 1968) 24-25.

[139]Louis Wirth, "Urbanism as a Way of Life," 46.

[140]Sjoberg, *Preindustrial City*, 159. Cf. also Oscar Lewis, "Further Observations on the Folk-Urban Continuum and Urbanization with Special Reference to Mexico City," *The Study of Urbanization*, 491-502.

[141]Sjoberg, *Preindustrial City*, 157-160.

[142]Ibid., 159.

[143]Ibid., 124.

[144]Ibid., 161.

[145]Ibid., 161. [Robert R. Wilson ("The Old Testament Genealogies in Recent Research," *JBL* XCIV [1975] 169-189) gives full documentation for the use of genealogies for political and social purposes in the ancient Near East, drawing considerably upon anthropological literature.]

[146]Judg 8:30; 9:2, 5; 2 Kgs 10:1, 6-7; cf. also 1 Chr 27:32 which speaks of two men "who attended the king's sons," presumably as their tutors. The number "seventy" is probably not to be taken literally, but is no doubt a figurative way of saying "a very large family." Cf. also the inscription of Panammuwa from Zincirli in *KAI*, No. 215.3: "And he killed his father BRSR and seventy of the relatives (*ʾyḥy*) of his father."

De Vaux (*Ancient Israel*, I, 119) believes that "sons" in the passages cited above should be taken in a literal sense and not be interpreted simply as descendants in general.

[147]Ruth 4:16; 2 Sam 4:4; Isa 49:23, and especially 2 Kgs 10:5. With regard to the last passage, in v 6 the "guardians" are referred to as "the great men of the city" (*gĕdōlê hā'îr*). Cf. also 1 Chr 27:32. Contra de Vaux (*Ancient Israel*, I, 119) who maintains that the "sons" in such references should be taken literally, there is the possibility that the "sons" of these rulers were administrative trainees, rather than the biological sons of the monarch. Evidence for such a use of "son" is found, e.g., in a tablet from Shechem, described by Albright ("A Teacher to a Man of Shechem about 1400 B.C.," *BASOR*, 86 [1942] 28-30). This tablet is a letter from a tutor to a member of the nobility at Shechem. One line says: "The children [or "sons," *bānîm*] who are with me continue to learn--their father and their mother every[day a]like am I." On the continuing use of son as a technical term for pupil in the OT, cf. Prov 2:1; 3:1, 21; etc. and Scott (*Proverbs-Ecclesiastes*, 37-38).

[148]On the problem of this relationship, cf. E. R. Daglish ("Ner," *IDB*, III, 536-537).

[149]This phrase is deliberately altered by the Chronicler to read: "and David's sons were the chief officials in the service of the king." (1 Chr 18:17) In the Chronicler's view, no one could be priests except the sons of Aaron, certainly not these laymen. Cf. Myers, *I Chronicles*, 139.

[150]De Vaux, *Ancient Israel*, I, 127. Cf. also Driver (*Notes on Samuel*, 285) who believes that it is not improbable that these "sons of David" were "domestic priests." Driver also notes the custom among the Phoenicians of the use of members of the royal family to fill priestly offices.

[151]1 Kgs 4:11. The appointment at Dor would have been especially important, if Dor served as a principal Israelite seaport as is maintained by Aharoni (*Land of the Bible*, 17).

[152]1 Kgs 22:26-27 = 2 Chr 18:25-26; Jer 36:26; 38:6; 2 Chr 28:7.

[153]De Vaux, *Ancient Israel*, I, 120.

[154]Millar Burrows, "Ancient Israel," *The Idea of History in the Ancient Near East* (ed. Robert C. Dentan; New Haven: Yale University Press, 1955) 105-106.

[155]The idea of a "prophetic word of God history" is borrowed from R. B. Y. Scott in a private communication.

[156]Raymond A. Bowman, "Genealogy," *IDB*, II, 363.

[157]Ibid., 363-364.

[158]Peter Farb, *Man's Rise to Civilization as Shown by the Indians of North America from Primeval Times to the Coming of the Industrial State* (N.Y.: E. P. Dutton, 1968) 138.

[159]Malamat, "Mari and the Bible," 147-150.

[160]Anson F. Rainey (*The Social Stratification of Ugarit* [unpublished Ph.D. dissertation, Brandeis University, 1962] 212) observes that the safeguarding of the family patrimony was

an important feature of the feudal grants made by Ugarit's kings. In most of them the award was confirmed to the recipient's heirs by a clause such as: "No man shall take these fields from the hand of PN or from the hand of his sons forever." *UT*, 15:136.13-17. Cf. also *UT* 1008.15-20; 1009.12-17.

[161]Laws concerning the patrimony are found in Num 36:1-13; Lev 25:13, 25-28; Num 27:8-11. Cf. also Deut 15:1-3 and Lev 25:8-17. As Scott (*Relevance of the Prophets*, 28) suggests:
> The owner held the land as representative of his family; he had the usufruct only, not the right of disposal. The principle at stake was fundamental from the religious viewpoint: 'The land shall not be sold in perpetuity, for the land is mine, and ye are strangers and sojourners with me.' (Lev 25:23)

[162]E. Hammershaimb, "The Ethics of the Prophets," VTSup, VII, (Leiden: E. J. Brill, 1960) 96. Cf. also J. Mauchline, "Kings," 347. De Vaux (*Ancient Israel*, I, 55) thinks that the outcome of the incident may point simply to a case of arbitrary confiscation and does not necessarily include the idea that the property of men condemned to death reverted to the king.

[163]Montgomery-Gehman, *Kings*, 322.

[164]It is interesting to note in this connection that in the several cases where reference is made to adding onto royal estates by purchase, the owner was a non-Israelite. Cf. 2 Sam 24:24; 16:24. On other means of acqusition of property by the crown see de Vaux (*Ancient Israel*, I, 124-125).

[165]Lev 25:29-30. Norman Snaith ("Leviticus," *PCB*, 252) sees the basis for this exclusion in the fact that the jubilee reversion laws are agricultural laws. Cf. also Pedersen, *Israel*, I-II, 88.

[166]Ezek 46:16-17 shows the importance of kinship even for kings. The property of the "prince" in Ezekiel's system is to be considered inalienable and must remain within his family. Property given to royal officials, however, is subject to reversion in "the year of liberty."

[167]von Rad, *Deuteronomy*, 143. Von Rad makes this statement with particular reference to Deut 21:13-29 and 27:20. However, his use of the "extended family" as a criterion for assigning these legal maxims to an early date is brought into question by the demonstration of the continued existence of the extended family in an urban setting.

[168]As de Vaux (*Ancient Israel*, I, 68) suggests, the basic framework of Deuteronomy, of which this law is a part, is largely municipal law.

[169]*Antiquities*, IV.23.

[170]Sjoberg, *Preindustrial City*, 109-110. Cf. also Talcott Parsons, *Essays in Sociological Theory* (Glencoe: Free Press) 171-172.

[171]According to Joachim Wach (*Sociology of Religion* [Chicago: University of Chicago, 1944] 211), status acquired by birth is disposed to favor more rigid class stratification than when the criterion is individual ability, strength, or cunning.

[172] Sjoberg, *Preindustrial City*, 113-114.

[173] The *RSV* translates this term with "nobles" except in Isa 34:12, where it is translated "princes" and in Eccl 10:17 where it is rendered "free men," probably on the basis of the meaing of the root *ḥrr*. Snaith ("Kings," 174) observes that the word *ḥōrîm* means "freeborn, freedman" in other Semitic languages, but that in Hebrew it refers to men of somewhat higher station in life, thus the translation "nobles." The word is probably an Aramaic one, used in the North, and not appearing in southern literature until the time of Nehemiah. It occurs in Jeremiah (27:30; 39:6) but neither of these verses is in the LXX.

[174] In the 2 Kings passage, the deportees are, in addition to the *śārîm*, the *gibbōrê haḥayil*.

[175] On the lateness of *ḥōrîm*, cf. BDB, 359 and S. R. Driver (*Introduction to the Literature of the Old Testament* [rev. ed., N.Y.: Chas. Scribner's Sons, 1913] 533 n). On *śārîm* as urban officials, see below, 122-124.

[176] The Arabic cognate of the Hebrew *ndb* is *naduba*, "to be noble, willing, generous," BDB, 621. In Prov 19:6, the term does not mean a member of the upper class and is translated simply "a generous man."

[177] De Vaux (*Ancient Israel*, I, 69-70) also notes that in other instances these men are called simply *gedōlîm*, "great ones" (2 Kgs 10:6, 11; Jer 5:5; Jonah 3:7).

[178] Sjoberg, *Preindustrial City*, 68. Cf., e.g., the taxation in kind for the support of Solomon's administration, court, and army (1 Kgs 4:7-19). It is interesting to note the situation reflected in the Amarna letters. Egypt, in an urban context in Palestine, cultivated the skills and leadership capacities of her subjects the more effectively to administer and exploit the resources of the region, and thereby sowed the seeds for her own downfall as these subjects became proficient in their art.

[179] 1 Sam 8:14-17. Cf. the prophetic injunctions cited by de Vaux (*Ancient Israel*, I, 73).

[180] Scott, *Relevance of the Prophets*, 31-32.

[181] De Vaux, *Ancient Israel*, I, 68, 73.

[182] For the late and sparse evidence for the application of the sabbatical and jubilee cycles see de Vaux (*Ancient Israel*, I, 174-176). One of the most complete analyses of the jubilee is that of Robert North (*Sociology of the Biblical Jubilee* [Rome: Pontifical Biblical Institute, 1954]).

[183] Emile Marmorstein, "The Origins of Agricultural Feudalism in the Holy Land," *PEQ* LXXXV (1953) 116-117.

[184] Deuteronomic legislation protecting the *gērîm* is found in Deut 12:12; 14:29; 26:12; 10:18; 24:19-21. In 12:12; 14:29 and 26:12, they are listed together with the Levites.

[185] Scott, *Relevance of the Prophets*, 183-185.

[186] P. M. Hauser, "Urbanization: an Overview," *The Study of Urbanization*, 26.

[187]Sjoberg, *Preindustrial City*, 244-245.

[188]Pedersen, *Israel*, I-II, 34-35. Pedersen also observes, on the basis of 1 Sam 20:6, that in a small town, the whole town considered itself one family. In the case of Nob, the city of priests, the ruling family may have been a family of priests (cf. 1 Sam 22:19).

[189]I. Rabbinowitz, "Government," *IDB*, II, 454. Cf. the traditions of Joshua in which the tribe is subdivided into cities and villages rather than into clans and families.

[190]The continuing tendency toward this form of political organization can also be seen in Mesopotamia. Cf. T. Fish, "The Place of the Small State in the Political and Cultural History of Ancient Mesopotamia," *BJRL*, March, 1944, 83-98.

[191]Weber (*Ancient Judaism*, 14) observes that the political constitution of the Syrian-Palestinian city represents a developed stage of urbanism which resembles that of the old Hellenic "polis of the gentes." Contra Westerman ("Concerning Urbanism," 82-83) who maintians that we must distinguish sharply between the type of urban life which developed during the two millenia of the pre-Greek oriental cultures and that which we find in the Hellenic city-states, a distinction which is basically political. Weber's position is probably nearer the truth since Westerman underestimates the political role of the city in pre-Hellenic times.

[192]Pedersen, *Israel*, I-II, 6-7. Canaanite city-state kings are mentioned in Josh 2; 10; 11; Judg 1:5-7; 5:19.

[193]Wright, *Shechem*, 21.

[194]Weber (*Ancient Judaism*, 19) maintains that in the period between Solomon and Josiah, the city elders receded more and more into the background, being completely displaced by the stewards and officials of the king. Our position is that, for the most part, the elders continued to regulate local affairs under the monarchy, except in the capital city.

[195]O. R. Gurney, *The Hittites*, Pelican Book (Harmondsworth: Penguin Books, 1954) 68-69. Cf. de Vaux, "'peuple de pays,'" 171.

[196]ARM, II.16, 75, as cited by John McKenzie ("The Elders in the Old Testament," AnBib, 10 [Rome: Pontifical Biblical Institute, 1959] 395-396).

[197]McKenzie, "Elders," 396. De Vaux (*Ancient Israel*, I, 138) believes, however, that in Mesopotamia, from the archives of Mari down to the correspondence of the Sargon dynasty in the eighth century B.C., the elders appear as the people's representatives but that they were without any administrative functions.

[198]Ezek 27:9. The "elders of Gebal" is equivalent to the "elders of Byblos." See BDB, 148 and Josh 13:5.

[199]McKenzie, "Elders," 396.

[200]Ibid., 396.

[201]Geoffrey Evans, "'Gates' and 'Streets:' Urban Institutions in Old Testament Times," *JRH* II (1962) 5-8.

[202]Ibid., 5. See also Evans' "Ancient Mesopotamian Assemblies, *JAOS* LXXVIII (1958) 1-11. Evans accepts and expands upon the original thesis of Thorkild Jacobsen ("Primitive Democracy in Ancient Mesopotamia," *JNES* II [1943] 159-172). Others who have posited two assemblies in Israel are: H. M. Orlinsky (*Ancient Israel* [Ithaca: Cornell University, 1954] 61); McKenzie ("Elders," 398); Ephraim Speiser ("'Coming' and 'Going' at the 'City' Gate," *BASOR* 144 [1956] 20-23); and Alt ("The Formation of the Israelite State," 231).

[203]*ANET*, 45-46, lines 11.1-2.

[204]Ibid., 11.3-8. According to Speiser ("'Coming' and 'Going,'" 23) the elders here are called the "city fathers" (*ABBA URU*).

[205]*ANET*, 45-46, 11.15-23. On *GURUŠ* as "able-bodied men," see Jacobsen ("Primitive Democracy," 166, n 44).

[206]*ANET*, 46, 11.24-39.

[207]These sources date from shortly after the beginning of the second millenium. For these documents see G. R. Driver and John C. Miles (*The Assyrian Laws* [Oxford: Clarendon, 1935] 376-379).

[208]Evans, "Ancient Mesopotamian Assemblies," 11.

[209]Speiser, "'Coming' and 'Going,'" 20-23.

[210]Ibid., 21. Speiser draws attention to Ruth 3:11 for this meaning of *ša'ar*. He also observes that in this sense *ša'ar* comes close to the Akkadian term *bābtu*, which is common in the Code of Hammurabi in the sense of "district, quarter" and is known to be an extension of *bābu*, "entrance, gate." Cf. the etymology of Babylon in Gen 11:9 and n. 234 below.

[211]Speiser, "'Coming' and 'Going,'" 22. Speiser observes that *yāṣā'* by itself can mean "to go forth to battle"(Amos 5:3; 1 Chr 20:1). He also cites Akkadian literary support for such an interpretation in the phrase: "I constructed siege works against him and the going out through his city gate I made utterly repugnant to him."

[212]Geoffrey Evans, "'Coming' and 'Going' at the City Gate--A Discussion of Prof. Speiser's Paper," *BASOR* 150 (1958) 33.

[213]John Wilson, "The Assembly of a Phoenician City," *JNES* IV (1945) 245. He sees the Egyptian *mw'd* as correctly rendering the Hebrew *mô'ēd*, "assembly, council."

[214]The LXX and Targum of Mic 6:9 contain a reference to the "assembly of the city," a reading which is to be preferred to the MT reading of "and who has appointed it." But this verse gives no information as to the composition of the body.

[215]C. Umhau Wolf, "Traces of Primitive Democracy in Ancient Israel," *JNES* VI (1947) 98-108.

[216]Ex 24:1, 9; Num 11:16, 24-25; Judg 8:14; 9:56; Ezek 8:11.

[217]Wolf ("Traces of Primitive Democracy," 100) cites as an example of such an interpretation that of G. F. Moore

(Judges, ICC, vol. 7 [N.Y.: Chas. Scribner's Sons, 1901] 224).

[218]Pedersen, *Israel*, I-II, 36.

[219]The number seventy is particularly suspect in this regard because of its frequent use as a round number.

[220]McKenzie, "Elders," 401.

[221]Sjoberg, *Preindustrial City*, 221-222.

[222]Pedersen, *Israel*, I-II, 36.

[223]Cf. Wolf, "Traces of Primitive Democracy," 99.

[224]Pedersen, *Israel*, I-II, 36.

[225]McKenzie, "Elders," 405.

[226]McKenzie, "Elders," 405. Cf. Pedersen (*Israel*, I-II, 36) who maintains that "It is a matter of course that they must belong to the *gibbôrê hayil*, the proprietors and warriors who are able to bear the burden of the community." Cf. also Weber (*Ancient Judaism*, 19). Both Pedersen and Weber interpret this term as a technical one designating a class of landed proprietors. The term is probably better understood as referring to the valiant men, the brave warriors, even if they possess no property of their own. The term was then, in its extended meaning, applied to those who were bound to armed service, and having to provide their own equipment, enjoyed a certain standard of living.

[227]McKenzie, "Elders," 405.

[228]De Vaux, *Ancient Israel*, I, 69, 138. As such, the elders are not to be equated with the entire male population in assembly. The elders as the heads of tribal groups became heads of cities as the two became identified.

[229]Josh 20:4; Judg 8:6, 14, 16; Ruth 4:2, 4, 9. Cf. also 1 Sam 11:3-4, where the elders of the city of Jabesh-gilead apparently have the power in an emergency to appoint a leader from the outside. Cf. also the situation in Judg 10:17-18; 11:8.

[230]So Gen 50:7 (Egypt); Num 22:4 (Midian); Judg 11:5, 7, 9 (Gilead); 1 Kgs 20:7; Jer 26:17 ("the land"); 1 Sam 30:26; 2 Sam 19:12; 2 Kgs 23:1 (Judah); passim (Israel); and Jer 19:1 ("the people").

[231]Aharoni (*Land of the Bible*, 259) observes that this list includes southern tribes which had been joined to greater Judah, e.g., the Kenites and the Jerahmeelites. David was thus trying to win over those groups who felt no great affinity with the Israelite alliance.

[232]This is apparently a continuation of the situation which prevailed in tribal organization, in which the elders were not in any formal sense the official representatives of the assembly of the people; rather, they were the assembly itself, in the characteristic manner of regarding a whole as completely present in its most characteristic parts (cf. Ps 107:32). Thus, whenever the assembly was required for some action or decision, yet could not be present, the elders would act for the entire body (cf. Ex 18:12; 24:1-2; Num 11:16; Deut 31:28, 30). There is also the possibility that these "early"

arrangements may, in fact, conceal the later arrangement. The
number "ten" mentioned in Ruth as evidently constituting a quo-
rum of elders, probably reflects a postexilic situation. In
Eccl 7:19 there is the phrase: "Wisdom gives more strength to
a wise man than a council of ten gives a city." Scott (*Proverbs-Ecclesiastes*, 236) concurs with Robert Gordis (*Koheleth--
The Man and His World* [N.Y.: Jewish Theological Seminary of
America, 1951] 269) who sees in this verse a reference to the
council of elders in a Hellenistic city.

[233] McKenzie, "Elders," 389-391.

[234] While the designation "elder" is not used as such at
Ugarit, Rainey (*Social Stratification*, 88, 227) mentions a
group which is called in Akkadian the *awīlu ša bābi*, "men of
the gate." These men represent Ugarit in international nego-
tiations and were empowered to take oaths in the name of the
citizenry of their city. Rainey also would compare these "men
of the gate" with the "judges" and "nobles" who held court in
the vicinity of the city gate (*UT*, 2 Aqht V.5-8). The gate as
the usual location of the urban assembly in the OT, together
with the representative function of these men at Ugarit, certainly suggests a comparison with the OT elders. The term "elder" is also lacking in the Amarna letters, but Pedersen (*Israel*, I-II, 7) believes that the "city lords" mentioned by Rib-
addi, the king of Gubla (Byblos), probably refers to a kind of
elder (*EA*, 138.49).

[235] The translation of this term as "prince" can be mis-
leading in view of the common use of the term in English to
designate a direct male heir of a monarch. C. U. Wolf
("Prince," *IDB*, III, 891) observes that in the OT, "sons of
the king" are quite distinct from the "princes," except when a
king's son has become pre-eminent by some other cause than his
heredity.

[236] KB, 929.

[237] In Num 22:7, the officials from Moab are called the
ziqnê mô'āb, while in v 14 of the same chapter they are referred to as the *śārê mô'āb*. Cf. also Judg 8:6; 5:15.

[238] Pedersen, *Israel*, I-II, 38-39.

[239] J. van der Ploeg ("Les chefs du peuple d'Israel et
leurs titres," *RB* LVII [1950] 43-44) observes that the *śārîm*
mentioned in Jeremiah are sometimes the ministers of the king,
sometimes the heads of important families, and sometimes high
military commanders. He adds that there is no means of establishing with certainty whether they represent one or the other
category in texts such as Jer 26:16. That the elders as a local ruling group retained some degree of independence from the
central authority seems to be implied by the fact that they
did not disappear with the collapse of the monarchy, but are
in evidence in exilic and postexilic times (Ezek 8:1; 14:1;
20:1, 3; Ezr 10:8, 14).

[240] In the list of Job 29:7-10, the terms *śārîm* and *něgî-
dîm* are used in a context which Rabbinowitz ("Government,"
454) terms a "classical description of an urban assembly." He
holds that these terms and others such as *něbîdîm* in Job 34:18
and *něśi'îm* in Josh 22:14 are practically synonyms for the

powerful elders, each emphasizing a particular nuance of the same basic conception. Cf. also Isa 3:14.

[241]De Vaux (*Ancient Israel*, I, 138) points out that we have no proof that there was a *śar hāˤîr* in any place other than in the capital cities. He does allow, however, for an indication to the contrary. We know, e.g., that under Ahab there were *śārê hammĕdînōt*, "governors of the districts," who in turn had *naˤărê* numbering some 232 (1 Kgs 20:15). The *naˤar*, as an assistant attached to a master's service, may here be an indirect reference to the *śārîm* in the communities who assisted the district governors in their responsibility of supplying the king and his court with food, of administering the crown property, and collecting other taxes (cf. 1 Kgs 4:7-28).

[242]McKenzie, "Elders," 390-391.

[243]Cf. Sjoberg, *Preindustrial City*, 244-247. It is interesting to note in this regard that, in the increasing differentiation of function in the monarchy, apparently the first office to become differentiated from that of the king was the military commander, a post which Saul filled with his relative Abner, who occupied an important position in Saul's court (cf. 1 Sam 20:25). Joab, the commander of the army of David, was also a blood relative of his superior (2 Sam 2:18; 1 Chr 2:16). On the continuing place of the military in the organization of the city, Oppenheim (*Ancient Mesopotamia*, 112) notes that according to the cylinder of Sennacherib, the citizens of Ekron fall into two or perhaps three classes: military leaders, nobles, and common people. It should also be noted in this context that at Ugarit, the officers of the higher echelons are occasionally referred to by the term *awîlu ša šarri*, "the king's man" (*UT*, 15:18.17). Foreigners who had no established family ties in Ugarit, but who had entered the service of the king were called *arad šarri*, according to Rainey (*Social Stratification*, 89). There is also at Ugarit an apparent equivalent to the OT term *śar hāˤîr* in the term *rb qrt*, "chief of the city" (*UT*, 1024, rev. 3). The expression *rb ntbtš*, "chief(s) of NTBTS" appears at the end of a list of four "prefects" (*skn*, cf. the Hebrew *sōkēn*, Isa 22:15) from four towns in the territory of Ugarit, where *rb=skn* (*UT*, 1033.6).

[244]Sjoberg, *Preindustrial City*, 245.

[245]1 Kgs 22:26. Cf. 2 Kgs 10:5; 23:8; 2 Chr 34:8.

[246]Cf. especially Neufeld, "Royal Urban Society," 31-53.

[247]Gray (*Legacy*, 240) observes that although this story relates a fictitious incident, it must have been true to life.

[248]Sjoberg, *Preindustrial City*, 247.

[249]Pedersen, *Israel*, I-II, 36.

[250]Von Rad (*Deuteronomy*, 135-136) maintains that the instructions given here represent, in their present form, a weaving together of ancient customs with recent institutions and the mature conceptions of a comparatively late period. According to him, it was originally the elders who performed the sacral operation, and the appearance of the priests, the sons of Levi in v 5, is a later addition.

[251]Cited by Ignatius Hunt (*World of the Patriarchs*

[Englewood Cliffs, N.J.: Prentice-Hall, 1967] 44). Hunt also
mentions a case where the citizens of a city are accused of
burglary and larceny, but declare under oath that they did not
steal the things mentioned. For the references to the Nuzi
tablets, Hunt cites Roger O'Callahan ("Historical Parallels to
Patriarchal Social Custom," *CBQ* VI [1944] 403-404).

[252] T. H. Gaster, *Thespis*, Harper Torchbook (rev. ed.,
N.Y.: Harper and Row, 1961) 364-366. The text in question is
UT, Aqat III.151b-169.

[253] Gaster (ibid., 365) also notes that a similar practice
was current in early Arabian society. With regard to Ugarit,
Rainey (*Social Stratification*, 226) observes that the *mārū Ugarit* (the Akkadian counterpart of the Ugaritic *bn ugrt*) shared
corporate responsibility for the murder of a foreign citizen
within their territory (*UT*, 17.142, 158, 234).

[254] Cf. von Rad, *Deuteronomy*, 97-98.

[255] Cf., e.g., 1 Kgs 22:10. The Hebrew term *gōren* is usually translated as "threshing floor," but as Gray contends
("Tell el Far'a by Nablus: A 'Mother' in Ancient Israel," *PEQ*
[1952] 112) the vicinity of the gate was a most unlikely place
for a threshing floor. He accordingly takes *gōren* in its primary meaning of "hollow, open space" for which he cites the
Arabic cognate *garana*, "to fray, rub." He cites an instance
of the juxtaposition of the gate and *grn* as the seat of judgment in 2 Aqht 5.6-7:

> . . .*b ap tgr*   . . .at the entrance of the gate
> *tht adrm dbgrn*   In the place of the notables who
>   are in the piazza.

[256] Evans, "'Gates' and 'Streets,'" 1.

[257] Mircea Eliade, *The Sacred and the Profane* (N.Y.: Harcourt and Brace, 1959) 25.

[258] De Vaux, "Tirzah," 377. Cf. 2 Kgs 23:8.

[259] Cf. 1 Kgs 21:13. While this phrase does not occur in
the passages where stoning is the sentence in Deuteronomy (21:
21; 22:21), it is nevertheless implied. Cf. also the numerous
references to "an unclean place outside the city" in Leviticus
(14:40, 41, 45, 53) and the reference to "outside the city" as
being the place of disposal of idols in Manasseh's reforms (2
Chr 33:15). The place where the heifer was to be killed in
the expiatory rite of Deuteronomy 21 is specified as a place
"which is neither plowed nor sown," (v 4) which intimates that
not only is the city to be cleansed from guilt, but that the
city's cultivated land is not to be profaned by the shedding
of blood. Cf. Gen 4:10-12, where the shedding of Abel's blood
on cultivated ground leads to the curse. The wilderness is
thus regarded as a profane area. It is interesting to note in
this connection that Tallqvist ("Namen der Totenwelt," 21)
sees the motive for the metonymic expression *EDIN/seru*,
"steppe" being applied to the world of the dead as stemming
from the fact that the wilderness, which began outside the
city's territory, was considered to be an unclean place, and
like the underworld, the residence of evil spirits and demons.

[260] Cf. also Deut 21:2: "your elders and your judges," but
in vv 3,4, and 6, only the elders are mentioned.

[261]Von Rad, *Deuteronomy*, 114. Cf. also Rolf Knierim ("Exodus 18 und die Neuordnung der mosaischen Gerechtsbarkeit," *ZAW* LXXIII [1961] 158-162) who argues that such royal functionaries had both military and judicial competence.

[262]Von Rad, *Deuteronomy*, 114.

[263]Cf. W. F. Albright ("The Judicial Reform of Jehoshaphat," *Alexander Marx Jubilee Volume* [ed. Saul Lieberman; N.Y.: The Jewish Theological Seminary of America, 1950] 61-82); and the earlier works of Albright cited there (77). Cf. also Knierim ("Exodus 18," 162); von Rad (*Deuteronomy*, 114) and Gordis ("Democratic Origins in Ancient Israel," *Marx Jubilee Volume*, 377, n 16).

[264]On other aspects of the reforms of Jehoshaphat see Jacob M. Myers (*II Chronicles*, AB, vol. 13 [Garden City: Doubleday, 1965] 108-109).

[265]Albright, "Judicial Reform," 76.

[266]Von Rad, *Deuteronomy*, 114.

[267]Sjoberg, *Preindustrial City*, 196-198.

[268]H. K. Beebe, "Ancient Palestinian Dwellings," *BA* XXXI (1968) 55. As specific examples he cites the existence of dye vats and loom weights in homes of Iron Age Debir, which attest to dyeing and weaving industries. He also points to the open hearth and underground water system in a house at Shechem which may have been equipment for baking lime or firing pottery. A third example is from Jericho, where several houses had considerably more than a normal number of saddle querns, which he believes may indicate a corn grinding business.

[269]Cf. the expression for factory in Israeli Hebrew, *bêt ḥārॅšet*. The etymology of the Hebrew word *ḥārāš* appears to be rather complex, involving the phoneme merger *š* and *t > š*. Both the root *ḥrt*, "to plow," and the root *ḥrš*, "craftsman," occur in Ugaritic (cf. *UT*, 19.903, 905). Similar roots also occur in Arabic and other Semitic languages (cf. the list of cognates in *WUS* for *ḥrš* and *ḥrt*, 108-109). The root *ḥrt* may be preserved in the *hapax legomenon* of Ex 32:16: *ḥārût ʿal-ḥallūḥot*, "graven upon the tablets." This phrase is duplicated in the Manual of Discipline at Qumran, 1QS 10.6, 8, 11. Cf. also Sir 45:11. In Hebrew, *ḥārāš*, "craftsman," is derived from the root *ḥrš*, meaning basically "to plow, engrave," and is related to *ḥrt* in Ugaritic and to the Arabic *ḥarata*; or alternatively from the root *ḥrš*, which has its cognate in the identical Ugaritic root, and is also apparently related to the Akkadian *eršu*, "wise or prudent." Cf. KB³, 343-345. Cf. also Isa 3:3.

[270]Woodworker: 2 Sam 5:11 = 1 Chr 14:1; 2 Kgs 12:12; 22:6 = 2 Chr 34:11; etc. Stoneworker: 2 Sam 5:11; Ex 28:11; etc. Metalworker: 1 Sam 13:19; Hos 8:6; 13:2; Deut 27:5; etc. Cf. the specialties listed at Ugarit: *ḥrš anyt*, "shipwrights" (*UT*, 170.1); *ḥrš bhtm*, "house builders" (*UT*, 80:1.16; etc.); *ḥrš mrkbt*, "chariot makers" (*UT*, 114.8; etc.) Cf. also *UT*, 903.

[271]For a partial listing, see C. U. Wolf ("Occupations," *IDB*, III, 589). Cf. also the list of J. P. Hyatt (*The Dictionary of the Bible* [ed. James Hastings, F. C. Grant, and H. H. Rowley; rev. ed., N.Y.: Chas. Scribner's Sons, 1963] 58-59).

[272]Sjoberg, *Preindustrial City*, 187-190.

[273]Cf. 1 Chr 4:21. On the head of such a guild as a "father," cf. 1 Chr 4:14. Cf. also Neh 3:8, 31; 1 Chr 2:55.

[274]Cf. laws 188, 189 in Hammurabi's Code, *ANET*, 174-175, and the Sumerian text translated by S. N. Kramer (*History Begins at Sumer* [Garden City: Doubleday, 1959] 15) which reads: "Is is in accordance with the fate decreed by Enlil for man that a son follows the work of his father."

[275]M. L. Geltzer, "The Organization of Craftsmanship at Ugarit," (Russian) *Palestinski Sbornik* XIII (1965) 47-60. Summary in *Internationale Zeitschriftenschau für Bibelwissenschaft und Grenzgebiete* XIII (1966-67) 213. David Weisberg (*Guild Structure and Political Allegiance in Early Achaemenid Mesopotamia* [New Haven: Yale University, 1967]) has argued that craftsmen in this period were not royal property, but independent artisans who formed themselves into autonomous guilds with bargaining power *vis-à-vis* the government. It was only in the less skilled types of labor that the government could impose its will and force men to work. Weisberg bases his thesis primarily on the existence of a text containing an *adû*, or loyalty oath. He argues that if the craftsmen had to work for the crown, there would have been no reason for them to take such an oath, but the king could merely force them to work at the forfeiture of their jobs if they went elsewhere. However, the OT pattern would appear to be closer to the Ugaritic pattern. Weisberg states:

> While in the Old Babylonian period we had agreed that 'Independence--in the sense of the independence of the medieval guild--is unlikely for economic reasons, such as the difficulty of procurement of raw materials and the absence of a market economy,' in the early Achaemenid period--a time of flourishing trade, a money economy, good markets, and a strong merchant class--independence in the sense of the independence of medieval guilds was most likely (103).

[276]N. Avigad, "Some Notes on the Hebrew Inscriptions from Gibeon," *IEJ* IX (1959) 130-133.

[277]W. L. Reed, "Gibeon," *AOTS*, 241; J. B. Pritchard, "Industry and Trade at Biblical Gibeon," *BA* XXIII (1960) 23-29; Pritchard, *Gibeon, Where the Sun Stood Still* (Princeton: Princeton University, 1962) 48-49; Pritchard, "Gibeon," *IDB*, II, 393. Photographs of the inscriptions can be found in Pritchard (*Hebrew Inscriptions and Stamps from Gibeon* [Phila.: University of Pennsylvania Museum, 1959]).

[278]Pritchard, "Gibeon," *IDB*, II, 393.

[279]Pritchard, "Industry and Trade," 25. Cf. also Myers (*I Chronicles*, 66) who suggests that the Gedor of 1 Chr 9:35; 8:31 which is related to Gibeon, may be the one which appears on the jar handles.

[280]Cf. Olga Tufnell ("Seals and Scarabs," *IDB*, IV, 259) who cites the continuing eastern Mediterranean tradition of stamping jar handles, which finally developed into the hallmarks of wine exporters in the Hellenistic world.

[281]Aharoni, "Beth-Haccherem," 174.

[282]Ibid., 174-175 and 184, notes 6-9.

[283]Cited by Aharoni (ibid., 183-184, notes 5 and 10).
The confusion results from the similarity between the letters
w and *r* in the Aramaic script of the period.

[284]David Diringer, "Seals," *Documents from Old Testament
Times* (ed. D. Winton Thomas. Harper Torchbook; N.Y.: Harper
and Row, 1959, 220). In the case of personal names, Diringer
believes them to be the names of the owners of the factories.
Cf. also I. Mendelsohn ("Guilds in Ancient Palestine," *BASOR*
80[1940] 17-21) and de Vaux (*Ancient Israel*, I, 77, 126).
Commenting on the passage in Chronicles, Myers (*I Chronicles*,
30) says: "Here is more than genealogy in the strict sense of
the word; it is rather more of a reference to the founders of
various guilds whose names were associated with localities
where their trade was carried on possibly for centuries." Cf.
also Weisberg (*Guild Structure*, 103) who shows that craftsmen
in Mesopotamia traced their descent to a common ancestor. In
this connection, Genesis 4 is concerned with the origin of
guilds and trades, and transfers them into prehistory. The OT,
in contrast to the rest of the ancient Near East, could scarce-
ly attribute inventions and patronage of individual guilds to
deities, and hence "demythologized" their origins. At Ugarit,
the artisans' patron deity was *Ktr-w-Hss*, who bore the epithet
hyn d hrš ydm, "H of the handicrafts." Cf. Rainey, *Social
Stratification*, 167. The connection of craftsmen with the city
can be seen in Gen 4:21-22, where Cain is both "father" of the
smith and the musician, and, at the same time, the founder of
a city.

[285]De Vaux, *Ancient Israel*, I, 202. R. B. Y. Scott
("Weights and Measures in the Bible," *BA* XXII [1959] 34) believes, on the basis of 2 Sam 14:16, that such royal standards
were already extant in the time of David.

[286]Albright, *Tell Beit Mirsim*, sections 36-40.

[287]Heaton, *The Hebrew Kingdoms*, 37. The city of Debir
covered about seven-and-one-half acres at this time.

[288]B. Mazar, "En-gedi," *AOTS*, 225. Cf. also the citations of later authors who speak of the cultivation of balm in
this region.

[289]Nelson Glueck, "Transjordan," *AOTS*, 438-439.

[290]Heaton, *The Hebrew Kingdoms*, 33.

[291]Reed, "Gibeon," 234-235, 238. A detailed description
of the Gibeon winery can be found in Pritchard (*Winery, Defenses and Soundings at Gibeon* [Phila.: University of Pennsylvania Museum, 1964]).

[292]Heaton, *The Hebrew Kingdoms*, 36-37.

[293]Reed, "Gibeon," 234.

[294]De Vaux, *Ancient Israel*, I, 126.

[295]Aharoni, *Land of the Bible*, 109.

[296]W. H. Morton, "Gederah," *IDB*, II, 361. Cf. also H. G.

May, ed. *Oxford Bible Atlas* (London: Oxford University, 1962) 126 and the map on 63.

[297]C. U. Wolf, "Fuller," *IDB*, II, 330.

[298]H. J. Franken, "The Excavations at Deir 'Allā in Jordan," *VT* X (1960) 388-393 and plates 8-9; and *VT* XII (1962) 380-382. Cf. also B. Rothnburg ("Ancient Copper Industries in the Western Arabah," *PEQ* [1962] 5-71).

[299]Pritchard, "The First Excavations at Tell es-Sa'idiyeh," *BA*, XXVIII (1965) 17.

[300]Sjoberg, *Preindustrial City*, 187-190.

[301]It should be noted in passing that the distinction between artisan and merchant in the OT is often a fuzzy one. Weisberg (*Guild Structure*, 103) notes that the bond between artisans was not merely professional, but extended into the social sphere. Social concern was evinced on behalf of widows of workers sold into slavery, and there is proof for a guild from which money was disbursed for various purposes.

[302]The Hebrew word translated "bazaars" by the *RSV* (cf. the *KJV*, "streets") is ḥûṣōt. Montgomery-Gehman (*Kings*, 329) points out that the Targum, Syriac, and Aquila translate with the plural of šûq.

[303]It is well known that merchants in the ancient Near East were often proteges of their own home government (cf. 1 Kgs 10:29). For a comprehensive study of this subject see W. F. Leemans (*The Old Babylonian Merchant* [Leiden: E. J. Brill, 1950]). Another instance of alien merchants in an OT city is reported in Neh 13:16, where it is said that Tyrians who lived in the city (Jerusalem), brought in fish and all kinds of wares and sold them. On Phoenician commercial agents see J. M. Myers ("Some Considerations bearing on the Date of Joel," *ZAW* LXXIV [1962] 178-90).

[304]Evans, "'Gates' and 'Streets.'" 9.

[305]Weber, *Ancient Judaism*, 33.

[306]Cf. de Vaux, *Ancient Israel*, I, 78.

[307]Marmorstein, "Feudalism," 116.

[308]Weber's contention that the "stone masons" of 1 Chr 22:2 were gērîm and thus royal artisans cannot be maintained. The verse actually refers to gērîm who were forced to do labor as quarrymen. In 2 Chr 2:17-18, the gērîm bear burdens, quarry stone, and act as supervisors, but are differentiated from the foreign and native craftsmen in vv 13-14, who are obviously not under the corvée, as are the gērîm.

[309]Cf. Ex 20:10; 23:12; Lev 16:29; 19:10; 23:22; Deut 24:14. On the status of the gērîm, cf. de Vaux (*Ancient Israel*, I, 74-75) and Pedersen (*Israel*, I-II, 40-42). Pedersen is quite specific in stating that the gērîm alluded to in the legal passages cannot be identified with the Aramean merchants who were established in the bazaars in Samaria.

[310]McCown, "City," 636.

[311]1 Kgs 9:19. On the translation "horses" instead of the *RSV* "horsemen," see W. R. Arnold ("The Word prš in the

Old Testament," *JBL* XXIV [1905] 45-53).

[312]Gen 41:35, 48 (in Egypt); Ex 1:11 (in Egypt); 1 Kgs 9:19, cf. 2 Chr 8:4, 6 (Solomonic); 2 Chr 16:4 (in Naphtali, associated with Baasha); 2 Chr 17:12 (Judean, built by Jehoshaphat) and 2 Chr 32:28 (associated with Hezekiah).

[313]H. N. Richardson, "Store-Cities," *IDB*, IV, 447.

[314]Wright, *Shechem* , 147. KB, 542, compares the Hebrew word with the Akkadian verb *šakānu*, "to store up" and to the noun *maškanu*, "magazine."

[315]Cf. Martin Noth, *The History of Israel* (2nd ed., N.Y.: Harper and Row, 1958), 210. The Samaria ostraca are concerned with the delivery of wine and oil due to the king. These ostraca were found in a room that may have been a store room of the type built by Hezekiah (2 Chr 32:28). Cf. J. N. Schofield, "Inscribed Potsherds from Samaria," in *Documents from Old Testament Times*, 204- 208. Cf. also the Arad ostraca, some of which are receipts for goods distributed from the royal storehouse at Arad. See Aharoni, "Hebrew Ostraca from Tel Arad," *IEJ* XVI (1966) 1-7.

[316]Cf., e.g., the list of administrative centers in Judah constructed by de Vaux on the basis of the province lists of Josh 15; 18:21-28 (*Ancient Israel*, I, 136). Aharoni has an interesting thesis regarding the royal seal impressions which bear the phrase *lmlk* and one of the four place names, Hebron, Sochoh, Ziph, and the unidentified *mmšt*. Instead of interpreting these impressions as the marks of royal potteries in the four towns mentioned, he believes that the four names represent new administrative centers where tribute was to be concentrated, or, in biblical terminology: store cities. The reorganization of tax-collecting procedures and concentration of tribute in kind at four main cities is a move attributed to Hezekiah, and may be alluded to in 2 Chr. 32:27-29. This represented a simplification of a complex system (*Land of the Bible*, 340). However, a difficulty in Aharoni's explanation of the seals, is that it fails to account for the dispersal of the seals throughout the towns of Judah. The thesis that the seals are the hallmarks of royal potteries, on the other hand, is not invalidated by this dispersal. Cf. David Diringer, "The Royal Jar-Handle Stamps of Ancient Judah," *BA* XII (1949) 70-86.

[317]Emerton, "Beth-Shemesh," 202. It is interesting to note that these dimensions, when converted to the long cubit of 518-520 mm., would give a silo of the dimensions 11 by 12.5 by 14.5 cubits.

[318]G. E. Wright, "Judean Lachish," *BAR*, II, 303.

[319]Wright, "Shechem," 366; Diringer, "Mizpah," 334; Yadin, "Hazor," 254-255. Gray (*The KRT Text*, 38) finds evidence for such structures at Ugarit in lines 81-82.of the KRT text: *ʿdb akl lqryt / ḥṭt lbt ḥbr*. The term *qryt* regularly means "city" but it may also be a cognate of the Akkadian *qarîtu* , "granary," to which Gray would compare the expression *bêt ḥāber* in Prov 21:9; 25:24. Other terms for "granary" or "storehouse" are listed by Richardson (Granary," *IDB*, II, 469).

[320] De Vaux, *Ancient Israel*, I, 223.

[321] The extensive stable complex at Megiddo, described by Wright ("The Discoveries at Megiddo, 1935-39," *BAR*, II, 235-239), is now assigned to the period of Ahab. This does not exclude the possibility that Solomonic Megiddo also had stables, but they are not the excavated ones. Cf. Yadin, "New Light on Solomon's Megiddo," *BAR*, II, 240-247. [Pritchard ("The Megiddo Stables: A Reassessment," *NEATC*, 268-276) sees the Megiddo "stable" complex as storehouses or barracks. Yadin ("The Megiddo Stables," *Magnalia Dei*, 249-252) has now questioned Pritchard's reassessment.]

[322] 2 Chr 11:11-12. Cf. also the reference to Jehoshaphat in 17:12.

[323] The *ʿîr hammĕlûkāh* of 2 Sam 12:26 is probably to be read as *ʿîr hammayim*. Cf. *BHK*.

[324] *Seren* is the OT term used exclusively for the "lord" or king of one of the five independent Philistine cities. On the political organization of the Philistines cf. Alt, "The Formation of the Israelite State," 225-228.

[325] De Vaux, *Ancient Israel*, I, 161-162.

[326] Cf. Moshe Greenberg ("The Biblical Concept of Asylum," *JBL* LXXVIII [1959] 125-132); de Vaux, *Ancient Israel*, I, 161-163); Bright ("Joshua," *IB*, II, 648); and Albright (*Archaeology and the Religion of Israel* [2nd ed. rev., Baltimore: Johns Hopkins Press, 1946] 121-123).

[327] In its present form, the Deuteronomy passage may well represent the earliest stratum. There are retouchings in the Josh. passage which are dependent upon the Numbers and Deuteronomy passages. Cf. Noth, *Das Buch Joshua*, HAT, vol. 7 (2d ed., Tübingen: J.C.B. Mohr, 1953) 97.

[328] Julius Wellhausen, *Prolegomena to the History of Israel* (Edinburgh: T. and T. Clark, 1885) 33. Quoted by Greenberg ("Asylum," 126).

[329] Cf. 1 Kgs 1:50-51; 2:28.

[330] Cf. von Rad (*Deuteronomy*, 128); Greenberg ("Asylum," 127-129); and the works cited by Greenberg in n. 6, 126. De Vaux (*Ancient Israel*, I, 162) seems to retain Wellhausen's position.

[331] Von Rad (*Deuteronomy*, 127) mentions such parallels, but does not deal with them in his explanation. Cf. also Greenberg, "City of Refuge," *IDB*, I, 638-639.

[332] Demosthenes, *Against Aristocrates*, XXIII.72. Quoted by Greenberg ("Asylum," 128).

[333] Greenberg, "Asylum," 128-130. Cf. the examples cited on 129 which refer to the punitive character of this detention.

[334] Ibid., 130.

[335] De Vaux, *Ancient Israel*, I, 162-163. De Vaux does not believe that the list of cities can be dated before Solomon. Albright (*Archaeology and the Religion of Israel*, 121-123) however, assigns the list to the time of David.

[336]The juxtaposition of the list of Joshua 21 with the list of cities of refuge in chap. 20 is interesting, but there is no apparent functional relationship between the two city-types.

[337]The lists are dealt with in respect to date, historical reliability, etc. by Alt ("Bemerkungen zu einigen judäischen Ortslisten des Alten Testaments," *KS*, II, 289-305). Cf. also Haran ("Levitical Cities: Utopia and Historical Reality," *Tarbiṣ*, XXVII[1957-58] 421-39 [in Hebrew with an English summary]); and de Vaux (*Ancient Israel*, I, 366-367).

[338]Such an explanation may also be applicable to Nob, "the city of priests" (1 Sam 22:19).

[339]B. Mazar, "The Cities of the Priests and Levites," VT Sup, VII (Leiden: E. J. Brill, 1960) 202.

[340]Cf. the extracts from this document in *ANET*, 260-262.

[341]Mazar, "Cities of the Priests and Levites," 205.

[342]Cf. Myers (*I Chronicles*, 181-183) who believes that the Levitical cities were administrative and fiscal centers, but maintains that the practice assigned to David is anachronistic.

[343]Aharoni, *Land of the Bible*, 273 and the list on 270-272.

[344]Ibid., 272.

[345]Aharoni, "Hebrew Ostraca," 1-7. Cf. also Aharoni, "Arad," 11-13.

CHAPTER IV

URBANIZATION IN THE OLD TESTAMENT

AND THE ISRAELITE VALUATION OF THE CITY

This chapter has two principal foci: (1) a survey of some of the more salient historical aspects of urbanization in the OT, including a brief sketch of urbanization in the ancient Near East before the formation of the Israelite state; and (2) an analysis of the Israelite valuation of the city as it is reflected in the various traditions of the OT, with special attention given to the prophetic traditions.

Pre-Israelite Urbanization in the Ancient Near East

A comprehensive survey of urbanization in the ancient Near East is obviously not within the range of this study, but for our purpose it will suffice to set forth some of the salient points in this historical process as it unfolded in that part of the world, particularly in Palestine, where the Bronze Age Canaanite cities constituted the forerunners of the Israelite cities.

The beginnings of urbanization are quite obscure, and of course the date assigned to the origins of this socio-historical process is dependent upon which set of criteria one adopts as being definitive of the city. Adopting the criteria which were provisionally outlined in our first chapter, we can perhaps say, admitting to oversimplification, that the transition to urban life took place somewhere between the seventh and third millennia and might be termed the "urban revolution," using this label to designate the emergence of the distinctive form of life which had its center in the city and which coincides with the transition from prehistory to history.[1] If, however, one accepts the claim that prepottery Neolithic Jericho was not an isolated phenomenon, but rather just one example of the emergence of the city in the Jordan valley area, then the beginning date for the transition to urban life would have to be revised upward considerably.[2]

Speaking of the origins of the city in Mesopotamia, Henri
Frankfort says:

> The differences between the various types of prehistoric
> farmers are insignificant beside the overriding similari-
> ty of their mode of life, relatively isolated as they
> were and almost entirely self-sufficient in their small
> villages. But by the middle of the fourth millennium B.C
> this picture changed, first in Mesopotamia and a little
> later in Egypt. . . It is important to realize that the
> change was not a quantitative one. If one stresses the
> increased food supply or the expansion of human skill and
> enterprise; or if one combines both elements by proclaim-
> ing irrigation a triumph of skill which produced abun-
> dance; even if one emphasizes the contrast between the
> circumscribed existence of the prehistoric villagers and
> the richer, more varied, and more complex life in the cit
> ies--one misses the point.[3]

Frankfort thus implies a circumscribed role for technology,
quantitatively speaking, in the formation of cities. In this,
he is in agreement with Sjoberg. Sjoberg differentiates three
types of societies: (1) folk, or preliterate; (2) preindustrial civilized society or literate preindustrial society; and
(3) industrial-urban society. In this threefold typology, he
views technology as the key independent variable, but technology seen not as some materialistic, impersonal force outside
the socio-cultural context or beyond human control; but technology as a human creation both requiring and making possible
certain social forms.[4]

Lampard has emphasized the fact that definitive urbanization in Mesopotamia was the achievement of social organization
He observes that technological, economic, and even the demographic features of the transition to urban life seem to have
been dependent on patterns of organization:

> To be sure, the appearance of cities on the alluvial
> plain also reflected the greater flexibility and more di-
> verse resource inventory of the riverine setting but by
> Ubaidian times, if not earlier, natural endowment was
> less the 'gift' of nature than a function of human re-
> sourcefulness and adaptive behaviour.[5]

While the first cities to leave historical records appear
in southern Mesopotamia, the transition to this form of social
organization and settlement can probably best be seen in
northern Mesopotamia in the Gawran and Ninevite periods, i.e.
ca. 3500-2700 B.C.[6] In this area at least some settlements of
village complexity gave way to towns of moderately greater
size and complexity. Jawad takes the sites of Tepe Gawra and

Brak as two cases in point. These "towns" occupy little more than 3.7 and 5 acres respectively. This fact is taken as an indication that these sites were at the initial stage of town development, and therefore can best be called townships, or to be more precise, townlets. A township, in the sense in which Jawad uses the term, is considered to be an intermediary form between village and city, a transition between rural and urban life.[7]

As a result of those innovations which were basically social, there appeared in southern Mesopotamia what can be called the city in the proper sense of the term. Since the emergence of the city in southern Mesopotamia corresponds with the transition from prehistory to history and thus the appearance of writing, we should not be too surprised to discover that the first known written documents are concerned with an aspect of the administration of the early cities. These earliest written tablets served the administration of the temple community, one of two interlocking but distinct social institutions of this time and area. The focal institution for administrative purposes was the temple, which actually functioned as the manorial house of an estate, with the members of the community laboring in its service.[8] Each city recognized the sovereignty of the particular god it held to be its owner. This conception not only was spelled out in the society's theology, but it also informed the practical organization of the society, in that the city was seen as ruled by its god.

The characteristic form of the temple which thus served as the administrative center was the artificial mound, called a ziggurat or temple tower. While many interpretations have been offered as to the significance of such towers, the most straightforward one seems to be that of Frankfort, who, instead of considering one or more aspects of the religious symbolism involved in such an "artificial mountain," sees the ziggurat as simply representing the primary notion that a mountain was a very significant religious symbol in the ancient Near Eastern world, and one which is related to the city in important ways, especially as cities were situated on or near mountains which were seen as a normal setting for divine activity.[9]

Under this early system of economic management one would theoretically expect one distinct temple community to have formed the original nucleus of each city, but there is no definitive evidence to verify this; and, in fact, some Early Dynastic period tablets mention cities which are made up of several temples with their estates.[10]

There was, as we have mentioned in the previous chapter, a separation between temple and palace in the Mesopotamian city, corresponding to the economic and the political administrative units. But, as we also remarked, this separation is not characteristic of the Palestinian city, and indeed may have been one of the factors in the development of Jerusalem as a holy city of special importance. In Mesopotamia, however, the temple community was not a political institution, that function being left to the "assembly" and the "elders" of the community. Thus, the idea of the city as a political unit lies close to the origins of the city itself and is of no little significance:

> It is well to recognize the extraordinary character of this urban form of political organization. It represents in the highest degree . . . intensified self-consciousness and self-assertion. . . It is a man-made institution overriding the natural and primordial division of society in families and clans. It asserts that habitat, not kinship, determines one's affinities. The city, moreover, does not recognize outside authority. It may be subjected by a neighbor or a ruler; but its loyalty cannot be won by force, for its sovereignty rests with the assembly of its citizens.[11]

This prevailing tendency toward local autonomy on the part of the city was never really lost sight of in the ancient Near Eastern world and was a factor which was operative even millennia later when the kings of Israel sought to weld autonomous units into a unified state, never with complete success.

While kings did arise in the early Mesopotamian cities, they were city-state kings, and their authority never entirely superseded that of the local assembly. The first ruler to claim sovereignty over the entire land and to establish a dynasty was Sargon of Akkad in the second half of the twenty-fourth century. In attempting to account for the emergence of this broader political unit, Frankfort has suggested that this political ideal was not unrelated to the fact that Sargon and his house were not bound to the traditional viewpoint which

grasped political problems exclusively in terms of the city.
Instead, he holds that it is possible that the Akkadian-speak-
ing inhabitants of middle and northern Mesopotamia had always
acknowledged loyalties which went beyond the city proper.
But, in spite of the attempts of the Akkadian kings for centuries to come, the particularism of the cities was never
overcome:

> At each new succession of a king in Akkad, the land rose
> in revolt. Far from rallying against the barbarians, the
> people attempted to revert to the local autonomy which
> had been the rule before the rise of Sargon.[12]

As a corollary to this tendency toward local autonomy, it
might also be noted that, in spite of forced urbanization policies instituted by kings, there was never an articulate opposition against the city in Mesopotamia. The city was always
accepted as the basic institution for civilized living.[13]

Pre-Israelite Urbanization in Palestine

Urban civilization is witnessed for the first time as a
common pattern in Palestine in the Early Bronze Age culture.
Emmanuel Anati, in his analysis of Palestine before the Hebrews, sees the city as the paramount characteristic of this
age; and in the place of the usual Early, Middle, and Late
Bronze Age terminology, he divides the period into Early Urban
(3300-1850 B.C.), Middle Urban (1850-1550 B.C.), and Late Urban (1550-1200 B.C.)[14]

Before discussing the Bronze Age city, mention should be
made of what might be called a *Vorform* of this city as it has
been excavated at Jericho in both levels of the prepottery
Neolithic community to which the designation Prepottery Neolithic A has been given. The date for the first of the permanent communities at this location goes back to about 7000
B.C.[15] This first community was succeeded by another, still
in the Prepottery Neolithic stage, which continued well into
the sixth millennium.

Whatever else might be said about this community, it certainly bears witness to the importance of an adequate water
source for the establishment of an urban community. Among the
factors which can be used to explain the emergence of this
community, certainly the existence of a large spring at the
site must be considered as one of prime importance.

The continuity of water supply furnished by this spring is demonstrated by the fact that even today, "No other oasis of the lower Jordan valley or around the Dead Sea can be compared to the Jericho oasis."[16] The importance of the spring in encouraging the development of a permanent settlement at this site can be seen even before the appearance of the Neolithic community. In the Mesolithic period, preceding the Neolithic by ca. 1,000 years, remains exist from what Kenyon believes was a temple, built by persons who were in transition from man as a wandering hunter to man as a member of a settled community.[17]

About a thousand years after the establishment of the first permanent structure at Jericho, a community of some complexity is attested, which is described in these terms:

> After the settlement had expanded to its full size, it was surrounded by massive defences, and assumes an urban character. The town wall was a solid, free-standing, stone affair 6 feet 6 inches wide. At the north and south ends as found it had been destroyed to its lower courses, but on the west side it was preserved to a height of 12 feet. At this point the excavated area coincided with the position of a great stone tower built against the inside of the wall, still surviving to a height of 30 feet. It is to be presumed that it was for the purpose of defence, and provision was made for manning the top by a passage entering from the eastern side, and leading to a steep flight of twenty-two steps climbing up to the top of the tower. The whole comprises an amazing bit of architecture.[18]

Certainly, this community at Jericho fulfills many of the criteria which go into the definition of a city. There is evidence for rather dense population. The size of the city was not much different from that of the Early Bronze Age cities, about ten acres according to Kenyon's estimate.[19] On the basis of 240 inhabitants per urban acre, the population would have been about 2,400 or just slightly less.[20] A settlement of such extent and population implies that a successful system of food production had been developed. Because Jericho lies in the rain shadow, it seems reasonable to assume that a system of irrigation was successfully maintained in order to provide water for the large fields which would be required to sustain a community of this size.[21] This, in turn, suggests planning and control on the part of the inhabitants, as do the rather elaborate defensive structures. Here again is witness to the achievement of considerable social organization:

> . . . the evidence that there was an efficient communal
> organization is to be seen in the great defensive system.
> The visual evidence that this provides links with the
> chain of reasoning based on the size of the settlement.
> The expansion of the settlement precedes the building of
> the defences, and thus the need for irrigation had called
> into being the organisation of which the defences are evi-
> dence.[22]

Thus, although several urban criteria find objective verification at Prepottery Neolithic A Jericho, Kenyon has been
taken to task for her application of the term "urban" to this
community.[23]   Childe, e.g., in his criticism of this terminology, contends that in addition to size, heterogeneity, public
works, etc., writing is essential to the categorization of the
city, implying as it does the existence of a highly specialized nonagricultural group that has the necessary leisure to
develop such a complex skill. Above all, he sees the use of a
writing system as the single firm criterion for distinguishing
the city, the nucleus of civilization, from other types of
early settlements.[24]   But certainly, the preconditions for the
development of writing are present at Jericho. Kenyon can
hardly be disputed in her contention that the archaeological
remains of this settlement witness to a high level of social
organization and thus point to the existence of a class which
had been freed from agricultural tasks. There is always the
possibility, especially in view of the extreme antiquity of
Neolithic Jericho, that the community did have at least an elementary system of writing, or at least of numerical notation
(which is what the earliest Sumerian writing was), but that
they wrote on perishable material, and thus the lack of evidence for writing at Jericho is but an accident of archaeology.
If the capacity for organization, with or without writing, is
the essential criterion, then Jericho should be regarded as a
city. But, if one insists on the presence of writing, then
not even the Early Bronze Age communities can be called cities,
for a form of writing was not developed on the Mediterranean
seabord until ca. 2,500 B.C., or halfway through the Early
Bronze Age.[25]   The earliest clear evidence for the use of
writing in Syria-Palestine is from the Middle Bronze Age.[26]

While Jericho is an interesting phenomenon as a *Vorform*
of the later Palestinian city, it does not represent the

beginning of an extended urban stage. The succeeding culture at Jericho, the Pottery Neolithic, is that of a people who lived in flimsy, partially recessed huts, who were probably seminomadic.[27]

It is in the Early Bronze Age that there emerged a developed urban society with many similar cities. In this period, the country began to assume the appearance which it would have in the Israelite era. Most of the principal Canaanite cities were founded at this time and assumed the names by which they were to be known throughout the OT period.[28]

Our knowledge of the Early Bronze Age city is, for the most part, limited to what has been gained through archaeology. The only legible written source extant from this period, concerning Palestine, is a cenotaph inscription from Abydos, Egypt. The inscription is from the tomb of Uni, commander of the army of Pepi I (ca. 2375-2350), and tells of military campaigns in Palestine, which was called the "land of the sand-dwellers:"

> This army returned in safety,
>   After it had crushed the land of the [sand]-dwellers.
> This army returned in safety,
>   After it had thrown down its [i.e. the land's] enclo-
>   sures.
> This army returned in safety,
>   After it had cut down its fig trees and vines.
> This army returned in safety,
>   After it had cast fire into all its dwellings.[29]

This text implies that the population of Palestine was living in fortified cities and practiced the cultivation of orchards and vineyards. In addition to this text, there is a tomb scene of the late Fifth or early Sixth Dynasty (ca. 2400-2300) in Egypt showing the Egyptians making a successful attack on a fortress defended by Asiatics.[30]

What is implied in these Egyptian sources is confirmed by the results of archaeology at a number of sites where the remains of Early Bronze cities have been unearthed. Perhaps the outstanding feature of these cities is the massive walls with which they were surrounded. At EB II Jericho, e.g., the city wall in one phase was 17 feet thick.[31] In an EB stratum at Megiddo (XVIII), a stone city wall was discovered which had an original thickness of between 13 and 16 feet, and was later made nearly 26 feet thick.[32] When discovered, this wall was

still some 13 feet high.[33] Even thicker walls were found at
Tell el Far'ah. Here, walls made of brick on an earth and
stone foundation were at one spot nearly 40 feet thick.[34]
Associated with the walls at Tell el Far'ah, there was a fortified gate with towers projecting from the line of the
wall.[35] A stone wall, about 8 feet thick, enclosing an area
of more than 20 acres was found at EB Arad.[36]

The motivation for the construction of such thick walls
in this period is probably to be seen in the particularism of
the city-state system, in which there was continuous rivalry
between these independent units.[37] There is no evidence, literary or archaeological, that any of the EB city-states in
Palestine achieved hegemony over the land.[38] Such a motivation does not rule out the possibility that such defenses may
also have been designed to provide protection from extra-Pal-
estinian threats, such as the attacks suggested by the above-
mentioned Egyptian document from the Early Bronze Age.[39]

In addition to the city walls, there is also archaeological evidence in this period for other urban structures which
indicate a considerable degree of social organization. At
Tirzah (Tell el Far'ah) there is evidence for city planning,
the likes of which are rare even in much later periods. The
houses of this EB community bordered on straight streets, e-
quipped with drains collecting the waste water and bringing it
into a sewer which led outside the settlement. There is also
evidence for the existence of a small sanctuary.[40] Another
notable structure is the sanctuary at 'Ai (et-Tell) which
seems to have foreshadowed the pattern of Solomon's Temple.[41]
One of the most intriguing urban structures of the period is
the large public structure at Beth-yerah (Khirbet Kerak).
This building covered some 2,500 square yards and had walls
over 30 feet thick. Inside, there was a number of circular
pits between 23 and 30 feet in diameter. The most satisfactory explanation of the function of this building, based on an
analogous structure at Melos, is that it was a public granary.[42] This granary then confirms the existence of social
organization and of an authority capable of extracting a considerable surplus for the support of an urban population.[43]

In attempting to account for the development of these EB cities, it is important to note that the major cities, and those appearing first and lasting the longest, are in the northern and central regions of Palestine. Kenyon attributes this partly to the accidents of archaeology, but also takes account of the preceding history of these regions. According to her analysis, the southern region does not witness the "Proto-Urban" culture and it seems that urbanization spread into the southern area from the North.[44] While Kenyon thus attributes the onset of urbanization in Palestine to an internal evolution, de Vaux et al. on the other hand believe this urban transformation cannot be explained by an evolution on the spot, but that it marks and requires the arrival of a new population group, with new crafts, especially an established tradition of architecture and urban life.[45] While the absence of written documents makes a definite decision impossible, there seems to be evidence for Mesopotamian influence in the onset of urbanization in Palestine, and it is possible that groups who ultimately stemmed from there provided the necessary leadership resulting in the formation of the EB Palestinian cities. De Vaux, for example, believes that the intensive use of brick, even in mountainous regions, suggests an origin in valleys or alluvial plains. Aharoni has observed that the semicircular towers which were set at certain intervals in the city walls of EB Arad, Jericho and ʿAi were similar to those discovered at Uruk in Mesopotamia.[46] Mesopotamian presence or influence in Palestine at this time is demonstrated by a number of seal impressions, particularly of cylinder seals with an animal frieze, which are to be compared with seals found in Mesopotamia dating from the first part of the Early Dynastic period.[47]

The fact that EB Palestinian cities demonstrate a cultural unity with Byblos and southern Syria seems to indicate that the impulse toward urbanization came from that area, which in turn was a mediator of Mesopotamian culture. The most recent evidence in support of the arrival of a new group into Palestine which developed the cities of Early Bronze Palestine has been provided by the excavations at Bâb edh-Dhrâʿ, at the entrance to the Dead Sea Lisan. Paul Lapp has interpreted the evidence from Bâb edh-Dhrâ' in the following way:

> The most satisfactory postulation seems to me to be the arrival of a large non-urban group in the area during the first phase followed by successive increments of closely related people. The introduction of town life during the third phase (ca. 29th-23rd centuries B.C.) may be considered a foreign imposition by an unrelated group. . . (During this period) Bâb edh-Dhrâ' was part of a network of such towns in Palestine established for commercial purposes and attendant security considerations. . . Striking confirmation of the fact that migrations from the northeast continued during the urban phase comes from Khirbet Kerak ware. . .[48]

The development from village to city was apparently a process in which village dwellings rapidly increased in EB IC and were soon enclosed by rapidly expanding defenses. Such a process is witnessed to at Jericho and Tell el-Far'ah, as we have noted. Lapp maintains that this is, however, only the first of two phases in the development of fortified sites. After already extant settlements were fortified, there was an intensification of occupation, but only after a major destruction does evidence of town planning occur, for which EB III Megiddo is cited as an example. Lapp would apply the designation "fortified towns" only to those sites where town planning is in evidence and the unplanned maze of village houses has been clearly superseded.[49]

Wright summarizes the developments of the Early Bronze Age in Palestine as follows:

> We may thus say that the age between about 3200 and 2800 B.C. was the first 'boom' age in Palestine. The great increase in the number and amount of archaeological deposits indicates a rapid increase in population. World trade was underway. . . fortified cities and monumental architecture were erected. . . Sudden acceleration in the arts of civilization is also evident . . . By this time, urbanism has begun . . .[50]

While the EB period in Palestine thus saw the beginnings of urbanization, it also saw urban life come to a rather abrupt end in the last centuries of the third millennium with an ensuing interlude in which city life gave way to a society of seminomadic pastoralists. Evidence for this interlude lies in the fact that there is not a single EB city excavated or explored to date in all Palestine which

does not have a gap in its occupation in this period. Evidence
for the presence of seminomads in this period comes from tombs
which Kenyon has analyzed at Jericho and Lapp has studied at
Bâb edh-Dhrâʿ.[51] Lapp posits a "posturban" phase at Bâb
edh-Dhrâʿ, beginning in the twenty-third century and links it
to the destruction of other Palestinian, Syrian and Anatolian
cities during the course of that century:

> The emerging picture would seem to place the origins of
> the non-urban EB Palestinians in the steppes of Soviet
> Central Asia. The fourth phase of the Bâb edh-Dhrâʿ
> cemetery seems to have its best overall parallels in
> this area, and scattered evidence of migrations may be
> noted along a route leading through Georgia and Eastern
> to Central Anatolia into Syria and Palestine.[52]

The evidence thus seems to point to the fact that newcomers
destroyed the urban civilization of the EB Age and substituted
something entirely different, in which walled cities played
no part at all.

But again, this interlude of about four centuries ended
as abruptly as it began, and the Middle Bronze Age ushers in
another period of urbanization. This period is of special
importance since, unlike the previous urban phase, it continues
uninterrupted, and it is the urban centers formed in this
period with which the Israelites come into contact with their
settlement in Palestine. While we cannot enter into the
history of individual sites in this period, the progress and
extent of urbanization in the MB age can be discerned from
the results of archaeology, supplemented in this period by
epigraphic sources.

With regard to written sources, a most important group
is the so-called Execration Texts from Egypt. There are two
kinds of texts included in this group: an early type which is
inscribed on bowls, known as the Berlin texts, and a later
type which is written on figurines, known as the Brussels
texts.[53] The dating of the texts is disputed, but is somewhere in the nineteenth-eighteenth centuries B.C.[54] For our
pruposes it is sufficient to observe that there is agreement
that the Brussels texts are later than the Berlin texts, and
that the date of these texts falls within the period of
re-urbanization at the beginning of the MB Age. The first
group of texts includes the names of about twenty cities or

regions in Palestine and Syria, together with the names of more than thirty rulers. Most of the names are unknown from other sources, and from this it has been inferred that they represent tribes which had settled in particular areas. This is then coupled with the fact that there are several rulers mentioned for each place, and the conclusion is drawn that the picture is one of a seminomadic society in the process of sedentarization, in which the tribe is still the basic form of social organization.[55] The second group includes sixty-four place names, most of which can be identified. In contrast to the earlier group, here the places mentioned generally have only one ruler.[56] The differences between the two collections of texts thus suggest that they stem from a period of transition, at the end of which there appears the pattern of city-states with their kings.

Just as there is no agreement on the exact date of the Execration Texts, neither is there a consensus on the function they were meant to fulfill. Helck has recently suggested that the texts played a role in Egypt's commercial activity in Palestine-Syria since they name cities that lay along principal trade routes. The texts were accordingly written and broken with the magical intent of keeping caravan routes open.[57] A more likely explanation is that the cities mentioned just happen to be on trade routes, because such strategic sites were the logical choice in the process of re-urbanization. The function attributed to the texts by Van Seters seems to be a more likely one. He contends that the texts reflect a situation in which Palestine was, or was in the process of becoming, the seat of many strong city-states whose kings and princes were in league with each other:

> The names of the kings in the Execration texts allow us to identify clearly the rising power in Syria-Palestine as an Amorite urban society; . . . . These city-states of Palestine presented an increasing threat to Egyptian security.[58]

As was the case in the EB Age, again in this period archaeology testifies to the fact that this period of urbanization was initiated by the appearance of a new group of people who carried with them a background of urban culture. This is indicated by the appearance of new types of pottery, new weapons and new burial customs.[59] Archaeology also shows that in this period there were noticeable improvements in building methods. It is in this period that a method of fortification which continued in use into the Israelite period made its first appearance. This method consisted of surrounding a city with a large mound of earth, whose surface was cemented or plastered to prevent erosion. This sloping type of earthen (*terre pisée*) construction was first identified at Tell el-Yehudiyeh and has been found subsequently in nearly every major Palestinian city of the period.[60] This huge sloping ramp at the foot of the city wall often had a moat or trench in front of it. The logical reason for this new type of defense would seem to lie in the advent of a new type of weaponry, and, indeed, Yadin has set forth the thesis that it was the development of the battering ram which prompted this defensive measure.[61]

Another urban structure which made its appearance at the same time as the new defensive structures is witnessed to at Hazor, Carchemish and Qatna.[62] It consists of a huge rectangular plateau adjacent to the tell, partly defended by topographical features and partly by a beaten-earth wall, still standing to a height of about 50 feet and a width at its base of over 325 feet at Hazor.[63] Equally mammoth is the area included within this enclosure, which is about 180 acres at Hazor.[64] Previous to the Rothschild expedition, it was thought that this area represented a "camp-enclosure," occupied only by temporary structures.[65] The results of this expedition made it clear that this great addition to the area of the city of Hazor represented true urban expansion, for within it were found temples and other buildings on a scale suggesting palaces or public buildings of some type, all dating from the MB period.[66] Yadin concludes that:

> . . . the whole enclosure was inhabited from the middle of the eighteenth to the end of the thirteenth century. The one important conclusion that can be drawn from the fact that the whole area of the enclosure was a real city, is that during the Middle and Late Bronze periods, Hazor was indeed one of the greatest cities in Canaan, and with its estimated 40,000 population justly deserved the description given it in the book of Joshua: 'For Hazor beforetime was the head of all those kingdoms.'[67]

The size of this city exceeds by far that of any other Palestinian city, either in this or a later period. While this large area can properly be considered to be a part of the city of Hazor, it seems likely that at least part of such an extensive area may have been utilized for cultivation. In the light of this possibility, Yadin's population estimate should probably be revised downward. The only cities with such a large population in Palestine were the capital cities Jerusalem and Samaria, which were able to exact tribute from their kingdoms and thus were able to maintain a large population.[68] Certainly, such a large population could not have been exclusively urban in the sense of being engaged in nonagricultural pursuits, for agriculture was so labor-intensive that it took many agricultural laborers to support one man in the city.[69]

It is usually acknowledged that these structures were introduced by an intrusive people who also superimposed a warrior aristocracy on the cities, possibly of Hurrian extraction, but as Kenyon stresses:

> It must . . . be strongly emphasized that though the system of defences was new, the life in the towns within them continued unbroken . . . there was no break in culture. The type of defensive system was something which was superimposed on the other elements of town life.[70]

The Late Bronze Age city-states were, in most respects, the heirs of those of the preceding period. The major change was in the area of urban administration brought about by the rise of the New Egyptian empire. Egyptian control over Palestine had an urban base, but just as in the Israelite monarchy, the interference of the central authority in local affairs focused on the functions of the exaction of tribute and the maintenance of order. Egyptian domination also served to preserve the city-state system in that it discouraged the formation of any alliances between city-states.

A point of basic importance for our study is the decline of urban population in this period. Excavations in many Late Bronze sites have shown a progressive thinning out and impoverishment of the population. It is also significant that few new towns appear to have been founded in this period.[71] The centers of population came more and more to be concentrated along the main branches of the *Via Maris*, while the interior regions were less heavily settled. This pattern may well represent an attempt to escape the urban-centered Egyptian rule.

The Amarna materials reflect this demographic situation and the corresponding political organization in the latter half of the LB Age, a situation which has greatly informed the reconstruction of the pattern of early Hebrew settlement.[72] These Egyptian materials also record certain disturbances in Palestinian cities which were caused by bands of ʿapiru. The discussion of the intricacies of the ʿapiru question would take us too far afield. It is sufficient for our purpose to describe them as groups of persons who have renounced their loyalty to the existing political regime and have become free agents.[73] On the basis of such an interpretation of the ʿapiru, Mendenhall has suggested that the Amarna letters represent a process of the withdrawal, not physically and geographically but politically and subjectively of large population groups from any obligation to the existing political regimes, and therefore the renunciation of any protection from these sources.[74] Thus, whatever else can be said of the ʿapiru, they are certainly associated with disturbances in the social and political organization of the LB Palestinian cities, a disruption caused in part by the progressive weakening of Egyptian control. There can be little doubt that the ʿapiru revolts also had a social basis and might well be compared to a peasants' revolt against the upper strata which were in control of the city-states.[75]

Early Israelite Settlement and Urbanization

With the end of the Bronze Age, we are in the period which saw the beginning of Israelite settlement in Palestine, a period of manifest socio-political instability. The various theories on the Israelite occupation of Palestine can be classified according to three ideal types: (1) the territorial and *traditionsgeschichtliche*, associated mainly with Alt and Noth; (2) the archaeological, associated with the Albright school; and (3) the socio-political type of Mendenhall and his students.[76]

Noth states the position of the first type:

> . . . the occupation was a long process which certainly did not begin with the conquest of cities. On the

contrary, the attacks on isolated Canaanite cities probably did not begin until the Israelite tribes had established themselves in their vicinity, and had gained a footing in uninhabited or sparsely inhabited areas in Palestine. The occupation of Canaanite cities which were situated for the most part on the borders of Israelite territory, may be thought of at the most as the very last stage in the process of occupation, and a coming to terms with the earlier inhabitants after the real occupation was over.[77]

The position of the Albright school has recently been set forth by Lapp:

A wealth of archaeological evidence seems to demonstrate clearly that all over Palestine there are tells that clearly have a characteristically poor occupation after the massive destruction of the Late Bronze site and before the coming of the Philistines . . . in the last half of the thirteenth century. . . The most satisfying explanation of the problem of the destruction of Lachish, Hazor, and other towns similarly destroyed is a concerted effort on the part of a sizeable group of Israelites.[78]

The ongoing debate between these two schools has been a lively one, and the literature stemming from the proponents of these two ideal types has been considerable.

The third type of solution seeks to find a way out of the impasse between the two previous types, which has been created by the problematic nature of the sources for this period coupled with the problem of the interpretation of archaeological data. In outlining his position, Mendenhall points out three tacit or expressed assumptions which lie behind the reconstructions of both the Alt-Noth school and the Albright school. The first of these assumptions is that the twelve Israelite tribes were an intrusive element, entering Palestine from some other area just prior to or simultaneously with the "conquest." Connected with this is the second assumption which pictures the Israelite tribes as seminomadic peoples who seized land and settled upon it during and after the conquest. The third assumption is that the solidarity of the twelve tribes was an ethnic one, and that kinship was the basis of contrast between the native Canaanites and the incoming Israelites. Commenting on these assumptions, Mendenhall admits that the first and third assumptions have some basis in the biblical traditions, but he holds that the assumption that the early Israelites were nomads in "entirely in the face of biblical and extrabiblical evidence, and it is here that the reconstruction of an alternative must begin."[79]

We shall not attempt to discuss the plusses and minuses of the first two types, but shall instead concentrate on the third type of solution, which we feel best takes account of the nature of the process of urbanization and of the Palestinian city itself, with its socio-political structures. With Mendenhall, we believe that early Israel cannot be understood totally within the framework of traditional ideas about a primitive people which gradually became urbanized at the end of a unilinear evolutionary process. The traditional evolutionary schema posits that "primitive man" evolved in the sequence of hunter, nomad, sedentary villager and finally, city-dweller. Most historical reconstructions of the early Israelite period have been bound to the last three stages in this sequence.

In view of the evidence against this concept of cultural evolution which we shall outline below, we shall attempt to show that the theory that sets up a nomadic invasion or infiltration followed by sedentarization and then urbanization is not adequate for describing the relations between early Israel and the Canaanite cities. In approaching the problem of nomadism in the history of Old Testament urbanization, we shall challenge the usual assumption of a universal hostility between sedentary and nomadic groups. As an alternative, we shall suggest that a much closer interaction between town and tribe existed than is generally supposed. An examination of the supposed "nomadic survivals" in the Old Testament will also be important in the context of our analysis of the "anti-urban" traditions embodied in the so-called "nomadic ideal."

An early scholar who spoke out against the traditional idea that village life in Near Eastern culture was necessarily preceded by a nomadic stage was Edouard Hahn:

> In the nineteenth century, when attention was first
> seriously devoted to the economies of primitive peoples,
> these hoary economic states met with little criticism
> from the ideas of unilinear evolution, themselves
> transferred uncritically from biology to human culture.
> Man had begun everywhere it was suggested as a hunter,
> had later learned to domesticate some of his animals
> and so became a pastoralist, and finally rose to the
> stage of agriculture.

Nor were any valid reasons adduced for supposing that pastoralism everywhere preceded cultivation. The German geographer Edouard Hahn performed the valuable service of attacking the dogma of pastoral priority.[80]

Decisive evidence against the theory of cultural evolution from the desert to the sown has been provided in more recent times by Robert Braidwood et al., who, in contrast to the older theory, trace the development of culture from food-gathering to incipient cultivation and domestication, primary village farming communities, and the era of towns. In this sequence there is no nomadic stage posited.[81]

Since this nineteenth-century idea of cultural evolution has thus been successfully challenged by the work of other disciplines, its continuing use in OT historiography is seriously called into question; and one should ask whether a nomadic stage should be posited in the history of the Israelites. Such a stage has usually been posited in connection with two periods--the patriarchal age and the period of the Israelite settlement in Palestine in the thirteenth century. In both instances the model for understanding the historical process has been the sedentarization of nomadic groups.

In seeking to determine the presence or absence of nomadism in the OT, one must first of all recognize the existence of different types of nomadism in the ancient Near East, and with this recognition, also guard against making descriptive statements about nomads which over-generalize on the basis of only one type. De Vaux has described three basic nomadic types. The true nomad or Bedouin, whose name derives from the Arabic term meaning "desert dweller," is a camel-breeder who can live and travel extensively in regions which are truly desert, that is where the rainfall is less than four inches annually. The Bedouin type has very little contact with settled people. The second type, which is usually termed a "semi-nomad," breeds sheep and goats and is thus prevented from living in true desert regions, but instead dwells in the steppes where the annual rainfall is four to ten inches. This type has a good deal more contact with the settled population, since his grazing grounds border on their fields. The third type might be called either a seminomad or a semisettler. This type has added cattle to his livestock and thus further limited his mobility. In addition, this type has taken up agricultural pursuits and may build semipermanent dwellings in village settlements. This third type has been described as having a double social morphology. De Vaux, in presenting his typology of nomadic groups, adds that in addition to these main types there are also intermediate stages and hybrid forms.[82]

Of these various types of nomadism, there can be no question of the existence of the Bedouin type either among the patriarchs or the Israelites of the occupation period. The desert existence of the Bedouin is made possible by the camel, and there is rather conclusive evidence that the dromedary was not domesticated before the twelfth century B.C., and it cannot be supposed that even then the elaborate institutions and customs of Bedouinism sprang up at once.[83] Not only does this fact place in question the use of Bedouin analogies in describing the institutions of the OT; but, in addition, this historical point makes even the analogies drawn from modern sheep-breeders of very limited applicability:

> The modern sheep-breeding tribes studied by modern
> writers are of the same general social type as the
> earliest Israelite groups, but there is a real dif-
> ference. The sheep-breeders of today were formerly
> camel-breeders. They retain the memory and some of
> the customs of that life of liberty in the open desert.
> The Israelites had no such memories, because neither
> they nor their ancestors had ever known this life.
> Besides, in their time, there was no real 'desert
> civilization' to lay down codes of behavior; in their
> eyes the desert was the refuge of outlaws, the
> haunt of brigands, the home of demons and wild beasts.[84]

The extent of the application of the Bedouin analogy to the OT ranges from an outright rejection of any applicability at all to a systematic application of it. Characteristic of the former position is Weber's observation that the collections of ancient Israelite laws show no trace of genuine Bedouin customs and that indeed, the biblical tradition holds that the Bedouins were the deadly enemies of Israel.[85] On the other end of the spectrum stand such works as that of Samuel Nyström.[86] The intent of such studies is to show that the "Bedouin ideal" is reflected in the OT through a compilation of so-called "survivals of Bedouin culture." Examples of such survivals cited by Nyström are hospitality, blood revenge, tribal organization, marriage customs, etc.[87]

While one cannot deny the existence of such institutions in the Old Testament, they need not be interpreted as Bedouin survivals. The principal defect of such interpretations as Nyström's is that they fail to take account of parallels in the general culture of the urban ancient Near East in their attempt to make such practices distinctive marks of nomadic culture and unequivocal evidences of a nomadic background.

An early attempt to apply nomadic ideals to the OT was that of John Flight.[88] Flight's essay was written in a period when efforts were being made to temper some of the sweeping generalizations of the "Pan-Babylonian" school. But, in spite of this mitigating circumstance, Flight's argument fails because of its circular character. He presupposes a stage of nomadism in the Israelite heritage on the basis of data from the OT, and then uses these same data to prove the existence of Israelite nomadism. He also makes the error of assuming that the use of pastoral imagery is a direct proof of nomadic survivals. The traditional language of the prophets, which Flight draws upon in support of his thesis, is a complex phenomenon which cannot be so used, as we shall see in our observations below concerning the supposed "nomadic ideal" in the prophets.

The second type of nomadism mentioned above has been called "ass nomadism." This term has been used particularly by Albright to describe the pastoralism of the early second millennium B.C., that is, the patriarchal period.[89] Albright, along with Gordon et al. have connected the "wandering" of Abraham not with the phenomenon of nomadism as such, but see the ass rather as related to the business enterprise of Abraham, whom they picture as a merchant.[90] It is quite true that the ass was a common transport animal in the second millennium B.C. and that trade flourished across the entire ancient Near East. Evidence of such trade is seen in Egypt in the relief depicting Amorite traders found in the tomb of Beni-Hasan.[91] Not only does Albright assemble an impressive amount of textual evidence referring to this type of caravan trade, but he also calls attention to some interesting phenomena such as Damascus having been called at one time the "land of the donkeys,"

Shechem being inhabited by the *běnê-ḥamôr* and Abraham having donkeys according to Gen 12:16; 22:3.[92] However, both Albright and Gordon have been criticized for their translation of the participle *sōḥēr* as "merchant."[93] While we cannot discuss their arguments in detail here, Albright and Gordon have performed an important service in calling into question the oversimplified picture of the patriarchal figures. Gordon makes the important observation that the fact that the patriarchs "wandered" and owned flocks has beclouded our understanding, for not only nomads but village farmers as well as city dwellers often owned cattle. In this connection, he observes that while Hammurapi's Code takes no notice of nomadism, it does deal with flocks belonging to the settled population, including urbanites. The patriarch's kinsmen in Aram-Naharaim owned livestock, but such passages as Gen 24:10, 13 leave no doubt that they lived in a city.[94]

While there may have been ass-nomads who combined trading and the smith's craft as pictured in the Beni-Hasan murals, it is with de Vaux's third type of nomadism, or a subtype thereof, that we encounter the only type of nomadism witnessed to in the OT. With only the patriarchal narratives as sources, it is almost impossible to state with any precision just what the patriarchs' way of life was. The migrations associated with Abraham need not be seen as instances of nomadism, and the patriarchal narratives as a whole certainly bear the imprint of at least a semisettled life in which the patriarchal groups are activated by what Talmon has termed an "agricultural orientation." Talmon sees the same ideals reflected in the patriarchal traditions as were crystallized in the post-Exodus traditions of the hope of a permanent settlement in Canaan.[95]

In the schematized chronological sequence of the patriarchal narratives, the first mention of agriculture is in connection with Isaac in the land of the city-state Gerar: "And Isaac sowed in that land, and reaped in the same year a hundredfold."[96] Isaac is thus described as a herder of sheep and an agriculturalist. His sons Jacob and Esau were not only brothers, but twins. The former is designated a shepherd; the latter a farmer. The blessing which Jacob

receives in Gen 27:27-28 is appropriate to an agriculturalist.
The herds of the patriarchs are made up of both sheep and
cattle, cattle being specifically mentioned when they are in
Canaan or Edom, implying a more settled state.[97] Jacob's
sons travel with their flocks, but Jacob remains at home
(Genesis 37). Jacob, at one stage of his life, is a shepherd
in the service of Laban, who is a resident in a city or
village. The predominance of either pastoral or agricultural
pursuits seems to have varied with the geography of the area
and the availability and suitability of its land for one or
the other occupation. Mendenhall suggests that:

> . . . the evidence from the Bible and the Mari documents
> strongly suggests . . . that the pastoralist was a
> villager who specialized in animal husbandry, primarily
> because there was not enough tillable land to support
> the entire population.[98]

Thus it appears that the later biblical writers have
described the patriarchs in a way resembling the third of de
Vaux's types or a variant thereof. The patriarchs might thus
be called village-pastoralists. As such they were in frequent
contact with cities, being either within the area of a city-
state or on the edge of its territory. It is with the nature
of this contact and its implications for urbanization that we
are concerned.

Because of the meagerness and problematic nature of the
patriarchal materials, attention has turned in recent years
to the eighteenth century B.C. documents from the Mesopotamian
city of Mari for the illumination of the relationships between
tribal groups and urban centers. While these documents are
of limited applicability in the verification of specifics in
the patriarchal narratives, they are certainly of importance
in illuminating the way in which tribal groups of varied character fit into the city-state political system.

The Mari texts portray a number of tribal groups, their
locations, their movements, their economies and a number of
situations involving them with urban government. The pioneer
in the study of these tribal groups at Mari has been J. R.
Kupper, a pupil of G. Dossin, who, in his *magnum opus*, *Les
nomades en Mésopotamie au temps des rois de Mari*, has collected
and interpreted historical data from Mari. Kupper has

provided important modifications of traditional theory on
Semitic nomadism at a number of points, but he has recently
been criticized for the perpetuation of certain presuppositions
regarding nomadism which have been allowed to color his work.
Kupper's critic in this regard is J. T. Luke, whose work reflects that of his teacher, G. Mendenhall, and in particular
Mendenhall's work on the "Conquest" which we have cited.
Luke attacks three basic assertions of Kupper's work: (1)
Kupper continues the evolutionary notion that nomadism necessarily precedes sedentarization. Thus, for him, the ancient
Semites were "originally" nomads or seminomads. On this model,
the tribal groups at Mari are then classified by him as being
somewhere on a continuum ranging from the "original nomadic
state" to full sedentarization. (2) Conflict between nomads
and sedentary groups is, according to Kupper, the normal
condition; that is, it has to him the character of a universally applicable historical constant. (3) Kupper understands
sociopolitical change in the ancient Near East largely in a
unidirectional framework, i.e., in terms of the impact of
intruding nomads upon the sedentary zone.[99]

One of Luke's prime objectives in his critique of Kupper
et al. is to challenge the theory that nomadic invasion or
infiltration and subsequent sedentarization is an adequate
model for describing the relations between tribal groups and
urban society. As an alternative, Luke proposes a political
model, à la Mendenhall, for the understanding of associations
between these two groups. At the heart of this model is the
attempt on the part of the urban authorities to maintain their
authority and constituency. To do this, they pursued various
policies which affected tribal territorial claims, migration
patterns and tribal independence per se. He criticizes the
traditional evolutionary theory and summarizes his own position in the following terms:

> The three major West Semitic tribal groups of the early
> second millennium B.C., the DUMU.MES Iaminites, Suteans
> and Haneans, cannot adequately be described by the tradi-
> tional theory that all Semites evolved from original no-
> madism to sedentarization.
> The theory creates a sharp contrast between the
> pastoralist and the villager which is untenable. The
> economy of these tribal groups combined village agri-
> culture with sheep pastoralism. . .

The theory also assumes that nomads from the desert or steppe constantly wait to infiltrate or invade the sown and take possession of territory, thus creating a constant conflict with the settled population. This process is not attested at Mari. Our data prove that the DUMU.MES Iaminites and the Haneans were established in villages and specific territories along the middle Euphrates and had claims to pastures. . . the tribal groups were political entities, aligned with local rulers. . . traditional theory applied to Mari evidence has produced a reversal of cause and effect--the tribal groups did not invade the kingdom of Mari; rather the rulers of Mari invaded their territory.[100]

Luke supports his thesis of interdependence between pastoral-tribal groups and sedentary groups by citing numerous examples; the earliest one cited is the Sumerian disputation over the marriage of the goddess Inanna, involving the shepherd Dumuzi and the farmer Enkimdu.[101] According to Luke, this myth also, like later sources, contains clear references to the phenomenon of double land use in which, after the harvest, flocks are allowed to graze the stubble. At the same time the flocks fertilize the fields. This double land use then is a clear indicator of pastoral-agricultural interrelationship.[102]

In those cases where there is hostility between pastoral groups and urban authorities, Luke again questions the usefulness of invasion theories as adequately explaining the process of sociopolitical change. He instead would see the source of conflict in the attempts of urban authorities to extend their authority over village-pastoral groups in ways which were considered repressive by the latter element:[103]

The success of the urban political center in the Near East, in attempting to extend authority over village-pastoral groups is rarely complete. The farther removed in distance and accessibility a given village or pastoral group may be, the less its gain in terms of protection and exchange, and the less its enthusiasm for submission. Since there is always this delicate nature to certain areas of government, the possibility of 'withdrawal' is always present, relative only to the performance and power of the urban center. Furthermore, the very factors which enrich the city and its elite threaten the village. If the economic and manpower drain on the village-pastoral groups is increased, the urban center may appear enhanced to the outsider, including the historian, but since these pressures may easily become oppressive they create, at the same time, the conditions in which 'withdrawal' may be expected. Therefore, the ability to maintain constituency was equally important to the ancient urban center as its position in broader patterns of conflict or alliance with similar cities and states.[104]

Luke's thesis, at this point, bears strong resemblance
to a point of Weber's, who also rejected reconstructions of
the beginnings of the Israelite state which were formulated
exclusively in terms of the conquest theory. For Weber,
external conflict was present, but it was balanced by endo-
genous developments:

> In the plains and on the coast, the military patrician of
> the cities was the enemy against whom the already settled
> and particularly the mountain peasant and seminomadic
> herdsman, at least in West Jordan, had to fight. The
> urban patrician sought through warfare to capture men and
> women slaves, to secure tribute and services, and to
> take . . . booty. In addition they fought for control
> over the caravan routes. The free peasant and the
> herdsman . . . fought not only for continuation of their
> domination of the caravan routes and control over their
> profits, but to defend their freedom from tribute and
> servitude to the patricians. They possibly strove, in
> turn, to conquer the cities, partly to destroy them,
> partly to establish themselves as overlords.[105]

While Mendenhall and his student perhaps claim too much
for their overall thesis, their critique of the usual assumptions regarding the model of nomadic incursion is apt and
incisive, and it may well be that these studies which minimize
the importance of the so-called "nomadic heritage" of Israel
provide a useful key in the reconstruction of early Israelite
history. Admittedly, the information preserved in the OT
about the relationships between Canaanite cities and Israelite
tribes is sporadic and more or less fortuitous. But there
are also instances which imply that a *modus vivendi* was
achieved by the tribes which lived within the area of a given
city-state. Noth, e.g., observes that the tribes of Issachar,
Zebulun and Asher, which were located on the borders of the
plain of Jezreel and the plain of Acco, apparently entered
into a "feudal" relationship with the governments of the
closely spaced cities of the plains. As a result of this
relationship, these tribes probably received a share of the
profits accruing from their rich estates in return for their
services.[106]

There are obvious references to hostility between town
and tribe in the OT. In the schematized conquest narratives
these hostilities are reported from the Israelite point of
view and are directly related to the occupation of the land.
In a critical historical reconstruction, however, such attacks

by the Israelites on isolated cities are better thought of as a coming to terms with the earlier inhabitants of the cities.[107] When viewed in this perspective, these attacks may have been prompted by an attempt on the part of the urban authorities to enact some oppressive measures against a previously independent Israelite tribe. An instance of an attempt to enlarge the sway of an urban center and resulting hostility is preserved in the traditions concerning Shechem in Judges 9. The tradition here records a particular instance of conflict which arose out of a relationship between the tribe of Manasseh and the city Shechem, but it has general significance in illustrating conditions which may well have existed elsewhere and is of help in answering the question of how a city came into Israelite hands. The account first of all presupposes a certain degree of connubium between tribe and city, since Abimelech was half Shechemite. Abimelech was made king by the ruling aristocracy of Shechem. Apparently in an attempt to enlarge the area controlled by his city-state, Abimelech moved his own residence to Arumah and installed Zebul as his "officer" $(p\check{e}q\hat{\imath}d\hat{o})$ or "ruler of the city" $(\check{s}ar\ h\bar{a}\,{}^{\backprime}\hat{\imath}r)$.[108] After a period, however, the Shechemites were incited to rebellion against Abimelech, but together with his mercenaries, he attacked and conquered the city. The ensuing attack on Thebez may have been an attempt by Abimelech to acquire a new center for his rule, but the battle ended in his death. While the specifics of this story are not our concern, this episode is no doubt illustrative of the struggles for power that went on between the Israelite tribes and the Canaanite cities in which a city could become Israelite as a result of a power struggle in which the Canaanite aristocracy was unseated.

In a similar manner Weber asserts that the normal relationship between small-stock breeders and farmers on the one hand, and the urban population on the other rested on contractually fixed pasture and traverse rights. Such a relationship could readily lead to full citizenship and the urbanization of wealthier sibs, be it accomplished by treaty or after violent conflict.[109] Presumably the violation of the contract by either party could result in the outbreak of hostilities.

In seeking to understand the nature of town-tribe relationships in the OT, we should perhaps say something of the
tribal organization found in Israel and its relationship to
the process of urbanization. With Mendenhall, we would assert
that the tribal organization of Israel is not dependent upon
the assumption of an original nomadic background, but existed
independently of such a background.[110] In contrast to the position which sees a necessary relationship between tribal organization and a preceding nomadic stage, together with an accompanying state of hostility between tribe and town, there
are features in Israel's tribal organization which actually
contributed to Israelite urbanization.

In his classic work on *Ancient Law*, Henry Maine posited a
sharp differentiation between two principles of uniting individuals for governmental purposes--the blood tie and the
territorial tie.[111] Maine's thesis has been tacitly accepted
in many of the reconstructions of the early Israelite period
which posit the disintegration of tribal organization as the
necessary result of settlement in a given area. Such reconstructions apparently assume that an original blood relationship bond was replaced by the bond of local contiguity. But,
Noth has shown in his study of the origins of the Israelite
tribes, that they consisted of clans or sibs which settled in
a particular limited area and were not held together by bonds
of kinship.[112] Thus, it would appear that the two principles
of kinship and local contiguity are not of necessity mutually
exclusive. This is the position taken by R. H. Lowie, who
holds that the apparently exclusive potency of blood relationship is seen to be appreciably limited by the recognition of
local contiguity as a basis for political action and sentiment.
In addition, he maintains that:

> Not only do local ties coexist with those of blood kin-
> ship, but it may be contended that the bond of relation-
> ship when defined in sociological rather than biological
> terms is itself in no small part a *derivative* of local
> contiguity.[113]

Thus the clan as a kinship unit in Israel could also be
closely associated with a given locality. An example of this
may perhaps be seen in the old name of Hebron, Kiriatharba,
meaning "fourfold city."[114] In this connection, Malamat has
suggested that the root *ḥbr* in Hebrew is related to the

Akkadian *hibrum*, which is used at Mari to designate a tribal
subdivision.[115] The name Hebron and the older name may thus be
related in the fact that the city was at one time constituted
of a specific confederation of the four tribal sub-groups of
Korah, Tappuah, Rekem and Shema, which are mentioned in
connection with Hebron in 1 Chr 2:43.

The clan, associated with a given locality, was a political unit in early Israel. The tribe on the other hand:

> . . . must be considered as a larger unit of society
> which transcended the immediate environment of an
> individual, usually a village, upon which the village
> could rely for aid against an attack.[116]

The tribe was thus the unit which backed up the administrative
authority of the clan or village, which actually became
practically interchangeable.[117]

The administrative body of the clan, and likewise of the
village and city was the elders. There are some references to
the "elders of the tribes," but we know nothing of any administrative function which they might have performed.[118] De
Vaux points out that the tribes in the early narratives have
no individual chiefs.[119] Thus, administratively, no great
social change was necessary for the Israelites in the development from village to city. An Israelite city could simply be
a former village which had developed into a city by the addition of fortifications, being governed by the same or a similar group of elders. If, as Mendenhall suggests, a process
of "withdrawal" is witnessed to in the early Israelite period,
what may have been involved was a declaration of independence
from the obligations imposed on Israelite villages by the
Canaanite city-states and consequently a surrendering of the
protection afforded by the city in favor of a reliance on
the tribal system for defense. The inability of the tribal
league to provide for this defense may then have been instrumental in stimulating urbanization on the part of these same
villages, in that it encouraged either Israelite "city-building," that is the fortification of villages, or the surrendering of independence in return for the protection and other
rewards afforded by incorporation into the city-state system.
Speaking of this phenomenon of "withdrawal," Mendenhall says:

The observation that Canaan is constantly presented as

> the polar opposite of that which early Yahwism represent-
> ed is best understood under the assumption that the
> earliest Israelites actually had been under the domina-
> tion of the Canaanite cities, and had successfully with-
> drawn. Having become independent, they were determined
> not immediately to reconstruct the same sort of power-
> centered, status-centered society as that which they
> had escaped, even though it was a constant temptation
> (Abimelech) to which they finally succumbed (Solomon).[120]

No doubt one of the factors which tended to draw city and
village together, in spite of yearning for independence, was
the fact that they formed a natural economic unit as we have
noted.

The fact that the Israelite tribal league was not primarily
a political unit was also a contributory factor in Israelite
urbanization. The apolitical nature of the tribal union has
often been noted:

> An Israelite confederacy existed, but without political
> organization. If there was not permanent organization,
> and if the improvisation in case of emergency functioned
> as haphazardly as the Deborah song reveals, 'Israel'
> never can have 'conquered' Canaan; . . . There was no
> political organization because no military effort on a
> national scale had been necessary.[121]

Politically, administration was left to the local level. The
failure of the tribal confederacy to provide for "national"
mobilization in the face of the growing Philistine threat led
to the development of the more complex form of social
organization provided by the monarchy, which operated from
an urban base.

Israelite Urbanization under the Monarchy and the Valuation of the City in the Old Testament

As we have noted, urbanization is a function of social
organization, in that urban growth is highly correlated with
the consolidation or extension of a political apparatus. In
speaking of the preindustrial city in general, Sjoberg says:

> The extension of the power-group's domain, notably
> through empire-building is the primary mechanism for
> introducing city life into generally non-urbanized
> territories. Administrative and military centers are
> required to control newly won territory; undoubtedly some
> of these have been established upon existing village
> sites. Around these settlements cluster artisans,
> merchants and other assorted groups who function to
> sustain the non-agriculturalists. Soon full-fledged
> cities develop. The military and other government
> officials seek in urban living to maximize their

contracts with one another and to take advantage of
the communication and transportation ties with the
societal capital; the small and isolated rural communities cannot perform this function. Even when roads
are built to outlying areas these connect only the
most important cities. These urban outposts, moreover,
are the channels through which is funneled the
economic surplus remitted to the heartland.[122]

Sjoberg's observations are certainly borne out under the
Israelite monarchy, and urbanization as royal policy is attested as well throughout the ancient Near East.[123]

While the monarchy stimulated urbanization in Israel,
there were other factors at work which limited the development
of cities. First among these was the static character of
agriculture which was bound to animate forms of energy and was
so labor-intensive that it took many cultivators to support
even a small urban population.[124] The technology of transport
was as labor-intensive as that of agriculture. Long-distance
transport was thus available only for goods of high value
and small bulk--primarily luxury goods for the elite. Other
limiting factors were the lack of scientific medicine, which
made any concentration of population a health hazard in the
face of infectious disease; the fixity of the peasant on the
land, which minimized rural-urban migration; the absence of
large-scale manufacturing, which would have derived more
advantage from urban concentration than did handicraft; the
bureaucratic control of the peasantry, which stifled free
trade in the hinterland; and the traditionalism of all classes,
which hampered technological and economic advance.[125]

One of the basic aims of the monarchy was to create a
unity out of the many isolated communities, which could then
be controlled by central authority. But the Late Bronze Age
city-state system and the tribal system of Israel which followed it were not amenable to this kind of development. While
the urbanization fostered by royal policy created and tena-
ciously maintained cities which evolved into political centers
of gravity, they in turn evoked anti-centralization reactions
in certain strata of the population. These anti-urban tendencies have to be recognized as social and political facts and
constituted one side of a perennial argument.

One of the first measures adopted by the monarchy to

gain control was the institution of a provincial system which
made use of key cities as stations for district administrators
who were responsible to the crown in Jerusalem. Where cities
did not exist in a given administrative region, they were
founded or rebuilt.[126] This whole process was begun under
David, but he only provided the groundwork for the more
extensive developments under Solomon:

> It seems clear that the material splendor of Solomon's
> reign was concentrated at Jerusalem, where little trace
> of the period is likely ever to be found. There, Phoe-
> nician civilization must have been firmly established.
> In lesser towns much of the old simplicity remained.
> It is true that the remains indicate comparatively order-
> ly towns with a homogeneous type of layout and archi-
> tecture; for the first time since the MB Age there was
> an appreciable number of true towns, instead of straggling
> villages, but there can have been few with any pretensions
> to architectural distinction, and we have no evidence of
> any particular luxury.[127]

City-building continued after Solomon as well, and we
have references to such activity on the part of Uzziah (2 Chr
26:9-10), Jotham (2 Chr 27:3-4), Hezekiah (2 Chr 32:5; Isa
22:8-11), and Manasseh (2 Chr 33:14). Such building activity
was concentrated for the most part in the capitals and in those
cities which were of strategic importance for the given
monarch. It was in these cities that the most important
changes took place. The "industrialization" of which the king
was the principal entrepeneur caused considerable changes in
the economic structure, which in turn brought about the social
pathology.

With the accelerated and more intensive urbanization
which took place during the monarchy, there also arose ex-
plicity anti-urban sentiments. It will be our purpose in the
remainder of this chapter to examine the nature and extent of
such sentiments, particularly with regard to their religious
basis. It is significant that the commitment of these sentiments to writing first appears in the monarchical period as
a product of urban culture.

In many respects the development of religion in Israel
paralleled the developments in the political sphere and should
therefore be viewed in the historical perspective of these
developments. Just as the tribal system of Israel interacted
with the city-state system of the Canaanites on the political

level, so, on the religious level as well, there was an interaction between tribal religion and urban religion.

Religion and the City in the Premonarchical Period

While we cannot treat the extensive subject of religion
in the premonarchical history of the Israelites, it is important to define the essential societal conditions which made
possible the cultural innovation of Yahwism which was originated by Israel in this period. One way of accounting for the
uniqueness of Yahwism has been to place the cultural origins
of Israel in the desert and to make of Yahweh a "nomads' God -
a God of the desert."[128] One of the most convincing challenges
to such an idea is the one developed by Frank Cross, who has
questioned the legitimacy of Alt's analogy between Nabatean
Arabs and ancient Israel on the basis of "Alt's tacit assumption that Israel, like the Nabateans, infiltrated Palestine
from the desert as simple nomads, untainted by the civilization of the settled country."[129] As an alternative, Cross
contends that:

> There seems to be no reason to doubt that these [patri-
> archal] clan or 'social' gods were high gods and were
> quickly identified with the gods in sanctuaries in the
> new land. Sometimes these gods of Patriarchal type seem
> to have been minor 'mediator' gods, sometimes the great
> figures of the pantheon. In either case, the movement
> is from an old culture to a new, an old pantheon to a
> new, not from anonymous gods to named gods, nor from a
> cultural blank into first contacts with civilization.[130]

Such a position is to be preferred to one which seeks to explain the origins of Israelite religion in terms of a radical
distinction between the "personal, intuitive realization of
God" deriving from the desert, and the "mythical, magical and
polytheistic" religion which originated in urban life.[131]

The questions which Graham asks concerning the uniqueness
of Yahwism are basic to our concern:

> Was the distinctive 'Mosaic' Yahwism born in the desert,
> or was it born in Canaan? Did it intrude into a going,
> culturally organized, social process wherein it succeeded
> at once in establishing itself, as a distinctive way of
> life, a functioning pattern of culture? Or did its later
> distinctiveness emerge from a cultural conflict in which
> an indigenous culture pattern was gradually modified,
> through the reactions of deviating individuals, under the
> stimulus of changing economic and political pressures?
> Was it born in the desert and carried into Canaan? Or
> did it come to birth in Canaan and, through its hardly

won sense of distinctiveness, endow itself with a
corresponding sense of its ancestry?[132]

In asking such questions, Graham favors the alternative which
sees the distinctiveness of Yahwism as resulting from a process of cultural conflict, a position which seems closer to
historical reality than the one which posits the desert origins. This is certainly not to say that the groups who made up
premonarchical Israel were devoid of religious traditions; it
is simply to confess that these traditions were not only
inextricably interwoven with the religious traditions of the
Canaanites, but were also continually molded and remolded by
later generations who understood them from a particular socio-
historical context.[133] The gradual crystallization of the
Yahwistic religion can thus be traced according to the principle of cultural contact. In this perspective the clash of
both internal and external elements is responsible for the
creation of new concepts of faith and institutions of religion.[134]

The early contact between the Israelite tribal system and
the Canaanite city-state system was quite influential in
setting the pattern of an alternation between the principles
of centralization and disintegration which can be seen in the
religious sphere as well as in the political. In this period,
von Rad calls for a distinction between national and tribal
religion, a distinction which stems from the fact that the
cult of Yahweh, to which the tribal alliance as a body regarded itself as pledged, still left a good deal of freedom in
its members' religious practice, with the result that in the
end the Yahwistic cult found entrance gradually into the sanctuaries of the tribal areas.[135] This characteristic of the
tribal confederacy thus combined with the Canaanite city-state
system, in which case each city had rival temples to the
Canaanite deities. Before the Davidic empire, there had been
no strong centralized government and consequently no central
temple in Canaan which could be said to be Baal's main abode:

The attempt, then, to localize a god's accessibility in a
sacred building, and the geographic disunity which encouraged the erection of rival shrines and temples to any
one god without a counter tendency toward centralization
--these two factors appear to have resulted in a greater
tendency toward splitting up and localizing divine beings

than was the case in Egypt or Mesopotamia. Thus it
could happen, as stated in the books of Deuteronomy and
Judges, that the more Israelites took over the Canaanite beliefs and practices, the greater the weakening
of the national unity and the accentuation of local
differences.[136]

Thus there was, in the very nature of the Canaanite religion
with its multiplicity of local shrines, an inherent element
disruptive of unity and fostering local particularism, an
element which the Hebrews inherited in the process of urbanization. On the local level, the religious traditions of the
clans could interact with those of the Canaanites. The results
of this cultural contact were both positive and negative.
Here, we shall deal with some of the negative or "anti-urban"
valuations in Israelite religion.

As we have seen, Israel's early social development in
Palestine was broadly from a pastoral and agricultural patri-
archalism to a loosely structured society of city-states
having upper classes, and lower classes which were generally
"clients" of the upper group. With the emergence of the
monarchy, Israel became a small empire with a "national"
cult, a patrician class centered in the cities, semi-free
peasant and artisan class, a patrimonial type of centralized
bureaucracy, considerable market trade and a corvée for mobili-
zing manpower. It is in this period then, that the first
anti-urban traditions were committed to writing.

Pre-Prophetic Anti-urbanism

The first so-called "anti-urban" traditions, both chron-
ologically and in terms of the present order of OT literature,
are recorded in the section of Genesis usually termed the
primeval history. Here the city is spoken of for the first
time in Gen 4:17b: ". . . and he (Cain) built a city, and
called the name of the city after the name of his son,
Enoch."[137] Cain is thus pictured as the father, or founder of
a city.[138] Connected with Cain's city-founding is the fact
that the patriarchs of three guilds are listed as Cain's
descendants.[139] As we have already indicated, the guild is a
distinctively urban phenomenon. The three guilds represented
here are metalworkers, musicians, and "those who dwell in
tents and have cattle" (Gen 4:20). While the third of these
groups has commonly been interpreted as a group of nomads,

Wallis may be correct in maintaining the unity of the passage
by seeing in this third group a guild as well. He holds that
they were professional cattle-breeders and herders who lived
near the city, where they were in charge of the herds of their
urban patrons.[140]

The story of Cain is made up of a number of strands of
tradition which have been woven together, either by J, or by
the source from which he drew. In the present form of the
story, the figure of Cain is thus a composite one, representing
a fusion of several distinct types. While a complete resolution of the Cain material into its component parts can only
be achieved with relative success, it is important to ascertain
the relationship of the Cain genealogy in 4:17-24 to the preceding account of Cain and Abel in order to determine what is
the "anti-urban" element in the chapter. Gressmann has observed that the whole story of Cain appears to be foreign to
the other stories in Genesis 1-11.[141] It certainly is independent of the tradition in chap. 5, which lists a variant
genealogy, culminating in Noah, and which does not know
Cain.[142]

The attempts to sort out the various components within
the Cain story and its relationship to the Seth tradition have
been numerous.[143] The first motif in the chapter is the one
which centers on the dispute between the shepherd, Abel, and
Cain, the farmer. It is this motif which has several parallels
in Mesopotamian mythology.[144] In its original form, this part
of the story may well have been a ritual myth ending in a
ritual banishment or flight, similar to the sending of Azazel
into the desert.[145] An interesting possibility would be to
see in Cain and Abel the representatives of two different
communities, each vying for the favor of its deity in a
struggle for hegemony in the land.[146]

However the Cain-Abel account is interpreted, the problem of its relationship to the Cainite genealogy remains.
The figure of Cain the farmer and the fratricide are often
held to be incompatible with the figure of Cain in the genealogy, who is the founder of the city and city culture.[147]
While this fact may point to different origins for the two
elements of the story, we must deal with the story in its

present composite form if we are to discern J's purpose and the "anti-urban" tendency. The point of the story would thus appear to be that J sees in Cain's city-building the human answer to God's curse on Cain which would have condemned him to be a "fugitive and wanderer on the earth." The "anti-urban" element thus appears in the fact that the first city was built as man's attempt to provide security for himself apart from the provisions of God, and indeed, "away from the presence of Yahweh." Cain builds his own "city of refuge" in order to escape from the divinely ordained blood-revenge.[148] There also seems to be a tacit implication that Cain's city could not be under the protection of Yahweh, since in the theology of the preexilic period, Yahweh's circle of rule was thought to be limited to Canaan, with other powers ruling elsewhere.[149] Cain's city is thus a foreign city. The motif of the city as a fortress, having its origins and *raison d'être* in man's attempt to provide for his own security instead of placing his final faith in Yahweh, is a recurring one as we shall see in our discussion of anti-urbanism in the prophetic literature.

In a manner not unlike that evidenced in the Cain story, the same redactor has utilized what may have been originally two independent stories, one dealing with a tower and the other dealing with a city in Gen 11:1-9.[150] This composite story, again like the Cain story, is out of harmony with its context, in this case chap 10. Genesis 10 accepts the phenomenon of a multiplcity of nations without negative comment. Genesis 11 opens with mankind still unified, and the dispersion to follow is viewed negatively.[151] While the story in Genesis 11 may be a composite one, the fact remains that in its present form it constitutes a unity, and we must seek out the meaning of that unity if we are to understand what concept of the city underlies it.

The city concept which this story communicates has been obscured by commentators' preoccupation with seeing in it the "Tower of Babel," a Mesopotamian temple-tower or ziggurat. In this perspective, attention has been diverted to this temple-type as a threat to the gods and their power. But, as von Rad maintains, the statement that the tower should reach to heaven should not be pressed as part of such an interpretation.

"That men wanted to storm heaven is not said. Rather, one will observe the subtlety of the narrative in the fact that it does not give anything unprecedented as the motive."[152]

The anti-urban judgment implied in this story lies on a different level, and is much more closely related to the concept of the city in Israelite thought than is assumed when it is made a condemnation of a Babylonian temple.[153] While he sees the ultimate inspiration for this narrative in Mesopotamian literature, Speiser suggests that the expression *ʿîr ûmigdāl* is an example of the phenomenon of hendiadys, attested elsewhere in the OT.[154] Taken in this sense then, *migdāl* is used in this story in its sense of "citadel," and the phrase *ʿîr ûmigdāl* can thus be translated " a city with a citadel."[155] The phrase *wərʾōšô bašāmayim*, "and its top (was) in the heavens," can also be interpreted as part of typical urban terminology in the OT, being employed as figurative language describing fortifications of monumental proportions. Such language is used, e.g., in Deut 1:28, ". . . the cities are great and fortified up to heaven . . ."[156] A rather striking example of such language, and perhaps even of a reminiscence of the Genesis 11 story can be seen in the oracle of Jeremiah which condemns Babylon:

> Though Babylon should mount up to heaven
>   and though she should fortify her strong height,
> yet destroyers would come from me upon her,
> says the Lord. (Jer 51:53)

Viewed in this way, the story becomes another example of man's futile attempt to gain security apart from God through city-building, even when the city purports to be a holy city, protected by a deity. Connected with this, there also seems to be a particular thrust directed against the city which represents the center of an empire. This is perhaps most clearly seen in the judgment of Yahweh, which "scattered them abroad from there over the face of all the earth."[157] The city here is thus the prototype of all the cities which were the visible centers of the centralized authority of the empire. The monumental architecture of the city was thus important as a symbol of the city's power, particularly when the city was the center of an empire. This story can thus be seen as an example of the recurring resistance against the concentration

of resources in the claims of a central authority for the
services of its subjects.[158]

All this is not to imply that the story in Genesis 11 has
nothing at all to do with Mesopotamian temple-towers. It is
rather to suggest that the story, as it now stands, is more
closely related to things which constituted more immediate
threats to the champions of the Yahwistic faith--viz., man's
attempt to provide for his own security apart from Yahweh,
seen perhaps most clearly for the Israelite in the two capital
cities of Jerusalem and Samaria and the whole spectrum of
socio-religious problems associated with these cities, as
representatives of the monarchy and its policies.

The Anti-Urbanism of the Prophets

While there are other anti-urban sentiments outside
the prophetic literature which we have not touched upon,[159]
it is especially in the prophets that there is articulated
an anti-urbanism which requires examination.

Von Rad connects the emergence of the prophets with
four factors: (1) the degeneracy of Yahwism because of syncretism, (2) the systematic emancipation, due to formation of
the state, from Yahweh and the protection which he offered,
(3) the social and economic developments of the monarchy, and
(4) the rise of Assyria.[160] Of these four factors, the first
three are internal ones which can be correlated with the urbanization and the religious, social, and economic developments
which accompanied it. Thus, it should be no surprise to
discover that there is much in the content of the works of the
classical prophets which suggests a concern with the problems
associated with the city. On a purely physical level, the
rise of cities gave the prophet the opportunity to deliver his
message many times to various groups, and the city crowds
contained individuals who were capable of retaining it. It
was also in the city that the prophets found the *literati*
who could preserve their message.

Before analyzing the anti-urbanism of the prophets, it
might be well to characterize the relation of the prophets
to the social order in general. Scott describes this relationship:

The prophets' quarrel with their existing social order

was that it did not enshrine and sustain the human and social values integral to Yahwism, but on the contrary destroyed them. . . The foundations upon which the economic and political structure must be reared are ethical and religious--a right-ness of human relationships by Yahweh's standards, and the dependable justice which maintains this norm in social life. . .

The evils condemned are not fastened on as individual aberrations from the normal mores of the society . . . They are characteristics of the society as such, permeating its political structure, its economic activities, its culture and its accepted morality, and profoundly affecting its religion. They correspond in some way to the form and ends of the social order itself, to the principles upon which it operates and to the values it enshrines.[161]

The city thus became an object of prophetic criticism as a social institution which was part of a corrupt whole, but an important part at that. In the city could be seen, in their most intensive form, the particular social evils, which, while having a political or economic base, were religious as well. The city, as a constituent element of the social order, stood under God's judgment.

The anti-urbanism of the prophets has often been seen as the negative pole of a position which has as its positive pole an adherence to a "nomadic ideal" or "desert ideal." The phrase "nomadic ideal" was introduced into Old Testament studies in 1895 by Karl Budde.[162] His point of departure was the figure of Jehonadab ben Rechab, whom he described as "the representative of the nomadic ideal." He then went on to point out that "the nomadic ideal meets us not only in the Rechabites, but also in the prophets of Israel," especially Hosea, but also Jeremiah and Isaiah.[163]

Budde's position was taken up and expanded with respect to the prophets, especially Hosea, by P. Humbert.[164] Humbert's methodology in establishing Hosea's ideal as a nomadic one is characteristic of many of the arguments which have been used to demonstrate the existence of such an ideal in the prophets. He began by asking what Hosea's basic viewpoint regarding Israel's life in Canaan was. He then observed that Hosea did not mention any aspect of Israel's life in the land without denouncing it. If then one were to take away from life in the land everything which Hosea condemned, what is left? Nothing but the desert and nomadism, "the austere

ethics of the simple religion of the fathers."[165]   Since every
aspect of agricultural and urban society is under judgment
there is nothing else left.   Humbert's argument presumes, however, that the prophets were reformers, but they were not
reformers; they were rather revolutionaries.[166]   When Hosea
pronounced judgment on the social fabric as a whole, what he
had in mind was a destruction of the whole and not a backward
social evolution.

Perhaps the most extended treatment of the nomadic ideal
is that of J. W. Flight.[167]   He took up Budde's position, am-
plified it, and recommended its adoption as a normative concept
in the prophets.   Commenting on the development of ideas
concerning the nomadic ideal, Talmon says:

> One can hardly fail to recognize the turn which the desert
> ideal took in the process of scholarly discussion.   It
> started as an analysis of one theme in the Old Testament
> thought and literature and ended up by becoming the ex-
> pression of the quintessence of Biblical religion.[168]

In attempting to analyze the role of the "nomadic ideal"
in the social critique of the prophets, we should perhaps
adopt as our point of departure the group with which Budde
began, viz. the Rechabites.   The literature on the Rechabites
is not very extensive, and for the most part proceeds along
lines similar to Budde's or presses his views with greater
confidence, largely without the benefit of any additional
information.[169]   The Rechabites are typically described as a
puritanical, reactionary clan, who lived in an extra-urban
nomadic setting and observed nomadic traditions as a living
protest against the way of life which prevailed in the Israelite cities.   The usual approach then goes on to say that the
Rechabites were only extreme examples of the ideal toward
which the prophets tended.   In the following discussion, we
shall have cause to challenge this interpretation at several
points and to question the position which sees an affinity
between the Rechabites and the prophets.

The first mention of a "Rechabite" in OT historical
narrative is in connection with Jehu's rebellion in the ninth
century B.C.:

> And when he (Jehu) departed from there (Beth-eked), he
> met Jehonadab the son of Rechab coming to meet him; and
> greeted him, and said to him, 'Is your heart true to my

> heart as mine is to yours?' And Jehonadab answered, 'It
> is.' Jehu said, 'If it is, give me your hand.' So he
> gave him his hand. And Jehu took him up with him into
> the chariot...And when he came to Samaria, he slew all
> that remained to Ahab in Samaria. . . (2 Kgs 10:15-17)

This piece of historical narrative concerning an event
in the ninth century actually tells us very little about the
Rechabite sect which can be harmonized with the later information about their peculiar discipline in the time of Jeremiah.
There seems to have been operative too great a tendency in OT
scholarship to superimpose a uniformity on all the references
to the Rechabites in the OT in order to make them support the
presupposed idea that they were a nomadic clan. In the above
passage, there is not the slightest indication that Jehonadab
ben Rechab is a representative of a "nomadic ideal," or even
that he lived a nomadic existence. The fact that Jehu met
Jehonadab between Samaria and Jezreel can hardly be used as
evidence for the nomadic nature of an unmentioned group with
which Jehonadab was connected as Causse has done.[170] The
importance of this passage is that it is usually taken to be
the *Grundlegende* of the Rechabite sect, since Jehonadab was
looked upon as its founder or father.

The identification of Jehonadab is quite problematic.
We are told nothing about him before his temporary alliance
with Jehu, and because of the dearth of information on the
twenty-eight year reign of Jehu, we know nothing of his fate.
If he in fact played the important role in Jehu's reform
that is often attributed to him, it would seem only natural
that he would have been rewarded with a position in Jehu's
administration. Even Jehonadab's name raises a number of problems. We cannot really determine whether the designation *ben-
rēkāb* is a true father-son designation, or whether it is rather
to be taken in one of the other ways in which *ben* is used in
the OT. In the latter sense it could mean simply a descendant
of one Rechab.[171] Also in this general sense, *ben* could mean
that the person in question is a member of an occupational
group, with the element of the name indicating the occupation.[172] The occupation here would probably be that of
charioteer. It does seem unlikely, however, that the founder
of a group known as Rechabites or *benê-rēkāb*, would himself
be described as *ben-rēkāb*.[173] One further possibility is to

understand *ben-rēkāb* as an indication of the fact that
Jehonadab was a native of place named Rechab. If Rechab here
is a place name, it might possibly be identified with Beth-
marcaboth (*bêt-hammārkābôt*, Josh 19:5; 1 Chr 4:31), which
according to Cohen derived its name from the fact that Solomon
selected the place as a good location for the manufacture and
storage of chariots (*markĕbôt*).[174] If interpreted in this way,
Jehonadab is again associated with chariotry, and it may not
be accidental that Jehu takes him into this chariot. The
question with which Jehu addresses Jehonadab and the latter's
reply should perhaps be compared with two other instances in
which there is a similar question and answer. The first of
these is found in 1 Kgs 22:4, where Ahab asks Jehoshaphat,
"'Will you go with me to battle at Ramoth-gilead?' And Jehoshaphat said to the king of Israel, 'I am as you are, my people
as your people, my horses as your horses.'" Jehoram similarly
addresses Jehoshaphat in 2 Kgs 3:7, "'. . . will you go with
me to battle against Moab?'" and Jehoshaphat's answer repeats
the words of 1 Kgs 22:4. In both of these instances the
dialogue serves to confirm a military alliance, and the conver-
sation between Jehu and Jehonadab apparently confirms a similar
agreement. Such an association between Jehu and Jehonadab may
have resulted from a prior association in the king's chariot-
corps. If this interpretation of Jehonadab is correct, it
would almost certainly mean that the person whom the later
Rechabites looked upon as their founder was a champion for
Yahweh in a militaristic manner, and also a city-dweller. If
Jehonadab did legislate the Rechabite discipline, the principles of holy war may have been behind it, and it may be an
evidence of a "withdrawal" from the domination of the central
authority which had its center in the city. Such a phenomenon
would be in harmony with Sjoberg's observation regarding the
origins of such sectarian groups:

> Sectarian groups seem to arise first in the cities,
> thence to diffuse to the rural areas. Although the pre-
> industrial city is quite stable compared to the industri-
> al one, it nonetheless has its moments of crisis and
> internal dissension. It is during these periods that
> new sects emerge and take hold, often around a charis-
> matic leader.[175]

Probably the most that can be said with certainty on the basis of this passage is that the Jehonadab who at least temporarily aligned himself with Jehu in his militant Yahwistic revolution was, like Elijah and Elisha, a militant supporter of Yahwism in the face of the increasing threat of Baalism under the Omrides. It is simply going beyond the facts to assert as does Ben-gavriel that he was "a naive man of the wilderness,"[176] or to assume that there was a large group of people living the nomadic life who were ready to follow the lead of this champion of the "nomadic ideal."[177] This passage, taken by itself, leaves the origin of the Rechabite sect in doubt. It is only some two-and-one-half centuries later that it is expressly said that this sect looked upon Jehonadab as its patriarch and the author of its discipline.

It is in Jeremiah 35 that we actually hear of the *bêt hā-rēkābîm*, "the house of the Rechabites," and of their program. In response to an offer of wine from Jeremiah, they answer:

> "We will drink no wine, for Jehonadab the son of Rechab, our father, commanded us, 'You shall not drink wine, neither you nor your sons for ever; you shall not build a house; you shall not sow seed; you shall not plant or have a vineyard; but you shall live in tents all your days, that you may live many days in the land where you sojourn.' (Jer 35:6-7)

The labelling of the Rechabites as nomads rests on several presuppositions, formulated on the basis of their program: (1) that teetotalism is a distinctive trait of a nomadic society; (2) that tent-dwelling necessarily indicates nomadism; and (3) that the disdaining of agriculture is a sure sign of nomadism. It is, however, questionable whether these cultural traits can be interpreted as characteristics peculiar to nomadic society. The teetotalism of the Rechabites, which is usually interpreted as a survival of the nomad's contempt for unnatural fermented beverages, need not be so interpreted, and it is questionable whether it is a trait of nomadism at all.[178] But it is a part of the purification ritual of the Israelite army when in camp. Here than is a combination of living in tents and avoiding fermented beverages.[179] Thus the fact that the Rechabites avoided drinking wine and lived in tents may point to an effort to be in a perpetual state of mobilization for holy war. The avoidance of agricultural pursuits may

similarly have been a measure adopted to insure mobility and
to avoid being tied to one place.

The Rechabites' discipline has led to their being compared with the Nazirites. Scott, for example, characterizes
the Rechabites as "a Nazirite family."[180] The Nazirites, like
the Rechabites, were closely related to the holy war ideology:

> There are many affinities between the Nazirite and the
> warrior. Samson, who is called a Nazirite, was a holy
> warrior much like Saul. . . . War in early Israel was a
> holy enterprise, and while on active duty the warrior
> was in a state of sanctity marked by a special pattern of
> conduct (Deut 23:9-14; 1 Sam 21:4-6; 2 Sam 11:11-12).
> The Naziriteship of Joseph (Gen 49:26; Deut 33:16) in
> relation to other tribes may rest on the military prowess
> of that tribe in Israel's early history in Canaan.
> Princes may have been Nazirites (Lam 4:7) in the sense
> that they were warrior chieftains.[181]

On the basis of a phrase in the prophecy of Jeremiah regarding the Rechabites, they may have been related to the Nazirites in the fact that they also had some relationship to the
cult:

> "Thus says the Lord of hosts, the God of Israel: Because
> you have obeyed the command of Jehonadab your father,
> and kept all his precepts, and done all that he commanded
> you, therefore thus says the Lord of hosts, the God of
> Israel: Jehonadab the son of Rechab shall never lack a
> man to stand before me." (Jer 35:18-19)

The phrase in this passage which bears cultic connotations is,
"Jehonadab the son of Rechab shall never lack a man to stand
before me (Yahweh)," which on the basis of its use elsewhere
in the Old Testament might be rendered, "The Rechabites will
always serve God in the sanctuary."[182] However, the connection of the Rechabites with the cult may be of postexilic
origin. The first oracle of Jeremiah (35:12-17) is addressed
to the people and contrasts the disobedience of the people
with the fidelity of the Rechabites. The second oracle
(35:18-19) is addressed to the Rechabites and may have been
a later addition explaining the employment of Rechabites as
cultic functionaries in post-exilic times.[183]

One or perhaps two isolated genealogical notices preserved in Chronicles may connect the Rechabites with the
Kenites. But, due to the nature of these texts, they provide
slight evidence for asserting that the Rechabites were
nomads.[184] Neither does the oft-cited parallel from Diodorus

Siculus concerning the Nabateans constitute such grounds, and one cannot ignore the difference in time, the caution with which classical witnesses to the Nabateans must now be used, and the totally different purpose of the rule in Nabatean society.[185]

In addition to the above arguments, it might also be observed, rather ironically, that in the time of emergency the Rechabites, who were supposedly "anti-urban nomads," fled to the city for protection. If they had in fact been nomadic shepherds it is unlikely that they would have fled to a fortified city in time of siege, for this would have meant the abandonment of their herds. It would have been a more sensible move to flee to the desert fringe with their flocks. Riemann's conclusion with regard to the Rechabites seems in line with the facts as we have observed them. He says:

> It is fair to say that the Rechabite oath is a datum to which the 'nomadic ideal' may perhaps be applied, but from which it cannot be conclusively demonstrated.[186]

While the Rechabite movement can be seen as a "protest movement," that protest did not necessarily involve the return to the nomadic life. The Rechabites were opposed to features of life in the land in which they lived, but their love of land forbade their return to the steppe. Their way of life was an attempt to simplify existence in order to lead the pure life which was required by the puritanical Yahwism associated with the ideology of holy war. It does not seem, however, that the Rechabites can be adduced in evidence of the presupposed prophetic "nomadic ideal!" They may have resisted the course of cultural development, but Abramsky's appraisal of them seems to be in line with the available data, without adding questionable interpretation:

> It would seem as if this were a limited, inherently conservative family association. Jehonadab, its patriarch, established its undeviable commandments. From the various nuances of the term ʾb in the Old Testament, the intent here is a founder of a religious association. In only one historical situation--under the house of Ahab and during Jehu's revolt--did such association arise in the face of pagan worship and the Phoenician-oriented rule of the house of Ahab. . . Of course, the commandments of this sect are not to be regarded as an idealization of desert life. . . Even though the Rechabite sect in itself was not a revisionary sect, it may be regarded-- in the light of its social withdrawal and its force of

discipline and belief--as the archetype of the Essenes and other sects which rose during the Second Temple period.[187]

If the Rechabites cannot be adduced in evidence of the "nomadic ideal," the question which naturally follows is whether there is any other basis for this ideal in the prophetic literature, and if so, does it constitute the basis of the prophetic criticism of the city. Perhaps the most thorough study of the "nomadic ideal" in the prophets is that of Paul Riemann cited above.[188] With Talmon, Riemann's purpose is to give a balanced view of the role of the desert in Israelite thought and to clear up the ambiguity which is displayed in so much of the writing on this subject. Such ambiguity shows up even in the work of careful scholars such as de Vaux. Talmon notes that de Vaux in one instance says that "our oldest Biblical texts show little admiration for nomadic life." . . that in the prophetic books "we do encounter what has been called the 'nomadic ideal' of the Old Testament. . . They condemn the comfort and luxury of urban life in their own day, and see salvation, etc."[189]

At the outset, the patriarchal era must be excluded as the basis for the reputed "nomadic ideal." The preexilic prophets make no use at all of the patriarchs as examples of the piety and godliness of the nomadic life. In fact, there is only one passing reference to Jacob in the prophetic literature, and the other patriarchs are not even mentioned.[190] We are thus left with the period of the Exodus and the wandering in the wilderness as the possible matrix for the concept. But, as Talmon observes:

> Historically and sociologically this hypothesis appears to be untenable. Whatever may in reality have been the length of time which the Israelites spent in the desert . . . even in that comparatively short period . . . the tribes of Israel are not presented in the organizational pattern of a typical nomad society. It is interesting to observe that the main characteristics of desert life and desert society, as they were abstracted from an analysis of the pre-Islamic tribes, finds little expression in the Pentateuchal books which record the desert trek. 'Tribal solidarity, desert hospitality and blood vengeance' . . . insofar as they are reflected in Old Testament literature, are to be found mirrored in the accounts of Israelite sedentary history. . . .[191]

How then do the prophets make use of the desert period?
Certainly they do not make extensive use of it. The tradition of the ancestral wandering in the desert is only mentioned
five times by the preexilic prophets.[192] Riemann believes it
to be significant that it was specifically the generation of
the Exodus, and not the ancestors of Israel in general, whom
the prophets associate with the desert (hammidbār). If, in
fact, Israel's forebears had lived for many generations in the
desert areas of northern Arabia before coming into Canaan,
there is no trace of this in the prophetic heritage.[193]

In seeking to determine the use made of the wilderness
tradition by the prophets, we should briefly examine some of
those passages which have been used in support of the "nomadic
ideal." Perhaps the parade example is Hos 2:14-16. In speaking of this passage, Budde says:

> Here the nomadic ideal comes into prominence by a round-
> about way. Its justification is not unconditional.
> Hosea sees in the return to the nomadic life a means of
> discipline and improvement which Yahweh will apply at
> his pleasure.[194]

De Vaux cites this passage when he says that the prophets "see
salvation in a return, at some future date, to the life of the
desert, envisaged as a golden age."[195] These statements should
be compared with the one of Causse, who in attacking the positions of Humbert and Gautier maintains that:

> Hosea did not only condemn sedentary culture. He declared
> expressly that it is Yahweh who gives to his people the
> blessings of the land--Yahweh and not the Baalim. The
> return to the desert is represented as an ordeal, the
> means of a divine education. After this ordeal, which
> should lead to reconciliation, Yahweh will return his
> people to their fields and vines. The ideal of Hosea is
> a peasant ideal much more than a nomadic ideal.[196]

Certainly, the return to the wilderness is here only a temporary halting place in an ultimate return to the land. The so-
journ in the wilderness is a punishment brought on the people
for their apostasy; the return to the fertile land is the
promise of Yahweh, based on his mercy. This passage is thus
in harmony with the rest of the first three chapters of Hosea,
of which it is a part. The motif in these chapters is Yahweh's
unfailing love for Israel, after the analogy of the love of a
husband for his unfaithful wife. Just as Hosea's wife is to
be punished for her conduct (3:3), so Israel is to be

chastised with a re-enactment of the desert trek.[197] It is
not the desert which is given a positive valuation, but rather
the deeds of Yahweh in the desert.[198] Here, as elsewhere,
when the "desert motif" seems to attain to the status of a
self-contained positive value, this attribution has resulted
from a mixing of motifs, which introduces subsidiary elements
into the "desert motif."[199]

Other passages often cited in support of the "nomadic
ideal" are Amos 2:10 and 5:25:

> Also I brought you up out of the land of Egypt,
> and led you forty years in the wilderness,
> to possess the land of the Amorites. (2:10)

> Did you bring to me sacrifices and offerings the forty
> years in the wilderness, O house of Israel? (5:25)

Commenting on these two verses, Wolff says:

> The forty years in the wilderness are to Amos not only a
> model of God's helping power (2:10), but also a time of
> normative character for the right kind of worship
> (5:25).[200]

However, rather than being a positive statement regarding the
desert, 2:10 seems instead to be an instance of God's special
care for his people in a time of their helplessness. Amos 5:25
can be understood as a protest against the deteriorating relationship with God that had developed as a result of a magical
concept of the efficacy of sacrifice in place of a dependence
on Yahweh: "Not in such terms of easy intimacy had the relationship between Israel and the dread storm-god Yahweh found
expression in the desert days."[201]

A final passage to be examined in this context is Jer
2:2-6. When used by those who would support the "nomadic
ideal," it has been said that this oracle of Jeremiah speaks
of the wandering in the wilderness as "the time when the
relationship [between Yahweh and Israel] was at its fairest,
the time of the first love of Yahweh and Israel."[202] But C.
Barth questions whether this oracle is really a salvation
oracle, in which Yahweh rewards the attitude of his people in
the desert. He suggests that the prophet here has used the
form of the *Heilsorakel* in an ironic manner, in order to say
in effect: "Certainly Yahweh helped you, since you *were* so
true to him in the desert." The *Heilsorakel* form is thus used
not to console the people, but to reproach them.[203] In fact,

this passage again illustrates the groundless mercy of Yahweh in contrast to the apostasy of the people. Barth's interpretation has in its favor the fact that elsewhere in his book, Jeremiah makes extensive use of a negative valuation of the wilderness, a valuation which we must now turn to.

It is with the negative valuation of the desert in the prophets that we come into contact with their anti-urban statements. The negative valuation of the city is not then a reaction to a pre-existent positive valuation of the desert. On the contrary, it is the negative picture of the desert which is used to express God's judgment on the city. Riemann deals at some length with the negative concept of the desert in Israelite thought. He summarizes his position:

> The return-to-desert motif is a salient feature of the prophetic literature, appearing at least twenty-two times in pre-exilic materials from Isaiah, Hosea, Zephaniah and Jeremiah. The phrase is regularly 'be made (like the) desert' (*not* 'return to the desert'), often elaborated with desert epithets or with a list of animals who will live at the abandoned site. The emphasis is unmistakably on radical reduction and utter desolation . . . return to the desert is accordingly a covenant curse, anticipating the end of the community and not a change of environment. Thus it can be explained why the motif is always an expression of divine judgment; why it is used as often against enemy nations as against Israel herself, with no difference in form or expression; and why it did not draw its imagery from the wilderness wandering tradition.[204]

In the course of his study, Riemann demonstrates that the prophets made frequent use of desert terms and figures, not because they had a peculiarly favorable view of the desert which they wished to impart, but because they shared the common antipathy toward the desert which they were thus able to use in their sentences of judgment. For our purpose, we should observe how desert imagery is used in those passages where the prophets pass judgment on Israelite cities.

The language used by the prophets in their connection of desert imagery with the judgment which would befall the cities has been likened to the language used in treaty-curses in the ancient Near East.[205] In the prophets the use of such language is most easily explained in the context of the lawsuit which Yahweh pressed for breach of covenant.[206] The treaty-curse form is well illustrated in the eighth-century B.C. treaty from Sefire:

> Its vegetation shall be destroyed to a desert and Arpad
> will become a tell for the lying down of the desert
> animal and the gazelle and the fox . . . And this city
> shall not be mentioned nor MDR' nor MDBH . . .207

This treaty curse should be compared with such passages as
Zeph 2:13-15:

> And he will stretch out his hand against the north, and
>   destroy Assyria;
> and he will make Nineveh a desolation, a dry waste like
>   the desert.
> Herds shall lie down in the midst of her,
>   all the beasts of the field;
> the vulture and the hedgehog shall lodge in her capitals;
>   the owl shall hoot in the window, the raven croak on
>   the threshold;
> for her cedar work shall be laid bare.
> This is the exultant city that dwelt secure, that said
>   to herself, 'I am and there is none else.'
> What a desolation she has become, a lair for wild beasts!
> Everyone who passes by her hisses and shakes his fist.208

The concluding line of this passage contains a common cliché
which is used to describe a ruined city, viz., that all those
who pass by will be appalled, shudder, hiss, nod the head, or
wave the hand in horror or derision.209   In a number of instances this cliché is joined with a curse which cites Sodom and
Gomorrah, and occasionally the other "cities of the plain."
The Sodom-Gomorrah curse does not occur in any ancient Near
Eastern treaty-curses, but may represent a curse which was
unique to Israelite tradition.   Sodom and Gomorrah are, to
the prophets, symbols of wickedness, but even more often are
used as parade examples for sudden and complete destruction.210

In these prophetic oracles, the same language is applied
to both Israelite and non-Israelite cities.   This represents
the development of the concept in Israelite thought that God
will punish his disobedient people in the same way as he
punishes his enemies.   Certainly, the destruction of cities
in ancient as well as modern times was the culminating act of
warfare and symbolic of the capitualtion of the land, especially when the city in question was the capital city.

John Dunne offers some intriguing suggestions on the significance of city-destruction in the ancient Near East:

> Although it would appear to be an act of singular barbar-
> ism, almost as if it were the destruction of civilization
> itself, in that the city is the very embodiment of civil-
> ization, the Sumerians listed 'the destruction of cities'
> as one of the divine institutions (*me*'s) upon which

civilization is founded (Kramer, *History begins at Sumer*, p. 100). Significantly, the institution which follows is 'lamentation.' To judge from the 'Lamentation over the destruction of Ur' (*ANET*, pp. 455 ff.), a poem occasioned by the fall of Ur to the Elamites and Subarians, the chief effect of destroying a city besides the obvious physical consequences was to force the abandonment of the city by its gods. The statement is made repeatedly in this poem that the ruined city's institutions and rites have become inimical, meaning that they have devolved upon the enemy. To destroy the city, apparently, meant not to destroy but to appropriate the civilization of the city.[211]

In historical terms, the city of Ur was destroyed by the Elamites, an enemy from the east:

The utter destruction of the city was wrought, in our terms, by the barbaric hordes which attacked it. Not so in terms of the Mesopotamian's own understanding of his universe: the wild destructive essence manifest in this attack was Enlil's. The enemy hordes were but a cloak, an outward form under which that essence realized itself. In a deeper, truer sense the barbaric hordes were a storm, Enlil's storm, wherewith the god himself was executing a verdict passed on Ur and its people by the assembly of the gods.[212]

Similarly, the prophets, in announcing the verdict of destruction on Israelite cities, had in mind, for the most part, particular national powers which would be the agents of destruction. But, behind these human armies there stood the verdict of God himself, who was the true destroyer. Hosea expresses this thought rather succinctly:

I will destroy you, O Israel
  who can help you?
Where is your king now,
  where is he that can save you in all your cities?[213]

Manifestly, both the monarchy and the city were institutions which arose in Israel for the purpose of defense from enemies, but neither of them was to be of any avail in the face of Yahweh's judgment. Certainly there could be no thought of protection for the cities on the part of the idols whom the Israelites might have counted on in this regard. They all are totally impotent in face of the judgment of Yahweh.

The prophets thus make use of the language of the treaty-curse to make clear to the people that their cities would be destroyed because they had failed to meet the obligations of their covenant with Yahweh, and hence he was going to carry out the terms of this covenant, one stipulation of which was the reduction of their cities to desert.

What is perhaps the most prevalent form which the anti-urbanism of the prophets takes, is related to one of the earliest and most basic concepts of the city in Israel--the physical concept of the city as a permanent fortified settlement. The city was conceived of as a fortress for the protection of its people. The prophetic criticism of the city in this particular form is not really concerned with the city as a political unit, nor with the social problems associated with the city, but concentrates on the city as a physical structure for defense. We have already commented on the monarchy's support of the building and fortifying of cities as a defensive and administrative measure, particularly in the time of Solomon and later. The prophetic reaction to this activity is put rather forcefully by Weiser, whose statement we reproduce in the original German because of its energetic quality:

> Politische Erfolge haben in der Zeit Jerobeams II. zu
> einer Kulturentfaltung geführt, die neben anderem in
> Tempelbauten und Vermehrung der festen Städte ihren
> stolzen Ausdruck fand. Der Prophet macht die Kultur-
> feligkeit seiner Zeit nicht mit. Er sieht auch hier
> hinter die Fassade und den oberflächlichen Augenschein
> und erkennt in dieser Kulturfreudigkeit jenen
> unbändigen titanischen Drang des Menschen, selbst
> etwas sein zu wollen neben Gott und ohne Gott. Tempel
> und Paläste sind ihm der Ausdruck des Stolzes und der
> Selbstüberhebung des Menschen, der das Kreaturgefühl
> vergisst, in seiner Welt selbst Schöpfer sein will und
> sich sichern möchte gegen die Fährlichkeiten des Lebens
> (vgl. 1. Mose 11:1-9). Und doch kann er durch dies alles
> nicht jenes Ungesichertsein der Lage aufheben, in der sich
> der Mensch seinem Schöpfer gegenüber befindet. Mensch
> sein heisst auch für Hosea in Abhängigkeit vom Schöpfer
> leben (vgl. 1. Mose 3:11), und darum sieht der Prophet in
> dem ungehemmten Selbstbewusstsein seiner Zeit ein
> Vergessen des Schöpfers. Das Drohwort, das wohl
> absichtlich eine in Fremdvölkerorakeln gebräuchliche
> Redeform (Amos 1:3 ff.) auf Israel selbst anwendet, weiss
> von dem Gegensatz, in dem Gott gegen solche menschliche
> Hybris steht, und von dem Untergang, der einer Kultur
> droht, die im Grunde 'gottlos' ist, weil sie nicht aus
> dem Wissen um die Verplichtung der Kreatur ihrem
> Schöpfer gegenüber lebt.[214]

The passage on which Weiser is commenting is Hos 8:14, which is a parade example of this kind of anti-urban expression in the prophets:

> For Israel has forgotten his Maker
>   and built palaces (or 'temples,' hêkālôt);
> and Judah has multiplied fortified cities ('ārîm bĕsurôt);

but I will send a fire upon his cities,
and it shall devour his citadels (ʾarmĕnōtehā).[215]

Hosea also preserves what must have been a rather stereotyped formula used to describe the full horror of the destruction of a fortified city:

Samaria shall bear her guilt,
because she has rebelled against her God;
they shall fall by the sword,
their little ones shall be dashed in pieces,
and their pregnant women ripped open.[216]

While the bulk of the "anti-urbanisms" in Amos has a
different basis, the element which condemns the city as a fortress is not absent. It is found in the context of those oracles dealing with Samaria. Apparently Amos saw the conditions
in Samaria as bringing to a focus the self-sufficiency and
self-assertion on the part of man over against God that prevailed in the national life generally.[217] This is expressed
in Amos 6:8:

I abhor the pride of Jacob,
and hate his strongholds;
and I will deliver up (his) city (or 'cities') and all
that is in it ('them').[218]

In Isaiah, the false security of the city is made an
expression of human pride:

For the Lord of hosts has a day
against all that is proud and lofty,
against all that is lifted up and high;
against all the cedars of Lebanon,
lofty and lifted up;
and against all the oaks of Bashan;
against all the high mountains,
and against all the lofty hills;
against every high tower,
and against every fortified wall. (Isa 2:12-15)

In some instances, the destruction of cities is specifically
related to the lack of trust in Yahweh:

In that day your strong cities will be like the deserted
places of the Hivites and the Amorites, which they deserted because of the children of Israel, and there will be
desolation. Because you have forgotten the God of your
salvation, and have not remembered the Rock (ṣûr) of your
refuge.[219]

In that day you looked to the weapons of the house of the
forest (or "arsenal"), and you saw that the breaches of
the city of David were many, and you collected the waters
of the lower pool, and you counted the houses of Jerusalem, and you broke down the houses to fortify the wall. . .
But you did not look to him who did it, or have regard

for him who planned it long ago. (Isa 22:8b-11)

Just as the city is not a secure refuge because of the people's apostasy, the keeping of the stipulations of the covenant could make a city strong:

We have a strong city;
to guard us he has set wall and rampart about us.

He who walks righteously and speaks uprightly;
    he who despises the gain of oppressions,
who shakes his hands, lest they hold a bribe,
    who stops his ears from hearing of bloodshed,
and shuts his eyes from looking upon evil.

He will dwell on the heights;
    his place of defense will be the fortresses of rocks.[220]

Jeremiah also makes extensive use of the motif of the city as a false refuge:

Behold, I am bringing upon you a nation from afar,
O house of Israel, says the Lord . . .
    your fortified cities in which you trust
        they shall destroy with the sword.

Behold, I am against you, O inhabitant of the valley,
    O rock of the plain, says the Lord;
you who say, 'Who shall come down against us,
    or who shall enter our habitations?'
I will punish you according to the fruit of your doings,
    says the Lord;
I will kindle a fire in her citadel (*běyaʿrāh*)
    and it shall devour all that is round about it.[221]

In one of the relatively few occurrences of the term *běrît*, "covenant," in the prophetic literature, Jeremiah gives a specific explanation for the destruction of a city, in the context of the "passer-by" cliché:

And many nations will pass by this city, and every man will say to his neighbor, 'Why has the Lord dealt thus with this great city?' And they will answer, 'Because they forsook the covenant of the Lord their God, and worshiped other gods and served them.' (Jer 21:8).

The thought of the prophets, which links unfaithfulness to the covenant with the failure of cities to fulfill their protective function, is also to be noted in the covenant curses in Deuteronomy. The thought inherent here seems to be that while the protective function of the city is a legitimate one, this function of the city had been perverted because of the unfaithfulness to the covenant. Thus, the city which had been given to the Israelites by God has been turned into a "demonic" structure, working against God:

And when the Lord your God brings you into the land which

he swore to your fathers, to Abraham, to Isaac, and to
Jacob, to give you, with great and goodly cities, which
you did not build . . .

And I commanded you at that time, saying, 'The Lord your
God has given you this land to possess; all your men of
valor shall pass over armed before your brethren the
people of Israel. But your wives, your little ones, and
your cattle . . . shall remain in the cities which I have
given you.'

They shall besiege you in all your towns, until your high
and fortified walls, in which you trusted, come down
throughout the land; and they shall besiege you in all
your towns throughout all the land which the Lord your
God has given you.[222]

The prophets saw confidence in arms and fortifications
as particularly incongruous and pitiable in the face of the
breakup of the social and political norms of their day:

The prophets condemned with a passion amounting to fierce-
ness the particular evils they saw about them in society--
oppression, violence, debauchery, greed, theft, dis-
honesty, lust for power, callous inhumanity, faithlessness
to trust. These are sins of individual men and women,
evils which, on the face of it, *may appear in any form of
society, and by which any society where they are prevalent
and tolerated stands condemned.*[223]

The last several words of this quotation from Scott raise an
important question. We have already seen that in their discussion of such phenomena as Scott lists, the prophets were
discussing effects of urbanization in some cases. The question
raised here is--to what degree did the prophets associate
evidences of social and personal pathology with the city?, or,
in other terms, how was the institution of the city seen to be
related to particular evils? Wallis is a representative of
those who see the relationship as one in which the prophets
articulate particular evils because of a pre-existent aversion
to the city:

Im Grunde aber wirkt in allen Propheten, die gegen diese
Mißstände ihre Stimme erhoben haben, jener alte Argwohn,
jene tiefe Abneigung gegen die städtische Gesellschaft
nach. Die grossen Geister Israels haben die alten For-
derungen der Sittlichkeit und Gerechtigkeit aus der
Wüstenzeit nicht vergessen und sie immer wieder vorgetra-
gen. Wenn aber irgendwo diesen ethischen Maximen wider-
sprochen wurde, so in den Palästen, an den Gerichts-
höfen und auf den Märkten der Großstadt.[224]

However, such a position attributes to the prophets a
general anti-urbanism, while in reality the prophets are not

moral generalists. They do not take positions based on a general aversion toward something, but whenever they pass judgment, it is in concrete and specific terms. This position also suggests that the prophets had a particular attachment to some social institutions, and a corresponding aversion toward others. It does not seem, however, that the prophets singled out any single institution as particularly responsible for the social pathology of their day. It would probably be more accurate to speak of a general despair of human institutions. The city as a social institution was but one constituent element in the social order which was corrupt throughout. The situation was not due to any one institution, but as Amos says, the whole nation is corrupt: "Behold, the eyes of the Lord God are upon the sinful kingdom, and I will destroy it from the surface of the ground" (Amos 9:8).

The repercussion of the nation's sin had affected every aspect of human society--its economic, social and political welfare--for the functioning of all institutions was dependent upon the maintenance of the harmonious relationship between God and man in which man stood under the will of God. What was wrong with Israelite society could not be remedied by reforms in any one institution. Certainly the prophets did not believe that any sort of "urban renewal" could get at the root of the problems, for there was no room in Hebrew thought for a theory of environmental causation. The nation's sin could not be blamed on the urban environment, nor was it just the result of the failure of this social form nor even of the people to adjust to it.

> Can we find, in the prophetic discourses, some radical vice which underlies all the moral evil which they find in the people of the Lord? It would be interesting if we could; but the prophets are not moralists nor psychoanalysts. To them, moral evil appears as a single unholy entity. The distinction between religious and moral evil would have no sense for the prophets, for they were unconscious of any such distinction. In our own language, however, we do make the distinction; and we would say that the prophets appear to view the religious corruptions of their people as basic, from which moral corruption flows of necessity. Morality was to 'know God;' if one does not know God, then one does not know good.[225]

With this recognition of the prophetic stance *vis-à-vis* human institutions and of the fact that they saw the basic problem as a religious one, we should make some preliminary remarks here regarding the "urban religion" of the prophets' time.

Whatever else they were, the prophets were above all else champions of Yahwism in the face of the threat posed to it by Canaanite religion. The problem with syncretism, or better, assimilation, was not so much that the Israelites had abandoned the worship of Yahweh for the Baalim, but rather that the distinguishing marks of Yahwism had become blurred, and Yahweh was regarded in practice as one of the Baalim, even if in a henotheistic sense.

> The religious situation in the time of the great prophets was . . . complex. The worship by many of . . . foreign deities was doubtless facilitated to some degree by the thought that they were subordinate to Yahweh, or operated in areas with which he was not directly concerned. He was the God of the nation as such, of its historic tradition, of its battles and its king. He did not seem to be concerned with the problems of the individual cultivator. Israel '*did not know* that it was I who gave her the grain, the wine and the oil' (Hos 2:8). So the farmer and the herdsman brought their offerings to the local shrine, but also made their appearance periodically at the temple of Yahweh.[226]

How then did the city contribute to this complex religious picture? Do the prophets condemn "urban religion," while endorsing the religion practiced in the rural areas? Was there, in fact, a fundamental difference between the religion of the city and the religion of the country; and if so, what was it? In answer to the last question, Sjoberg offers the following observations:

> The fundamental cleavage within the religious hierarchy has its counterparts in the religious beliefs and attitudes and practices of the population: distinctly upper and lower-class norms can be discerned. The folk religious rites of the lower class, whether in country or city, may bear little resemblance to the more formal observances of the upper stratum. Local deities dot the religious scene for the lower classes. A number of factors are responsible for the divergencies of religious behavior of the different classes: (1) the sacred writings are read and understood by a minute, but influential sector of the city and society. The religious behavior of this group is consequently standardised through time and displays striking homogeneity within and among cities. The uneducated, lacking acquaintance with many of these ideal norms, rely upon verbal interpretation of these by priests. But the lower clergy and their followers are cut off from direct communication with the elite

learning. (2) Another reason is the heavy expenditure of
time, effort and financial resources required if one is to
fulfill the exacting religious requirements set forth in
the sacred writings.[227]

The religious situation pictured by Sjoberg is thus dependent upon his analysis of the class structure in the preindustrial city, and does not posit a simple rural-urban split
since the lower class is both urban and rural. In Israel,
the two types of religious practice were connected with the
temples in the cities, on the one hand, and the open-air
"high-places" on the other. Of the former, there is considerable evidence in the prophetic literature for a great number
of such temples and for the frequency, abundance and expen-
siveness of the sacrifices which were offered in them.[228]
The $b\bar{a}m\hat{o}t$ are also mentioned by the prophets.[229] Any attempt
which seeks to align the prophets with one of these expressions
of religion, and to portray them as the champions of one class
against the other, is seriously challenged both by the theoretical perspective afforded by the preindustrial city, relative to the class structure, and by the more specific information regarding the prophets and the way in which they identified themselves.

Finkelstein is probably the leading proponent of those
who would see in the prophets the representatives of the
peasantry over against the aristocracy.

> . . . the prophetic . . . traditions were the products of
> a persistent cultural battle . . . between the submerged,
> unlanded groups and their oppressors, the great land-
> owners. Beginning in the primitive opposition of the
> semi-nomadic shepherd and the settled farmer, the struggle
> developed into a new arraignment of the small peasant . . .
> against the more prosperous farmer . . . From the province
> the conflict was transferred to the cities, where it
> expressed itself in the resistance of traders and artisans
> to the nobles and courtiers. Finally, it appeared in the
> sancturary in the bitter rivalry between the Levite and
> the priest.[230]

In the development of his thesis, Finkelstein classifies the
prophets on the basis of their having either a rural or urban
identification. For example, he explains the lack of invective
against social injustice on the part of Hosea as an indication
of his rural identification. "We can trace, however, a development in the mind of this prophet as he grows out of his

early village simplicity into the later metropolitan sophis-
tication."[231]

Certainly, we can, for the most part, identify the origins of the prophets. Amos, the dresser of sycamore trees
and $n\bar{o}q\bar{e}d$, "sheep-breeder" was from the town of Tekoa (Amos
1:1), which was but ten miles south of Jerusalem.[232] Hosea's
actual birthplace is not named, but he may have been a city-
dweller.[233] Isaiah appeared exclusively in Jerusalem, and is
usually assumed to have been a Jerusalemite, as was Zephaniah
(Zeph 1:4). Micah was from the city of Moresheth-gath.[234]
Jeremiah was a native of the priestly city of Anathoth (Jer
1:1).[235] But an identification with the city was not crucial
for the prophets, and was not really determinative of their
message as Finkelstein suggests. Weber's analysis of the
social context of the prophets' message is much nearer the
truth:

> In status origin the prophets were diverse (*uneinheit-
> lich*). It is out of the question that they were, for
> the most part, derived from proletarian or negatively
> privileged or uneducated strata. Moreover their social
> ethical attitude was by no means determined by their per-
> sonal descent. For they share the same attitude despite
> their very diverse social origins.[236]

On the one side, prophetic denunciation is directed against
the urban upper stratum for their social and religious sins,
but on the other hand, the prophets also declaimed against the
tainted rural places of worship, the $b\bar{a}m\hat{o}t$.[237]

The basic attitude of the prophets toward the institution of the city is perhaps echoed in the wisdom saying preserved in Psalm 127:1:

> Unless the Lord builds the house,
>   those who build it labor in vain.
> Unless the Lord watches over the city,
>   the watchman stays awake in vain.

Thus, in the final analysis, we might say that the prophets adopted a view which regarded the institution of the city
merely as one instrument that could be used in the plan of God.
As such, the city had no final value. Certainly the particular socio-religious forms of the city were, in the long run,
immaterial to the fulfillment of God's purpose for Israel.
There is no element of hope in the prophets which is based
upon the human will. If man wishes to provide for his welfare

he must learn that there are some things that are beyond his
power and can only be achieved by Yahweh. The city, as a
symbol of man's attempt to provide for his own material
security, stands condemned.

NOTES

[1]The phrase "urban revolution" was coined by V. Gordon Childe (*Man Makes Himself* [London: Watts, 1936]). While Childe distinguished himself among archaeologists by his early atten- tion to the socio-economic developments related to city ori- gins, he has been criticized for overplaying the role of tech- nological and economic factors to the extent that "his point of view has assumed a Marxist slant which applies to ancient Near East conditions inappropriate categories." (Frankfort, *The Birth of Civilization*, 61, n.10). Frankfort, however, in criti- cizing Childe's early position, admits to a modification of that position in some of Childe's later works, esp. in his ar- ticle, "The Urban Revolution," which was cited in our first chapter.

[2]Kenyon, *Digging up Jericho* (London: Benn, 1957) 65-76. Cf. also Paul Lapp ("Palestine in the Early Bronze Age"), an article to appear in the forthcoming Festschrift for Nelson Glueck. [The Glueck Festschrift, *NEATC*, has Lapp's article on 101-131].

[3]Frankfort, *The Birth of Civilization*, 49-50.

[4]Sjoberg, *Preindustrial City*, 7-10.

[5]Lampard, "Historical Aspects of Urbanization," 533.

[6]These two periods in northern Mesopotamia roughly corres- pond to Uruk, Jemdet Nasr and Early Dynastic I in southern Mes- opotamia and to the end of the Ghassulian and Early Bronze I and II in Palestine. On these chronological periods, cf. Ed- ward F. Campbell, Jr. ("The Ancient Near East: Chronological Bibliography and Charts, *The Bible and the Ancient Near East* [ed. G. E. Wright; Garden City: Doubleday, 1965] 281-282).

[7]Jawad, *Townships*, 70-71.

[8]Cf. Frankfort, *The Birth of Civilization*, 54, 64-66.

[9]Ibid., 56. For the various interpretations which have been proposed regarding the temple towers, see André Parrot (*Ziggurats et tour de Babel* [Paris: Michel, 1949]).

[10]Frankfort, *The Birth of Civilization*, 64-66.

[11]Ibid., 77.

[12]Ibid., 85, 88.

[13]Cf. Fish, "The Place of the Small State," 83-86.

[14]Anati, *Palestine before the Hebrews*, 317-318. The more common divisions are ca. 3100-2100 B.C. for the Early Bronze

Age; ca. 2100-1500 B.C. for the Middle Bronze Age; and ca. 1550-1200 B.C. for the Late Bronze Age. Cf. Noth, *Old Testament World*, 122.

[15]Kenyon, *Archaeology*, 43-46. Note the Carbon-14 date of 6850 + 210 years given by Kenyon for the timbers of one of the houses built in the late phase of the PPNA community.

[16]Jean Perot, "Palestine-Syria-Cilicia," *Courses toward Urban Life* (eds. R. J. Braidwood and G. R. Willey; Chicago: Aldine, 1962) 152.

[17]Kenyon (*Archaeology*, 42) cites a Carbon-14 date of 7800 B.C. + 210 years for this structure. Cf. also her description of this structure and her reasons for calling it a temple on 41-43 and in her "Excavations at Jericho, 1954," *PEQ* (1954) 51.

[18]Kenyon, *Archaeology*, 44-45. Cf. also her "Excavations at Jericho, 1955," *PEQ* (1955) 110. [R. B. Y. Scott has pointed out, in a private communication, that six feet six inches equals four Babylonian cubits of .495 meters each].

[19]Kenyon, *Archaeology*, 43. Perot ("Palestine-Syria-Cilicia," 152) cites a figure of ca. 36,000 sq. meters which would be about 9 acres. Cf. also S. Yeivin ("The Land of Israel and the Birth of Civilization in the Near East," *Antiquity and Survival*, II[1957] 115) who gives an estimate of 7-8 acres. An exact figure is impossible, owing to modern structures.

[20]On this demographic estimate, cf. above, 79.

[21]The average annual rainfall for this area, based on records for 1859-1948, is between 3.9 and 7.8 inches. Cf. the rainfall map from Ashbel, reproduced by Scott ("Palestine, Climate of," *IDB*, III, 624). H. G. May (*Oxford Bible Atlas*, 50) gives a figure of 6.4 inches for Jericho.

[22]Kenyon, *Archaeology*, 46. Cf. also her "Excavations," *PEQ* (1955) 109-111.

[23]M. Wheeler ("The First Towns?" *Antiquity* XXX (1956) 132-134, 225) also accepts Kenyon's classification of Jericho as urban. He takes as the chief elements of civilization a settled community of a size sufficient to support non-agricultural specialists, and public works that imply an organized and durable administration. Although he views these traits as preconditions for the development of writing, he does not consider writing a necessary component of civilization.

[24]Childe, "Civilization, Cities, and Towns," *Antiquity* XXXI(1957) 36-39. Cf. also Sjoberg, *Preindustrial City*, 32-33.

[25]R. J. Williams ("Writing and Writing Materials," *IDB*, IV, 912) mentions a stela from Balu'ah in Moab which bears an inscription in a linear script which has been dated to the late third millennium. He believes that this may be an example of the first indigenous script in the area.

[26]Cf. the inscriptions from Gezer, Lachish, and Shechem in

G. R. Driver (*Semitic Writing from Pictograph to Alphabet* [London: G. Cumberlege, 1948] 98-99).

[27]Kenyon, "Jericho," *AOTS*, 266.

[28]On the continuity of toponyms, cf. Aharoni (*Land of the Bible*, 96-100).

[29]*ANET*, 228.

[30]Ibid., 227.

[31]Kenyon, *Archaeology*, 106-107. Cf. her "Jericho," *AOTS*, 266-267.

[32]Schofield, "Megiddo," 312.

[33]Kenyon, "Some Notes on the Early Middle Bronze Strata of Megiddo," *Eretz Israel* V (1958) 51-52.

[34]Wright, "The Archaeology of Palestine," *The Bible and the Ancient Near East*, 101.

[35]De Vaux, "Tirzah," *AOTS*, 372-373.

[36]Y. Aharoni and R. Amiran, "Arad: a Biblical City in Southern Palestine," *Archaeology* XVII (1964) 43-47.

[37]Lapp ("Palestine in the Early Bronze Age," 21) has challenged this motivation for EB defenses. He says:
We are faced with the choice between the newcomers quickly taking hegemony and just as rapidly dividing into warring factions building defenses against each other, or viewing the newcomers as a more unified and cooperating group building defenses against a common threat whether indigenous or external. The homogeneity of the culture of the newcomers . . . favors the second alternative, and their peaceful coexistence with their predecessors in EB IC, when the first defenses were being built, points to an external foe.

[38]Kenyon, *Amorites and Canaanites* (London: The British Academy, 1966) 6-7.

[39]John Wilson (*ANET*, 227) suggests that for the most part it is an argument from silence to assume that military contacts between Egypt and Asia were slight under the Old Kingdom.

[40]De Vaux, "Tirzah," 372-373.

[41]Kenyon, *Archaeology*, 116.

[42]Wright, "The Archaeology of Palestine," 101.

[43]Additional evidence for the existence of communal granaries comes from Arad. Cf. Aharoni, "The Negeb," *AOTS*, 387.

[44]Kenyon, *Archaeology*, 120-121.

[45]De Vaux, *Palestine in the Early Bronze Age*, CAH, rev. ed., vol. 1, ch. 15 (Cambridge: Cambridge University, 1964) 27. Cf. also de Vaux, "Tirzah," 373.

[46]Aharoni, "Arad," 3-6.

[47]Wright, "The Archaeology of Palestine," 101. For a list of these seals with references, cf. the works cited by Wright on 130, n.50.

[48]Lapp, "Bâb edh-Dhrâ', Perizzites and Emim," *Jerusalem through the Ages*, the Twenty-Fifth Archaeological Convention (Jerusalem: Israel Exploration Society, 1968) 12-14. Cf. also Lapp, "Bâb edh-Dhrâ' Tomb A 76 and Early Bronze I in Palestine," *BASOR* 189 (1968) 26-29.

[49]Lapp, "Palestine in the Early Bronze Age," 14-15, 20.

[50]Wright, "The Discoveries at Megiddo," 227.

[51]Kenyon, *Amorites and Canaanites*, 17-18.

[52]Lapp, "Bâb edh-Dhrâ', Perizzites and Emim," 14.

[53]The Berlin texts were published by K. Sethe (*Die Achtung feindlicher Fürsten, Völker und Dinge auf altägyptischen Tongefässcherben des mittleren Reiches* [Berlin: Verlag der Akademie der Wissenschaften, 1926]. The later texts were published by G. Posener (*Princes et pays d'Asie et de Nubie* [Brussels, 1940]. Cf. the excerpts in *ANET*, 328-329.

[54]For suggested dates see Wilson (*ANET*, 328, n.1).

[55]Cf. Aharoni, *Land of the Bible*, 131-132. See also the map in Aharoni and M. Avi-Yonah (*Macmillan Bible Atlas* [N.Y.: Macmillan, 1968] 26).

[56]Cf. Aharoni's arrangement of the list according to regions (*Land of the Bible*, 133).

[57]H. W. Helck, *Die Beziehungen Ägyptens zu Vorderasien im 3. und 2. Jahrtausend v. Chr.* (Wiesbaden: Harrassowitz, 1962) 63.

[58]John Van Seters, *The Hyksos: A New Investigation* (New Haven: Yale University, 1966) 80.

[59]An excellent survey of the archaeological finds of this period, site by site, is given by Kenyon (*Palestine in the Middle Bronze Age*, CAH, rev. ed., vol. II, ch. 3 [Cambridge: Cambridge University, 1966].

[60]Wright, "The Archaeology of Palestine," 107. Cf. also Yadin ("Hyksos Fortifications and the Battering-Ram," *BASOR* 137[1955] 23-26). An illustration of this type of defense can be found in Kenyon (*Archaeology*, 178, fig. 43).

[61]Cf. Yadin, "Hyksos Fortifications," 23-34.

[62]Qatna, like Hazor, extended from the foot of the mound over an area of ca. 247 acres. It reached its peak at about the same time as Hazor, and it is probable that both towns were founded by the Hyksos. It is also interesting to note that Qatna and Hazor are mentioned together in the Mari archives, *ARM*, VI.78, cited by Malamat ("Hazor 'The Head of all those Kingdoms," *JBL* LXXIX [1960] 19).

[63]Yadin, "Excavations at Hazor," *BAR*, II. 193=194.

[64]Ibid., 224.

[65]Cf. John Garstang, *The Foundations of Bible History: Joshua, Judges* (London: Constable, 1931) 185.

[66]Yadin, "Excavations at Hazor," 209-211.

[67]Ibid., 212. Yadin's population estimate is apparently based on his estimate of about 240 inhabitants per urban acre. In this case it figures out to about 222.

[68]De Vaux (*Ancient Israel*, I, 67) gives a figure of about 30,000 for Samaria at the time of its fall and believes that the population of Jerusalem at its pre-exilic peak was about 25,000 - 30,000. However, he warns that any calculation of urban population in the OT is precarious, owing to the nature of the city as a place of refuge.

[69]Kingsley Davis ("The Origin and Growth of Urbanism in the World," *AJOS* LX [1955] 432) estimates that the percentage of non-agricultural urban dwellers was probably not more than 1-2 per cent, and that 50-90 farmers were required to support one man in the city. Applying this yardstick to the estimate of de Vaux (*Ancient Israel*, I, 67) that Palestine could hardly have supported a population of more than one million, the number of non-agriculturally employed city dwellers could not have exceeded ca. 20,000.

[70]Kenyon, *Archaeology*, 181. Cf. Van Seters (*The Hyksos*, 37) who holds that there is no reason for postulating, for the so-called Hyksos defenses, an immigration either of a new people or of a new warrior aristocracy. On the contrary, he believes that the fortifications are the product of developments inspired in part by the Amorite and Egyptian worlds, and in part by native inventiveness applied to materials and geography.

[71]Albright (*From the Stone Age to Christianity*, 208) attributes this situation both to the oppressive Egyptian domination and the inner weakness of Canaanite civilization. Cf. also Aharoni (*Land of the Bible*, 139).

[72]Cf. esp. Alt, "The Settlement of the Israelites in Palestine," *Essays on Old Testament History and Religion*, 179-182.

[73]For a concise summary and bibliography on the ʿapiru problem, see Mary Gray ("The Habiru-Hebrew Problem," *HUCA* XXIX [1958] 135-202).

[74]George Mendenhall, "The Hebrew Conquest of Palestine," *BA* XXV (1962) 73.

[75]Ibid., 71-73.

[76]A recent survey and up-to-date bibliography of these three types is that of Manfred Weippert (*Der Landnahme der israelitischen Stämme in der neueren wissenschaftlichen Diskussion* [Göttingen: Vandenhoeck und Ruprecht, 1967]). Cf. the review by W. L. Moran (*CBQ* XXX [1968] 644-645).

[77]Noth, *The History of Israel*, 149.

[78]Lapp, "The Conquest of Palestine in the Light of Archaeology," *Concordia Theological Monthly* XXXVIII (1967) 298-299.

[79]Mendenhall, "The Hebrew Conquest," 66-67.

[80]Hahn's main work is *Von der Hacke zum Pflug*, published in 1914. The quotation here is from D. Forde (*Habitat, Economy and Society*, 461) quoted by John T. Luke (*Pastoralism and Politics in the Mari Period: a Re-examination of the Character and Political Significance of the Major West Semitic Tribal Groups on the Middle Euphrates, ca. 1828-1758 B.C.* [unpublished Ph.D. dissertation, University of Michigan, 1965] 22-23). The traditional sequence has also been challenged by Louis Wallis (*A Sociological Study of the Bible* [Chicago: University of Chicago, 1912] 56-57) and lately by G. Widengren in his review of Sabatino Moscati's *Le antiche divinita semitiche* (*JSS* I (1956) 397-399.

[81]R. J. Braidwood and Bruce Howe, *Prehistoric Investigations in Iraqi Kurdistan* (Chicago: University of Chicago, 1960) 170-172. Cf. also Burchard Brentjes ("Wer war zuerst da: Nomade oder Bauer?," *Wissenschaft und Fortschritt* [1965] 86-89. A summary of Brentjes' conclusions is found in *IZBG* XIII (1966-67) 198.

[82]De Vaux, *Ancient Israel*, I, 3-4. Cf. also his "Les patriarches hebreux," 17-20. [A recent bibliography on nomadism can be found in the work of Norman K. Gottwald ("Nomadism," *IDBSup*, 630-631)].

[83]The most thorough studies on the domestication of the camel are those of Reinhard Walz ("Zum Problem des Zeitpunkts der Domestikation der altweltlichen Cameliden," *ZDMG* CI [1951] 29-51, and "Neue Untersuchungen zum Domestikationsproblem der altweltlichen Cameliden," *ZDMG* CIV [1954] 45-87).

[84]De Vaux, *Ancient Israel*, I, 4. Cf. below, 220-222.

[85]Weber, *Ancient Judaism*, 13. Cf. also Eric Voegelin (*Order and History, I, Israel and Revelation* [Baton Rouge: Louisiana State University, 1956] 208-210) who not only questions the applicability of the Bedouin analogy but points out instances of an outright disregard of Bedouin mores in even the earliest strata of the OT.

[86] Samuel Nyström, *Beduinentum und Jahvismus: Eine sozio-logisch-religionsgeschichtliche Untersuchung zum A.T.* (Lund: C. W. K. Gleerup, 1946). [For a perceptive study of how such assumptions have functioned in OT studies, see Norman K. Gott-wald ("Domain Assumptions and Societal Models in the Study of Pre-monarchic Israel," VTSup, Edinburgh Congress Vol. [1975] 1-12)].

[87] Ibid., 24-27.

[88] J. Flight, "The Nomadic Idea and Ideal in the Old Testament," *JBL* XLII (1923) 158-226.

[89] Cf. Albright (*From the Stone Age to Christianity*, 164-166) and R. Walz ("Gab es ein Esel-Nomadentum im alten Orient?" *Akten des xxiv internationalen orientalisten Kongresses*, H. Franke, ed. [Wiesbaden, 1959] 150-152).

[90] Albright, "Abram the Hebrew," 36-54; Gordon, "Abraham and the Merchants of Ura," *JNES* XVII (1958) 28-31; Gordon, "Abraham of Ur," *Hebrew and Semitic Studies Presented to Godfrey Rolles Driver* (eds. D. W. Thomas and W. D. McHardy; Oxford: Oxford University, 1963) 77-84; and Loren Fisher, "Abraham and his Priest-King," *JBL* LXXXI (1962) 264.

[91] Cf. Percy E. Newberry, *Beni Hasan*, I (London: Trubner and Co., 1893-1900) pl. XXX-XXXL, XXXVIII. Cf. also the interpretation of S. Yeivin ("Topographic and Ethnic Notes," *Atiqot* II [1959] 157-158).

[92] Albright, "Abram the Hebrew," 40-42.

[93] Cf., e.g., the criticism of Hunt (*World of the Patriarchs*, 48-49).

[94] Gordon, "Abraham and the Merchants of Ura," 29.

[95] Shemaryahu Talmon, "The 'Desert Motif' in the Bible and in Qumran Literature," *Biblical Motifs: Origins and Transformations* (ed. A. Altmann; Cambridge: Harvard University, 1966) 34.

[96] Gen 26:12. Note that in 26:6 it is said that Isaac dwelt "in Gerar." For other references to patriarchal agricultural activity see Gen 30:14; 37:7; 33:17, 19.

[97] Gen 13:5; 15:9; 18:7-9; 32:6, 8-16; 33:13.

[98] Mendenhall, "The Hebrew Conquest," 69. [Cf. also now, Mendenhall, "Social Organization in Early Israel," *Magnalia Dei*, 132-151].

[99] Luke, *Pastoralism and Politics*, 29-31.

[100] Ibid., 277-278.

[101] Luke bases his discussion on the text as it appears in Kramer (*History Begins at Sumer*, 136-138). For other texts

with a similar theme, cf. the discussion below of the Cain-Abel theme, 205-207.

[102]Luke, *Pastoralism and Politics*, 29-31.

[103]It might be noted in passing, that the sources from Mari are written from the viewpoint of the urban group, while the OT sources dealing with the Israelite "conquest" reflect the interests of the opposite group.

[104]Luke, *Pastoralism and Politics*, 37.

[105]Weber, *Ancient Judaism*, 54.

[106]Noth, *The History of Israel*, 145. Noth's observation is apparently based on the references to these tribes in the Testament of Jacob in Gen 49. E. Speiser (*Genesis*, AB, vol. 1 [Garden City: Doubleday, 1965] 371) assigns this passage "to an early stage in the Israelite settlement in Canaan, with some of the allusions resting perhaps on still earlier traditions. In no instance is there the slightest indication of a setting later than the end of the second millennium."

[107]Noth, *The History of Israel*, 149.

[108]Ibid., 153. Noth identifies Arumah with the modern el-'Orme, ca. six miles SE of Shechem. Cf. Aharoni, *Land of the Bible*, 372.

[109]Weber, *Ancient Judaism*, 39.

[110]Mendenhall, "The Hebrew Conquest," 69.

[111]See Chapter I, 5.

[112]Noth, *The History of Israel*, 106. According to Noth, the clan was the largest unit still held together by ties of blood relationship.

[113]R. H. Lowie, *The Origins of the State* (N.Y.: Russell and Russell, 1962) 62.

[114]Cf. Gen 23:2; 35:27; Num 13:22; Josh 15:54; 20:7; 21: 11; Neh 11:25.

[115]Malamat, "Mari and the Bible," 144-145. Malamat cites *ARM*, I:119,10; VII:267.2 as references in which the phrase *ḥibrum ša nawîm* occurs. He defines *ḥibrum* as a "separate union of families linked together within the larger unit of the clan or tribe." On the meaning of *nawîm*, see above, 59-60.

[116]Mendenhall, "The Hebrew Conquest," 70.

[117]Cf. de Vaux, *Ancient Israel*, I, 12. He observes that in many of the genealogies of Chronicles names of villages are used to replace the names of ancestors. In this regard, cf. esp. 1 Chr 2.

[118] Deut 31:28; 1 Sam 30:26; 2 Sam 19:12; Ezek 8:1; Judg 11:5. Cf. Noth, *The History of Israel*, 108.

[119] De Vaux, *Ancient Israel*, I, 12. Albright (*From the Stone Age to Christianity*, 283) observes that only in the administrative lists which are incorporated into the Priestly Code and the Book of Chronicles do we find reference to tribal chieftains.

[120] Mendenhall, "The Hebrew Conquest," 77.

[121] Voegelin, *Order and History*, I, 204-205.

[122] Sjoberg, *Preindustrial City*, 70.

[123] Cf. Oppenheim, *Ancient Mesopotamia*, 118.

[124] Cf. the figures cited above in n.69. It is also interesting to note that in the Gezer calendar, there is some agricultural task listed for every month of the year.

[125] Davis, "The Origin and Growth of Urbanism," 431-432.

[126] G. E. Wright, "The Provinces of Solomon (1 Kgs 4:7-19)" *Eretz Israel* VIII (1967) 59-62.

[127] Kenyon, *Archaeology*, 285-286.

[128] Flight, "The Nomadic Ideal," 197.

[129] Frank M. Cross, Jr., "Yahweh and the God of the Patriarchs," *HTR* IV (1962) 321. Alt's position is set forth in his essay, "The God of the Fathers," *Essays on Old Testament History and Religion*, 1-86.

[130] Cross, "Yahweh and the God of the Patriarchs," 232.

[131] Alfred Guillaume, *Prophecy and Divination among the Hebrews and other Semites* (London: Hodder and Stoughton, 1938) 61-64.

[132] W. C. Graham, "Recent Light on the Cultural Origins of the Hebrews," *JR* XIV (1934) 319.

[133] Cf. Gerhard von Rad, *Old Testament Theology*, I (N.Y.: Harper and Row, 1962) 15.

[134] Cf. Raphael Hallevy, "The Canaanite Period: A Culture Clash," *Tarbiz* XXXV (1965) 95-102 (Hebrew). For an English summary see *IZBG* XIV (1967-68) 245.

[135] Von Rad, *Old Testament Theology*, I, 20. Cf. also Parsons, *Societies: Evolutionary and Comparative Perspectives*, 96.

[136] Wright, "The Provinces of Solomon," 173.

[137] This verse is usually attributed to J, but O. Eissfeldt (*The Old Testament: An Introduction*, [N.Y.: Harper and Row,

1965] 195) assigns 4:17a, 18-24 to his "L" source, which he considers to be the oldest narrative strand in the OT because it presents "an outline of . . . history which places nomads at the beginning,"and must therefore "be older than one (viz., J) which pictures the first men as husbandsmen." On this theory, then, he excludes 4:17b from this source. Eissfeldt's separation of his L source appears thus to rest on the concept of cultural evolution which we have called into question.

[138]Cf. the genealogies of 1 Chr 1-6, where cities are listed as the "sons" of their supposed founders or "fathers." See also Josh 21:11 and Judg 9:28.

[139]Cf. J. Gabriel ("Die Kainitengenealogie," *Bib* [1959] 409-427) and also Albright ("Dedan," *Geschichte und Altes Testament* [Fs. A. Alt; Tübingen: J. C. B. Mohr, 1953] 9-11).

[140]Gerhard Wallis, "Die Stadt in den Uberlieferungen der Genesis," *ZAW*, LXXIII(1966) 134. Cf. also 2 Chr 14:14 where, in an account dealing with the destruction of a city, it is said that "they smote the tents of those who had cattle."

[141]Hugo Gressmann (*The Tower of Babel* [N.Y.: Jewish Institute of Religion, 1928] 25) contends that it was added later, probably to illustrate the corruption of mankind before the flood.

[142]Cf. Gen 9:20 with 4:2b. Hermann Gunkel (*Genesis* [Göttingen: Vandenhoeck und Ruprecht, 1910] 53), however, sees *qenān* (5:12) as a variant of Cain (*qayin*). Enoch also appears in the Sethite genealogy.

[143]For a partial list see Wallis ("Die Stadt," 137, n.24). To this list should be added John Skinner (*Genesis*, ICC, vol. 1 [2d ed., Edinburgh: T. and T. Clark, 1930] 114-116) and esp. S. Hooke (*Middle Eastern Mythology*, Pelican Book [Baltimore: Penguin Books, 1963] 123-126).

[144]Kramer, *History Begins at Sumer*, 136-142. See also Castellino ("Les origines de la civilisation," 133-134). It is interesting to note that these stories do not presuppose a normal state of conflict between the nomad and the farmer. In the biblical account it is the farmer and not the nomad who is the aggressor. It might also be noted that the agriculturalist, in the person of Cain, is older than the nomad, Abel.

[145]Hooke, *Middle Eastern Mythology*, 123-125. Cf. Lev 16: 8, 10, 26. Hooke sees in the story an expiatory ritual which J has used for his own purpose, viz., the aetiological one of explaining the origin of the blood feud.

[146]Such an interpretation is suggested by John S. Dunne (*The City of the Gods* [N.Y.: Macmillan, 1965) 30-31). He contends that in Mesopotamian mythology, quarrels between cities over hegemony in the land could accordingly be understood as a dispute between their kings for the hand of the goddess. Sometimes the dispute took the form of claims and counterclaims of rival cities to be the dwelling place of the goddess, and sometimes, with the implicit acknowledgment that the rival city

was the actual habitation of the goddess, it took the form of a demand that the goddess be brought from one city to another. Dunne thus sees in the dispute between Enkidu and Dumuzi (*ANET*, 41-42) a contention between two cities for the goddess since both of the rivals for the hand of Inanna are said to be kings, and Dumuzi is known to have been king of Erech. While the banishment of Cain is hard to reconcile with Dunne's interpretation, there is a parallel for the motif of the banishment of a city in Ugaritic mythology; cf. Gaster, *Thespis*, 364-365.

[147]Skinner (*Genesis*, 116-117) would solve this seeming contradiction by emending the *kĕšēm bĕnô* of v17 to read *kišmô*, thus making Enoch the builder of the city which is called by his name. This emendation is suggested in order to avoid "the ascription to Cain of two steps in civilization--agriculture and city-building." It thus appears to have been made on tendentious grounds rather than textual ones, and is neither necessary nor convincing.

[148]As Wallis ("Die Stadt," 137) observes, the curse on Cain was not that of being condemned to nomadism so much as it was being expelled from the tribal structure with its protection.

[149]Cf. 1 Sam 26:19; 2 Kgs 5:17-18; Jonah 1:3; Lev 16:7-10.

[150]Advocates of a two-source theory include: Gunkel (*Genesis*, 92-93); W. Zimmerli (*l Mose l-ll, die Urgeschichte* [2. Aufl., Zurich: Zwingli, 1957] 159-161); von Rad (*Genesis* [Philadelphia: Westminster, 1961] 144-146); S. Hooke ("Genesis," *PCB*, 185); and C. A. Simpson ("Genesis," *IB*, I, 562-563).

[151]Cf. Jean Daniélou, *Au commencement: Genèse l-ll* (Paris: Editions du Seuil, 1963) 112-114.

[152]Von Rad, *Genesis*, 145. Such an explicit motive is attributed to the building in this story as it appears in *Jub.* 10:18-20: "'Behold the children of men have become evil through the wicked purpose of building for themselves a city and a tower, saying, 'Go to, let us ascend thereby into heaven.'" Translation from R. H. Charles (*The Apocrypha and Pseudepigrapha of the Old Testament in English*, vol. II [Oxford: Clarendon, 1913] 28-29).

[153]Note in this connection that the "tower" is not mentioned after v5, and the antecedent of the phrase, "Therefore its name was called Babel," in v9 is the word "city" in v8.

[154]E. Speiser, "Word Plays on the Creation Epic's Version of the Founding of Babylon," *Orientalia* XXV (1956) 318-320.

[155]Cf. O.E. Ravn's translation, "eine Stadt und Burg" ("Der Turm zu Babel: Eine exegetische Studie über Gen. 11.1-9," *ZDMG* XVI [1937] 353). Note that in the story, the *migdāl* is completed. The expansion of the city around the citadel is what is interrupted.

[156]Cf. Deut 2:36; 9:1; and Isa 1:12-15.

[157] In *Jub.* 10:23-25, the judgment is expressed in terms which indicate that the point of the story is not a general anti-urbanism, but rather a judgment against the empire city: ". . . they may be dispersed into cities and nations, and one purpose will no longer abide them. . ." Quoted from Charles (*Apocrypha and Pseudepigrapha*, II, 29).

[158] Cf. I. Mendelsohn, "Samuel's Denunciation of Kingship in the Light of the Akkadian Documents from Ugarit," *BASOR* 143(1956) 17-22. The phrase "Let us make a name for ourselves" (v4) may be related to this aspect of the city if, as R. Abba suggests ("Name," *IDB*, III, 501), šēm can be derived from the root šmh, "to be high," and hence have the primary meaning of "monument" or "memorial." Cf. 2 Sam 8:3; Isa 55:13.

[159] Cf. Wallis, "Die Stadt," 143-145. It seems, however, that in some instances Wallis is overeager in his association of the condemnation of any social evil in OT literature with anti-urban sentiments.

[160] Von Rad, *Old Testament Theology*, I, 64-65.

[161] Scott, *Relevance of the Prophets*, 180, 182.

[162] K. Budde, "The Nomadic Ideal in the Old Testament," *The New World* IV (1895) 726-745.

[163] Ibid., 727-729.

[164] P. Humbert, "Osée le prophète bédouin," *Revue d'histoire et de philosophie religieuses* I (1921) 97-118. Cf. also his "La logique de la perspective nomade chez Osée," *Festschrift Marti* (ed. K. Budde; Giessen: Töpfelmann, 1925) 158-166.

[165] Humbert, "Osée le prophète bédouin," 115.

[166] Cf. Scott, *Relevance of the Prophets*, 185.

[167] Flight, "The Nomadic Ideal," 158-226.

[168] Talmon, "The 'Desert Motif,'" 33.

[169] Literature on the Rechabites beyond articles in Bible dictionaries and notes in general works includes: Lucien Gautier, *A propos des Récabites; un chapitre de l'histoire religieuse d'Israel avant l'exil* (Lausanne, 1927); M. Y. Ben-Gavriel, "Das nomadische Ideal in der Bibel," *Stimmen der Zeit* 171(1962-63) 253-263; P. Seidensticker, "Prophetensöhne-Rechabiter-Nasiräer," *Studii Biblici Fransiscani, Liber Annus* X(1959) 65-119; S. Talmon, "1 Chronicles 2:55," *Eretz-Israel* V (1958) 111-113 (Hebrew with English summary); S. Abramsky, "The House of Rechab--Genealogy and Military League," *Eretz-Israel* VIII (1967) 255-264 (Hebrew with English summary). [This author now sees the Rechabites as a group of metallurgists or smiths whose peculiar life-style was derived from their occupational pattern. See "Rechabites," *IDBSup*, 726-728 and the bibliography cited there].

[170]Causse, *Du groupe ethnique*, 67. Neither is there support for the idea of Pope ("Rechab," *IDB*, IV, 15) that the "proto-Rechabites" were probably a nomad clan who pastured their flocks in the marginal areas of the northern kingdom."

[171]If it is taken in this way, the particular Rechab in question cannot be identified with certainty. It might be the Rechab mentioned in 2 Sam 4:2, who is an army officer.

[172]In this sense, cf. the use of the expression "sons of the prophets" to designate a group who separated themselves from society and devoted themselves to Yahweh's service under a prophet who was their "father." Cf. J. G. Williams ("The Prophetic Father," *JBL* LXXXV [1966] 344-348) and Mendelsohn ("Guilds in Ancient Israel," 17-19).

[173]Cf. W. H. Bennet, "Rechab, Rechabites," *A Dictionary of the Bible* (ed. J. Hastings; N.Y.: Scribner's, 1902, vol. IV, 204).

[174]S. Cohen, "Beth-marcaboth," *IDB*, III, 220. Cf. 2 Chr 9:25.

[175]Sjoberg, *Preindustrial City*, 263.

[176]Ben-gavriel, "Das nomadische Ideal," 256.

[177]Causse (*Les 'pauvres d'Israël'* [Strasbourg: Librairie Istra, 1922] 39-40) believes that Budde overstates the importance of the Rechabites in Jehu's reform.

[178]Cf. the story of Sinuhe (*ANET*, 19-21) and Albright (*The Biblical Period from Abraham to Ezra* [N.Y.: Harper and Row, 1963] -1-12).

[179]Cf. 2 Sam 11:11 and also von Rad (*Der heilige Krieg*, 6-8).

[180]Scott, *Relevance of the Prophets*, 52. On the Nazirites, cf. Amos 2:11-12; Num 6; Judg 13:5; 1 Sam 1:11. Scott observes that 4QSam[a] at 1 Sam 1:22 preserves the reading, "I will make him a Nazirite forever." Cf. also the reference in *UT*, 144.4 to a *bn ndr*, "son of a vow," i.e., "a Nazirite."

[181]J. C. Rylaarsdam, "Nazirite," *IDB*, III, 526. Cf. also Weber, *Ancient Judaism*, 94-95.

[182]Cf. Seidensticker ("Prophetensöhne-Rechabiter-Nasiraer," 98) and A. Weiser (*Das Buch Jeremia*, ATD, vols. 20-21 [5. Aufl., Göttingen: Vandenhoeck und Ruprecht, 1966] 320, n.2). On the phrase ʿōmēd lifnê yhwh, cf. Gen 18:22; Judg 20:28; Deut 10:8; 18:5, 7; Pss 133:1; 134:1; Jer 15:19.

[183]On the later traditions concerning the Rechabites as cultic personnel see Pope ("Rechab," 16).

[184]1 Chr 2:55; 4:12. Far from proving the nomadic nature of either group, the intent of these genealogical notes seems

to have been to give them local connections. Cf. Myers, *l Chronicles*, 15-16, 26-28.

[185]The passage is found in *Diodorus of Sicily*, vol. X, xix, 94.2-4: "They neither sow grain nor plant fruit-bearing plants, nor drink, nor build a house; whoever acts to the contrary is punished with death." On the use of Nabatean sources cf. S. Cohen ("Nabateans," *IDB*, III, 491). The purpose of the Rechabite vow was to deserve long life in the land.

[186]Paul Riemann, *Desert and Return to Desert in the Pre-Exilic Prophets* (unpublished Ph.D. dissertation, Harvard University, 1963-64) 53.

[187]Abramsky, "The House of Rechab," 76.

[188]Cf. also Talmon ("The 'Desert Motif,'"); Chr. Barth ("Zur Bedeutung der Wüstentradition," VTSup, XV[Leiden: E. J. Brill, 1966] 14-23); R. T. Anderson ("The Role of the Desert in Israelite Thought," *JBRL* XXVII [1959] 41-44); U. Mauser (*Christ in the Wilderness* [London: SCM Press, 1963] 15-17); and H. W. Wolff ("Das Thema 'Umkehr' in der alttestamentlichen Prophetie," *ZTK* XLVIII [1951] 129-148).

[189]Talmon ("The 'Desert Motif,'" 33), quoting de Vaux (*Ancient Israel*, I, 13-14).

[190]Hos 12:12. Cf. Guillaume, *Prophecy and Divination*, 86.

[191]Talmon, "The 'Desert Motif,'" 35. Cf. also Hammershaimb, "The Ethics of the Prophets," 79-81.

[192]Amos 2:10; 5:25; Hos 13:5; Jer 2:2, 6.

[193]Riemann, *Desert and Return to Desert*, 114-115. On the amalgamation of the Exodus and wilderness themes, cf. Mauser (*Christ in the Wilderness*) 15-18.

[194]Budde, "The Nomadic Ideal," 732.

[195]De Vaux, *Ancient Israel*, I, 14.

[196]Causse, "Les prophètes et la crise sociologique de la religion d'Israel," *Revue d'histoire et de philosophie religieuse* (1932) 118. Cf. also his *Du groupe ethnique*, 87.

[197]Cf. Talmon, "The 'Desert Motif,'" 50.

[198]Barth, "Zur Bedeutung der Wüstentradition," 19. Cf. also Hos 9:10; 12:9.

[199]Talmon, "The 'Desert Motif,'" 37.

[200]Wolff, "Das Thema 'Umkehr,'" 129-130. Cf. also G. H. Williams, *Wilderness and Paradise in Christian Thought* (N.Y.: Harper and Row, 1962) 15-18.

[201]H. E. W. Fosbroke, "Amos," *IB*, VI, 821.

[202]Von Rad, *Old Testament Theology*, I, 281.

[203]Barth, "Zur Bedeutung der Wüstentradition," 18-19.

[204]Riemann, *Desert and Return to Desert*, 391-393. On the Israelite concept of the desert, cf. Anderson ("The Role of the Desert in Israelite Thought," 41-44) and A. O. Haldar (*The Notion of the Desert in the Sumero-Akkadian and West-Semitic Religions* [Uppsala: A. B. Lundequist, 1950]).

[205]D. J. McCarthy, *Treaty and Covenant: A Study in Form in the Ancient Oriental Documents and in the Old Testament* (Rome: Pontifical Biblical Institute, 1963); Hillers, *Treaty-Curses and the Old Testament Prophets*; F. C. Fensham, "Maledictions and Benedictions in Ancient Near Eastern Vassal-Treaties and the Old Testament," *ZAW* LXXIV (1962) 1-9; and Fensham, "Common Trends in Curses of the NE Treaties and *Kudurru*-inscriptions compared with Maledictions of Amos and Isaiah," *ZAW* LXXV (1963) 155-175.

[206]Cf. George Mendenhall, "Law and Covenant in Israel and the Ancient Near East," *BA* XVII (1954) 26-46; 49-76, esp. 43.

[207]Sefire I A.32-34. Text in *KAI*, no. 22.

[208]This same theme appears with minor variations in Isa 13:19-22; Jer 50:39; Isa 34:11-13; 17:1-2; 27:10; 32:14; Jer 10:22; 49:33; 51:37; Ezek 25:5. Cf. also Deut 29:20-22.

[209]Hillers, *Treaty Curses*, 76. Cf. Jer 19:8.

[210]Ibid., 74. Cf. Deut 29:22-23; 32:32; Isa 1:9; Jer 20:16; 49:17-18; 50:39-40; Hos 11:8; Amos 4:11; Zeph 2:9.

[211]Dunne, *City of the Gods*, 29.

[212]Thorkild Jacobsen, "Mesopotamia: The Cosmos as a State," *Before Philosophy* (eds. H. and H. A. Frankfort; Harmondsworth: Penguin Books, 1951) 154.

[213]Hos 13:9-10a. For the text on which this translation is based, cf. *BHK*, but retain *bĕkol-'ārekā* with LXX and Vulgate.

[214]A. Weiser, *Das Buch der zwölf kleinen Propheten*, ATD, vol. 24 (4. verbesserter Aufl, Göttingen: Vandenhoeck und Ruprecht, 1963) 70-71.

[215]On "citadel" as a translation of *'armon*, see above, 49-50. Gottwald (*All the Kingdoms of the Earth*, 132) believes that the echo in 8:14b of the foreign-oracle framework of Amos 1-2 is probably drawn from the same execration traditions that were used by Amos and Joel.

[216]Hos 14:1 (English 13:16). These same atrocities are associated with the conquest of cities in Isa 13:16-18; 2 Kgs 8:12; and in attenuated form in Hos 10:14.

[217] Fosbroke, "Amos," 803.

[218] The reference in the second half of the verse may be to Samaria, or to all the cities of the northern kingdom. The word "city" lacks the definite article. Cf. also Amos 4:1-3.

[219] Isa 17:9-10. Only Isaiah makes use of the term *ṣûr* in referring to Yahweh as the defense of his people. Cf. 26:4; 30:29. This imagery is frequent in the Deuteronomic history and in the Psalms.

[220] Isa 26:1 (*JB*); 33:15-16a. Cf. also 23:11; 25:11b-12; 28:17.

[221] Jer 5:15a, 17e; 21:13-14. For this translation of *yaʿar*, see above, 50-52. It is also possible that in some instances *yʿr* is a textual error, caused by the transposition of the letters of *ʿyr*, "city," and is thus the usual term; with its meaning of "citadel." The phrase here: *wĕhiṣṣatî ʾēš bĕyaʿrāh wĕʾākĕlāh kol-sĕbîbĕhā*, should be compared with the phrase *wĕhiṣṣatî bĕʿîrhā wĕʾākĕlāh kol-sĕbîbĕhā*, which occurs in Jer 17:27; 49:27; 50:32. Cf. also 49:27. According to *BHK*, the Syriac of 21:14 reads *bĕʿārêhā*.

[222] Deut 6:10 (cf. Josh 24:13); 3:18; 28:52.

[223] Scott, *Relevance of the Prophets*, 180-181. Underlining is that of this author.

[224] Wallis, "Die Stadt," 147.

[225] John L. McKenzie, *The Two-Edged Sword: An Interpretation of the Old Testament* (Milwaukee: Bruce, 1957) 159-160.

[226] Scott, *Relevance of the Prophets*, 190-191.

[227] Sjoberg, *Preindustrial City*, 261-262.

[228] Cf. Scott, *Relevance of the Prophets*, 201. Cf. also Amos 4:4, 5; 5:21-23; Hos 8:11; 10:1; Isa 1:11; 2:8; Jer 3:1; 11:13.

[229] Cf. Hos 4:11-14; Jer 2:27-28.

[230] Louis Finklestein, *The Pharisees: The Sociological Background of Their Faith* (Phila.: Jewish Publication Society, 1938) 2.

[231] Ibid., 295. He would also divide Jeremiah and Micah into rural and urban sections. He further classifies the prophets in this manner: Nahum, rural; Habakkuk, urban; Zephaniah, "an urban patrician who identified himself with the masses"; Ezekiel, a prophet of rural origin who was converted to the urban point of view during the Exile.

[232] On the meaning of *nōqēd*, see Bič ("Der Prophet Amos--ein Haepatoskopos," *VT* I [1951] 293-296) and the reply of Murtonen ("The Prophet Amos--a Hepatoscoper," *VT* II [1952] 170-171).

On the classification of Tekoa as a city, cf. 2 Chr 11:6; Jer 6:1.

[233]Scott (*Relevance of the Prophets*, 175) infers this on the basis that he, like Isaiah and Zephaniah, was identified only by his paternal ancestry.

[234]On the identification with Tell el-Judeideh and its probable inclusion in the list of sites fortified by Rehoboam, cf. Aharoni (*Land of the Bible*, 292).

[235]Anathoth is probably a shortened form of Beth-Anathoth, which would indicate that the city had a temple of Anath. Cf. Aharoni, *Land of the Bible*, 97. Anathoth is listed among the Levitical cities in Josh 18.

[236]Weber, *Ancient Judaism*, 277.

[237]Ibid., 279-281. Cf. also Scott, *Relevance of the Prophets*, 181-182.

SELECTED BIBLIOGRAPHY

I. General Reference Works and Exegetical Aids

Aharoni, Y. *The Land of the Bible: A Historical Geography.* Translated by A. F. Rainey. London: Burns and Oates, 1962.

Aharoni, Y., and M. Avi-Yonah. *The Macmillan Bible Atlas.* N.Y.: Macmillan, 1968.

Aistleitner, J. *Wörterbuch der ugaritischen Sprache.* Edited by O. Eissfeldt. 3rd ed. Berlin: Akademie-Verlag, 1963.

Barucq, Andre. *Le livre des Proverbes.* Paris: Gabalda, 1964.

Bauer, Hans, and Pontus Leander. *Historische Grammatik der hebräischen Sprache des Alten Testaments.* Vol. 1. Hildesheim: Georg Olms, 1962.

Black, M., and H. H. Rowley (eds). *Peake's Commentary on the Bible.* London: Nelson, 1962.

Bright, J. "Isaiah," *PCB*, 489-515.

_____. *Jeremiah.* AB, 21. Garden City: Doubleday, 1965.

_____. "The Book of Joshua, Introduction and Exegesis," *IB*, Vol. II, 541-673.

Brockelmann, C. *Grundriss der vergleichenden Grammatik der semitischen Sprachen.* 2 vols. N.Y.: Lemcke and Buechner, 1908-1913.

Brockington, L. H. "I and II Samuel," *PCB*, 318-337.

Brown, F., S. R. Driver, and C. A. Briggs. *A Hebrew and English Lexicon of the Old Testament.* Oxford: The Clarendon Press, 1907 (reprinted with corrections, 1953, 1957, 1959).

Budde, K. *Die Bücher Samuel, erklärt.* KHAT, Vol. 8. Tübingen: J. C. B. Mohr, 1902.

Buttrick, G. B. (ed.). *The Interpreter's Dictionary of the Bible.* 4 vols. N.Y.: Abingdon, 1962.

Caird, G. B. "The First and Second Books of Samuel, Introduction and Exegesis," *IB*, Vol. II, 853-1176.

Charles, R. H. (ed.). *The Apocrypha and Pseudepigrapha of the Old Testament in English.* 2 vols. Oxford: The Clarendon Press, 1913.

Clements, R. E. *God's Chosen People: A Theological Interpretation of the Book of Deuteronomy.* London: SCM, 1968.

Cowley, A. E. *Aramaic Papyri of the Fifth Century B.C.* Oxford: The Clarendon Press, 1923.

[Crim, K. (ed.). *The Interpreter's Dictionary of the Bible: Supplementary Volume.* N.Y.: Abingdon, 1976.]

Dahood, M. *Psalms I, 1-50.* AB, 16. Garden City: Doubleday, 1965.

_____. *Psalms II, 51-100*. AB, 17. Garden City: Doubleday, 1968.

Danby, Herbert. *The Mishnah: Translated from the Hebrew with introduction and brief explanatory Notes*. London: Oxford University Press, 1933.

Daniélou, J. *Au commencement: Genèse 1-11*. Paris: Editions du Seuil, 1963.

Dillmann, A. *Der Prophet Jesaia, erklärt*. 5th ed. Leipzig: S. Hirzel, 1890.

Donner, H., and W. Röllig. *Kanaanäische und aramäische Inschriften*. 3 vols. Wiesbaden: O. Harrassowitz, 1962.

Driver, G. R. *Canaanite Myths and Legends*. Edinburgh: T. and T. Clark, 1956.

Driver, S. R. *A Critical and Exegetical Commentary on the Book of Deuteronomy*. ICC, Vol. V. N.Y.: Scribner's Sons, 1902.

_____. *Introduction to the Literature of the Old Testament*. rev. ed. N.Y.: Scribner's Sons, 1913.

_____. *Notes on the Hebrew Text and Topography of the Books of Samuel*. 2nd ed. Oxford: The Clarendon Press, 1913.

Eichrodt, W. *Der Prophet Hezekiel*. ATD, Vol. XIII. Göttingen: Vandenhoeck und Ruprecht, 1966.

Eissfeldt, O. *The Old Testament: an Introduction*. Translated by P. Ackroyd. N.Y.: Harper and Row, 1965.

Etheridge, J. W. *The Targums of Onkelos and Jonathan ben Uzziel on the Pentateuch with the Fragments of the Jerusalem Targum from the Chaldee*. 1862. N.Y.: Ktav, 1968.

Fosbroke, H. E. W. "The Book of Amos, Introduction and Exegesis," *IB*, Vol. VI, 763-853.

Fuerst, J. *A Hebrew and Chaldee Lexicon to the Old Testament*. Translated by Samuel Davidson. 3rd ed. Leipzig: Bernhard Tauchnitz, 1867.

Galling, K. *Biblisches Reallexikon*. Tübingen: J. C. B. Mohr, 1937.

Garstang, John. *The Foundations of Bible History: Joshua and Judges*. London: Constable and Co., 1931.

Gelb, I. J., et al. (eds.). *The Assyrian Dictionary of the Oriental Institute of the University of Chicago*. 9 vols. to date. Chicago: The Oriental Institute, 1956- .

Gesenius, W. *A Hebrew and English Lexicon of the Old Testament*. Translated by E. Robinson. 20th ed. Boston: Crocker and Brewster, 1854.

_____. *Wilhelm Gesenius' hebräisches und aramäisches Handwörterbuch über das Alte Testament*. Edited by F. Buhl. 15th ed. Leipzig: C. W. Vogel, 1910.

Gordon, C. H. *Ugaritic Textbook*. (AnOr, Vol. XXXVIII). Rome: Pontifical Biblical Institute, 1965.

Gray, J. *I and II Kings*. Philadelphia: Westminster Press, 1963.

Gunkel, H. *Genesis*. Göttingen: Vandenhoeck und Ruprecht, 1910.

Haag, H. (ed.). *Bibel-Lexikon*. 2nd ed. Zurich: Benziger Verlag, 1968.

Harper, W. R. *A Critical and Exegetical Commentary on Amos and Hosea*. ICC, Vol. XXIII. Edinburgh: T. and T. Clark, 1905.

Hastings, J. (ed.). *Dictionary of the Bible*. 5 vols. Edinburgh: T. and T. Clark, 1898-1904.

_____. *Dictionary of the Bible*. Rev. ed. by F. C. Grant and H. H. Rowley. N.Y.: Charles Scribner's Sons, 1963.

Hertzberg, H. W. *I and II Samuel*. Translated by J. S. Bowden. London: SCM, 1964.

The Holy Bible. Revised Standard Version. N.Y.: Nelson, 1953.

Hooke, S. H. "Genesis," *PCB*, 175-207.

Jastrow, M. (compiler). *A Dictionary of the Targum, the Talmud Babli and Yerushalmi, and the Midrashic Literature*. 2 vols. N.Y.: Pardes, 1950.

Jean, C. F., and J. Hoftizer. *Dictionnaire des inscriptions sémitiques de l'ouest*. Leiden: E. J. Brill, 1965.

The Jerusalem Bible. Garden City: Doubleday, 1966.

Johnson, A. R. "The Psalms," *The Old Testament and Modern Study*. Edited by H. H. Rowley. Oxford: The Clarendon Press, 1951.

Josephus, Flavius. *The Life and Works of Flavius Josephus*. Translated by W. Whiston. Phila.: John C. Winston, 1957.

Kautzsch, E. (ed.). *Gesenius' Hebrew Grammar*. Revised by A. E. Cowley. Oxford: The Clarendon Press, 1910.

Kittel, R. (ed.). *Theologisches Wörterbuch zum Neuen Testament*. 8 vols. Stuttgart: W. Kohlhammer Verlag, 1933- .

_____. *Biblia Hebraica*. 3rd ed. Stuttgart: Privilegierte Württembergische Bibelanstalt, 1937.

Knudtzon, J. A. (ed.). *Die El-Amarna Tafeln*. Leipzig: J. C. Hinrichs, 1908.

Köhler, L., and W. Baumgartner. *Hebräisches und aramäisches Lexikon zum Alten Testament*. 3rd ed. Edited by W. Baumgartner et al. Leiden: E. J. Brill, 1967- .

_____. *Lexicon in Veteris Testamenti Libros*. Leiden: E. J. Brill, 1953.

Kraus, H.-J. *Worship in Israel*. Translated by G. Buswell. Richmond: John Knox Press, 1966.

Lidzbarski, M. *Handbuch der nordsemitischen Epigraphik*. 2 vols. Weimar: Verlag von Emil Felber, 1898.

Lisowsky, G. *Konkordanz zum hebräischen Alten Testament*. 2nd ed. Stuttgart: Württembergische Bibelanstalt, 1958.

Mandelkern, S. *Veteris Testamenti concordantiae hebraicae atque chaldaicae*. Schocken: Cura F. Margolin, 1937.

Mauchline, J. "I and II Kings," *PCB*, 338-356.

May, H. G. "Joshua," *PCB*, 289-303.

_____. (ed.). *Oxford Bible Atlas*. London: Oxford University Press, 1962.

Montgomery, J. A., and H. S. Gehman. *A Critical and Exegetical Commentary on the Book of Kings*. ICC. Edinburgh: T. and T. Clark, 1951.

Moore, G. F. *A Critical and Exegetical Commentary on the Book of Judges*. ICC, Vol. VII. N.Y.: Charles Scribner's Sons, 1901.

Moscati, S. *An Introduction to the Comparative Grammar of the Semitic Languages: Phonology and Morphology*. Wiesbaden: O. Harras

Mowinckel, S. *The Psalms in Israel's Worship*. Translated by D. R. Ap-Thomas. 2 vols. N.Y.: Abingdon, 1962.

Myers, J. M. *I Chronicles*. AB, 12. Garden City: Doubleday, 1965.

_____. *II Chronicles*. AB, 13. Garden City: Doubleday, 1965.

_____. *Ezra-Nehemiah*. AB, 14. Garden City: Doubleday, 1965.

_____. "The Book of Judges, Introduction and Exegesis," *IB*, Vol. II, 677-826.

Nicholson, E. W. *Deuteronomy and Tradition*. Phila.: Fortress Press, 1967.

Noth, M. *Das Buch Josua*. HAT, Vol. VII. 2nd ed. Tubingen: J. C. B. Mohr, 1953.

_____. *Exodus: A Commentary*. Philadelphia: Westminster Press, 1962.

Parrot, A., and G. Dossin (eds.). *Archives royales de Mari*. 13 vols. to date. Paris: Imprimerie Nationale, 1950- .

Pritchard, J. B. (ed.). *Ancient Near Eastern Texts relating to the Old Testament*. 2nd ed. Princeton: Princeton University Press, 1955.

Von Rad, G. *Deuteronomy: A Commentary*. London: SCM, 1966.

_____. *Genesis: A Commentary*. Translated by J. Marks. Phila.: Westminster Press, 1961.

_____. *Studies in Deuteronomy*. Translated by D. Stalker. London: SCM, 1961.

Rahlfs, A. *Septuaginta*. 2 vols. 7th ed. Stuttgart: Württembergische Bibelanstalt, 1935.

Reicke, B., and L. Rost (eds.). *Biblisch-historisches Handwörterbuch*. 3 vols. Göttingen: Vandenhoeck und Ruprecht, 1962-1966.

Roberts, B. J. *The Old Testament Text and Versions*. Cardiff: University of Wales Press, 1951.

De Saulcy, J. M., et al. *Corpus inscriptionum semiticarum ab Academia inscriptionum et litterarum humaniorum conditum atque digestum.* Vol. 1. Paris: E Rei publicae Typographeo, 1881.

Scott, R. B. Y. "Isaiah 1-39, Introduction and Exegesis," *IB*, Vol. V, 151-381.

_____. *Proverbs - Ecclesiastes.* AB, 18. Garden City: Doubleday, 1965.

Simpson, C. A. "The Book of Genesis, Introduction and Exegesis," *IB*, Vol. I, 439-829.

Skinner, J. *A Critical and Exegetical Commentary on the Book of Genesis.* ICC, Vol. I. 2nd ed, Edinburgh: T. and T. Clark, 1930.

Snaith, N. H. "The First and Second Book of Kings, Introduction and Exegesis," *IB*, Vol. III, 1-348.

_____. "Leviticus," *PCB*, 241-253.

Speiser, E. A. *Genesis.* AB, 1. Garden City: Doubleday, 1964.

Sperber, A. *A Historical Grammar of Biblical Hebrew.* Leiden: E. J. Brill, 1966.

Weiser, A. *Das Buch der zwölf kleinen Propheten I: die Propheten Hosea, Joel, Amos, Obadja, Jona, Micha.* ATD, Vol. XXIV. 4th ed. Göttingen: Vandenhoeck and Ruprecht, 1963.

_____. *Das Buch Jeremia.* ATD, Vols. XX/XXI. 5th ed. Göttingen: Vandenhoeck und Ruprecht, 1966.

_____. *The Psalms: A Commentary.* Translated by H. Hartwell. Philadelphia: Westminster Press, 1962.

Williams, R. J. *Hebrew Syntax: An Outline.* Toronto: University of Toronto Press, 1967.

Wolfe, R. "The Book of Micah, Introduction and Exegesis," *IB*, Vol. VI, 897-952.

Wright, G. E. "The Book of Deuteronomy, Introduction and Exegesis," *IB*, Vol. II, 311-540.

Young, G. D. *Concordance of Ugaritic.* (AnOr, Vol. XXXVI). Rome: Pontifical Biblical Institute, 1956.

Zimmerli, W. *1 Mose 1-11, die Urgeschichte.* 2nd ed. Zürich: Zwingli, 1957.

II. Urban and Sociological Studies

Adams, R. M. "The Rise of Cities," *Scientific American*, Sept., 1960, 153-172.

Beals, R. L. "Urbanism, Urbanization and Acculturation," *American Anthropologist* LIII (1951) 1-10.

Becker, H. "Constructive Typology in the Social Sciences," *American Sociological Review* V (1940) 40-55.

_____. "Sacred and Secular Societies," *Social Forces* XXVIII (1950) 361-376.

_____. *Through Values to Social Interpretation.* Durham: Duke University Press, 1950.

Braidwood, R. "The Agricultural Revolution," *Scientific American*, Sept., 1960, 130-152.

Braidwood, R., and G. R. Willey (eds.). *Courses toward Urban Life*. Chicago: Aldine, 1962.

Braidwood, R., and B. Howe. *Prehistoric Investigations in Iraqi Kurdistan*. ("Studies in Ancient Oriental Civilization," XXXI.) Chicago: University of Chicago Press, 1960.

Childe, V. G. "Civilization, Cities and Towns," *Antiquity*, XXXI(1957) 36-38.

_____. *Man Makes Himself*. London: Watts, 1936.

_____. *Social Evolution*. London: Watts, 1951.

_____. "The Urban Revolution," *Town Planning Review* XXI (1950) 3-17.

Comhaire, J. D., and W. J. Cahnman. *How Cities Grew*. Madison, N.J.: Florham Park Press, 1959.

Coulborn, Rushton (ed.). *Feudalism in History*. Princeton: Princeton University Press, 1956.

_____. *The Origin of Civilized Societies*. Princeton: Princeton University Press, 1959.

Davis, Kingsley. "The Origin and Growth of Urbanism in the World," *AJOS* LX (1955) 429-437.

Dewey, R. "The Rural-Urban Continuum: Real but Relatively Unimportant," *AJOS* LXVI (1960) 60-66.

Durkheim, Émile. *Émile Durkheim on the Division of Labor in Society*. Translated by G. Simpson. N.Y.: Macmillan, 1933.

Farb, P. *Man's Rise to Civilization as Shown by the Indians of North America from Primeval Times to the Coming of the Industrial State*. N.Y.: E. P. Dutton, 1968.

Foster, G. M. "What is Folk Culture?" *American Anthropologist* LV (1953) 159-173.

Frankfort, H. *The Birth of Civilization in the Near East*. Anchor Book. Garden City: Doubleday, 1956.

_____. "Town Planning in Ancient Mesopotamia," *Town Planning Review* XXI (1950) 99-115.

Fustel de Coulanges, N. D. *The Ancient City: A Study on the Religion, Laws, and Institutions of Greece and Rome*. Translated by W. Small. N.Y.: Charles T. Dillingham, 1882.

Geertz, C. *Agricultural Involution*. Berkeley: University of California Press, 1963.

Gist, N. P., and S. F. Fava. *Urban Society*. 5th ed. N.Y.: Thomas Y. Crowell, 1964.

[Gottwald, Norman K. "Domain Assumptions and Societal Models in the Study of Pre-monarchic Israel," VTSup, Edinburgh Congress Vol. (1975) 1-12. Leiden: E. J. Brill, 1976.]

[_____. "Nomadism," *IDBSup*, 630-631.]

[Gulick, John. "Village and City: Cultural Continuities in Twentieth Century Middle Eastern Cultures," *Middle Eastern Cities*. Edited by I. M. Lapidus. Berkeley: University of California Press, 1969].

Hatt, P. K., and A. J. Reiss (eds.). *Reader in Urban Sociology*. Glencoe, Ill.: The Free Press, 1951.

Hauser, P. M., and L. F. Schnore (eds.). *The Study of Urbanization*. N.Y.: Hohn Wiley and Sons, 1965.

Hauser, P. M. "World Urbanism," *AJOS* LX (1955) 427-428.

Jawad, A. J. *The Advent of the Era of Townships in Northern Mesopotamia*. Leiden: E. J. Brill, 1965.

Kenyon, K. M. "Reply to Professor Braidwood," *Antiquity* XXXI (1957) 82-84.

_____. "Jericho and its Setting in Near Eastern History," *Antiquity* XXX (1956) 184-195.

Kraeling, C. H., and R. M. Adams (eds.). *The City Invincible: A Symposium on Urbanization and Cultural Development in the Ancient Near East*. Chicago: University of Chicago Press, 1960,

Lampard, E. E. "Historical Aspects of Urbanization," *The Study of Urbanization*. Edited by Hauser and Schnore, 519-554.

Lenski, G. E. *The Religious Factor: A Sociological Study of Religion's mpact on Politics, Economics, and Family Life*. Anchor Book. Garden City: Doubleday, 1963.

Lewis, O. "Further Observations on the Folk-Urban Continuum and Urbanization with Special Reference to Mexico City," *The Study of Urbanization*. Edited by Hauser and Schnore, 491-502.

Lowie, R. H. *The Origins of the State*. N.Y.: Russell and Russell, 1927.

Maine, H. *Ancient Law*. London: J. Murray, 1861.

Mann, P. H. *An Approach to Urban Sociology*. London: Routledge and Kegan Paul, 1965.

Martindale, D. "Prefatory Remarks: The Theory of the City," in Weber, M. *The City*. Translated and edited by D. Martindale and G. Neuwirth. N.Y.: The Free Press, 1966, 9-62.

[Mendenhall, George E. "Social Organization in Early Israel," *Magnalia Dei*. Edited by F. M. Cross et al., 132-151.]

Miner, H. "The Folk-Urban Continuum," *American Sociological Review* XVII (1952) 529-537.

Mumford, L. *The City in History*. N.Y.: Harcourt, Brace and World, 1961.

Park, R. E. "The City: Suggestions for the Investigation of Human Behavior in the Urban Environment," *Reader in Urban Sociology*. Edited by Hatt and Reiss, 2-31.

Parsons, Talcott. *Essays in Sociological Theory*. Glencoe: The Free Press, 1949.

_____. _Societies: Evolutionary and Comparative Perspectives._ Englewood Cliffs, N.J.: Prentice-Hall, 1966.

_____. _The Structure of Social Action._ Glencoe: The Free Press, 1949.

_____. "The Theoretical Development of the Sociology of Religion," _Journal of the History of Ideas_ V (1944) 176-190.

Perot, J. "Palestine-Syria-Cilicia," _Courses toward Urban Life._ Edited by Braidwood and Willey, 147-164.

Piganiol, A. "City-State," _Reader in Urban Sociology._ Edited by Hatt and Reiss, 71-74.

Piggott, S. "The Role of the City in Ancient Civilizations." _The Metropolis in Modern Life._ Edited by R. M. Fisher. Garden City: Doubleday, 1955, 5-17.

Pirenne, H. _Medieval Cities._ Translated by F. D. Halsey. Princeton: Princeton University Press, 1946.

Radcliffe-Brown, A. R. "Religion and Society," _Structure and Function in Primitive Society._ Glencoe: Free Press, 1965.

Redfield, R., and M. Singer. _The Cultural Role of Cities._ Chicago: University of Chicago Press, 1961.

Redfield, R. "The Folk Society," _AJOS_ LII (1947) 293-308.

_____. _The Primitive World and its Transformations._ Ithaca, N.Y.: Great Seal Books, 1953.

Reiss, A. J., Jr. "An Analysis of Urban Phenomena," _The Metropolis in Modern Life._ Edited by R. Fisher, 41-54.

Schneider, W. _Überall ist Babylon: die Stadt als Schicksal des Menschen von Ur bis Utopia._ Düsseldorf: Econ-Verlag, 1960.

Sjoberg, G. "Comparative Urban Sociology," _Sociology Today._ Edited by R. K. Merton, et al. Harper Torchbook. N.Y.: Harper and Row, 1959, Vol. II, 334-359.

_____. "Folk and 'Feudal' Societies," _AJOS_ LVIII (1952) 231-239.

_____. "The Preindustrial City," _AJOS_ LX (1955) 438-445.

_____. _The Preindustrial City: Past and Present._ Glencoe: The Free Press, 1960.

_____. "Theory and Research in Urban Sociology," _Study of Urbanization._ Edited by Hauser and Schnore, 157-189.

Stewart, C. T., Jr. "The Rural-Urban Dichotomy: Concepts and Uses," _AJOS_ LXIV (1958) 152-158.

Tönnies, F. _Community and Association._ Translated by C. P. Loomis. London: Routledge and Kegan Paul, 1955.

Wach, Joachim. _Sociology of Religion._ Chicago: University of Chicago Press, 1944.

Weber, M. _The City._ Translated and Edited by D. Martindale and G. Neuwirth. N.Y.: The Free Press, 1966.

_____. _The Sociology of Religion._ Boston: Beacon Press, 1922.

[Wheatley, Paul. *The Pivot of the Four Quarters*. Chicago: Aldine, 1971].

Wheeler, M. "The First Towns?" *Antiquity* XXX (1956) 132-136, 225.

Wirth, L. "Urbanism as a Way of Life," *Reader in Urban Sociology*. Edited by Hatt and Reiss, 32-49.

[Wolf, E. R. *Peasants*. Englewood Cliffs: Prentice-Hall, 1966].

Woolley, C. L. "The Urbanization of Society," *Journal of World History* IV (1957) 246-258.

III. Archaeology and Individual Sites

Ackroyd, P. "Samaria," *AOTS*. Edited by D. W. Thomas, 343-354.

Aharoni, Y. "Arad: Its Inscriptions and Temple," *BA* XXXI (1968) 1-32.

_____. "Beth-haccherem," *AOTS*. Edited by Thomas, 171-184.

[_____. "Excavations at Tel Beer-sheba," *BA* XXXV (1972) 111-127].

_____. "The Date of Casemate Walls in Judah and Israel and Their Purpose," *BASOR* 154 (1959) 35-39.

_____. "Hebrew Ostraca from Tel Arad," *IEJ* XVI (1966) 1-7.

_____. "The Negeb," *AOTS*. Edited by Thomas, 385-404.

[_____. "Nothing Early and Nothing Late: Re-Writing Israel's Conquest," *BA* XXXIX (1976) 55-76].

Albright, W. F. *The Archaeology of Palestine*. Pelican Book. Harmondsworth: Penguin Books, 1951.

_____. *The Archaeology of Palestine and the Bible*. 3rd ed. N.Y.: Fleming H. Revell, 1935.

_____. *Archaeology and the Religion of Israel*. 2nd ed. rev. Baltimore: Johns Hopkins Press, 1946.

_____, et al. *The Excavation of Tell Beit Mirsim. III The Iron Age*. *AASOR* XXI/XXII (1941-1943).

Alt, A. "Der Stadstaat Samaria," *KS*, III, 258-302.

Avigad, N. "Some Notes on the Hebrew Inscriptions from Gibeon," *IEJ* IX (1959) 130-133.

Barrois, G. A. *Manuel d'archaéologie biblique*. 2 vols. Paris: A. Picard, 1939-1953.

_____. "Salem," *IDB*, IV, 166.

Beebe, H. K. "Ancient Palestinian Dwellings," *BA* XXXI (1968) 38-57.

[Biran, Avram. "Tel Dan," *BA* XXXVII (1974) 26-51].

Braidwood, R. J. "Jericho and Its Setting in Near Eastern History," *Antiquity* XXXL (1957) 73-81.

Cohen, S. "Beth-marcaboth," *IDB*, III, 220.

_____. "Havvoth-Jair," *IDB*, II, 537-538.

Crowfoot, J. W., et al. *Samaria-Sebaste II: The Buildings at Samaria*. London: Palestine Exploration Fund, 1942.

Diringer, D. "Mizpah," *AOTS*. Edited by Thomas, 329-342.

Emerton, J. A. "Beth Shemesh," *AOTS*. Edited by Thomas, 197-206.

Franken, H. J. "The Excavations at Deir ʿAllā," *VT* X (1960) 386-393; XII (1962) 378-382.

Glueck, N. "Transjordan," *AOTS*. Edited by Thomas, 429-452.

Gold, V. R. "Beth-Shemesh," *IDB*, I, 401-403.

_____. "Hazor," *IDB*, II, 539-540.

Gray, J. "Hazor," *VT* XVI (1966) 26-52.

_____. "Tell el Farʿa by Nablus: A 'Mother' in Ancient Israel," *PEQ* (1952) 110-113.

Hamilton, R. W. "Waterworks," *IDB*, IV, 811-816.

Kapelrud, A. S. "Tyre," *IDB*, IV, 721-723.

Kenyon, K. M. *Archaeology in the Holy Land*. New York: Frederick A. Praeger, 1960.

_____. *Digging up Jericho*. London: Benn, 1957.

_____. "Excavations at Jericho," *PEQ* (1954) 45-63; (1955) 108-117.

[_____. "Israelite Jerusalem," *NEATC*. Edited by Sanders, 232-253].

_____. "Jericho," *AOTS*. Edited by Thomas, 264-276.

_____. *Palestine in the Middle Bronze Age*. CAH, Vol. II, ch. III. rev ed. Cambridge: The University Press, 1966.

[_____. *Royal Cities of the Old Testament*. London: Barrie and Jenkins, 1971].

_____. "Some Notes on the Early Middle Bronze Strata of Megiddo," *Eretz Israel* V (1958) 51-60.

Kirkbride, A. S. "Desert Kites," *JPOS* XX (1946) 1-5.

[Lapp, Nancy L. "Casemate Walls in Palestine and the Late Iron II Casemate at Tell el-Fûl (Gibeah)," *BASOR* 223 (Oct., 1976) 25-42].

Lapp, P. W. "Bâb edh-Dhrâʿ, Perizzites and Emim," *Jerusalem through the Ages*. 25th Archaeological Convention. Jerusalem: Israel Exploration Society, 1968, 1-25.

_____. "Bâb edh-Dhrâʿ Tomb A76 and Early Bronze I in Palestine," *BASOR* 189 (1968) 12-41.

_____. "The Conquest of Palestine in the Light of Archaeology," *Concordia Theological Monthly* XXXVIII (1967) 242-357.

_____. "Palestine in the Early Bronze Age," *NEATC*. Edited by Sanders, 101-131.

Loud, G. *Megiddo II: Seasons of 1935-39*. ("Oriental Institute Publications," 62). Chicago: The Oriental Institute, 1948.

McCown, C. C. *The Ladder of Progress in Palestine*. N.Y.: Harper and Row, 1943.

_____, et al. *Tell en-Nasbeh, I*. Berkeley: Palestine Institute of Pacific School of Religion and the American Schools of Oriental Research, 1947.

Malamat, A. "Hazor 'The Head of All Those Kingdoms,'" *JBL* LXXIX (1960) 12-19.

Mazar, B. "En-gedi," *AOTS*. Edited by Thomas, 223-230.

Morton, W. H. "Gederah," *IDB*, II, 361.

Nielsen, E. *Shechem, a Traditio-historical Investigation*. Copenhagen: Gad, 1955.

Parrot, A. *Samaria--the Capital of the Kingdom of Israel*. London: SCM, 1958.

[Pettinato, Giovanni. "The Royal Archives of Tell Mardikh--Ebla," *BA* XXXIX (1976) 44-52].

Pritchard, "Gibeon," *IDB*, II, 391-393.

_____. *Gibeon, Where the Sun Stood Still, the Discovery of the Biblical City*. Princeton: Princeton University Press, 1962.

_____. *Hebrew Inscriptions and Stamps from Gibeon*. Philadelphia: University of Pennsylvania Museum, 1959.

_____. "Industry and Trade at Biblical Gibeon," *BA* XXIII (1960) 23-29.

[_____. "The Megiddo Stables: A Reassessment," *NEATC*. Edited by Sanders, 268-276].

_____. *Winery, Defenses and Soundings at Gibeon*. Philadelphia: University of Pennsylvania Museum, 1964.

Reed, W. L. "Gibeon," *AOTS*. Edited by Thomas, 231-244.

[Sanders, J. A.(ed.). *Near Eastern Archaeology in the Twentieth Century: Essays in Honor of Nelson Glueck*. Garden City: Doubleday, 1970].

Schofield, J. N. "Inscribed Potsherds from Samaria," *DOTT*. Edited by Thomas. Harper Torchbook. N.Y.: Harper and Row, 1958, 204-209.

_____. "Megiddo," *AOTS*. Edited by Thomas, 309-328.

Thomas. D. W. (ed.). *Archaeology and Old Testament Study*. Oxford: The Clarendon Press, 1967.

Toombs, L. E., and G. E. Wright. "The Fourth Campaign at Balaṭah (Shechem)," *BASOR* 169 (1963) 1-60.

Van Beek, G. "Samaria," *IDB*, IV, 182-188.

De Vaux, R. "Tirzah," *AOTS*. Edited by Thomas, 371-384.

Watzinger, C. *Denkmäler Palästinas: eine Einführung in die Archäologie des heiligen Landes*. Leipzig: Hinrichs, 1933-1935.

Wright, G. E. "The Archaeology of Palestine," *The Bible and the Ancient Near East*. Edited by G. E. Wright. Anchor Book. Garden City: Doubleday, 1965, 85-139.

262

_____. "The Discoveries at Megiddo," *BAR, 2.* Edited by D. N. Freedman and E. F. Campbell, Jr. Anchor Book. Garden City: Doubleday, 1964, 301-312.

_____. "Shechem," *AOTS.* Edited by Thomas, 355-370.

_____. *Shechem, the Biography of a Biblical City.* N.Y.: McGraw-Hill, 1965.

_____. "The Temple in Palestine-Syria," *BAR.* Edited by Wright and Freedman. Anchor Book. Garden City: Doubleday, 1961, 169-184.

Yadin, Y. "Excavations at Hazor," *BAR, 2.* Edited by Freedman and Campbell. Anchor Book. Garden City: Doubleday, 1964.

_____. "Hazor," *AOTS.* Edited by Thomas, 245-263.

[_____. "The Megiddo Stables," *Magnalia Dei.* Edited by F. M. Cross, et al., 249-252].

_____. "New Light on Solomon's Megiddo," *BAR, 2.* Edited by Freedman and Campbell, 240-247.

_____. "Note on Megiddo," *IEJ* XVI (1966) 278-280.

_____. "Solomon's City Wall and Gate at Gezer," *IEJ* VIII (1958) 80-86.

Yeivin, S. *A Decade of Archaeology in Israel: 1948-1958.* Istanbul: Nederlands historisch-archaeologisch Institue in het Nabije Oosten, 1960.

IV. General

Abba, R. "Name," *IDB,* III, 500-508.

Abramsky, S. "The House of Rechab - Genealogy and Military League," *Eretz Israel* VIII (1967) 255-264. (Hebrew with an English summary on 76).

Ahlström, G. W. *Aspects of Syncretism in Israelite Religion.* Lund: C. W. K. Gleerup, 1963.

_____. "Der Prophet Nathan und der Tempelbau," *VT* XI (1961) 113-127.

Albright, W. F. "Abram the Hebrew: A New Archaeological Interpretation," *BASOR* 163 (1961) 36-54.

_____. "Baal Zaphon," *Festschrift Alfred Bertholet zum 80. Geburtstag.* Edited by W. Baumgartner et al. Tübingen: J. C. B. Mohr, 1950, 1-14.

_____. *The Biblical Period from Abraham to Ezra.* Harper Torchbook. N. Y.: Harper and Row, 1963.

_____. "Canaanite ḥofši, 'free', in the Amarna Tablets," *JPOS* IV (1924) 169-170.

_____. "A Case of Lèse-Majesté in Pre-Israelite Lachish, with some Remarks on the Israelite Conquest," *BASOR* 87 (1942) 32-38.

_____. "Earliest Forms of Hebrew Verse," *JPOS* II (1922) 69-86.

_____. *From the Stone Age to Christianity.* 2nd ed. Anchor

Book. Garden City: Doubleday, 1957.

_____. "The High Place in Ancient Palestine," *VTSup*, IV (1957) 242-258.

_____. "The Judicial Reforms of Jehoshaphat," *Alexander Marx Jubilee Volume*. Edited by S. Lieberman. N.Y.: The Jewish Theological Seminary of America, 61-82.

_____. "The Names 'Nazareth' and 'Nazorean.'" *JBL* LXV (1946) 397-401.

_____. "The Names Shaddai and Abram," *JBL* LIV (1935) 173-204.

_____. "Note on Lacheman on the Word ḫupšu at Nuzi," *BASOR* 86 (1942) 37.

_____. "A Revision of Early Hebrew Chronology," *JPOS* I (1921) 49-79.

Alt, A. "Der Anteil des Königtums an der sozialen Entwicklung in den Reichen Israels und Juda," *KS*, III, 348-372.

_____. "Bemerkungen zu einigen judäischen Ortslisten des Alten Testaments," *KS*, II, 289-305.

_____. "The Formation of the Israelite State in Palestine," *Essays in Old Testament History and Religion*. Translated by R. A. Wilson. Garden City: Doubleday, 1967, 223-310.

_____. "Gedanken über das Königtum Jahwes," *KS*, I, 345-357.

_____. "The God of the Fathers," *Essays on Old Testament History and Religion*, 1-86.

_____. "Judas Gaue unter Josia," *KS*, II, 276-288.

_____. *Kleine Schriften zur Geschichte des Volkes Israel*. 3 vols. Munich: C. H. Beck, 1953-1959.

_____. "The Monarchy in the Kingdoms of Israel and Judah," *Essays on Old Testament History and Religion*, 311-335.

_____. "Neue assyrische Nachrichten über Palästina," *KS*, II, 226-241.

_____. "The Settlement of the Israelites in Palestine," *Essays on Old Testament History and Religion*, 173-222.

_____. "Zelte und Hütten," *KS*, III, 233-242.

Anati, E. *Palestine before the Hebrews*. London: Jonathan Cape, 1963.

Anderson, B. W. "God, Names of," *IDB*, II, 407-417.

Anderson, R. T. "The Role of the Desert in Israelite Thought," *JBRL* XXVII (1959) 41-44.

Arnold, W. R. "The Word prš in the Old Testament," *JBL* XXIV (1905) 45-53.

Baron, S. W. *A Social and Religious History of the Jews*. 3 vols. 2nd ed. N.Y.: Columbia University Press, 1952.

Barr, J. *Comparative Philology and the Text of the Old Testament*. Oxford: The Clarendon Press, 1968.

Barrois, G. A. "Pillar," *IDB*, III, 815-817.

_____. "Trade and Commerce," *IDB*, IV, 677-683.

Barth, C. "Zur Bedeutung der Wüstentradition," VTSup, XV (1965) 14-23.

Beegle, D. M. "Proper Names in the New Isaiah Scroll," *BASOR* 123 (1951) 26-30.

Ben-gavriel, M. Y. "Das nomadische Ideal in der Bibel," *Stimmen der Zeit* CLXXI (1962/1963) 253-263.

Bennet, W. H. "Rechab, Rechabites," *A Dictionary of the Bible*. Edited by Hastings, 203-205.

Bentzen, A. "The Cultic Use of the Story of the Ark in Samuel," *JBL* LXVII (1948) 37-53.

Bertholet, A. *A History of Hebrew Civilization*. Translated by A. K. Dallas. N.Y.: Brentano's, 1926.

Beyerlin, W. *Origins and History of the Oldest Sinaitic Traditions*. Translated by S. Rudman. Oxford: Blackwell, 1965.

Borée, W. *Die alten Ortsnamen Palästinas*. Leipzig: E. Pfeiffer Verlag, 1930.

Bowman, R. A. "Arameans, Aramaic and the Bible," *JNES*, VII (1948) 65-90.

_____. "Genealogy," *IDB*, II, 362-365.

Bright, J. "Hebrew Religion, History of," *IDB*, II, 560-570.

_____. *A History of Israel*. Philadelphia: Westminster Press, 1959.

Brinker, R. *The Influence of Sanctuaries in Early Israel*. Manchester: Manchester University Press, 1946.

Budde, K. "The Nomadic Ideal in the Old Testament," *The New World* IV (1895) 726-745.

Burrows, M. "Ancient Israel," *The Idea of History in the Ancient Near East*. Edited by R. C. Dentan. New Haven: Yale University Press, 1955.

Campbell, E. F., Jr. "The Amarna Letters and the Amarna Period," *BA* XXIII (1960) 2-22.

_____. "The Ancient Near East: Chronological Bibliography and Charts," *The Bible and the Ancient Near East*. Edited by Wright, 281-299.

Castellino, G. R. "Les origines de la civilisation selon les textes bibliques et les textes cunéiformes," VTSup, IV (1957) 116-137.

Causse, A. *Du groupe ethnique à la communauté religieuse. Le problème sociologique de la religion d'Israel*. Paris: Alcan, 1937.

_____. *Les 'pauvres d'Israel.'* Strasbourg: Librairie Istra, 1922.

_____. "Les prophètes et la crise sociologique de la religion d'Israel," *RHPR* (1932) 97-140.

_____. *Les prophètes contre la civilisation*. Alencon: Imprimeries typographiques A. Coueslant, 1913.

Chamberlayne, J. H. "Kinship Relations among the early Hebrews," *Numen* X (1963) 153-164.

Childs, B. S. *Isaiah and the Assyrian Crisis*. Naperville,
Ill.: Allenson, 1967.

_____. *Myth and Reality in the Old Testament*. London: SCM,
1960.

Claburn, W. E. *Deuteronomy and Collective Behavior*. Unpublished Ph.D. dissertation. Princeton University, 1968.

Clements, R. E. "Deuteronomy and the Jerusalem Cult Tradition," *VT* XV (1965) 300-312.

_____. *God and Temple. The Idea of the Divine Presence in
Ancient Israel*. Oxford: Blackwell, 1965.

_____. "Temple and Land: A Significant Aspect of Israel's
Worship," *TGUOS* XIX (1961-1962) 16-28.

Cohen, S. "Nabateans," *IDB*, III, 491-493.

Coon, C. S. *Caravan: The Story of the Middle East*. Rev. ed.
N.Y.: Holt, 1958.

Cross, F. M., and D. N. Freedman. "The Blessing of Moses," *JBL*
LXVII (1948) 191-210.

Cross, F. M., and G. E. Wright. "The Boundary and Province
Lists of the Kingdom of Judah," *JBL* LXXV (1956) 202-226.

[Cross, F. M., W. E. Lemke, and P. D. Miller, Jr. (eds.) *Mag-
nalia Dei: The Might Acts of God--Essays on the Bible and
Archaeology in Memory of G. Ernest Wright*. Garden City:
Doubleday, 1976].

_____. "Yahweh and the God of the Patriarchs," *HTR* LV
(1962) 225-259.

Dahood, M. "Congruity of Metaphors," *Hebräische Wortforschung:
Festschrift zum 80. Geburtstag von W. Baumgartner*. Edited
by B. Hartmann, et al. VTSup XXL (1967) 40-49.

_____. "The Phoenician Background of Qoheleth," *Bib* XLVII
(1966) 264-282.

_____. *Proverbs and Northwest Semitic Philology*. Rome:
Pontifical Biblical Institute, 1963.

_____. "Proverbs 8:22-31: Translation and Commentary,"
CBQ XXX (1968) 512-521.

Davies, G. H. "Ark of the Covenant," *IDB*, I, 222-226.

Diringer, D. "The Royal Jar-Handle Stamps of Ancient Judah,"
BA XII (1949) 70-86.

_____. "Seals," *DOTT*. Edited by Thomas, 63-66.

[Dreyer, H. J. "The Roots *qr*, *ʿr*, *g̣r* and *ṣ/ṭr* = 'stone, wall,
city, etc.," *De Fructu Oris Sui*. Edited by I. H. Eybers
et al. Leiden: E. J. Brill, 1971, 17-25].

Driver, G. R. "Hebrew Notes on Prophets and Proverbs," *JTS*
XLI (1940) 162-175.

_____. "Linguistic and Textual Problems: Jeremiah," *JQR*
XVIII (1937-1938) 97-129.

_____. "Problems in the Hebrew Text of Job," VTSup, III (1955) 72-93.

_____. *Semitic Writing from Pictograph to Alphabet.* London: G. Cumberledge, 1948.

Dunne, J. S. *The City of the Gods; a Study in Myth and Mortality.* N.Y.: Macmillan, 1965.

Edzard, D. O. "Altbabylonisch nawûm," *ZA* LIII (1959) 168-173.

Eichrodt, W. *Theology of the Old Testament, I.* Translated by J. A. Baker. Philadelphia: Westminster Press, 1961.

Eissfeldt, O. *Baal Zaphon, Zeus Kassios und der Durchzug der Israeliten durchs Meer.* Halle: M. Niemeyer, 1932.

Eliade, M. *Patterns in Comparative Religion.* N.Y.: Sheed and Ward, 1958.

_____. *The Sacred and the Profane.* N.Y.: Harcourt, Brace and Co., 1959.

Evans, G. "Ancient Mesopotamian Assemblies," *JAOS* LXXVIII (1958) 1-11.

_____. "'Coming' and 'Going' at the City Gate - A Discussion of Prof. Speiser's Paper," *BASOR* 150 (1958) 28-33.

_____. "'Gates' and 'Streets': Urban Institutions in Old Testament Times," *JRH* II (1962) 1-12.

Fensham, F. C. "Common Trends in Curses of the Near Eastern Treaties and *Kudurru*-inscriptions compared with Maledictions of Amos and Isaiah," *ZAW* LXXV (1963) 155-175.

_____. "Maledictions and Benedictions in Ancient Near Eastern Vassal-Treaties," *ZAW* LXXIV (1962) 1-9.

Finklestein, L. *The Pharisees: The Sociological Background of their Faith.* 2 vols. Philadelphia: The Jewish Publication Society, 1938.

_____. *The Jews, Their History, Culture and Religion.* 2 vols. 2nd ed. N.Y.: Harper and Brothers, 1955.

Fish, T. "The Place of the Small State in the Political and Cultural History of Ancient Mesopotamia," *BJRL* 1944) 83-98.

Fisher, L. R. "Abraham and his Priest-King," *JBL* LXXXI (1962) 264-270.

_____. "The Temple Quarter," *JSS* VIII (1963) 34-41.

Fitzmeyer, L. A. *The Genesis Apocryphon of Qumran Cave 1.* Rome: Pontifical Biblical Institute, 1966.

Flight, J. "The Nomadic Idea and Ideal in the Old Testament," *JBL* XLII (1923) 158-226.

Frankfort, H., and H. A. (eds.). *Before Philosophy.* Pelican Book. Baltimore: Penguin Books, 1949.

Free, J. P. "Abraham's Camels," *JNES* III (1944) 187-193.

Fretheim, T. E. "Psalm 132: a Form-Critical Study," *JBL* LXXXVI (1967) 289-300.

[Frick, F. S. "Rechabites," *IDBSup*, 726-728].

[Frick, F. S. "The Rechabites Reconsidered," *JBL* XC (1971) 279-287].

Fuss, W. "2 Samuel 24," *ZAW* LXXIV (1962) 145-164.

Gabriel, J. "Die Kainitengenealogie," *Bib* XL (1959) 409-427.

Gadd, J. "Tablets from Kirkuk," *RA* XXIII (1926) 4-161.

Galling, K. "Die Ausrufung des Namens als Rechtsakt in Israel," *TLZ* LXXXI (1956) 65-70.

Garstang, J. *The Heritage of Solomon: an Historical Introduction to the Sociology of Ancient Palestine*. London: Williams and Norgate, 1934.

Gaster, T. H. *Thespis*. rev. ed. Harper Torchbook. N.Y.: Harper and Row, 1961.

Gautier, L. *A propos des Récabites; un chapitre de l'histoire religieuse d'Israel avant l'exil*. Lausanne, 1927.

Gelb, I. "The Early History of the West Semitic People," *JCS* XV (1961) 27-47.

_____. "Hittites," *IDB*, II, 612-615.

_____. *A Study of Writing*. Chicago: University of Chicago Press, 1963.

Gibson, J. C. L. "Light from Mari on the Patriarchs," *JSS* VII (1962) 44-62.

Ginsberg, H. L. "Baal's Two Messengers," *BASOR* 95 (1944) 25-30.

_____. "Two North-Canaanite Letters from Ugarit," *BASOR* 72 (1938) 18-19.

_____. "The Ugaritic Texts and Textual Criticism," *JBL*. LXII (1943) 109-115.

Goetze, A. *Kleinasien*. 2nd ed. ("Handbuch der Altertumswissenschaft," Abt. 3, T. 1, Bd. 3, Abschnitt 3:1). Munich: C. H. Beck, 1957.

Gordis, R. "Democratic Origins in Ancient Israel - the Biblical 'ēdāh," *Alexander Marx Jubilee Volume*. Edited by S. Lieberman. N.Y.: Jewish Theological Seminary, 1950, 369-388.

_____. "Sectional Rivalry in the Kingdom of Judah," *JQR* XXV (1934-1935) 237-259.

Gordon, C. H. "Abraham and the Merchants of Ura," *JNES* XVII (1958) 28-31.

_____. "Abraham of Ur." *Hebrew and Semitic Studies Presented to G. R. Driver*. Edited by D. W. Thomas and W. D. McHardy. Oxford: The Clarendon Press, 1963, 78-84.

_____. *The Common Background of Greek and Hebrew Civilizations*. N.Y.: W. W. Norton and Co., 1965.

_____. "Hebrew Origins in the Light of Recent Discovery," *Biblical and Other Studies*. Edited by A. Altmann. Cambridge: Harvard University Press, 1963, 3-14.

_____. *Ugaritic Literature*. Rome: Pontifical Biblical Institute, 1949.

Gottwald, N. K. *All the Kingdoms of the Earth. Israelite Prophecy and International Relations in the Ancient Near East*. N.Y.: Harper and Row, 1964.

Graham, W. C. "Recent Light on the Cultural Origins of the Hebrews," *JR* XIV (1934) 306-329.

Gray, J. *The Canaanites*. N.Y.: Frederick A. Praeger, 1964.

_____. "The Desert God ʿAttr in the Literature and Religion of Canaan," *JNES* VIII (1949) 72-83.

_____. "Feudalism in Ugarit and Early Israel," *ZAW* LXIV (1952) 49-55.

_____. "The Goren at the City Gate: Justice and Royal Office in the Ugaritic Text 'Aqht," *PEQ* (1953) 118-123.

_____. "The Kingship of God in the Prophets and Psalms," *VT* XI (1961) 1-29.

_____. *The KRT Text in the Literature of Ras Shamra. A Social Myth of Ancient Canaan*. 2nd ed. Leiden: E. J. Brill, 1964.

_____. *The Legacy of Canaan*. 2nd ed. Leiden: E. J. Brill, 1965.

Gray, M. "The Habiru-Hebrew Problem," *HUCA* XXIX (1958) 135-202.

Greenberg, M. "The Biblical Concept of Asylum," *JBL* LXXVIII (1959) 125-132.

_____. "City of Refuge," *IDB*, I, 638-639.

Gressmann, H. *The Tower of Babel*. N.Y.: The Jewish Institute of Religion, 1928.

Guillaume. *Prophecy and Divination among the Hebrews and other Semites*. London: Hodder and Stoughton, 1938.

Gurney, O.R. *The Hittites*. 2nd ed. Pelican Book. Harmondsworth: Penguin Books, 1954.

Haldar, A. O. *The Notion of the Desert in the Sumero-Akkadian and West-Semitic Religions*. Uppsala: A. B. Lundequist, 1950.

Halévy, J. *Études sabéenes*. Paris: Imprimerie nationale, 1875.

Hallevy, R. "The Canaanite Period: A Culture Clash," *Tarbiz* XXXV (1965) 95-102 (Hebrew).

Hammershaimb, E. "The Ethics of the Prophets," VTSup VII (1960) 75-101.

Haran, M. "The Disappearance of the Ark," *IEJ* XIII (1963) 46-58.

_____. "Levitical Cities: Utopia and Historical Reality," *Tarbiz* XXVII (1957-1958) 421-439 (Hebrew).

_____. "The Nature of the 'Ohel Moʿedh' in Pentateuchal Sources," *JSS* V (1960) 50-65.

Hartmann, B. "Mögen die Götter dich behüten und unversehrt bewahren," *Hebräische Wortforschung: Festschrift zum 80. Geburtstag von W. Baumgartner*. VTSup XVI (1967) 102-105.

Heaton, E. W. *The Hebrew Kingdoms*. ("New Clarendon Bible, Vol. III). London: Oxford University Press, 1968.

Heidel, A. *The Gilgamesh Epic and Old Testament Parallels*. Phoenix Book. Chicago: University of Chicago Press, 1949.

Helck, H. W. *Die Beziehungen Ägyptens zu Vorderasien im 3. und 2. Jahrtausend v. Chr.* Wiesbaden: O. Harrassowitz, 1962.

Henry, K. H. "Land Tenure in the Old Testament," *PEQ* LXXXVI (1954) 5-15.

Hillers, D. R. "Ritual Procession of the Ark and Psalm 132," *CBQ* XXX (1968) 48-55.

_____. *Treaty-Curses and the Old Testament Prophets*. Rome: Pontifical Biblical Institute, 1964.

Holt, J. M. *The Patriarchs of Israel*. Nashville: Vanderbilt University Press, 1964.

Hooke, S. H. "Cain and Abel," *Folk-Lore* L (1939) 58-65.

_____. *Middle Eastern Mythology*. Pelican Book. Baltimore: Penguin Books, 1963.

Humbert, P. "La logique de la perspective nomade chez Osée," *Festschrift Marti*, BZAW XLI (1925) 158-166.

_____. "Osée le prophète bédouin," *RHPR* I (1921) 97-118.

Hunt, I. *World of the Patriarchs*. Englewood Cliffs, N.J.: Prentice-Hall, 1967.

Isserlin, B. S. J. "Israelite and Pre-Israelite Place-Names in Palestine," *PEQ* LXXXIX (1957) 133-144.

Jacobsen, T. "Mesopotamia: The Cosmos as a State," *Before Philosophy*. Edited by H. and H. A. Frankfort. Pelican Book. Harmondsworth: Penguin Books, 1951, 125-219.

_____. "Primitive Democracy in Ancient Mesopotamia," *JNES* II (1943) 159-172.

Johnson, A. R. *Sacral Kingship in Ancient Israel*. 2nd ed. Cardiff: University of Wales Press, 1967.

Kapelrud, A. S. "Temple Building, a Task for Gods and Kings," *Or* XXXII (1963) 56-62.

Kassis, H. E. "Gath and the Structure of the 'Philistine' Society," *JBL* LXXXIV (1965) 259-271.

Kenyon, K. M. *Amorites and Canaanites*. London: The British Academy, 1966.

Klengel, H. "Die Rolle der 'Ältesten' (LÚ^{meš}SU.GI) im Kleinasien der Hethiterzeit," *ZA* XXIII (1965) 223-236.

_____. "Zu einigen Problemen des altvorderasiatischen Nomadentums," *ArOr* XXX (1962) 585-596.

Knierim, R. "Exodus 18 und die Neuordnung der mosaischen Gerechtsbarkeit," *ZAW* LXXV (1961) 146-171.

Köhler, L. *Hebrew Man*. London: SCM, 1956.

270

Kramer, S. N. "The 'Babel of Tongues': A Sumerian Version, *JAOS* LXXXVIII (1968) 108-111.

_____. *History begins at Sumer*. Anchor Book. Garden City: Doubleday, 1959.

_____. "Man's Golden Age: A Parallel to Genesis XI.1," *JAOS* LXIII (1943) 191-194.

_____. *Sumerian Mythology*. rev. ed. Harper Torchbook. N.Y.: Harper and Row, 1961.

Kupper, J. R. *Les nomades en Mésopotamie au temps des rois de Mari*. Paris: Societé d'edition "les belles lettres," 1957.

_____. "Le rôle des nomades dans l'histoire de la Mesopotamiene," *Journal of the Economic and Social History of the Orient* II (1959) 113-127.

Lambert, W. G. "A New Look at the Babylonian Background of Genesis," *JTS* XVI (1965) 287-300.

Leemans, W. F. *The Old Babylonian Merchant; his Business and his Social Position*. Leiden: E. J. Brill, 1950.

Van der Leeuw, G. *Religion in Essence and Manifestation*. 2 vols. Translated by J. E. Turner. N.Y.: Harper and Row, 1963.

Lehming, S. "Erwägungen zur Zelttradition," *Gottes Wort und Gottes Land*. Edited by H. G. Reventlow. Göttingen: Vandenhoeck und Ruprecht, 1965.

Lewy, J. "Les textes paléo-assyriens et l'Ancien Testament," *RHR* CX (1934) 29-65.

Lindblom, J. *Prophecy in Ancient Israel*. Philadelphia: Fortress Press, 1965.

Lindhagen, C. *The Servant Motif in the Old Testament*. Uppsala: Lundequistska bokhandeln, 1950.

Lovejoy, A. O., and G. Boas. *A Documentary History of Primitivism and Related Ideas, I. Primitivism and Related Ideas in Antiquity*. Baltimore: Johns Hopkins Press, 1935.

Luke, J. T. *Pastoralism and Politics at Mari in the Mari Period: A Re-examination of the Character and Political Significance of the Major West Semitic Tribal Groups on the Middle Euphrates, ca. 1828-1758 B.C.* Unpublished Ph.D. dissertation. University of Michigan, 1965.

Macalister, R. A. S. "The Craftsmen's Guild of the Tribe of Judah," *PEFQS* (1905) 243-253.

McCarthy, D. J. *Treaty and Covenant: A Study in Form in the Ancient Oriental Documents*. (AnBib, Vol. XXL). Rome: Pontifical Biblical Institute, 1963

McCown, C. C. "City," *IDB*, I 632-638.

McKenzie, J. L. "The Elders in the Old Testament," *Bib* XL (1959) 522-540.

_____. "Mythological Allusions in Ezekiel 28:12-18," *JBL* LXXV (1956) 322-327.

_____. *The Two-Edged Sword: An Interpretation of the Old Testament*. Milwaukee: Bruce Publishing Co., 1957.

Mackenzie, R. A. F. "The City and Israelite Religion," *CBQ* XXV (1963) 60-70.

Maier, J. *Das altisraelitische Ladeheilgitum*. Berlin: A. Tö-pelmann, 1965

Malamat, A. "Mari and the Bible: Some Patterns of Tribal Organization and Institutions," *JAOS* LXXXII (1962) 143-150.

Marmorstein, E. "The Origins of Agricultural Feudalism in the Holy Land," *PEQ* LXXXV (1953) 111-117.

Matous, L. "Einige Bemerkungen zum Beduinenproblem im alten Mesopotamien," *ArOr* XXVI (1958) 631-635.

Mauser, U. *Christ in the Wilderness: the Wilderness Theme in the Second Gospel and its Basis in the Biblical Tradition*. London: SCM, 1963.

May, H. G. "The Ark - A Miniature Temple," *AJSL* LII (1936) 215-234.

_____. "'Ephod' and 'Ariel,'" *AJSL* LVI (1939) 44-69.

_____. "A Sociological Approach to Hebrew Religion," *JBRL* XII (1944) 98-106.

Mazar, B. "The Cities of the Priests and Levites," VTSup VII (1960) 193-205.

_____. "The Tobiads," *IEJ* VII (1957) 137-145; 229-238.

Mendelsohn, I. "The Canaanite Term for 'Free Proletarian.'" *BASOR* 83 (1941) 36-39.

_____. "Guilds in Ancient Palestine," *BASOR* 80 (1940) 17-21.

_____. "New Light on the Ḫupšu," *BASOR* 139 (1955) 9-11.

_____. "Samuel's Denunciation of Kingship in the Light of the Akkadian Documents from Ugarit," *BASOR* 143 (1956) 17-22.

Mendenhall, G. E. "The Hebrew Conquest of Palestine," *BA* XXV (1962) 66-87.

_____. "Law and Covenant in Israel and the Ancient Near East," *BA* XVII(1954) 26-46; 49-76.

Menes, A. "Die sozialpolitische Analyse der Urgeschichte," *ZAW* II (1925) 33-62.

Meyer, E. *Die Israeliten und ihre Nachbarstämme*. Halle: A. S., 1906.

Moran, W. L. "Gen 49:10 and its Use in Ezek 21:32," *Bib* XXIX (1958) 405-425.

Mordtmann, J. H. *Himjarische Inschriften und Alterthümer in den königlichen Musseen zu Berlin*. Berlin: W. Spemann, 1893.

Morgenstern, J. "The Ark, the Ephod, and the Tent," *HUCA* XVII (1943) 153-265; XVIII (1944) 1-52.

Moscati, S. *The Face of the Ancient Orient*. Anchor Book. Garden City: Doubleday, 1960.

_____. *The Semites in Ancient History. An Inquiry into the*

Settlement of the Bedouin and their Political Establish-ment. Cardiff: University of Wales Press, 1959.

Newberry, P. E. *Beni Hasan, I.* London: Trubner and Co., 1893.

Neufeld, E. "The Emergence of a Royal Urban Society in Ancient Israel," *HUCA* XXXI (1960) 31-53.

Nicholson, E. W. "The Meaning of the Expression ʿm hʾrṣ in the Old Testament," *JSS* X (1965) 59-66.

Nielsen, E. "Some Reflections on the History of the Ark," VTSup VII (1960) 61-74.

North, R. "The Cain Music," *JBL* LXXXIII (1964) 373-389.

_____. *Sociology of the Biblical Jubilee.* Rome: Pontifical Biblical Institute, 1954.

Noth, M. "David und Israel in 2 Sam 7," *Mélanges bibliques rédigées en l'honneur de André Robert.* Paris: Bloud and Gay, 1956, 122-130.

_____. *The History of Israel.* 2nd ed. N.Y.: Harper and Row, 1958.

_____. "Old Testament Covenant-Making in the Light of a Text from Mari," *The Laws in the Pentateuch and Other Studies.* Translated by D. R. Ap-Thomas. Philadelphia: Fortress Press, 1966, 108-117.

_____. *The Old Testament World.* Translated by V. I. Gruhn. Philadelphia: Fortress Press, 1966.

Nourry, E. "Le tour de la ville et la chute de Jericho," *Essais de folklore biblique.* Paris: Alcan, 1923, 177-204.

Nyberg, H. S. "Studien zum Religionskampf im Alten Testament," *ARW* XXXV (1938) 329-337.

Nyström, S. *Beduinentum und Jahvismus: eine soziologisch-religionsgeschichtliche Untersuchung zum Alten Testament.* Lund: C. W. K. Gleerup, 1946.

Oppenheim, A. L. *Ancient Mesopotamia.* Chicago: University of Chicago Press, 1964.

_____. "The Mesopotamian Temple," *BAR.* Edited by G. E. Wright and D. N. Freedman. Anchor Book. Garden City: Doubleday, 1961, 158-168.

Orlinsky, H. M. *Ancient Israel.* Ithaca: Cornell University Press, 1954.

_____. "Ḥāṣēr in the Old Testament," *JAOS* LIX (1939) 22-37.

_____. "The Kings-Isaiah Recensions of the Hezekiah Story," *JQR* XXX (1939) 33-50.

Parrot, A. *The Tower of Babel.* London: SCM, 1955.

_____. *Ziggurats et tour de Babel.* Paris: Michel, 1949.

Pedersen, J. *Israel, its Life and Culture.* 4 vols in 2. Translated by A. Møller and A. I. Fausbøll. London: Cumberlege, 1946-1947.

_____. "Note on Hebrew Ḥofšī," *JPOS* VI (1926) 103-105.

Van der Ploeg, J. "Les chefs du peuple d'Israël et leurs

titres," *RB* LVII (1950) 40-61.

_____. "Le sens de *gibbôr ḥail*," *Vivre et penser* I (1941) 120-125.

Pope, M. H. "Rechab," *IDB*, IV, 14-16.

_____. *El in the Ugaritic Texts*. Leiden: E. J. Brill, 1955.

Posener, G. *Princes et pays d'Asie et de Bubie: textes hiera-tiques sur les figurines d'envoutement du moyen empire*. Brussels, 1940.

Praetorius, F. "Himjarische Inschriften," *ZDMG* XXVI (1872) 417-440.

Rabinowitz, I. "Government," *IDB*, II, 451-462.

Rabin, C. "Hittite Words in Hebrew," *Or* XXXII (1963) 113-139.

Von Rad, G. *Der heilige Krieg im alten Israel*. 4th ed. Göttingen: Vandenhoeck und Ruprecht, 1965.

_____. *The Message of the Prophets*. Translated by D. M. G. Stalker. London: SCM, 1968.

_____. *Old Testament Theology*. 2 vols. Translated by D. M. G. Stalker. N.Y.: Harper and Row. 1962-1965.

_____. "Promised Land and Yahweh's Land," *The Problem of the Hexateuch and Other Essays*. Translated by E. W. T. Dicken. N.Y.: McGraw-Hill, 1966, 103-124.

Rainey, A. F. *The Social Stratification of Ugarit*. Unpub-lished Ph.D. Dissertation. Brandeis University, 1962.

Ravn, O. E. "Der Turm zu Babel: eine exegetische Studie über Gen 11:1-9," *ZDMG* XCI (1937(352-372.

Richardson, H. N. "Store-cities," *IDB*, IV, 447.

_____. "A Ugaritic Letter of a King to his Mother," *JBL* LXVI (1947) 321-324.

Riemann, P. A. *Desert and Return to Desert in the Pre-Exilic Prophets*. Unpublished Ph.D. Dissertation. Harvard Uni-versity, 1963-1964.

Ringgren, H. *Word and Wisdom: Studies in the Hypostatization of Divine Qualities and Functions in the Ancient Near East*. Lund: H. Ohlssons boktryckerie, 1947.

Rössler, O. "Ghain im Ugaritischen," *ZA* XX (1961) 158-172.

Rylaarsdam, J. C. "Nazirite," *IDB*, III, 526-527.

Schmidt, W. *Königtum Gottes in Ugarit und Israel*. BZAW LXXX (1961).

Scott, R. B. Y. "Jachin and Boaz," *IDB*, II, 780-781.

_____. "Palestine, Climate of," *IDB*, III, 621-626.

_____. "Postscript on the Cubit," *JBL* LXXIX (1960) 368.

_____. *The Relevance of the Prophets*. rev. ed. N.Y.: Mac-millan, 1968.

_____. "Weights and Measures of the Bible," *BA* XXII (1959) 22-40.

274

_____. "Weights, Measures, Money, and Time," *PCB*. Edited by Rowley and Black, 37-41.

Segert, S. "Die Sprache der moabitischen Königsinschrift," *Archiv Orientální* XXIX (1961) 197-267.

Seidensticker, P. "Prophetensöhne-Rechabiter-Nasiräer," *Studii Biblici Franciscani Liber Annus* X (1959) 65-119.

Serra, R. "Una raiz, afin a la raiz ugaritica ġyr 'guardar,' en algunos textos biblicos," *Claretianum* IV (1964) 161-176.

Sethe, K. *Die Achtungfeindlicher Fürsten, Völker und Dinge auf altägyptischen Tongefässcherben des mittleren Reiches*. Berlin: Verlag der Akademie der Wissenschaften, 1926.

Simons, J. J. *Jerusalem in the Old Testament*. Leiden: E. J. Brill, 1952.

Soggin, J. A. "Der judäische ʿAm-haʾares und das Königtum im Juda," *VT* XIII (1963) 187-195.

Speiser, E. A. "'Coming' and 'Going' at the 'City' Gate," *BASOR* 144 (1956) 20-23.

_____. "The etymology of ʾarmōn," *JQR* XIV (1924) 329.

_____. "Hurrians," *IDB*, II, 664-666.

_____. "The Verb shr in Genesis and Early Hebrew Movements," *BASOR* 164 (1961) 23-28.

_____. "Word Plays on the Creation Epic's Version of the Founding of Babylon," *Or* XXV (1956) 317-323.

Tallqvist, K. "Sumerisch-akkadische Namen der Totenwelt," *Studia Orientalia* V (1934) 1-39.

Talmon, S. "The 'Desert Motif' in the Bible and in Qumran Literature," *Biblical Motifs: Origins and Transformations*. Edited by A. Altmann. Cambridge: Harvard University Press, 1966, 31-64.

_____. "1 Chronicles 2:55," *Eretz Israel* V (1958) 111-113 (Hebrew with English summary on 90).

Tufnell, O. "Seals and Scarabs," *IDB*, IV, 254-259.

Van Buren, E. D. "The *salmê* in Mesopotamian Art and Religion," *Or* X (1941) 65-92.

Van Seters, J. *The Hyksos: A New Investigation*. New Haven: Yale University Press, 1966.

De Vaux, R. *Ancient Israel: Its Life and Institutions*. Translated by J. McHugh. N.Y. McGraw-Hill, 1961.

_____. *Palestine in the Early Bronze Age*. CAH, rev. ed. Vol. I, Ch. 15. Cambridge: The University Press, 1965.

_____. "Les patriarches hébreux et l'histoire," *RB* LXXII (1965) 5-28.

_____. "Le sens de l'expression 'peuple de pays' dans l'ancien testament et le rôle politique du peuple en Israël," *RA* LVIII (1964) 167-172.

Virolleaud, C. "Les villes et les corporations du royaume d' Ugarit," *Syria* XXI (1940) 123-151.

Voegelin, E. *Order and History, I. Israel and Revelation*. Baton Rouge: Louisiana State University Press, 1956.

Wallis, G. "Die Stadt in den Überlieferungen der Genesis," *ZAW* LXXVIII (1966) 133-148.

Wallis, L. *God and the Social Process*. Chicago: University of Chicago Press, 1935.

_____. "Sociological Significance of the Bible," *AJOS* (Jan., 1907) 532-552.

_____. *A Sociological Study of the Bible*. Chicago: University of Chicago Press, 1912.

Walz, R. "Gab es ein Esel-Nomadentum in alten Orient?" *Akten des xxiv internationalen orientalisten Kongresses, Munich*. Wiesbaden: Deutsche morgenländische Gesellschaft, 1959, 150-152.

_____. "Neue Untersuchungen zum Domestikationsproblem der altweltlichen Cameliden," *ZDMG* CIV (1954) 45-87.

_____. "Zum Problem des Zeitpunkts der Domestikation der altweltlichen Cameliden," *ZDMG* CI (1951) 29-51.

Weber, M. *Ancient Judaism*. Translated and Edited by H. H. Gerth and D. Martindale. Glencoe: The Free Press, 1952.

Weippert, M. *Die Landnahme der israelitischen Stämme in der wissenschaftlichen Diskussion*. ("Forschungen zur Religion und Literatur des Alten und Neuen Testaments," No. 92). Göttingen: Vandenhoeck und Ruprecht, 1967.

Weisberg, D. B. *Guild Structure and Political Allegiance in Early Achaemenid Mesopotamia*. ("Yale Near Eastern Researches," 1). New Haven: Yale University Press, 1967.

Wensinck, A. J. *The Ideas of the Western Semites concerning the Navel of the Earth*. Amsterdam: J. Muller, 1916.

Westerman, W. L "Concerning Urbanism and Anti-Urbanism in Antiquity," *Bulletin of the Faculty of Arts, Farouk I University* V (1949) 81-96.

Williams, G. H. *Wilderness and Paradise in Christian Thought*. N.Y.: Harper and Row, 1962.

Williams, J. G. "The Prophetic 'Father.'" *JBL* LXXXV (1966) 344-348.

Williams, R. J. "Moabite Stone," *IDB*, III, 419-420.

_____. "Writing and Writing Materials," *IDB*, IV, 909-921.

Wilson, J. "The Assembly of a Phoenician City," *JNES* IV (1945) 245.

[Wilson, R. R. "The Old Testament Genealogies in Recent Research," *JBL* XCIV (1975) 169-189].

Wiseman, D. J. *The Alalakh Tablets*. London: The British Institute of Archaeology at Ankara, 1953.

[_____. "Alalakh Texts," *IDBSup*, 16-17].

Wolf, C. U. "Nomadism," *IDB*, III, 558-560.

_____. "Terminology of Israel's Tribal Organization," *JBL*

LXV (1946) 45-49.

_____. "Traces of Primitive Democracy in Ancient Israel," *JNES* VI (1947) 98-108.

_____. "Village," *IDB*, IV, 784.

Wolff, H. W. "Das Thema 'Umkehr' in der alttestamentlichen Prophetie," *ZTK* XLVIII (1951) 129-148.

Van der Woude, A. S. "Micah and the Pseudo-Prophets," *VT* XIX (1969) 244-260.

Wright, G. E. (ed.). *The Bible and the Ancient Near East. Essays in Honor of W. F. Albright.* Anchor Book. Garden City: Doubleday, 1965.

_____. "The Provinces of Solomon (1 Kings 4:7-19)," *Eretz Israel* VIII (1967) 58-68.

Wurthwein, E. *Der ʿam haᵓrez im Alten Testament.* Stuttgart: W. Kohlhammer, 1936.

Yadin, Y. *The Art of Warfare in Biblical Lands.* Translated by Moshe Pearlman. London: Weidenfeld and Nicolson, 1963.

_____. "Hyksos Fortifications and the Battering-Ram," *BASOR* 137 (1955) 23-34.

_____. "Some Aspects of the Material Culture of Northern Israel during the Canaanite and Israelite Periods in the Light of the Excavations at Hazor," *Antiquity and Survival* II (1957) 165-186.

Yeivin, S. "The Land of Israel and the Birth of Civilization in the Near East," *Antiquity and Survival* II (1957) 111-120.

_____. "Topographic and Ethnic Notes," *Atiqot* II (1959) 155-158.

Zeitlin, S. "The Am Haarez," *JQR* XXIII (1932) 45-61.

Zeivit, Z. "The Use of ʿebed as a Diplomatic Term in Jeremiah," *JBL* LXXXVIII (1969) 75-77.

Van Zyl, A. H. *The Moabites.* Leiden: E. J. Brill, 1960.

INDEX OF BIBLICAL PASSAGES

283